INTERNATIONAL COMMERCIAL CON

APPLICABLE SOURCES AND ENFORCEABILITY

Any practising lawyer and student working with international commercial contracts faces standardised contracts and international arbitration as the mechanism for dispute settlement. Transnational rules may be applicable, but national law is still important. Based on extensive practical experience, this book ~~analyses international contract practice and its interaction with the vari-~~

ous a
by na
these
inter

GIU
of O
cial
arbit
in It

INTERNATIONAL COMMERCIAL CONTRACTS

APPLICABLE SOURCES AND ENFORCEABILITY

GIUDITTA CORDERO-MOSS

CAMBRIDGE
UNIVERSITY PRESS

CAMBRIDGE
UNIVERSITY PRESS

University Printing House, Cambridge CB2 8BS, United Kingdom

Cambridge University Press is part of the University of Cambridge.

It furthers the University's mission by disseminating knowledge in the pursuit of
education, learning and research at the highest international levels of excellence.

www.cambridge.org
Information on this title: www.cambridge.org/9781107029187

© Cambridge University Press 2014

First published 2014

Printed in the United Kingdom by Clays, St Ives plc

A catalogue record for this publication is available from the British Library

Library of Congress Cataloguing in Publication data
Cordero-Moss, Giuditta, author.
International commercial contracts : applicable sources and enforceability / Giuditta Cordero-Moss.
pages cm
ISBN 978-1-107-02918-7 (Hardback) – ISBN 978-1-107-68471-3 (Paperback)   1. Conflict of laws–Contracts.
2. Conflict of laws–Commercial law.   3. Contracts (International law) I. Title.
K7350.C67 2014
346.02′2–dc23
2013040438

ISBN 978-1-107-02918-7 Hardback
ISBN 978-1-107-68471-3 Paperback

CONTENTS

PREFACE

This is the book that I would have liked to have read when I started my career as an in-house lawyer in an Italian multinational company about thirty years ago. Working with international contracts, I soon started wondering about various aspects of contract drafting. Why are international contracts written in a style that is completely different from their domestic counterparts and why are they written in the same style irrespective of the law that governs them? Is there some sort of transnational law that allows for the governing law to be disregarded and requires that contracts be written in a certain way, independently of the jurisdiction in which they will be implemented? Is national law made redundant by the extremely detailed style of the contracts? Does the choice-of-law clause written in the contract mean that the parties may exclude the applicability of any other rules from any other laws? Does the arbitration clause written in the contract mean that the parties may rely fully on the terms of the contract and the choice of law made therein, and need not be concerned with any other sources?

These questions continued presenting themselves after I went over to a Norwegian multinational company, and became even more pressing when I started following this company's legal interests in what was soon to become the former Soviet Union.

After numerous years as a corporate lawyer, in which a thorough analysis of these questions inevitably had to yield to new projects and more urgent matters, my generous employer gave me the opportunity to spend some time researching some of these issues. The result was a PhD thesis at the Institute of State and Law in the Russian Academy of Sciences, Moscow, under the knowledgeable supervision of Professor August A. Rubanov. This was the introduction to my academic career: the Russian PhD was followed by a PhD at the University of Oslo, under the invaluable supervision of Professors Sjur Brækhus and Helge J. Thue. Since then, about fifteen years have elapsed, during which I have devoted my research and teaching at the University of Oslo to the list of questions that I had compiled in my nearly fifteen years as a corporate lawyer, and to the additional questions that continue to arise in connection with arbitration proceedings that I am involved in or legal advice that I am requested to render.

The results of these almost thirty years of dwelling on the practical and academic aspects of international contracts, their sources and their enforceability are reflected in this book. Academically, the questions arising from international contracts fall into separate disciplines: contract law, comparative contract law, private international law, civil procedure and international arbitration. Scholars may specialise in a couple of these disciplines, but rarely in all of them. Therefore, it is not very common for all of the implications of international contracts to be dealt with in one book. In practice, however, questions arise out of international contracts in their complexity, irrespective of the academic discipline within which they fall. This explains the opening sentence of this preface, stating that this is the book that I would have liked to have read when I started working with international contracts.

In addition to the text being based on my own research and my practical experience, the material presented here takes advantage of the results of two research projects that I have organised at the University of Oslo.

The first project, the so-called 'Anglo project', was financed by the Norwegian Research Council and it ran from 2004 to 2009. It started from the observation that international contracts are written on the basis of common law models, even when they are subject to a civil governing law, and a series of so-called boilerplate clauses were analysed to assess their function in the original common law models and to verify what legal effects these clauses could achieve under civil laws. The project produced three PhD theses and a series of master's theses (a list may be found at www.jus.uio.no/ifp/english/research/projects/anglo/index.html) and resulted in a book: Giuditta Cordero-Moss (ed.), *Boilerplate Clauses, International Commercial Contracts and the Applicable Law* (2011).

The second research project, the so-called 'APA' (Arbitration and Party Autonomy) project, is still running, and is financed by the University of Oslo and the Norwegian multinational companies Statoil ASA, Orkla ASA, Yara ASA, as well as the law firms Selmer and DLAPiper. This project verifies to what extent party autonomy meets restrictions when a contract contains an arbitration clause. The project has so far resulted in various international conferences and a series of masters theses (a list may be found at www.jus.uio.no/ifp/english/research/projects/choice-of-law/), as well as in a book: Giuditta Cordero-Moss (ed.), *International Commercial Arbitration: Different Forms and their Features* (2013).

In addition, this book benefits from my lecturing activity, first of all at the University of Oslo, but also at the Centre for Energy, Petroleum and Mineral Law and Policy, Dundee, at the LLM in International Trade Law organised by the ILO, the University of Turin and the University Institute of European Studies, at The Hague Academy of International Law, as well as at the numerous universities and organisations where I have lectured as a guest. The questions and discussions following a lecture or the presentation of a paper are often useful to illustrate or clarify matters, and can give inspiration for new issues.

Another important source that this book takes advantage of is my participation in the UNCITRAL Working Group on Arbitration, where I was the delegate for Norway during the revision of the UNCITRAL Arbitration Rules and the preparation of a standard of transparency for treaty-based arbitration. The discussions in the Working

Group and the assistance given by the UNCITRAL Secretariat have provided an invaluable insight into the different approaches to various aspects of arbitration, as well as into the logic of international cooperation.

I would like to thank the members of the Department of Private Law of the Law Faculty, University of Oslo, of which I am presently the Director, for their support and for having borne with me while I was finalising this book. Thanks also to research assistants Nanette Christine Flatby Arvesen and Øivind K. Foss, of the APA-project, who have compiled the bibliography.

I would like to thank Cambridge University Press, and particularly Senior Commissioning Editor Sinead Moloney, for their very pleasant and professional cooperation in connection with the publication of this book.

Finally, I would like to express my sincere appreciation and gratitude to Finola O'Sullivan, Editorial Director of Law at Cambridge University Press, for her intelligent and continuing support.

GIUDITTA CORDERO-MOSS
Oslo, August 2013

Introduction

It may seem intuitive to some observers as to what an international commercial contract is, yet it is difficult to find an accepted definition for the term. What is even more difficult is identifying the legal rules to which international commercial contracts are subject. Are international contracts subject to some sort of international law? What are the sources of this law and what is its scope of application? To the extent that international contracts are subject to national rules, which law's rules are applicable? These questions become even more pressing when the practice of international contracting is taken into consideration: contracts are often written as if their terms were the only source with which to regulate the parties' relationship and as if any sources of law were irrelevant. This self-sufficiency is attempted through drafting the contract in great detail, by writing clauses that attempt to exclude any interference from external sources and by stipulating that disputes between the parties shall be solved out of court via arbitration. Contracts tend to be drafted in the same way, irrespective of the legal system in which they will be implemented. Ambitions regarding self-sufficiency, standardisation and arbitration clauses make one wonder about the relationship between the contract and the governing law.

This book will analyse the interaction between international commercial contracts and the sources that govern them.

In the first chapter, I will present the practice of international contract drafting and will highlight how its peculiarities may fit with the applicable sources of law when the contract has to be interpreted and enforced.

In Chapter 2, I will go through the most important sources of non-national law and will analyse to what extent they may contribute to the harmonised interpretation and regulation of international contracts.

In Chapter 3, I will examine how international contracts may be influenced by the national governing law.

In Chapter 4, I will discuss how the governing law is chosen and what role the will of the parties has in this process.

In Chapter 5, I will analyse the extent to which the role of the parties' will is enhanced when the contract stipulates that any disputes arising between the parties out of the contract shall be solved by arbitration.

Before starting the analysis of the role played by the parties' will and by the applicable sources of law in the interpretation and enforcement of international contracts, however, it is necessary to define the starting point of the analysis; namely, international commercial contracts.

Two elements require explanation: the term 'commercial' and the term 'international'.

1 Explanation of the term 'commercial'

To explain the term 'commercial', it will be sufficient here to specify that it refers to transactions entered into between parties in the course of their business activities. This leaves consumer contracts outside of the scope of the subject, as well as other aspects of private law, such as family or inheritance law. It is not the intention here to contribute to the old and extensive debate, which particularly seems to characterise some civil law legal traditions, concerning the difference between private law and commercial law; the difficulty in precisely defining the term 'commercial' appears clearly in the explanation of the term provided by the Model Law on International Commercial Arbitration made by the United Nations Commission on International Trade Law (UNCITRAL), which, in footnote 2 relating to Article 1, uses a tautology; that is, it explains the term 'commercial' by referring to the same concept, without imparting any additional explanation other than a long, non-exclusive list of transactions that are deemed to be of a commercial nature:

> The term 'commercial' should be given a wide interpretation so as to cover matters arising from all relationships of a commercial nature, whether contractual or not. Relationships of a commercial nature include, but are not limited to, the following transactions: any trade transaction for the supply or exchange of goods or services; distribution agreement; commercial representation or agency; factoring; leasing; construction of works; consulting; engineering licensing; investment; financing; banking; insurance; exploitation agreement or concession; joint venture and other forms of industrial or business co-operation; carriage of goods or passengers by air, sea, rail or road.[1]

As unsatisfactory as it may be to operate with a non-exhaustive list rather than with a clear definition of the scope of the content, we will follow the guidelines laid down by UNCITRAL, and will consider the kinds of transactions listed above as the objects for this book.

This seems to cover only private law matters and leave out questions of public law. However, this distinction is not clear cut. Leaving aside that the private–public law divide is not necessarily recognised in all legal systems

---

[1] United Nations Commission on International Trade Law, Model Law on International Commercial Arbitration 1985, as amended in 2006, (www.uncitral.org/pdf/english/texts/arbitration/ml-arb/07-86998_Ebook.pdf)

(notably, not in the common law tradition), there are aspects of public international law that may well be relevant to commercial activity, as mentioned in Section 3 of this Introduction.

2 Explanation of the term 'international'

As far as the term 'international' in the name 'international commercial law' is concerned, there are two possible interpretations: (i) the law is international because it stems from international sources; or (ii) it is not the law that is international, but the object that the law regulates which is international. Although the former is not completely irrelevant, as mentioned in Section 3 of this Introduction, it is the latter construction that correctly describes the subject of this book. We will focus on the law that governs international commercial relationships; however, the definition of 'international' varies according to the criteria used by the interpreter. Different state laws and different international conventions have different definitions of what international is.

For example, the Vienna Convention on the International Sale of Goods of 1980 (also known as the CISG) specifies, in Article 1.1, that a sale falls within the scope of the Convention (and therefore is to be deemed as international) if the parties have their place of business in different states:

> This Convention applies to contracts of sale of goods between parties whose places of business are in different States.

Therefore, under the CISG, a contract between, for example, a French seller and a Norwegian buyer, is considered as an international contract. A contract between two companies based in France, however, would not be considered as international under the CISG, even if the contract requires one party to import certain goods from a foreign state to sell them to the other party.

The Hague Convention on the Law Applicable to the International Sale of Goods of 1955[2] does not define the term international, and simply states in Article 1 that the mere determination by the parties is not sufficient to give a sale international character (indirectly accepting that a sale may be international if there are some foreign elements to the transaction, but that this is not necessarily the place of business of the parties):

> The mere declaration of the parties, relative to the application of a law or the competence of a judge or arbitrator, shall not be sufficient to confer upon a sale the international character provided for in the first paragraph of this Article.

[2] This Convention has been ratified by eleven European states, and is largely absorbed, as between EU member states, by the EU Rome I Regulation on the Law Applicable to Contractual Obligations (Regulation EC 593/2008 of 17 June 2008). The Convention is applicable when one of the parties belongs to a signatory state, which is not an EU member state, notably, Norway. The Hague Conference in 1986 drafted a more modern convention on the same subject; this convention, however, never entered into force.

Therefore, a contract between two Italian parties for the sale of a product manufactured in Italy according to which both delivery and payment will be made in Italy, will not qualify as international under The Hague Convention, even if the contract has a clause choosing German law as the law governing the transaction. However, the above-mentioned contract between two French companies for the import and successive domestic sale of certain goods might be considered as international for the purpose of The Hague Convention because there is a foreign element involved in the import of the goods.

The EU Rome I Regulation on the Law Applicable to Contractual Obligations (Regulation EC 593/2008 of 17 June 2008), which is the European Union's (EU's) instrument regulating the choice of law for contracts, speaks in Article 1.1 of any situation involving a conflict between the laws of different states; thus, indirectly, it opens the door even for the eventuality that the only foreign element to a transaction is the choice made by the parties of a foreign law – although, in such situations, the applicability of party autonomy, which is the most important conflict rule contained in the Convention, is limited by Article 3.3 thereof:

3.3. Where all other elements relevant to the situation at the time of the choice are located in a country other than the country whose law has been chosen, the choice of the parties shall not prejudice the application of provisions of the law of that other country which cannot be derogated from by agreement.

Therefore, the above-mentioned import and subsequent domestic sale between two companies based in France would fall within the scope of Article 1.1 of the Rome I Regulation and allow for a wide choice of law, as regulated for in Article 3.1, because the import of the goods is an element that connects the situation with more than one state. The domestic contract between the two Italian companies mentioned above, however, even though it falls within the scope of Article 1.1, would be subject to Article 3.3 of the Rome I Regulation, and would allow a more restricted party autonomy.

The UNCITRAL Model Law on International Arbitration defines, in Article 1.3, an arbitration as international if one or more conditions are met, also including the mere determination by the parties that the subject matter of the dispute relates to more than one state:

An arbitration is international if:

(a) the parties to an arbitration agreement have, at the time of the conclusion of that agreement, their places of business in different states; or
(b) one of the following places is situated outside the state in which the parties have their places of business:
    (i) the place of arbitration if determined in, or pursuant to, the arbitration agreement;
    (ii) any place where a substantial part of the obligations of the commercial relationship is to be performed or the place with which the subject matter of the dispute is most closely connected; or

(c) the parties have expressly agreed that the subject matter of the arbitration
    agreement relates to more than one state.

Therefore, a dispute arising out of the above-mentioned domestic agreement
between two Italian companies would qualify as international for the purpose of
the UNCITRAL Model Law, if the parties have chosen a foreign governing law or a
foreign state as a venue for the arbitration.

Bearing in mind these discrepancies, and that it is therefore necessary to verify in
each specific case (on the basis of the applicable law) whether the transaction is
international or not, it will suffice for the purpose of this book to define a transaction
as international whenever there is a foreign element to it that connects it with at least
two different states.

The most evident example would be a contract entered into by two parties that are
resident in different states: for example, an Italian clothes producer entering into an
agency contract with a Norwegian agent for the promotion and sale of the products in
the Norwegian territory, or a Russian aluminium producer entering into a contract
for the export of its products to Norway.

There might be, however, less evident cases, where an inquiry is necessary before
the transaction may be defined as either international or domestic. Where a contract
is entered into between a company located in a certain state and the local, wholly
owned subsidiary of a foreign company, for example, some state laws will permit
disputes connected therewith to be defined as international,[3] whereas others focus on
the formal aspect of the common nationality of the parties and consider the disputes
as domestic.[4]

3 The public international law dimension

Public international law is the branch of the law that regulates the relationship
between states. States are sovereign, and are therefore free to regulate their internal
affairs through legislation, administrative regulation and the exercise of the judicial
function; their sovereignty, however, does not extend beyond their respective territory. In terms of their relationship with other states, when states act as sovereign
states and need to determine their respective positions towards each other, they are
subject to the principles and rules of public international law.

A state does not act as a sovereign when it engages in commercial activity, and
public international law, therefore, is not relevant. Commercial transactions will be
subject to commercial and private law, even when one of the parties involved is a
state. Generally, there is no overlap between these branches of the law.

---

[3] For example, the Russian Law on International Commercial Arbitration of 1993 provides, in Article 1.2, that
disputes arising out of contracts between two Russian companies may be submitted to international
arbitration if one of the Russian companies is (wholly or even partially) owned by a foreign entity.
[4] For example, the Swiss Private International Law Act, Article 176.1.

In some situations, however, there is interference. This happens mainly when an investor engages in a business activity in a foreign country. The investor will enter into a series of contracts of a commercial nature with other private parties, or even with the host state, and these contracts will be subject to private or commercial law in accordance with the rules of private international law. The investor's activity will, in addition, have a series of implications in terms of administrative or public law, and these will be regulated by the law of the host country – for example, the enterprise will generate income that is subject to the local tax law, it will perhaps involve production activities, with implications for the local environmental law, it will have employees who are subject to the local labour law, it will have access to natural resources or infrastructure subject to administrative concessions, it will have export activity subject to licensing, etc. All these regulations to which the investor is subject are part of the legal system of the host country, and the host country, in its sovereignty, legislates and administrates within these fields as it deems fit and in accordance with its evaluation of what is in the public interest. This regulatory activity is within the sovereignty of the state, and, as a general rule, it is not subject to any other constraints other than the rule of law and the constitutional principles of the state itself.

Should the host country regulate these matters in a way that violates fundamental principles, for example, because it engages in discriminatory behaviour or because it confiscates property without paying compensation, it may encounter limitations being placed on it through public international law.

Public international law, particularly through treaties entered into on a bilateral or multilateral basis for the protection of investments made by nationals of one state in the territory of the other state, contains some principles that may be invoked by the foreign investor who is affected by the state's conduct. Traditionally, individuals are not considered to be subjects of public international law, and must present their claims against the host country via their respective country of origin, mainly through diplomatic protection. This gives the process a political, rather than a legal dimension, and is not necessarily favourable to the investor. The Washington Convention of 1965 on the Settlement of Investment Disputes between States and Nationals of other States (ICSID) established a legal proceeding in which foreign investors could pursue their claims directly against the host country in a special arbitration proceeding – the so-called investment arbitration. This arbitration largely resembles the procedure for commercial disputes, but permits the investor to raise claims based on alleged violations by the host country of its public international law obligations regarding the treatment of foreign investors, mainly based on treaties on investment protection. In the past decades, bilateral investment treaties (BITs) have proliferated, as well as some multinational treaties, giving investors the possibility of being able to directly bring an action against the host country in an arbitration form known as investment arbitration. Many of these treaties allow for the possibility of being able to choose not only a dedicated ICSID arbitration, but also forms of arbitration that are designed for commercial disputes, such as arbitration under the UNCITRAL Arbitration Rules or under the rules of the Arbitration Institute of the Stockholm Chamber of Commerce (SCC). In the past few decades, investment arbitration has been frequently used by investors and it has become a significant instrument in foreign business activity. Investment arbitration does not fall within the scope of this book, but will be mentioned occasionally when it is relevant.

The great number of international treaties on investment protection has led in the past decade or two to a boom in so-called investment disputes, in which foreign investors initiate an arbitration procedure against the host country by claiming that the public international law rules protecting foreign investment have been violated. This public international law protection may be wrongly interpreted as encouraging international transactions to be considered as detached from national law and subject to international law instead.[5]

In reality, investment protection does not replace national law; it adds a corrective dimension to national law, without, however, excluding its applicability. If a certain activity qualifies as an investment and enjoys the relevant protection, it will still be subject to the applicable state law, with corrections available through the fundamental principles of public international law such as non-discrimination, compensation upon expropriation, fair and equitable treatment, full protection and security. Any rules and regulations of national law that do not violate these fundamental principles will still be applicable to the investment.

However, the borderline between public international law and international commercial law is somewhat blurred, particularly in the context of transnational sources. This book will, therefore, discuss the public international law dimension when examining transnational sources that may be applicable to international contracts. In addition, the question of courts' international jurisdiction will be seen in the context of public international law. Questions specifically related to investment arbitration will be touched upon only marginally, mainly in respect of investment proceedings that are carried out under commercial arbitration rules.

---

[5] See Giuditta Cordero-Moss, 'Commercial Arbitration and Investment Arbitration: Fertile Soil for False Friends?', in Christina Binder, Ursula Kriebaum, August Reinisch, and Wittich Stephan (eds.), *International Investment Law for the 21st Century: Essays in Honour of Christoph Schreuer* (Oxford University Press, 2009), pp. 782–97, Section 2.

Contract practice and its expectations in terms of the governing law

1 The rationale of contract drafting

International contracts are often written on the basis of rather standardised models that are mainly drafted in English and, therefore, they employ a common law drafting style. This does not mean, however, that the parties intend the contract to be subject to English law. Often, contracts are governed by a law that does not belong to the common law family, and this may create tensions between the contractual provisions and the governing law. To minimise the risk of the governing law interfering with the agreed terms, international contracts are drafted in a style that aims to create an exhaustive, and as precise as possible, regulation of the underlying contractual relationship, thus attempting to render redundant any interference from external elements such as the interpreter's discretion or the rules and principles of the governing law.

To a large extent, this degree of detail may achieve the goal of rendering the contract a self-sufficient system, thus enhancing the impression that, if only they are sufficiently detailed and clear, contracts will be interpreted on the basis of their own terms and without being influenced by any governing law. This impression, however, has been proven to be illusionary, and not only because governing laws may contain mandatory rules that may not be derogated from by the contract. As a matter of fact, not many mandatory rules affect international commercial contracts, although there are important mandatory rules, for example, in the field of the limitation of liability, that are also relevant in the commercial context.[1] Perhaps more importantly, the governing law, which may vary from contract to contract, will affect consciously or not the way in which the contract is interpreted and applied. Notwithstanding any efforts by the parties to include as many details as possible in the contract in order to minimise the need for interpretation, the governing law will necessarily project its own principles regarding the function of a contract, the advisability of ensuring a fair balance between the parties' interests, the role of the interpreter in respect of obligations that are not explicitly regulated in the contract, the existence of a duty of the parties to act loyally towards each other and the existence and extent of a general

---

[1] Some examples are discussed in Chapter 3, Section 6. To what extent mandatory rules of the governing law have an impact in the context of international commercial arbitration will be analysed in Chapter 5, Section 2.

principle of good faith – in short, the balance between certainty and justice. That the same contract wording may be interpreted differently depending on the legal tradition of the interpreter largely deprives of its meaning the self-sufficiency goal, since it entails that the legal effects of the contract do not flow solely from the contract, but from the interaction of the contract with the governing law. Neither is much help afforded by the observation that legal systems converge on an abstract level and that, consequently, very similar results may be achieved in the various systems, albeit by applying different legal techniques.

First, convergence can rarely be said to be complete, as Chapter 3, Section 3 will show. Even within one single legal family there are significant differences, for example, between the US and English law regarding exculpatory clauses. Even within the same system, there may be divergences, as the same clause may have different legal effects in the different states within the US.[2]

Reducing the divergence to a mere question of technicalities, furthermore, misses the point: it is precisely the different legal techniques that matter when a specific wording has to be applied. It would not be of much comfort for a party to know that it could have achieved the desired result if only the contract had had the correct wording as required by the relevant legal technique. The party is interested in the legal effects of the particular clause that was written in the contract, not in the abstract possibility of obtaining the same result from a different clause.

Neither can the inconsistency of a contract wording's legal effects be overcome by invoking transnational sources to provide a uniform system that is independent of the peculiarities of national laws. As Chapter 2 will show, there do not seem to be any generally acknowledged transnational principles that are sufficiently specific to give uniform guidance on the interpretation of contracts.

The question of contract interpretation, thus, has to be addressed under the governing law.

To avoid external interferences, contracts often contain a series of clauses in which the parties try to take into their own hands those aspects where the balance between certainty and justice may be challenged – the so-called boilerplate clauses. These clauses relate to the interpretation and general operation of contracts, and are to be found in most contracts irrespective of the subject matter of the contract. They are relatively standardised and their wording is seldom given attention to during the negotiations. Some examples of these clauses will be presented in Section 4 below.[3] Their interpretation under transnational sources will be discussed

---

[2] Edward T. Canuel, 'Comparing Exculpatory Clauses under Anglo-American Law: Testing Total Legal Convergence', in Giuditta Cordero-Moss (ed.), *Boilerplate Clauses, International Commercial Contracts and the Applicable Law* (Cambridge University Press, 2011), pp. 80–103 Section 2.

[3] For a more extensive list of boilerplate clauses and an analysis of their legal effects under a variety of legal systems, see Giuditta Cordero-Moss (ed.), *Boilerplate Clauses, International Commercial Contracts and the Applicable Law* (Cambridge University Press, 2011).

in Chapter 2, Section 4.2 and their interpretation under various governing laws will be presented in Chapter 3, Section 4.

2 The models for international contract drafting

English is undeniably the common language for international business transactions. Communication between the business parties is mainly carried out in English and contracts that formalise the deals are written in English. Searching for models for specific contract terms or for entire contracts, English language wording will be the most common result. This has bigger consequences than the mere linguistic aspect: contracts that are originally written in the English language are usually drafted by lawyers educated in the common law tradition, and are developed to meet the requirements of and satisfy the criteria for contracts that are subject to the common law. Consequently, most of the internationally distributed publications offering model contract collections reproduce common law style contracts. As a result, law firms and corporate lawyers in a variety of jurisdictions (not only in common law jurisdictions) learn to draft international contracts on the basis of these models. International financial institutions impose the use of US or English style contracts for the transactions that they are financing, irrespective of whether the financed entities or the investors involved come from common law states or not, or whether most of the related contracts are governed by English law, or another system of common law, or not. As a result, operators in civil law states become accustomed to drafting in the common law style to meet the expectations of financial institutions. During the former Soviet Union's and the East European countries' transition to market-driven economies in the 1990s, for example, the European Bank for Recon-struction and Development, an international organisation devoted to financing East European and former Soviet Union projects, almost exclusively adopted common law contract models for projects that were to be carried out in those civil law countries, even when all of the parties involved belonged solely to the civil law tradition. Contract types developed through practice, such as, for example, swap contracts and other contracts for the trade of financial derivatives, are standardised by branch associations following the common law contract style. As a result, new types of transactions are regulated exclusively by common law style contracts, and these contracts are used to regulate not only international transactions, but even domestic transactions within civil law systems. Contracts for the hedging of financial risk, for example, might be written in English and inspired by English law, even if they are entered into by a Norwegian company and a Norwegian bank and are governed by Norwegian law.

The above-described widespread use of common law models is such that it is increasingly affecting even traditional contract types and domestic legal relationships, such as the rental of real estate or sale agreements within the borders of the same country. Even contract models applied by the Norwegian public sector for public procurement, to name one example, are increasingly drafted on the basis of these models, which are generally considered to represent state-of-the-art contracting among the law firms that might be hired by the relevant state body to draft the tender documentation. The Anglo-Americanisation of contract models, therefore, influences not only firms and companies that engage in international commerce, but also individuals, companies and even public bodies with purely domestic interests.

Extensive contracts do not reflect the tradition of civil law. As will be seen in Chapter 3, a civilian judge reads the contract in the light of the numerous default rules provided in the governing law for that type of contract. Therefore, extensive provisions are not required in the contract.[4] The common law drafting tradition, in turn, requires extensive contracts that spell out all of the obligations between the parties and leave little to the judge's discretion or interpretation, because the common law judge sees it as his or her function to enforce the bargain agreed upon between the parties, and not to substitute for the bargain actually made by the parties, a bargain which the interpreter deems to be more reasonable or commercially sensible.[5] Thus, English judges will be reluctant to read obligations that were not expressly agreed on by the parties into the contract. Since English judges often affirm that a sufficiently clear contract wording will be enforced, parties are encouraged to increase the level of detail, and to write around mechanisms that have proven to be problematic by formulating clauses that will fall outside the scope of the pitfall.

This drafting style follows the same approach that inspired the original common law models: *caveat emptor.*[6] A commercial contract between professionals, often written by expert lawyers, is expected to reflect careful evaluations made by each of the parties of its respective interests. The parties are assumed to be able to assess the relevant risks and to make provisions for them. The negotiations are expected to be carried out in a way that adequately takes care of each of the parties' positions, and the final text of the contract is deemed to reflect this. The contract is deemed to have been written accurately, so that each party may use the contractual terms to objectively quantify its risk and, for example, insure against it. Contracts may also be assigned to third parties, for example, as collateral for other obligations or in the context of other transactions. Contracts should therefore contain all elements according to which they will be interpreted, and interpretation must be made objectively and on the basis of the contract's wording. Third parties who come into contact with the contract have no possibility of being able to assess the subjective position of each of the parties, their respective assumptions, their non-expressed

---

[4] See Chapter 3. For a more extensive argumentation and references see Giuditta Cordero Moss, 'International Contracts between Common Law and Civil Law: Is Non-state Law to be Preferred? The Difficulty of Interpreting Legal Standards such as Good Faith, Article 3', (2007) 7(1) *Global Jurist Advances*, 1–38.

[5] *Charter Reinsurance Co Ltd* v. *Fagan* [1997] AC 313.

[6] This formula was pronounced by Lord Mansfield in *Stuart* v. *Wilkins* [1778] I Dougl. 18, 99 Eng. Rep. 15 and has since been used to characterise the approach of English contract law, whereby each party has to take care of its own interests.

intentions and the content of their communications during the negotiations or even after the conclusion of the contract. Under these circumstances, a literal and thus predictable application of the contract is perceived as the only fair application of contracts. It might be unfair to draw on external elements in addition to the wording of the contract, such as, for example, the conduct or silence by one of the parties that may have created expectations in the other party at some stage during the negotiations or even after the contract was signed. How can a contract circulate and be used as a basis for calculating an insurance premium, granting financing or be assigned to a third party if its implementation depends on elements that are not visible in the contract itself?

This heightens the impression that a well thought through formulation may solve all of the problems that may arise under the governing law. When adopting the common law style, drafters may apparently be tempted to overdo things, and to write provisions that seek to elevate the contract to the level of law.[7] This indulgence in self-referencing (also known as 'boot-strapping') makes one think of one of the tales featuring the Baron of Münchhausen, namely the tale where the Baron attempts to lift himself (and his horse) up from a swamp by pulling his own hair.

The eagerness in drafting may reach excesses that have been defined as 'nonsensical' by a prominent English expert.[8] For example, the ubiquitous representations and warranties clause[9] may list, among the matters that the parties represent to each other, that their respective obligations under the contract are valid, binding and enforceable.[10] This representation and warranty is itself an obligation under the

---

[7] A similar attempt to elevate the contract to the level of law may be found in the assumption that the contract's choice of law clause has the ability to move the whole legal relationship out of the scope of the application of any law but the law chosen by the parties. The choice of law made by the parties, however, has effect mainly within the sphere of contract law. For areas that are relevant to the contractual relationship, but are outside the scope of contract law, the parties' choice does not have any effect. Areas such as the parties' own legal capacity, the company law implications of the contract, or the contract's effects on third parties within property law are governed by the law applicable to those areas according to the respective conflict rule, and the parties' choice is not relevant. See Chapters 4 and 5.

[8] Edwin Peel, 'The Common law Tradition: Application of Boilerplate Clauses under English law', in Giuditta Cordero-Moss (ed.), *Boilerplate Clauses, International Commercial Contracts and the Applicable Law* (Cambridge University Press, 2011), pp. 129–78, footnote 160.

[9] See Chapter 3, Section 5.1.

[10] A representation clause on the validity and enforceability of the contract is a typical part of boilerplate clauses. See, for example, section 5.2, article V, form 8.4.01 (Form Asset Purchase Agreement), M. D. Fern, *Warren's Forms of Agreements* (LexisNexis, 2004), vol. 2. This is also the first representation recommended in Contract Standards, a site that analyses both public and private document collections with the purpose of creating standard forms and providing contract benchmarking (www.contractstandards.com/contract-structure/representations-and-warranties, last visited on 14 February 2013). On the basis of its survey, the site comments on this clause as follows: 'States that the execution of the agreement will not violate any law or conflict with any contractual obligation agreement. The language is typically consistent across a range of transaction types' (www.contractstandards.com/contract-structure/representations-and-warranties/no-conflicts, last visited on 14 February 2013). See also Sample Representations and Warranties, section 3.2, Documents for Small Businesses and Professionals, (www.docstoc.com/docs/

contract, and is itself subject to any ground for invalidity or unenforceability that might affect the contract, so what value does it add? A contract clause affirming that the contract is valid has a classical precedent in the known paradox of Epimenides the Cretan saying that all the Cretans are liars.

It is particularly interesting that this particular representations and warranties clause is criticised by an English lawyer, because it shows that the attempt to detach the contract from the governing law may go too far, even for English law, and this is notwithstanding that the drafting style adopted for international contracts is no doubt based on the English and American drafting traditions.

The representation clause on the validity and enforceability of the contract is not the only attempt to detach the contract from the governing law: as will be seen below, other clauses, which often recur in contracts, regulate the interpretation of the contract and the application of remedies independently from the governing law.

Chapter 3 will show that some of these clauses will not achieve the desired results if the contract is subject to civil law. This is due to the overarching principle of good faith that, in different ways, prevents a literal interpretation and application of the contract leading to unfair results.

Interestingly, some of these clauses do not seem to achieve the desired results, even under English law. As noted by Peel,[11] observers may tend to overestimate how literally English courts may interpret contracts.

Be that as it may, contract practice shows that it is based on the illusion that it is possible, by writing sufficiently clear and precise wording, to draft around problems and circumvent any criteria of fairness that may inspire the court in the interpretation of the contract. Peel actually confirms that this is supported indirectly by English courts themselves, who often found their decisions on the interpretation of the wording rather than on substantial considerations such as the balance between the parties' interests. In respect of some contract clauses, which interestingly attempt to regulate the interpretation of the contract precisely, it seems that the drafting efforts are not likely to achieve results that might be considered unfair by the court, no matter how clearly and precisely the wording was drafted, and in spite of the English courts insistance on making this a question of interpretation. For these clauses, therefore, English courts will not decide in the over-formalistic way that is often assumed to be typical of English courts.

9515308/Sample-Representations-and-Warranties, last visited on 14 February 2013). Numerous examples of the actual use of this representation clause may be found in the contracts filed with the US Securities and Exchange Commission; for example, section 25.1.3 of the contract dated 21 November 2004, between Rainbow DBS and Lockheed Martin Commercial Space Systems for the construction of up to five television satellites (www.wikinvest.com/stock/Cablevision_Systems_(CVC)/Filing/8-K/2005/F2355074, last visited on 14 February 2013) and section 5.02 of the merger agreement dated 14 May 2007, between eCollege.com and Pearson Education Inc. and Epsilon Acquisition Corp. (www.wikinvest.com/stock/ECollege.com_(ECLG)/Filing/DEFA14A/2007/F4972482, last visited on 14 February 2013).

[11] Peel, 'The Common Law Tradition under English Law',

In respect of other clauses, however, the criteria of certainty and consistency seem to be given primacy by the English courts. This ensures a literal application of the contract notwithstanding the result, as long as the clause is written in a sufficiently clear and precise manner. The clause on liquidated damages, for example, is designed to escape the common law prohibition of penalty clauses. In addition, this clause, and the possibility of being able to convert it into a price variation clause, provide a significant example of how drafting may be used to achieve a result that otherwise would not be enforceable: this is defined as the possibility of the parties being able to manipulate the interpretation to avoid the intervention of the courts,[12] as will be seen in more detail in Chapter 3, Section 5.2. The common law terminology is also adopted in contracts governed by civil laws, even when the applicable law permits contractual penalties, and where it would not be necessary to structure the penalty as a pre-estimation of damages. This creates problems of coordination with the civil governing law, as will be seen in Chapter 3, Section 5.2.

The liquidated damages clause is one example of the different approaches taken to drafting and interpretation in the common law and in the civil traditions. Whereas the former permits circumventing the law's rules by appropriate drafting, the latter integrates the language of the contract with the law's rules and principles.

The possibility of writing around problems is thus quite rooted in the common law tradition; international contracts adopt models developed under the common law, and they are often written as if they were assuming that any issues might be solved by properly drafted clauses, quite irrespective of the governing law.

3 The dynamics of contract drafting

As was seen above, the drafting style of commercial contracts usually attempts to create a self-sufficient system. The assumption is that, if the parties had wanted to restrict or qualify the application of the contract provisions, then they would have written the restrictions or the qualifications in the contract. Rules regarding the interpretation of the governing law, principles of good faith and other mandatory rules would interfere with the contract and create uncertainty.

As Chapter 3 will show, this goal for self-sufficiency may not be fulfilled.

There is a gap between the parties' reliance on the self-sufficiency of the contract and the actual legal effects of the contract under the governing law. This gap does not necessarily derive from the parties' ignorance of the legal framework surrounding the contract. More precisely, the parties may often be aware of the fact that they are unaware of the legal framework for the contract. The possibility that the wording of the contract is interpreted and applied differently from what a literal application would seem to suggest may be accepted by some parties as a calculated risk.

---

[12] Peel, 'The Common Law Tradition under English Law' Section 2.7.

Often, some of the clauses in a contract are inserted without the parties having given any particular consideration to their content. This applies particularly to the already mentioned boilerplate clauses, which are inserted more out of habit than out of a specific need or intention to regulate those matters in that particular way. In addition, parties may often negotiate details of their deal and draft the corresponding provisions before even considering the question of which law will govern the contract. This practice may be surprising, considering the importance that the governing law has for the application and even the effectiveness of contract terms, as was seen above. However, the practice of negotiating detailed wording without regard to the governing law is not necessarily always unreasonable. From a merely legal point of view, it may make little sense; from the overall economic perspective, however, it is more understandable.

A contract is the result of a process in which both parties participate from opposite starting points. This means that the final result is, necessarily, a compromise. In addition, time and resources are often limited during negotiations. This means that the process of negotiating a contract does not necessarily meet all of the requirements that would ideally characterise an optimal process under favourable conditions. What could be considered as an indispensable minimum in the abstract description of how a legal document should be drafted, does not necessarily match with the commercial understanding of the resources that should be spent on such a process. This may lead to contracts being signed without the parties having negotiated all of the clauses, or without the parties having complete information regarding each clause's legal effects under the governing law. What may appear, from a purely legal point of view, as unreasonable conduct, is actually often a deliberate assumption of contractual risk.[13]

Considerations regarding the internal organisation of the parties are also a part of the assessment of risk. In large multinational companies, risk management may require a certain standardisation, which in turn prevents a high degree of flexibility in drafting individual contracts. In balancing the conflicting interests of ensuring internal standardisation and permitting local adjustment, large organisations may prefer to enhance the former.[14]

It is, in other words, not necessarily the result of thoughtlessness if a contract is drafted without having regard for the governing law. Neither is it a symptom of a refusal of the applicability of national laws. It is the result of a cost–benefit evaluation, leading to the acceptance of a calculated legal risk.

---

[13] See more extensively, David Echenberg, 'Negotiating International Contracts: Does the Process Invite a Review of Standard contracts from the Point of View of National Legal Requirements?', in Giuditta Cordero-Moss (ed.), *Boilerplate Clauses, International Commercial Contracts and the Applicable Law* (Cambridge University Press, 2011), pp. 11–19. See also the debate in the APA seminar mentioned in section 3.7.2 below.

[14] See more extensively, Maria Celeste Vettese, 'Multinational Companies and National Contracts', in Giuditta Cordero-Moss (ed.), *Boilerplate Clauses, International Commercial Contracts and the Applicable Law* (Cambridge University Press, 2011), pp. 20–31.

Thus, it is true that clauses, originally meant to create certainty, upon interaction with the governing law, may create uncertainty.[15] The uncertainty about how exactly a clause will be interpreted by a judge is deleterious from a merely legal point of view. However, this uncertainty may turn out to be less harmful from a commercial perspective: faced with the prospects of employing time and resources to pursue a result that is unforeseeable from a legal point of view, the parties may be encouraged to find a commercial solution. Rather than maximising the legal conflict, they may be forced to find a mutually agreeable solution. This may turn out to be a better use of resources once the conflict has arisen.

In addition, this kind of legal uncertainty is evaluated as a risk, just like other risks that relate to the transaction. Commercial parties know that not all risks will materialise, and this will also apply to the legal risk: not all clauses with uncertain legal effects will actually have to be invoked or enforced. In the majority of contracts, the parties comply with their respective obligations and there is no need to invoke the application of specific clauses. In the situations where a contract clause actually has to be invoked, the simple fact that the clause is invoked may induce the other party to comply with it, irrespective of the actual enforceability of the clause. An invoked clause is not necessarily always contested. There will be, thus, only a small percentage of clauses that will actually be the basis of a conflict between the parties. Of these conflicts, we have seen that some may be solved amicably, exactly because the uncertainty of the clause's legal effects acts as a deterrent against litigation and as an incentive to find a commercial solution rather than pursuing legal avenues. This leaves quite a small percentage of clauses upon which the parties may eventually litigate. Some of these litigations will be won; some will be lost. The commercial thinking requires a party to assess the value of this risk of losing a law suit on enforceability of a clause (also by considering the likelihood that it will materialise), and compare this value with the costs of the alternative conduct. The alternative conduct would be to assess every single clause of each contract that is entered into, verify its compatibility with the law that will govern each of these contracts and propose adjustments to each of these clauses to the various other contracting parties. This, in turn, requires the employment of internal resources to revise standard documentation, and external resources to adjust clauses to the applicable law, and possibly to engage in negotiations to convince the other contracting parties to change a model of the contract that they are well acquainted with. In many situations, the costs of adjusting each contract to its applicable law will exceed the value of the risk that is run by entering into a contract with uncertain legal effects.

Often, the final draft of the contract is submitted to a local law firm, with the request to verify that it is in compliance with the applicable law. This review, however, would normally be limited to verifying that no mandatory rules were being

---

[15] This observation is made by Viggo Hagstrøm, 'The Nordic Tradition: Application of Boilerplate Clauses under Norwegian Law', in Giuditta Cordero-Moss (ed.), *Boilerplate Clauses, International Commercial Contracts and the Applicable Law* (Cambridge University Press, 2011), pp. 265–75, section 2.

violated. It would not extend to the compatibility of the drafting style with the applicable legal tradition, nor would it explain how the contract would be interpreted or supplemented by the governing law.

The sophisticated party, aware of the implications of adopting contract models that are not adjusted to the governing law and consciously assessing the connected risk, will identify the clauses that matter the most, and concentrate its negotiations on those, leaving the other clauses untouched and accepting the corresponding risk.

A further element that may be relevant is the specialisation of lawyers. Often, lawyers who draft contracts are specialised in negotiating and drafting contracts, but not in litigation. When a contract that they have drafted is signed, they will turn to the negotiation of the next contract. If a dispute arises out of one of the contracts that they have drafted, it will not be the drafting lawyers who will be involved, but litigation lawyers. Therefore, the drafting lawyers will not have the possibility of verifying how the clauses work in practice. The success of a clause will not be measured against the way in which the clause is interpreted or in terms of its effectiveness in avoiding disputes, because the drafting lawyer is not involved in this phase. The success of a clause will be measured against the frequency with which the clause is accepted by the other party during the negotiations. That the drafting lawyer rarely sees how the clauses work in practice may contribute to enhancing the gap between the drafting style and the legal effects of international contracts. As will be seen in Chapter 2, Section 1 below, litigation lawyers have quite a different approach to contract terms. A litigation lawyer works on a specific dispute and has the goal of solving that dispute on the basis of the applicable sources. To permit an assessment of whether the dispute shall be litigated or whether a commercial settlement is to be preferred, the contract's legal effects and enforceability are central in the evaluation of the litigation lawyer. The contract will, therefore, be read in light of the governing law, and all applicable sources will be assessed.

4 Examples of self-sufficient contract drafting

Below follow some examples of some contract clauses that often recur in international commercial contracts. With these clauses, the parties try to take into their own hands those aspects that are usually decided by the governing law. In the matters regulated by these clauses, however, the balance between certainty and justice may be challenged; Chapter 2 will show that the interpretation of these clauses is not uniform under transnational sources and Chapter 3 will show that the wording of the clauses may have differing legal effects depending on the governing law.

4.1 Boilerplate clauses

Some clauses are frequently part of international commercial contracts, irrespective of the type of contract. Not only are they generally expected as an integral part of contract drafting, they are also immediately recognised and thus very seldom discussed during the negotiations. The drafting of these clauses is often considered to be a mere 'copy and paste' exercise. They are often referred to as having 'boilerplate', standard language with a general applicability that follows automatically and does not require any particular attention. Through these clauses, the parties attempt to regulate the contract's interpretation, the exercise of remedies for breach of contract and the legal effects of future conduct. At the same time, these clauses attempt to exclude any rules that the applicable law may have on these aspects.

The following are examples of some of the most typical boilerplate clauses.

4.1.1 Entire agreement clause

The purpose of the entire agreement clause (also known as the merger clause or integration clause) is to attempt to isolate the contract from any source or element that may be external to the document. This is also often emphasised by referring to the four corners of the document as the borderline for the interpretation or construction of the contract. The parties' aim is thus to exclude terms or obligations that do not appear in the document. A typical entire agreement clause might read as follows:

> This Agreement constitutes the entire agreement between the Parties and supersedes any prior understanding or representation of any kind preceding the date of this Agreement.

As Chapters 2 and 3 will show, there does not seem to be a uniform transnational standard for interpreting this clause, and the ability of this clause to obtain the desired result varies considerably depending on the governing law.

To understand the origin of the entire agreement clause, it is necessary to keep in mind that many international contracts are based on English models. English contracts are written to meet the requirements and to take advantage of the possibilities contained in the English law of contracts. Traditionally, an interpreter of English law contracts is bound by the language of the contract. As a general rule, the interpreter would not be allowed to take into consideration external circumstances when construing the contract, such as the parties' conduct during negotiations or after the signature of the contract.[16] This is traditionally known as the *parol evidence* rule, which prevents the parties from producing any evidence to add to, vary or contradict the wording of a contract when its terms are being construed, and imposes that the contract be read exclusively on the basis of the provisions that are written therein.[17] The purpose of this rule is to enhance predictability in the course of commerce; in balancing the interests of establishing the real intention of the parties and preserving

---

[16] *Wilson v. Maynard Shipbuilding Consultants AG Ltd* [1978] QB 665.
[17] *Adams v. British Airways plc* [1995] IRLR 577.

predictability within commercial transactions, the parol evidence rule favours the latter. In the interests of certainty, therefore, a written contract is to be interpreted objectively and independently from extrinsic circumstances that are characteristic of the factual transaction. Gradually, however, a series of exceptions to the parol evidence rule has been created by court practice, mainly to ensure that the interpreter is aware of what the factual background of the parties was when they entered into the contract. Thus, it is permitted that evidence is produced of the factual background existing at or before the date of the contract (but not after that date, as is the case in the civil law systems), at least in respect of facts that were known to both parties.[18] The entire agreement clause is, in part, a countermove to this exception to the parol evidence rule. The parties may seek to prevent the admission of evidence of the factual background by inserting an entire agreement clause in their contract, stating that the document contains the entire contract.[19] This explains the origin of the entire agreement clause: it is mainly meant to avoid the exceptions to the parol evidence rule that have evolved in court practice, and to reinstate the original regime of strict adherence to the text of the contract.

4.1.2 No waiver clause

The purpose of a no waiver clause is to ensure that the remedies described in the contract may be exercised in accordance with their wording at any time and irrespective of the parties' conduct. This clause is originally meant to exclude the effects of the rule on acquiescence under English law. The rule on acquiescence would lead to a result that is similar to the requirement of exercising rights and remedies in good faith, present in many civil law regimes and in the transnational sources analysed in Chapter 2: if the party entitled to a remedy behaves in such a clear and unequivocal way that the other party may understand it as a representation of the former to waive its remedy, then the former party loses the possibility of exercising its remedy. Inserting a no waiver clause in the contract is meant to prevent any passive behaviour of the former party to be interpreted as a clear and unequivocal representation, and therefore prevents the effects of the rule on acquiescence.[20]

The parties try, with this clause, to create a contractual regime for the exercise of remedies without regard to any rules that the applicable law may have on the time frame within which remedies may be exercised and the conditions for such exercise. Many legal systems have principles that protect one party's expectations and prevent the abuse of formal rights. These rules may affect the exercise of remedies in a way

---

[18] *Investors Compensation Scheme Ltd* v. *West Bromwich BS* [1998] AU ER 98 and *Bank of Scotland* v. *Dunedin Property Investments Co Ltd* [1998] SC 657.
[19] *McGrath* v. *Shaw* [1987] 57 P & CR 452.
[20] For an analysis of this clause and its implications, with further references, see Peel, 'The Common Law Tradition under English Law', Section 2.2.

that is not visible in the language of the contract. The no waiver clause is inserted to avoid these 'invisible' restrictions on the possibility of exercising contractual remedies. A typical no waiver clause reads as follows:

> The failure of any party at any time to require performance of any provision or to resort to any remedy provided under this Agreement shall in no way affect the right of that party to require performance or to resort to a remedy at any time thereafter, nor shall the waiver by any party of a breach be deemed to be a waiver of any subsequent breach.

As Chapters 2 and 3 will show, there does not seem to be a uniform transnational standard for interpreting this clause. The ability of this clause to obtain the desired result varies considerably depending on the governing law.

4.1.3 No oral amendments clause

The purpose of this clause is to ensure that the contract is implemented at any time according to its wording and irrespective of what the parties may have agreed later, unless recorded in writing. This clause is useful, particularly when the contract is going to be exposed to third parties, either because it is meant to circulate, for example, in connection with the raising of finance or because its performance requires the involvement of numerous officers of the parties, who are not necessarily all authorised to represent the respective party. In the former scenario, third parties who assess the value of the contract must be assured that they can rely on the contract's wording. If oral amendments were possible, an accurate assessment of the contract's value could not be made simply on the basis of the document. In the latter scenario, the parties must feel sure that the contract may not be changed by an agreement given by some representatives who are not duly authorised to do so. In a large organisation, it is essential that the ability to make certain decisions is reserved for the bodies or people with the relevant formal competence. A typical no oral amendments clause reads as follows:

> No amendment or variation to this Agreement shall take effect unless it is in writing, signed by authorised representatives of each of the Parties.

As Chapters 2 and 3 will show, there does not seem to be a uniform transnational standard for interpreting this clause. The ability of this clause to obtain the desired result varies considerably depending on the governing law.

4.2 Subject to contract clause

In connection with larger commercial contracts with long-lasting and complicated negotiations, a widespread practice is to sign various documents in the course of the negotiations, usually named 'Letter of Intent', 'Heads of Agreement' or 'Memorandum of Understanding'. In the traditional picture of contract formation, a letter of intent is hard to categorise: it is not an offer, it is not an acceptance and it is not the final contract text. It is a pre-contractual document with an unclear function.[21]

The legal effects of a letter of intent cannot be assessed once and for all, mainly because the content and function of letters of intent vary considerably from case to case. What is common to all of these forms is that they have a clause, usually the last one, stating something along the following lines:

> This document is a letter of intent and is not binding on the parties. Failure to reach an agreement shall not expose any party to liability towards the other party.

Letters of intent may be quite detailed, so much so that they sometimes could be mistaken to be the final contract – if it were not for the subject to contract clause. One reason for entering into such a detailed a letter of intent in advance of the final contract is that the parties may not yet have negotiated all of the specific aspects of their cooperation and may therefore not be in a position to be able to write the contract with the degree of detail that they would feel comfortable with. As the details may have a significant impact on the evaluation of the transaction, it is understandable that the parties do not want to be bound until all technical, financial, commercial etc. elements have finally been agreed upon.

If the parties do not, and with good reason, want to be bound until they have agreed on all the aspects of their cooperation, why do they describe their cooperation in such a precise way in the letter of intent? What is this document meant to achieve? The document is said to not be binding, not only in respect of the freedom not to finalise the cooperation, but also in respect of the content of the cooperation: should one party, during the negotiations, depart from some of the parameters that were set forth in the letter of intent, it would not be in breach of contract because the document is not a binding contract. During the detailed negotiations, numerous issues may arise that have an impact on the parties' respective evaluation of their own and the other party's contribution to the cooperation, and this may have consequences relating to the split of the profit and liabilities between themselves. It is, therefore, understandable that the parties do not want to be bound to some items of the deal as long as the others are unclear.

While it may from a legal point of view be possible to argue that a certain parameter was not binding, its disregard may create practical difficulties during the negotiations, and a sudden change of position in such an important respect might undermine the mutual trust that is necessary for successful cooperation.

Therefore, the letter of intent may be seen as an attempt to convey a certain moral pressure against unjustified modifications to the terms contained therein, sometimes

---

[21] More extensively, see Giuditta Cordero Moss, 'The Function of Letters of Intent and their Recognition in Modern Legal Systems', in Reiner Schulze (ed.), *New Features in Contract Law* (Sellier European Law Publishers, 2007), pp. 139–59.

coupled (possibly unconsciously) with a malicious thought that this might restrict the other party's freedom, while one's own freedom remains unaffected due to the non-binding character of the document. Sometimes the moral pressure is expressed in the same clause determining the non-binding character of the document, which continues with a provision according to which 'the parties shall continue negotiations in good faith', or 'the parties shall use their best efforts to reach an agreement'. Often these clauses are not considered to be particularly binding: they are defined as being 'only' best effort obligations and, therefore, they are deemed to be without any binding content. The legal effects of these obligations will be touched upon in Chapter 3, Section 4.2.1.

It is not unusual for one party to emphasise the last article of the letter of intent regarding the parties not being bound. In these cases, a party may deem that the most important function of a letter of intent consists in establishing that the parties are not bound. A party may, for example, wish to keep all possibilities open to start similar cooperation with a third party, or to enter that specific market on its own. A letter of intent specifically stating that the parties are not bound may create the illusion that any break-off of the negotiations is acceptable. If the parties want to maintain full liberty in respect of the negotiations, why do they execute a document describing in relative detail the result that the negotiations are supposed to achieve? Sometimes the explanation may be found in a malicious use of the ambiguity of this document. The non-binding character will be invoked if one party wishes to break off the negotiations or to modify the terms set forth in the letter of intent, whereas the moral commitment will be invoked if it wishes to prevent the other party from doing so. Also in this case, as we saw for the previous clauses, Chapters 2 and 3 will show that there is no uniform standard according to which the clause can be interpreted.

4.3 Early termination clause

Early termination clauses stipulate that the contract may be terminated prior to its planned expiry if certain events occur; for example, one party may be given the power to terminate the contract early upon breach by the other party of certain obligations. The clause is meant to be operative irrespective of the consequences of the breach or of the early termination. By this clause, the parties attempt to avoid the uncertainty connected with the evaluation of how serious the breach is and what impact it has on the contract. This evaluation is due to the requirement, to be found in most applicable laws, that a breach must be fundamental if the innocent party shall be entitled to terminate the contract. By defining certain terms as essential in the contract, or by spelling out that certain breaches give the innocent party the power to terminate the contract, the parties attempt to specify effects that arise automatically, instead of allowing for an evaluation that takes all of the circumstances into consideration.

As Chapters 2 and 3 will show, the effects of these clauses may vary depending on the governing law, and transnational sources do not seem to provide a sufficiently detailed standard of interpretation that could provide any harmonisation.

4.4 Arbitration clauses

The wording of arbitration clauses is another good example of the importance of English law requirements to the drafting of international contracts. It is also an example of international contract drafting's resistance to change: as will be seen below, international arbitration clauses gradually assumed a wording that was originally meant to respond to some needs for clarity under English law. English law does not have this need for clarity anymore, but arbitration clauses continue to use the same wording.

Arbitration clauses are very detailed in the definition of their scope. This seems to have been a reaction particularly to some English court decisions that placed considerable emphasis on the language of the arbitration clause and drew (out of words that actually were not intended to restrict the scope of the arbitration agreement) unexpected conclusions as to which disputes could be deemed to fall within the scope of the arbitration clause. To name one example, a court interpreted a clause that referred to the arbitration of any disputes 'arising under' a certain contract. The court found that the clause covered only those disputes which may arise regarding the rights and obligations created by the contract itself. A clause referring to arbitration disputes 'in relation to' the contract or 'connected with' the contract, on the contrary, was held to have a wider scope.[22] This lead to more and more detailed formulations aimed at clarifying that the arbitration agreement covers all possible disputes between the parties. These fine verbal distinctions have now been abandoned by English courts: in the words of the House of Lords, these distinctions:

> reflect no credit upon English commercial law. It may be a great disappointment to the judges who explained so carefully the effects of the various linguistic nuances if they could learn that the draftsman ... obviously regarded the expressions 'arising under this charter' ... and 'arisen out of this charter' ... as mutually interchangeable. ...[T]he time has come to draw a line under the authorities to date and make a fresh start.[23]

The House of Lords affirmed that the parties:

> are unlikely to trouble themselves too much about [the clause's] precise language or to wish to explore the way it has been interpreted in the numerous authorities, not all of which speak with one voice. ....[I]f the parties wish to have issues as to the validity of their contract decided by one tribunal and issues as to its meaning or performance decided by another, they must say so expressly.[24]

In spite of the new approach by the English courts, the London Court of International Arbitration (LCIA) still determines the scope of its Model Arbitration clause by

---

[22] *Overseas Union Insurance Ltd* v. *AA Mutual International Insurance Co Ltd* [1988] 2 Lloyd's Rep 63.
[23] *Fiona Trust & Holding Corporation and others* v. *Privalov and others* [2008] 1 Lloyd's L Rep 254 at 257.
[24] *Ibid.*, p. 259.

reference to 'any dispute arising out of or in connection with this contract, including any question regarding its existence, validity or termination'.[25] This detailed
formulation has even spread beyond the area of English law: the Model Arbitration
clause recommended by the Arbitration Institute of the Swedish Chamber of
Commerce refers to 'any dispute, controversy or claim arising out of or in connection with this contract, or the breach, termination or invalidity thereof'.[26] Similarly,
the Model clause of the Swiss rules refers to 'Any dispute, controversy or claim
arising out of, or in relation to, this contract, including the validity, invalidity,
breach or termination thereof',[27] and the Model clause of the UNCITRAL Arbitration Rules to 'Any dispute, controversy or claim arising out of or relating to this
contract, or the breach, termination or invalidity thereof'.[28] Along the same
lines, although somewhat more succinctly, the Model clause of the International
Chamber of Commerce (ICC) refers to 'All disputes arising out of or in connection
with the present contract'.[29]

A detailed arbitration clause is meant to counteract restrictive interpretations
that may be imposed by the applicable arbitration law. A simple clause may
probably have the same effect in many jurisdictions, including those considered
above. The detailed wording of many model clauses is, therefore, redundant.
What a detailed arbitration clause may not achieve, however, no matter how clear
and precise it is, is to extend the scope of what the applicable arbitration law
considers to be arbitrable. The matter of arbitrability will be analysed in Chapter 5,
Section 2.7 below.

4.5 Other clauses

Numerous other clauses could be mentioned to illustrate the attempts at self-
sufficient drafting style of international contracts. In the course of this book, we will
mention clauses on liquidated damages, *force majeure*, hardship, irrevocability of the
offer, amendments to contracts and representations and warranties. These clauses
will serve to show that the same wording, in combination with different governing
laws, may lead to dramatically different results.

Elsewhere, I have published the results of research analysing a large number of
boilerplate clauses and their effects under a variety of legal systems.[30]

---

[25] www.lcia.org/Dispute_Resolution_Services/LCIA_Recommended_Clauses.aspx, last visited on 18 July 2013.
[26] sccinstitute.se/engelska-16.aspx, last visited on 18 July 2013.
[27] www.swissarbitration.org/sa/en/clause.php, last visited on 18 July 2013.
[28] www.uncitral.org/pdf/english/texts/arbitration/arb-rules-revised/arb-rules-revised-2010-e.pdf, last visited on 18 July 2013.
[29] www.iccwbo.org/products-and-services/arbitration-and-adr/arbitration/standard-icc-arbitration-clauses/, last visited on 18 July 2013.
[30] Cordero-Moss (ed.), *Boilerplate clauses.*

5 Conclusion

As was seen above, the text of the final contract is a mixture of legal analysis, the exercise of bargaining power, deference to widespread contract practice, reliance on one's own drafting experience, the need for standardisation, the need for efficiency and the assumption of risk. The proportion of the various components may vary, and in some situations, the assumed risk is well considered, whereas in other situations, it may remind one more of recklessness than of the assumption of calculated risk. Whether calculated or not, a risk is often taken, and is taken as a consequence of the dynamics of contract negotiations, as described in Section 3.

A judge or an arbitrator who assumes that all contracts are always written following the optimal drafting process (i.e. by carefully considering every single clause and its compliance with the governing law), will assume a coherent and conscious will by the parties to comply with the applicable law. If the contract terms are not well coordinated with the applicable law, which is likely to happen considering the dynamics of contract drafting explained above, the judge or arbitrator may react by proposing ingenious constructions in an attempt to reconcile the two aspects. The parties, however, may have taken it as a calculated risk that there was no conformity between the contract terms and the applicable law. The ingenious reconciliation made by an interpreter who assumes that the drafters had a high degree of awareness of the applicable law, may come as a larger surprise to the parties than that of the incompatibility of the contract terms with the applicable law.

Additionally, observers may induce from the practice whereby contracts are drafted without considering the applicable law that international contract practice refuses to acknowledge national laws. On this assumption, observers may propose that contracts should be governed by transnational rules instead of national laws. However, that the parties may have disregarded the applicable law as a result of a cost–benefit evaluation does not necessarily mean that they want to opt out of the applicable law. When interpreting international contracts, it is important to acknowledge that contract drafting's disregard for the governing law is a consequence of calculated risk, and not a symptom that implies that the drafters refuse to be subject to the governing law. The parties are still interested in enforcing their rights, and enforceability is ensured only by the judicial system of the applicable law.

An important shift in attitude occurs between the contract drafting phase and the contract interpretation or litigation phase. The phase of negotiations and drafting may be characterised by the above-described commercially inspired cost–benefit evaluations, which induce the parties to minimise the resources employed in tailoring the contract to the governing law, and to rely on a detailed and as exhaustive as possible description of the deal instead. Once a contract is signed, however, a new phase starts. The drafting lawyers (often termed 'transaction lawyers') are not involved with that contract anymore, and contract implementation is usually taken over by engineers or commercial people. When a dispute arises between the parties, or a difference in the interpretation becomes apparent, other lawyers are involved, who usually deal with dispute resolution (often termed 'litigation lawyers'). These litigation lawyers have a different approach from their negotiating counterparts: they often do not even talk to the drafting lawyers, so that the transaction lawyer is never informed about the problems arising out of his or her contracts, and the litigation lawyer never gets insight into the reasoning behind a specific wording. Litigation lawyers carefully analyse the specific contract and its effects under the governing law, and try to assess as precisely as possible the chances of winning a case in court or securing a favourable arbitration result on the basis of the contract wording, the applicable law and the degree of factual background that the governing law allows. On the basis of this assessment, they will develop a strategy that may range from seeking to reach a commercial solution if the probability of winning in court is not high, to insisting on the party's own position in cases where the prospects of a successful legal suit are high. In this phase, therefore, predictability of the legal framework and of the criteria applied for a decision are of the utmost importance.

In the context of such a picture, it is doubtful that the effects of the governing law on the contract should be disregarded to permit the drafter's ambitions of self-sufficiency to be realised.

2

The role of transnational law

1 Introduction

That international contracts are drafted without taking into consideration the requirements and assumptions of any particular contract law seems hard to reconcile with the necessity of interpreting and applying international contracts in accordance with a particular governing law. Taking contract practice as a starting point, the observer could be tempted to question how an international contract shall be subject to a law that was not considered during the drafting. Scholarly writings have been proposing a uniform international commercial law as a desirable alternative to the traditional system that sees international contracts subject to a national law chosen by the parties or selected on the basis of conflict rules.[1]

This literature presents various arguments aimed at showing that national laws are not adequate sources for governing international contracts. Arguments range from the rather pragmatic (and irrefutable) observation that it is costly and time consuming to analyse, for every contract, all potentially applicable laws, to the not necessarily always appropriate statement that conflict rules are a confusing and complicated mechanism and thus should be avoided, or to the usually unsubstantiated statement that national laws' content is adequate to regulate domestic but not international contracts. This latter argument seems to be less frequently invoked following the publication of principles and rules made specifically for international contracts (such as the UNIDROIT Principles of International Commercial Contracts (UPICC) or the Principles of European Contract Law (PECL) described in Section 4.2). As these rules and principles – tailored to international contracts – show no structural differences from those of national laws, it is difficult to affirm that national laws are not adequate for governing international contracts.

When seeking solutions that adequately cater to the peculiarities of international contract drafting, however, it is necessary to consider their feasibility

---

[1] Literature on the subject matter is vast. Among the works most frequently referred to are Filip De Ly, *International Business Law and Lex Mercatoria* (TMC Asser Institute, 1992); Klaus Peter Berger, *The Creeping Codification of the Lex Mercatoria*, 2nd edn (Kluwer Law International, 2010); and Ole Lando, 'The *Lex Mercatoria* in International Commercial Arbitration', (1985) 34 *International and Comparative Law Quarterly*, 747–68. For extensive references, see Roy Goode, Herbert Kronke, and Ewan McKendrick, *Transnational Commercial Law: Texts, Cases and Materials* (Oxford University Press, 2007), pp. 24ff.

and effectiveness. Are harmonised sources available on a transnational level that are capable of fully regulating the interpretation and application of contracts, thus making national contract laws redundant? Moreover, do the drafting style and practice constitute a sufficiently clear basis for selecting the applicable sources, thus justifying an approach that does not require the application of choice-of-law rules?

Certainly, the variety of national laws to which an international contract may be subject requires awareness of the different systems, and contract practice must be adapted to the applicable law under any given circumstances. This is costly and time consuming. As Chapter 1 showed, many drafters accept the consequences of these difficulties and draft contracts that are not adjusted to the applicable law – considering this as a calculated legal risk. The alternative envisaged by the proponents of a transnational law, is a uniform law applied in the same way all over the world. This would obviously be much more efficient.[2]

As this chapter will show,[3] however, there are no real alternatives to a state governing law when it comes to principles of general contract law upon which the interpretation and application of the agreed wording is based. Restatements of soft law, compilations of trade usages, digests of transnational principles and other international instruments may be invaluable in determining the content of specific

---

[2] That such efficiency would be desirable is not evident: just as the diversity in languages makes communication less efficient but enriches the cultural picture, so should the various legal traditions be seen as a strength rather than a weakness. There does not seem to be an evident or unified need for harmonisation, and voices are raised to underline that it might be 'better to celebrate our diversity rather than continue the quest for (a dull) uniformity' (Ewan McKendrick, 'Harmonisation of European Contract Law: The State We Are In', in Stefan Vogenauer and Stephen Weatherill (eds.), *The Harmonisation of European Contract Law*, (Hart Publishing, 2006), pp. 5–29, 28). Voices are also raised to warn against being lead 'into accepting the view that all non-state norms are a panacea for all ills, or that State laws or borders are the enemy' (Simeon Symeonides, 'Party Autonomy and Private-law Making: The Lex Mercatoria That Isn't' (19 November 2006), ssrn.com/abstract=946007, 24, last accessed 27 August 2013). That harmonisation of substantive law is not necessarily the only way to go seems to be reflected in a recent move within the European Commission: in February 2009, the work on a European contract law and, in particular, the Common Frame of Reference (CFR) project was transferred from the Commission's Consumer Affairs Directorate to its Justice, Freedom and Security Director, of which Jonathan Faull was Director General. Mr Faull stated, in the evidence he gave to the House of Lords' inquiry on European contract law, that 'the thrust is very much one of mutual recognition rather than harmonization', see the UK House of Lords European Union Committee, Social Policy and Consumer Affairs (Sub-Committee G), 12th Report of Session 2008– 09, *European Contract Law: The Draft Common Frame of Reference, Report with Evidence*, (10 June 2009), www.publications.parliament.uk/pa/ld200809/ldselect/ldeucom/95/9502.htm, last accessed 27 August 2013, question 143. See also Sections 53 and 93 of the Report. Recently, a law and economics-inspired view has received attention in Europe, according to which legal systems compete with each other to offer the most attractive regulation. For an overview and a criticism of this view in the context of contract law, see Stefan Vogenauer, 'Regulatory Competition through Choice of Contract Law and Choice of Forum in Europe: Theory and Evidence', (2013) 1 *European Review of Private Law*, 13–78.

[3] See also Giuditta Cordero-Moss, 'Does the Use of Common Law Contract Models give Rise to a Tacit Choice of Law or to a Harmonised, Transnational Interpretation?', in Giuditta Cordero-Moss (ed.), *Boilerplate Clauses, International Commercial Contracts and the Applicable Law* (Cambridge University Press, 2011), pp. 37–61.

contract regulations, such as the INCOTERMS used for the definition of the place of delivery in international sales.[4] However, these sources do not, for the moment, provide a sufficiently precise basis for addressing questions such as the function of a contract, the advisability of ensuring a fair balance between the parties' interests, the role of the interpreter in respect of obligations that are not explicitly regulated in the contract, the existence of a duty of the parties to act loyally towards each other and the existence and extent of a general principle of good faith. Some of the mentioned transnational sources – in particular, the UPICC and the PECL, as well as the various products of the on-going work on a European contract law, such as the Draft Common Frame of Reference (DCFR) and the proposal for a regulation on a common European sales law (CESL), both based on the PECL – solve these questions by making extensive reference to good faith; however, good faith is a legal standard that requires specification, and there does not seem to be any generally acknowledged legal standard of good faith that is sufficiently precise to be applied uniformly, irrespective of the governing law, as Sections 4.2 and 4.3 below will show.

Moreover, these instruments grant the interpreter much room for interference regarding the wording of the contract – based on the central role given to the principle of good faith. This seems to contradict the very intention of the parties as it is embodied in contract practice: as was seen in Chapter 1, contract practice has ambitions of being exhaustive and self-sufficient. Any correction by principles such as good faith would run counter to the expectations of the parties. In turn, this makes it difficult to see these transnational sources as an emanation of the parties' will and practice.

It is legitimate to wonder whether the cure is perhaps worse than the disease. If the alternative is less than a uniformly applied and exhaustive law, the result is a mixture of national laws and partly harmonised rules – some of which are not necessarily applicable, and others of which may be subject to a variety of interpretations. The advantages of embracing such a fragmented system are less evident.

Practitioners are remarkably absent from this debate,[5] in spite of the obvious relevance of their point of view. This results in the paradox of scholars disputing what is best for contract practice, without the benefit of receiving input from those who have practical experience of the issues.

Legal practice seems sceptical regarding a transnational law, mainly because of the difficulties in determining the exact content of such a harmonised non-national law. As will be seen in the following sections, the principles that can be determined as

---

[4] The INCOTERMS, however, do not cover all legal effects relating to the delivery: for example, they do not determine the moment when the title passes from the buyer to the seller, as pointed out by Maria Celeste Vettese *Multinational Companies and National Contracts'* in Giuditta Cordero-Moss (ed.), *Boilerplate Clauses, International Commercial Contracts and the Applicable Law* (Cambridge University Press, 2011), Section 2.

[5] As Lord Mustill incisively put it twenty years ago: 'The commercial man is a conspicuous absentee from the writings on the *lex mercatoria*', in Lord Mustill, 'The New *Lex Mercatoria*: The First Twenty-five Years', (1988) 4 *Arbitration International*, 86–119, 86. The same may be affirmed today.

being part of a transnational law are mainly quite vague and therefore cannot be used to decide on specific disputes of a legal–technical character. Furthermore, this law is quite fragmentary, leaving many areas of a dispute uncovered.

It has been argued that the open and incomplete character of the transnational law is not a disadvantage, but a positive characteristic: by not containing specific solutions or clear criteria, the transnational law would permit an arbitral tribunal to develop solutions in a creative way, acting as a 'social engineer'.[6] The parties would delegate to the arbitral tribunal the task of developing the criteria according to which the decision will be taken. This approach exhibits a deep trust in the capability of the arbitral tribunal as a lawmaker, but it seems to disregard the criterion of predictability. As this chapter will show, transnational law lacks a framework within which arbitrators would develop their solutions – this would make the arbitrators' creative work even less predictable. Fascinating as the idea of arbitrators as social engineers may be, the prospect of having to plead in front of a tribunal that develops its own criteria for decision-making alarmingly reminds one of the position of Josef K. in Franz Kafka's dystopian novel *Der Prozess*.

To the extent that the difficulty in identifying transnational rules and their fragmentation are seen as a negative aspect of the transnational law, a remedy may be found in the restatements, systematisations and standardisation that have been produced in the past decades, such as the UPICC or the PECL (which, together with the 1980 Vienna CISG, are sometimes referred to as the 'Troika'; a body of transnational law that is particularly apt for governing commercial contracts).[7]

Subjecting a contract to regulation by commercial practices or generally acknowledged principles or restatements thereof, however, would leave too much room for discretion, as will be seen below, thus representing an uncertain ground for the solution of potential disputes.

The theory of a harmonised transnational law seems to be based on the misconception that commercial parties desire a flexible system that the interpreter (judge or arbitrator) can adapt to their needs. Practitioners, however, emphasise that they desire a predictable legal system that can be objectively applied by the interpreter. The task of adapting the contract to the specific needs of the case is a task for the contract drafters, not for the interpreter.[8] We have commented in Chapter 1, Section

---

[6] Lando, 'The *Lex Mercatoria*', 752; Ole Lando, 'The Law Applicable to the Merits of the Dispute', (1986) 2 *Arbitration International*, 104–15, 112.

[7] See, for example, Ole Lando, 'CISG and its Followers: A Proposal to Adopt Some International Principles of Contract Law', (2005) 53 *American Journal of Comparative Law*, 379–402.

[8] For an interesting analysis of this aspect see W. Grosheide, 'The Duty to Deal Fairly in Commercial Contracts', in Stefan Grundmann and Denis Mazeaud (eds.), *General Clauses and Standards in European Contract Law* (Aspen Publishers, 2006), pp. 197–204, 201. The practitioners' reluctance to agree on the assumption that international contracts are drafted and should be interpreted outside of a domestic system of law was recently confirmed in Marcel Fontaine and Filip De Ly, *Drafting International Contracts. An Analysis of Contract Clauses* (Brill Academic Publishing, 2006), pp. 629ff. The book is an analysis of contract terms based on the reports prepared by the Working Group on International Contracts, a group that has

3 on the different approaches taken by transaction lawyers, who draft the contracts, and by litigation lawyers, who deal with the disputes arising out of the contracts. One of the aspects that interests litigation lawyers is the enforceability of rights (whether these are based on a contract or on an arbitral award). Also, it is extremely important that the parameters for enforceability be predictable:[9] if the criteria upon which the dispute will be decided are uncertain, it will be impossible to assess the risk connected with the dispute. How can a party embark on a costly proceeding that might last for years, without having been able to assess the risks connected with it?

2 Sources of transnational law

There is no standard definition of a non-national set of rules and principles that is held to apply to international contracts. The sources that are often mentioned in the international literature as a basis for such a transnational law have different places in the system:

(i) *Usages of the trade or customs* are, under the traditional view, the proper content of what goes under the name of *lex mercatoria*.[10] They are a source of law to all effects and, once proven, they are binding. A statutory confirmation of the quality of customs as sources of law can be found in various national laws. Contract practice and arbitration practice – if sufficiently proven and generalised – may be seen as a trade usage or custom.

(ii) *General principles of law* are part of the law and, once established, they are applied and given effect to. There does not seem to be a consensus on the definition of these principles.[11] Generally recognised principles are usually identified by assessing a convergence among various legal systems, case law and scholarly works.

(iii) *Soft law* is a term that has recently started being used as a synonym for transnational law.[12] Originally, the term is to be found in the field of public international law, and refers to sources that do not have binding force, but that are taken into consideration to such an extent that parties voluntarily apply

existed since 1975 and consists of practising lawyers who specialise in drafting, interpreting or litigating international contracts, as well as of academics. Criticising the possibility of a contract that is independent from any governing law see also Symeonides, *Party Autonomy and Private-law Making*, pp. 6ff.

[9] See the survey by the School of International Arbitration, Queen Mary University of London, *International Arbitration Survey: Choices in international arbitration*, www.arbitrationonline.org/docs/2010_InternationalArbitrationSurveyReport.pdf, p. 13. See also the survey published by the Law Society of England and Wales, *Firms' Cross-border Work*, December 2010, ec.europa.eu/justice/news/consulting_public/0052/contributions/224_en.pdf, last accessed 27 August 2013, p. 8.

[10] Substantiating this position, see Goode, Kronke, McKendrick, *Transnational Commercial Law*, pp. 25ff.

[11] For an overview of the various theories see De Ly, *International Business Law and Lex Mercatoria*, pp. 193ff.

[12] For example T. Wilhelmson, 'International *Lex Mercatoria* and Local Consumer Law: An Impossible Combination?' (2004) 3 *Revue européenne de droit de la consommation*, 138.

them (such as codes of conduct or ethical rules). A notable source of soft law concerns the restatements of general principles of contract law (such as the UPICC or the PECL). To the extent that these restatements of principles can be deemed to reflect generally recognised principles, they will be relevant in determining the content of the general principles of law; otherwise, they will be considered for their persuasive authority. According to some, even standard contracts may be considered as a source of soft law.

(iv) Sometimes, general principles of public international law, often as determined in state–investor arbitration, are deemed to be a source of transnational commercial law.[13]

(v) Sometimes a broader definition is used that covers, in addition, authoritative national and international sources (such as treaties and conventions), as long as they regulate international business activity.[14]

Some of the instruments listed above are extremely widely acknowledged, and after years or even decades of general use in practice, are, in some cases, deemed to have become an international trade practice, and are therefore applied even if the parties have not made reference to them (if the applicable law directs or permits the judge to apply trade usages). Others are in the process of obtaining a generalised acknowledgement, and cannot be considered as customary law yet; therefore, they are applicable only to the extent that the parties have made reference to them in their agreement.

Irrespective of the degree of acknowledgement of all the above-mentioned sources of transnational law, their application faces the question of the relationship with the state law that governs the transaction: is transnational law a replacement of state law, or does it integrate it, and to what extent can the state law be replaced or integrated?

These questions will be dealt with in the following sections by analysing some examples. The examples will show that transnational law is an extremely useful tool with which to integrate the law applicable to an international transaction, but it is not capable of replacing it completely, and it cannot prevail in the case of a conflict with the mandatory rules of applicable national or international rules.

Moreover, we will see that transnational sources are not so detailed as to provide a uniform basis for understanding principles such as that of good faith – and this in spite of the circumstance that many transnational sources attach great significance to the principle of good faith in the interpretation of contracts, as well as in respect of contract performance and the exercise of remedies for non-performance. There is, therefore, no harmonised standard for contract interpretation in the transnational law, nor harmonised guidelines for contract performance and for the exercise of remedies.

---

[13] For example, the Trans-Lex Transnational Law Digest and Bibliography (www.trans-lex.org/, last visited on 11 August 2013), uses investment awards to substantiate numerous principles listed therein as part of the 'new *lex mercatoria*'.

[14] Lando, 'The *Lex Mercatoria*', 748f.

Before analysing these questions, however, it may be useful to present more detail on the three sources that are sometimes referred to as the Troika.[15] A characteristic goal of the Troika is to act as the general contract law that governs all aspects of the legal relationship between the parties. The Troika should therefore, according to the supporters of this concept, replace the state governing law. As will be seen below, this creates various challenges in terms of enforceability that should not be underestimated. An instrument with the task of harmonising different legal traditions must be precise and leave little to the judge's discretion; otherwise, the harmonised rules are applied differently by the different countries' courts.[16]

2.1 The CISG

The CISG was drafted by the United Nations Commission on International Trade Law (UNCITRAL) and adopted in Vienna in 1980.[17] The Vienna Convention is based on two previous attempts to achieve a uniform law on international sales: the conventions relating to the Uniform Law on the Formation of Contracts for the International Sale of Goods (ULF) and to the Uniform Law on the International Sale of Goods (ULIS), both adopted in The Hague in 1964. These two predecessors of the CISG did not obtain widespread success, among other reasons, because their provisions were said to primarily reflect the legal traditions and economic situation of Western Europe. Western Europe was also the region that had been most active in the drafting of the conventions, thus enhancing the impression that these instruments expressed the interests of a certain part of the world. In 1968, the UNCITRAL was given the task of elaborating these two conventions into a text that could enjoy broader support. After having involved states from every geographical region in the process, the UNCITRAL presented the CISG as an elaboration of its two predecessors, with modifications that rendered it acceptable to states with different legal, economic and social backgrounds.[18]

The CISG has been signed by seventy-nine parties so far, and it is looked upon with extreme interest, especially in academic circles,[19] as the first example of a

---

[15] See, for example, Lando, 'CISG and Its Followers', 379ff. For further references see Goode, Kronke, McKendrick, *Transnational Commercial Law*, pp. 46ff.

[16] H. Eidenmüller, F. Faust, H. C. Grigoleit, N. Jansen, G. Wagner and R. Zimmermann, 'The Common Frame of Reference for European Private Law: Policy Choices and Codification Problems', (2008) 28(4) *Oxford Journal of Legal Studies*, 659–708.

[17] The full text can be found on the UNCITRAL's homepage, www.uncitral.org, which also contains an updated list of the countries that have ratified it, the reservations that were made etc.

[18] See the Explanatory Note by the UNCITRAL Secretariat on the United Nations Convention on Contracts for the International Sale of Goods, p. 1. The Note can be found at www.cisg.law.pace.edu/cisg/text/p23.html.

[19] See, for example, Bernard Audit, 'The Vienna Sales Convention and the *Lex Mercatoria*', in Thomas E. Carbonneau, (ed.), *Lex Mercatoria and Arbitration* (Juris Publishing, 1998), pp. 173–94. For a thorough analysis of the enormous impact of the CISG on scholars, see F. Ferrari (ed.), *The CISG and its Impact on National Legal Systems* (Sellier, 2008), pp. 436ff. Ferrari also shows, however, that the level of awareness about the CISG in the business community and among practising lawyers is strikingly low, see pp. 421ff.

uniform law that not only creates binding law as an international convention that is ratified by so many states, but that even gives recognition to the spontaneous rules born out of commercial practice[20] and itself becomes an autonomous body of international regulation that adapts to the changing circumstances independently from the legal systems of the ratifying states.[21] For the sake of completeness, however, it must be mentioned here that the CISG has not been ratified by such an important country in international commerce as the UK, nor by several states in Central and South America, as well as most Arabic and African countries, India and other South-Asian countries.

The CISG is a binding instrument; therefore, its rules are the prevailing law in the countries that ratified it – unless the parties made use of the possibility, contained in Article 6, to exclude the application of the Convention. Article 6 of the CISG gives the parties the possibility of being able to write in their contract that the CISG shall not be applied. The CISG covers the formation of contracts and the substantive rights and obligations of the buyer and the seller arising out of a contract of sale, such as delivery, conformity of the goods, payment and remedies for breach of the related obligations. The CISG is a binding convention; nevertheless, it is sometimes referred to as having, in addition to its direct binding effect, an authoritative effect that goes beyond its territorial and substantive scope of application, and supposedly makes it one of the most important sources of soft law for general contract law.

2.2 The Principles of International Commercial Contracts (UPICC) and the Principles of European Contract Law (PECL)

A trend of the last few decades has been the attempt to achieve the harmonisation of legal traditions by creating sources of soft law that address the general contract law.

Two prominent examples are the UPICC[22] and the PECL.[23] The UPICC were published first in 1994 by the UNIDROIT, an international organisation established in 1926 with the purpose of unifying private law. The work on the UPICC had started in 1981, in a working group under the direction of the Italian professor Michael Bonell. A second edition was published in 2004 and a third in 2010.

---

[20] This is because of the Convention's many references to trade usages.

[21] This is because of the particular rules on the Convention's interpretation laid down in its Article 7, which require an autonomous interpretation based on the principles underlying the Convention. On the opinion that the CISG is so widely recognised that it is applicable even without having been ratified, see below, Chapter 4, Section 5.3.

[22] UNIDROIT Principles of international commercial contracts, 3rd edn (2010), www.unidroit.org/english/ principles/contracts/principles2010/blackletter2010-english.pdf.

[23] Ole Lando and Hugh Beale (eds.), *Principles of European Contract Law: Parts I and II* (Kluwer Law International, 2002), and Ole Lando, André Prüm, Eric Clive and Reinhard Zimmermann (eds.), *Principles of European Contract Law: Part III* (Kluwer Law International, 2003).

The PECL were published in three volumes, from 1995 to 2002, by the so-called Commission on European Contract Law, a group of academics established in 1982 under the leadership of the Danish professor, Ole Lando. The work on the PECL proceeded largely in parallel with the work on the UPICC, and many members of one working group were also members of the other.

As a result of the partial overlap in these academic groups, the content, structure and terminology of these two collections of principles are largely similar to each other, with certain key differences that will be highlighted below.

Neither the PECL nor the UPICC are international conventions or have a binding effect. They are meant to systematically formulate the main rules prevailing in the field of cross-border contracts in a way that may be interpreted equally in all countries where they are applied. They are not merely a record of existing practices: they are, in part, a codification of generally adopted principles of international contracts and, in part, new rules ('best solutions') developed by a large group of experts from around the world.

As the outcome of the work is not binding, and conflicting mandatory rules or principles of the governing law prevail, the working group could agree to rules and formulations more easily than if it were drafting a convention destined to become binding. Moreover, the work did not require unanimity, and controversial matters could be regulated more easily than if a large consensus was expected – as happens when drafting a convention. These two aspects rendered it easier to codify the 'best rules' in a restatement rather than in binding instruments; however, these same aspects render such a restatement less representative than an instrument based on a larger consensus and to which most members are committed.[24]

These restatements of principles have multiple goals, mentioned in their respective preambles. As they are the result of an extensive comparative study and offer modern and functional solutions, they may be used by legislators as a source of inspiration when legislating in the field of general contract law. Due to the persuasive authority that derives from the high quality of the working group that prepared them, they could be used by courts or arbitrators to interpret existing international instruments. Moreover, as a guide to the drafting, they may be used by contractual parties during the preparation of their contract. The parties to an international contract might decide to subject their contract to the regulation of the restatements, as an expression of a balanced, international set of rules, rather than choosing a national governing law (on this particular use of the principles, it is necessary to make some reservations; see below, section 6). The restatements of principles might be useful for arbitrators, especially when deciding a dispute on

---

[24] See, extensively, Goode, Kronke, McKendrick, *Transnational Commercial Law*, pp. 509 and 528ff, explaining, in this light, why the principle of good faith and fair dealing was given such a central role in the UNIDROIT Principles but not in the CISG. See also McKendrick, 'Harmonisation of European Contract Law', pp. 5–29, 8.

the basis of the transnational law: rather than having to search for what could constitute international usages of trade or other sources of the transnational law that are difficult to identify, arbitrators could rely on a readily available set of rules. Finally, the restatements of principles aspire to be used by courts or arbitrators, instead of the governing law, should the content of the law be impossible or extremely difficult to establish. A significant difference between the two restatements is that the UPICC have no specific territorial scope and apply to any international contract, whereas the PECL have defined Europe as their scope of application. This has prompted higher goals for the PECL: in addition to aspiring to the status of a source of soft law, as described above, the PECL aspire to become the prevailing (on a long-term basis, binding) contract law within the EU and to replace the national laws that exist in every state today. The PECL have actually been used as a basis for the on-going work on a European contract law. The work was initiated at the beginning of this millennium,[25] and in 2004,[26] the European Commission entrusted a joint network on European Private Law with the preparation of a proposal for a Common Frame of Reference (CFR). The CFR was intended to be a toolbox for the Community legislator: it could be used as a set of non-binding guidelines by lawmakers at the Community level as a common source of inspiration, or for reference in the law-making process. It was intended to be a set of definitions, general principles and model rules in the field of contract law, to be derived from a variety of sources – such as a systematisation of the existing EU law and a comparative analysis of the Member States' laws. The Study Group on a European Civil Code and the Research Group on the Existing EC Private Law[27] jointly used the PECL as a basis for a DCFR that was finalised at the end of 2008.[28] The DCFR is subject to debate, both by politicians[29] and scholars,[30] and is referred to as 'academic', to underline that it is the result of the work of two academic groups and is not to be confused with what will be the final result of the European political process.

---

[25] Resolution of the European Parliament on the Annual Legislative Programme of March 16, 2000, 29/12/ 2000 OJ C 377, p. 323.

[26] Communication from the European Commission to the European Parliament and the Council 'European Contract Law and the Revision of the Acquis: The Way Forward', COM (2004) 651 final.

[27] The Acquis Group also published the Acquis Principles, a systematisation of the existing European law: Research Group on the Existing EC Private Law (Acquis Group), *Principles of the Existing EC Contract Law (Acquis Principles) – Contract II: General Provisions, Delivery of Goods, Package Travel and Payment Services* (Sellier, European Law Publisher, 2009).

[28] Study Group on a European Civil Code/Research Group on EC Private Law (eds.), *Principles, Definitions and Model Rules of European Private Law: Draft Common Frame of Reference (DCFR)* (Sellier European Law Publishers, 2009).

[29] Discussion on the topic of the Common Frame of Reference (CFR) in the Council of the European Union, initiated by the Presidency on 28 July 2008, 8286/08JUSTCIV 68 CONSOM 39.

[30] Eidenmüller, *et al.* 'The Common Frame of Reference'; Nils Jansen and Reinhard Zimmermann, '"A European Civil Code in All but Name": Discussing the Nature and Purposes of the Draft Common Frame of Reference', (2010) 69 *Cambridge Law Journal*, 98–112.

Another project of the Commission is the CESL, contained in a proposal for a Regulation dated 11 October 2011.[31] This is meant to be an optional instrument that applies only if the parties expressly agree on its application. The CESL is meant to apply to contracts between businesses and consumers, as well as to contracts between businesses and small- and medium-sized enterprises. Additionally, the CESL is, like the Academic DCFR, largely based on the PECL.

Depending on the development of these processes,[32] the PECL may become the basis of a European body of rules that eventually may be subject to interpretation or application by the European Court of Justice (ECJ). In such a case, over time, a coherent body of case law would be formed, and the content of the general clauses contained in these instruments would be easier to determine. As long as there is no centralised court creating a uniform jurisprudence, it will be difficult to have a harmonised interpretation of these instruments, as Section 4 will show.

3 Sources harmonising specific sectors

Transnational sources have proven to be successful, particularly in harmonising specific areas of international commercial law – as opposed to the general contract law, which will be examined in Section 4. Harmonisation of specific areas can be achieved in various ways: (i) through binding instruments such as the 1980 Vienna Convention (CISG), which creates a uniform law for certain aspects of sale contracts; (ii) through instruments issued by international bodies but without binding effect, such as the 1985 UNCITRAL Model Law on International Commercial Arbitration, revised in 2006 and meant to be a model for legislators,[33] or the UNCITRAL Arbitration Rules of 1976, revised in 2010 and meant to be adopted by the parties as an integration of the arbitration agreement;[34] and (iii) through instruments issued by private organisations such as the ICC, and without binding effect, unless the parties to the contract adopt them – such as the International Commercial Terms (INCOTERMS) or the Uniform Customs and Practices for Documentary Credits (UCP) 600 (formerly 500).

Common to these instruments is the fact that they have a specific scope of application: certain aspects of the contract of sale for the CISG, the procedural aspects of arbitration for the Model Law on Arbitration and the UNCITRAL Arbitration Rules, the passage of risk from seller to buyer and other specific obligations between

---

[31] COM (2011) 635 final.

[32] The developments relating to the CFR may be followed at ec.europa.eu/consumers/rights/contract_law_en.htm#cfr. The developments relating to the CESL may be followed at ec.europa.eu/justice/newsroom/news/20111011_en.htm.

[33] This instrument is not binding, as it is a model for legislators. If adopted, it will have the force of law in the system that has enacted it.

[34] This instrument is not binding, as it is a model for regulating the arbitral proceeding that the parties to the dispute may decide to adopt. If adopted by the parties, the Arbitration Rules will have the same status as a contract between them.

the parties for the INCOTERMS and the mechanism of documentary credits for the UCP 600. These instruments do not have the goal of regulating all aspects of the relationship between the parties, such as the validity of the contract, its interpretation or all remedies for breach of contract.

Thanks to this specific scope of application, the enforceability of these instruments is easy to predict and achieve. As their scope of application is specified and usually well within the scope of the freedom of contract, they are generally enforced without any difficulties, as long as they are adopted by the parties or enacted by the legislator.

If the instruments are not incorporated into the contract by the parties, they may nevertheless be applicable as an expression of trade usages. In spite of the undeniably wide recognition of these sources, however, they are not unanimously considered as trade usages; in some countries, they are considered as standard terms of contract that become effective between the parties only if they were expressly incorporated.[35] Furthermore, not all publications issued, for example, by the ICC, enjoy the same degree of recognition as the INCOTERMS and the UCP 600; thus, the simple fact that there is an ICC publication is not sufficient evidence that there is a corresponding trade usage.

Some examples of instruments that harmonise specific sectors are made below.

3.1 INCOTERMS

The INCOTERMS, a publication by the ICC, illustrate how transnational sources may reach harmonisation by supplementing national law. The INCOTERMS apply to the cross-border delivery of goods, and are divided into eleven different terms, all expressed by three-letter acronyms (such as FOB, CIF etc.). Each of these abbreviations is a term that allocates specific obligations between the seller and the buyer – primarily, the responsibility for customs clearance, as well as the arranging and paying for transportation and insurance. In addition, each abbreviation defines where delivery is deemed to have been made, and the consequent passage of risk from the seller to the buyer. By writing the abbreviation in the contract and specifying the place of delivery, the parties incorporate the corresponding allocation of obligations, and do not need to regulate all these matters in the contract. For example, writing that delivery has to be made FOB at a named port, means that the seller has to clear the goods for export, transport the goods to the named port and have them loaded on the ship that was organised by the buyer. The goods are deemed to be delivered when they are loaded on the ship, and any damage to the goods occurring after the delivery will be at the risk of the buyer. The buyer is responsible for arranging the ship and the rest of the transportation to the destination, arranging insurance and import clearance.

---

[35] See for references, H. van Houtte, *The Law of International Trade*, 2nd edn. (Sweet & Makwell, 2002), Section 8.15. On the challenges that courts may face in applying the UCP in spite of their general acknowledgement, see Christian Twigg-Flesner, 'Standard Terms in International Commercial Law: The Example of Documentary Credits', in Reiner Schulze (ed.), *New Features in Contract Law* (Sellier European Law Publishers, 2007), pp. 325–39.

A dispute regarding whether the seller is obliged to clear the goods for export, who bears the risk of loss until delivery or who was supposed to pay for the insurance during transportation will be easily solved by verifying which term of the INCO-TERMS the parties have chosen.[36] Other disputed matters, such as the validity of the contract or what remedies are available in case of default, are not regulated by the INCOTERMS. For these matters, it will be necessary to consult the governing law. Even matters that are within the scope of the INCOTERMS may be subject to different regulation by the governing law. For example, the question of liability for damages to the goods under transportation, normally directly regulated by the INCOTERMS, may be decided differently under the governing law in the case of exceptional circumstances beyond the parties' control, discharging the seller from the obligations that the contract has imposed on it. Thus, the INCOTERMS are based on the principle that the buyer bears the risk for loss of the goods if the loss occurs after the goods were delivered or were deemed to have been delivered. If the goods are lost after the risk has passed to the buyer, the buyer still has to pay the price to the seller. This, however, may be affected by the governing law. Assuming, for example, that both parties belong to countries that have ratified the CISG, the sale will be subject to the Convention's provisions. Article 66 of the CISG states that, in cases where the goods are lost due to an act or omission by the seller, the buyer is not bound to pay the price to the seller, even if the loss occurred after the risk had passed to the buyer. In a sale that incorporates the INCOTERMS and is subject to the CISG, both rules are applicable. The apparent contradiction may be explained in view of the limited scope of application of the INCOTERMS: this instrument is not concerned with questions regarding the validity of the contract, negligence by the parties etc. These aspects are left to the general contract law to govern. The general rule of the CISG actually confirms the allocation of risk made in the INCOTERMS (Article 66); however, the CISG also regulates the eventuality of negligence by the seller, which is not regulated in the INCOTERMS; hence, the difference between the two rules.

3.2 UCP 600

The UCP 600, a publication by the ICC regulating the payment mechanism of letters of credit (L/C, also called documentary credits), are another example of soft law that supplements the governing law. Like the INCOTERMS, they regulate a specific

---

[36] The eleven terms are divided into seven rules for any mode of transport and four rules for sea and waterway transport. Until 2010, the terms were divided into four groups. This division is not expressly made in the 2010 version, but it is still useful and applicable: the so-called E-terms (such as Ex Works), determining that delivery is made at the place of departure and the goods need not be cleared or loaded; the F-terms (such as Free on Board, FOB), determining that the main carriage is unpaid by the seller, but the goods must be cleared for export; the C-terms (such as Cost Insurance Freight, CIF), determining that the risk passes, although the main carriage is paid by the seller; and the D-terms (such as Duty Delivery Paid, DDP), determining that delivery is made on arrival of the goods to the destination.

mechanism and do not have the goal of covering general matters of contract law. However, they have a larger scope of application and in some situations they may conflict with mandatory rules of the governing law, as will be seen in Section 6.2 below.

Letters of credit are a widely used method of payment, applied when the creditor does not intend to take the commercial risk connected with the creditworthiness of the debtor. Letters of credit are mainly used as a method of payment in sale contracts. In this case, it is the buyer who is requested to open a letter of credit in favour of the seller. However, letters of credit may be used in any situation where a party owes a determined amount of money to another party. Often, for example, letters of credit are used to support payment under performance guarantees – for example, in a long-term supply contract the buyer may request the supplier to guarantee that the supplies will comply with the agreed time schedule and quality specifications. In case of non-compliance, the supplier will have to make payment under the guarantee. In this case, it will be the seller who is required to open a letter of credit in favour of the buyer.

A letter of credit is structured as follows: the debtor (called the applicant) requests a bank (called the issuing bank) to issue a letter of credit in favour of the creditor (called the beneficiary). The application contains the instructions for the issuing bank, and must state the precise amount of money that has to be paid, as well as the documents, upon the presentation of which the bank has to effect payment. This is the main characteristic of a letter of credit: the bank has to effect payment upon presentation of the documents that are named in the instructions. The bank simply has to verify the conformity on the face of the presented documents, and is not requested to assess the proper performance of the underlying transaction, or any other matter. Presentation of the documents is necessary and sufficient to trigger payment by the bank (which explains why letters of credit are also known as documentary credits); the obligation to pay is the bank's own obligation, which means that the beneficiary bears the commercial risk connected with the credit-worthiness of the bank, and not of the applicant. An implication of this fact is that the bank's obligation is autonomous, as the bank does not have any dealings with the underlying transaction upon which the beneficiary's credit towards the applicant is based. The bank's obligation to pay is based on the letter of credit alone. Therefore, the bank cannot invoke defences arising out of the underlying transaction to withhold payment, as long as the listed documents have been presented for payment. The autonomous character of the bank's payment obligation is one of the most charac-teristic aspects of a letter of credit, and is codified in the UCP 600, Articles 4 and 5.

The UCP 600 enjoy, as already mentioned, a general recognition as regulations for letters of credit; they are, at the same time, a source of regulation and a codification of generally acknowledged practices within that area. In particular, the two aspects mentioned above – the autonomy of the payment obligation and the implication of the roles as the advising or corresponding bank – are uniformly applied in letters of credit, irrespective of the fact that the particular letter of credit may or may not make express reference to the UCP 600.

3.3 *Summing up*

Transnational rules regulating specific aspects of a legal relationship are a useful complement to the governing law, and are enforceable if they are incorporated into the contract by the parties and do not violate the mandatory rules of the governing law. If these rules represent trade usages, they will be applicable even without incorporation by the parties, since most of the legal systems refer to trade usages. Even if they are incorporated by the parties into the contract, however, these sources do not replace the governing law. Both the contract and the incorporated sources will be subject to the applicable law, as will be seen in Section 6.2. If these rules are enacted in binding instruments, such as national laws or international conventions, they may also have the ability to prevail over mandatory rules.

4 The difficult task of harmonising legal traditions

As was seen in Section 3, transnational sources are a useful integration of the parties' will and the governing law when they regulate the details of specific aspects within the area of the freedom of contract. In this section, we will examine whether transnational sources achieve the harmonisation of legal traditions through instruments of general contract law and general clauses such as good faith or general contract practice. We will examine four types of sources below: general principles, restatements of principles such as the UPICC and the PECL, digests of principles and trade usages.

4.1 *General principles*

General principles are traditionally listed in scholarly writings as one of the important sources of transnational law that may contribute to the harmonisation of different legal traditions.[37] There does not seem to be a consensus on the definition of these principles;[38] the most recognised criteria for identifying what principles are generally recognised seem to be the reliance on a convergence among various legal systems, case law and scholarly works.

A widely appreciated paper by Lord Mustill identified, nearly three decades ago, twenty-five principles that, in arbitration practice and the literature, were considered as being generally recognised.[39] According to Lord Mustill's evaluation, these principles are 'so general that they are useless',[40] and it is tempting to agree with this evaluation: principles such as *pacta sunt servanda* or *rebus sic stantibus* can hardly be

---

[37] De Ly, *International Business Law and Lex Mercatoria*, pp. 193ff.

[38] For an overview of the various theories see De Ly, *International Business Law and Lex Mercatoria*, pp. 193ff. Goode, Kronke and McKendrick, *Transnational Commercial Law*, pp. 50ff., 100f., convincingly argues that their meaning and content is so uncertain, that they are rarely invoked in practice.

[39] Mustill, *The New Lex Mercatoria*.   [40] *Ibid.*, p. 92.

of guidance when solving a dispute with specific questions of a technical–legal character. The former states the sanctity of an agreement, and the latter states that an agreement is not binding when the conditions under which it was entered into change substantially. Both principles are important fundaments of most laws, and there is no reason to criticise them. However, these principles have such a high degree of abstraction that it may be very difficult to solve a dispute simply on their basis. The sanctity of a contract, for example, assumes that a contract has been entered into; however, the principle does not contain any specific guidelines as to when and how a contract is considered as being entered into. Take the typical example of the so-called 'battle of the forms'. A company that produces and sells certain products may have developed a set of general conditions of sale and endeavours to apply these conditions for each sale contract that it enters into. If the buyer of these products has developed its own general conditions of purchase, each of the parties' desire to apply its own general conditions may lead to a battle of the forms. The legal question that arises in connection with battles of forms is to be solved on the basis of the rules on the formation of contracts under the applicable law. Broadly speaking, there are various approaches: traditionally, an acceptance has to conform to the offer; otherwise, it would be considered as a rejection of the offer and thus as a counter-offer. According to this so-called mirror-image rule, therefore, in the eventuality that one party's offer makes reference to that party's general conditions, and the other party's acceptance makes reference to that other party's general conditions, there is no conformity between the offer and acceptance, and the response to the offer is to be considered as a counter-offer. If the first party, not paying attention to the exchange of conflicting general conditions, starts performing the contract, this will be considered as a tacit acceptance of the other party's counter-offer. This is the so-called 'last-shot theory', according to which the battle of the forms is won by the party who sent its conditions in last. Some legal systems contain a rule according to which, in the case of a conflicting offer and acceptance, a contract may be deemed concluded to the extent that the acceptance was in conformity with the offer, while the general conditions knock each other out to the extent that they are not in conformity with each other, so that none of them will be applicable (the so-called 'knock-out theory'). The principle of *pacta sunt servanda* does not give a basis for choosing between the two approaches.

Moreover, Lord Mustill found that several of these principles cannot be deemed to be generally recognised because they are not known in the common law system; for example, the principle prohibiting the abuse of a right and the principle requesting good faith in the pre-contractual phase.[41] Both principles will be touched upon in section 4.2 below, because they are part of the UPICC, the PECL, the DCFR and the CESL. As will be seen in Chapter 3, there are few principles in respect of good faith

---

[41] *Ibid..*, p. 111, respectively footnotes 85 and 87.

and fair dealing that may be considered as common to the civil law and common law systems; even among civil law systems, there are considerable differences.[42]

4.2 Restatements of principles: the UPICC and the PECL

Since the compilation made by Lord Mustill, a number of initiatives flourished to collect, systematise or restate generally acknowledged principles, thus aiming to reduce the gap between the different legal traditions. The UPICC and the PECL are the most prominent. They were briefly presented in section 2.2 above, and we will here examine to what extent they succeed in achieving the harmonisation of different legal traditions.

These restatements may contain principles and rules that do not reflect generally acknowledged standards, but represent what the restatements' authors considered to be the best rule. Hence, they may not be used as evidence of the general acknow-ledgement of the principles contained therein; however, they could become evidence if they are used consistently and widely in practice.[43]

The UPICC and the PECL give considerable importance to the principle of good faith, which underlies all of the restatements.[44] For example, the parties are under a duty of loyalty to each other, which receives various manifestations under the negotiations, and they are liable for the unjustified break-off of negotiations: contracts shall be interpreted in good faith, performance shall be made in good faith, remedies shall be exercised in good faith. The general principle of good faith, in other words, is, in these restatements, an overriding principle that functions as a corrective action to the mechanisms regulated in the contract whenever a literal application leads to results that seem too harsh, as applied to one of the parties. In order to apply this principle, the interpreter shall look beyond the wording of the contract. An accurate implementation of the contract according to its terms

---

[42] Even Reinhard Zimmermann and Simon Whittaker (eds.), *Good Faith in European Contract Law* (Cambridge University Press, 2000), p. 678, despite the observation that the principle of good faith is relevant to all or most of the doctrines of modern laws of contract, conclude that each system draws a different line between certainty and justice.

[43] See Symeonides, *Party Autonomy and Private-law Making*; Silvia Ferreri points out in The Italian National Report, XVII Congress of the International Academy of Comparative Law, Section II-B1, Private International Law, Utrecht, 16–26 July 2006, in item 6a: 'Paradoxically the success of such soft law instruments depends … on their success'. See also Goode, Kronke, McKendrick, *Transnational Commercial Law*, pp. 521ff.

[44] See Article 1.7 of the UPICC and Article 1:201 of the PECL. Comment No. 1 to Article 1.7 (www.unidroit. org/english/principles/contracts/principles2010/integralversionprinciples2010-e.pdf, last accessed on 30 July 2013) mentions the following provisions: Articles 1.8 and 1.9(2); 2.1.4(2)(b), 2.1.15, 2.1.16, 2.1.18 and 2.1.20; 2.2.4(2), 2.2.5(2), 2.2.7 and 2.2.10; 3.2.2, 3.2.5 and 3.2.7; 4.1(2), 4.2(2), 4.6 and 4.8; 5.1.2 and 5.1.3; 5.2.3 and 5.3.4; 6.1.3, 6.1.5, 6.1.16(2) and 6.1.17(1); 6.2.3(3)(4); 7.1.2, 7.1.6 and 7.1.7; 7.2.2(b)(c); 7.4.8 and 7.4.13; and 9.1.3, 9.1.4 and 9.1.10(1). Also the PECL have numerous specific rules applying the principle of good faith, for example, in Articles 1:202, 2:102, 2:104, 2:105, 2:106, 2:202, 2:301, 4:103, 4:106, 4:109, 4:110, 5:102, 6:102, 8:109, 9:101, 9:102 and 9:509.

may be considered to be against the principle of good faith if it amounts to an abuse of a right. An abuse of a right is defined by the official commentary on Article 1.7 of the UPICC as follows:

> It is characterised by a party's malicious behaviour which occurs for instance when a party exercises a right merely to damage the other party or for a purpose other than the one for which it had been granted, or when the exercise of a right is disproportionate to the originally intended result.[45]

This approach does not seem to be very compatible with the self-sufficiency of the contract that seems to be assumed by international commercial practice, as was described in Chapter 1. At first sight, the regime of the UPICC and of the PECL seems to substantially correspond to the civil law tradition and deviate from the common law approach, which will be described in Chapter 3. Harmonisation seems to be sought by embracing one legal tradition.

A more careful analysis of the matter, however, makes the resemblance between the restatements and the civil law tradition less evident: this is because the standard of good faith, against which the restatements measure pre-contractual liability, interpretation of the contract, performance of the contract and the exercise of remedies is to be established not on the basis of a national legal tradition, but on the basis of the standard generally recognised in international trade.[46]

In the commentary on Article 1.7, the UPICC affirm that the standard of good faith must always be understood as 'good faith in international trade', and that no reference has to be made to any standard that has been developed under any state law.[47] This approach is in line with the requirement of autonomous interpretation of the UPICC contained in Article 1.6 thereof: the UPICC are an instrument with an international character, and it would not serve the purpose of becoming a uniform law if the courts of every state interpreted them each in a different way, in light of their own legal culture. While the requirement of autonomous interpretation of the UPICC, and the corresponding requirement in Article 1:106 of the PECL are understandable in light of the ambitions of harmonising the law of contracts, they do not contribute to creating clarity in respect of the content of good faith as a standard, as will be seen below.[48]

Legal standards, or general clauses, are, per definition, in need of a specification of their content that depends to a large extent on the interpreter's discretion. When the general clause belongs to a state system, the interpreter's discretion is restricted or guided by principles and values underlying that particular system – for example, in

---

[45] Comment No. 2 to Article 1.7 (last accessed on 30 July 2013).

[46] See Article 1.6 of the UNIDROIT Principles of International Commercial Contracts and Article 1:106 of the PECL.

[47] Comment No. 3 to article 1.7 (last accessed on 30 July 2013).

[48] See Cordero-Moss, 'Does the Use of Common Law Contract Models Give Rise to a Tacit Choice of Law?', pp. 52ff (discussing the lack of a recognised standard of good faith in international contract law).

the Constitution, in other legislation or in society at large.[49] How would the interpreter evaluate the wording of an international contract that seems to provide for and permit the very conduct prohibited by the principle of good faith? An interpreter belonging to a tradition where there is no general principle of good faith might tend to consider that the clear wording of the contract indicates that the parties had considered all eventualities, made provision for them and accepted the consequences, and that therefore the articles of the UPICC and the PECL are not applicable. An interpreter belonging to a legal tradition with a strong general principle of good faith, on the other hand, may consider that consequences of a literal application of the contract must be mitigated if they disrupt the balance of interests between the parties. To the former interpreter, a fairness or good faith interpretation consists of an accurate interpretation of the contract. To the latter, it consists of intervening and reinstating a balance between the parties. There does not seem to be any uniform transnational principles or values that are sufficiently precise to permit choosing between these two approaches.[50]

One of the most important sources of generally acknowledged principles of international trade is international contract practice; and international contract practice, as described in Chapter 1, seems to show that the parties expect their contract to be interpreted solely on the basis of its terms. Therefore, it does not seem correct to construe the principle of good faith in the restatements as if it imposed obligations or duties that are in clear contradiction with contract practice, which is one of the most important sources that is used precisely to establish the content of the principle of good faith.

On the other hand, the principle of good faith is undoubtedly given a central role in the restatements; therefore, it does not seem logical to construe it, albeit in accordance with internationally recognised contract practice, in such a restrictive way that it is deprived of any significant role.

This paradox renders the regime of the restatements quite unpredictable in its application, and therefore not fully adequate in terms of regulating commercial relationships where the foreseeability of the legal positions and of the remedies is deemed to be very important.

In Section 4.3 below, we will analyse other sources that may be used to specify the content of the general clauses contained in the restatements of principles.

---

[49] See Peter Schlechtriem, 'The Functions of General Clauses, Exemplified by regarding Germanic Laws and Dutch Law', in Stefan Grundmann, and Denis Mazeaud, (eds.) *General Clauses and Standards in European Contract Law* (Aspen Publishers 2006), pp. 41–55, 49ff (analysing the application of general clauses, with particular, but not exclusive reference to the German system).

[50] See, for more details, Cordero-Moss, 'Does the Use of Common Law Contract Models Give Rise to a Tacit Choice of Law?', pp. 52ff. More extensively, see also Giuditta Cordero-Moss, 'Consumer Protection Except for Good Commercial Practice: A Satisfactory Regime for Commercial Contracts?', in Reiner Schulze (ed.), *CFR and Existing EC Contract Law* (Sellier European Law Publishers, 2009), pp. 78–94.

The dilemma described in connection with the UPICC will affect the interpretation of the corresponding provision in the PECL.

More recently, the already mentioned DCFR[51] and the proposal for a CESL[52] followed the same approach, giving ample room to the principle of good faith. These instruments define the content of the general principle of good faith for commercial contracts by making reference to 'good commercial practice'. As will be seen below, defining a general clause by reference to another general clause does not seem to bring the interpreter any closer to a specification of the former.

Depending on the development of the on-going process to develop a European contract law, described in Section 2.2, the PECL may become the basis of a European body of rules that eventually may be subject to interpretation or application by the ECJ. In such a case, over time, a coherent body of case law would be formed and the content of the principle of good faith would be easier to determine.

The UNIDROIT has taken a commendable role in contributing to the development of a body of case law that may enhance a harmonised interpretation and thus the predictability of the UPICC: following the example of CLOUT, a system established by the UNCITRAL for the collection and dissemination of court decisions and arbitral awards relating to UNCITRAL instruments, the UNIDROIT has established Unilex,[53] a database collecting case law and a bibliography on the UPICC and the CISG. In 1992, Unilex started collecting and publishing, *inter alia*, arbitral awards that contain references to the UPICC. Making available the case law that (if at all published) otherwise would be scattered among the publications issued by different arbitral institutions all over the world is a valuable step in promoting the development of a uniform body of law. When the number of the collected decisions becomes significant and their level of detail is such that they can be used to determine the specific scope of general clauses such as the principle of good faith, the UPICC will be in a position to contribute to the harmonisation of the general contract law – assuming that the decisions do not give contradictory interpretations. As the example of the regulation of entire agreement clauses in Section 4.2.1 will show, however, for the moment, the body of cases is not sufficient to ensure a harmonised interpretation of the principles.

We will see below how the restatements of principles regulate some of the clauses that were described in Chapter 1.

---

[51] This is confirmed in the House of Lords Sub-Committee G Report on European Contract Law Sections 24 ff., and, particularly, 27, 28, 32 and 33. See also Sections 78 and 79, stating the disagreement in principle on a generally interventionist law of contracts as taken by the DCFR, and criticising the generalisation of consumer protection as made in the DCFR. Attached to the Report is a Memorandum by S. Vogenauer, Professor of Comparative Law, University of Oxford, which singles out several areas where the DCFR certainly deviates from English contract law (Section 22) – also including the areas discussed in this book. For similar criticism, see also Eidenmüller, *et al.*, *The Common Frame of Reference for European Private Law.*

[52] Point 31 in the preamble and Articles 23, 49, 86 and 170.   [53] www.unilex.info/

4.2.1 Entire agreement

As seen in Chapter 1, a boilerplate clause that often recurs in contract practice is the entire agreement clause, according to which the document signed by the parties contains the whole agreement and may not be supplemented by evidence of prior statements or agreements.

This clause is recognised in Article 2.1.17 of the UPICC and Article 2:105 of the PECL, with some restrictions: the provisions specify that prior statements or agreements may be used to interpret the contract. This is one of the applications of the general principle of good faith; it is, however, unclear how far the principle of good faith goes in overriding the clause inserted by the parties. If prior statements and agreements may be used to interpret the contract, does this mean that more terms may be added to the contract, because, for example, the parties have discussed certain specifications at length during the negotiations and this has created in one of the parties the reasonable expectation that they would be implied in the contract? Article 1.8 of the UPICC would seem to indicate that this would be the preferred approach under the UPICC. According to this provision, a party may not act in a way that is inconsistent with the reasonable expectations that it has created in the other party. This is spelled out in respect of the entire agreement clause in the PECL, which, in paragraph 4 of Article 2:105, states that 'A party may by its statements or conduct be precluded from asserting a merger clause to the extent that the other party has reasonably relied on them'.

According to this logic, the detailed discussion during the phase of negotiations regarding certain characteristics for the products may create the reasonable expectation that those specifications have become part of the agreement, even if they were not written down in the contract; their subsequent exclusion on the basis of the entire agreement clause may be deemed to be against good faith.

According to the opposite logic, however, the very fact that the parties have excluded from the text of the contract some specifications that were discussed during the negotiations, indicates that no agreement was reached on those matters. Exclusion of those terms from the contract, combined with the entire agreement clause, strongly indicates the will of the parties not to be bound by those specifications. Their subsequent inclusion on the basis of the good faith principle would run counter to the parties' intention.

The foregoing shows that the application of the UPICC and of the PECL requires a specification of the principle of good faith. Is it to be intended as an overriding principle, possibly creating, restricting or modifying the obligations that flow from the text of the contract? Or is it meant to take the text of the contract as a starting point, ensuring that the obligations contained therein are enforced accurately and precisely as the parties have envisaged them? This represents the dichotomy between, on the one hand, the understanding of fairness as a principle ensuring balance between the parties notwithstanding the regulation that the parties may have agreed on, and, on the other hand, the understanding of fairness as a principle ensuring predictability, leaving it to the parties to evaluate the desirability of their contract regulation.

To test the ability of the UPICC to harmonise contract law with the help of the above-mentioned Unilex database, it may be interesting to examine the case law collected in respect of Article 2.1.17 of the UPICC.

At the date of writing this book, the Unilex database contains five decisions on Article 2.1.17 of the UPICC.[54]

In the first decision, ICC award no 9117 of 1998, the arbitral tribunal emphasises that an entire agreement clause is to be considered as typical in a commercial contract, and says that 'there can be no doubt for any party engaged in international trade that the clauses mean, and must mean, what they say'.[55] The contract also contained a no oral amendments clause, which is recognised in Article 2.1.18 of the UPICC. This Article contains a provision containing the same restrictions as Article 2.1.17 regarding conduct that has created expectations in the other party. The arbitral tribunal said that 'the explicit integration clause and the written modification clause, as contained in the Contract, operate as a bar against the assumption that a certain behaviour or practice could reach the level of becoming legally binding between the Parties'. Thus, according to this award, the principle of good faith contained in Articles 1.7 and 1.8 of the UPICC, and specified in Articles 2.1.17 and 2.1.18, does not affect a literal application of the contract's language. This approach seems to be consistent with the ideology underlying the drafting style of international contracts, as described in Chapter 1. Consequently, it considerably restricts the applicability of the principles underlying the UPICC.

Another decision mentioned in Unilex under Article 2.1.17 is by the English Court of Appeal.[56] There, Lord Justice Mummery stated that, under English law, extrinsic evidence could be used to ascertain the meaning of a term contained in a written contract if the term was ambiguous or unclear. On the contrary, extrinsic evidence could not be used to ascertain the content of the contract.[57] Lady Justice Arden considered this distinction as too conservative and argued for a broader use of extrinsic evidence, referring to the UPICC in support of her view.[58]

The narrow use of extrinsic evidence supported by Lord Justice Mummery can be found in another decision listed in the Unilex, rendered on 30 November 2012 by the Sheriffdom of Tayside Central and Fife in Scotland.[59] The dispute arose between a

---

[54] www.unilex.info/dynasite.cfm?dssid=2377&dsmid=13621&x=1 (last accessed on 19 July 2013). This page lists six cases, but one of them, ICC award No. 9117 of 1998, is listed twice.

[55] The award may be found at www.unilex.info/case.cfm?pid=2&do=case&id=661&step=FullText, last accessed on 19 July 2013. The paragraphs are not numbered.

[56] *Proforce Recruit Limited* v. *The Rugby Group Ltd* [2006] EWCA Civ 69, www.unilex.info/case.cfm?id=1119, last accessed on 19 July 2013.

[57] *Ibid.*, 41.   [58] *Ibid.*, 57.

[59] *Scotia Homes (South) Ltd* v. *Mr James Maurice McLean and Mrs Linda Isabella McLean*, www.unilex.info/case.cfm?id=1679, last accessed on 19 July 2013.

property developer and the buyer of one of the flats. The parties had entered into a contract relating to a flat then under construction, committing themselves to finalising the sale once the construction was fulfilled. When the construction was completed, the buyer refused to finalise the contract, alleging that the object of the contract had not been sufficiently specified. The developer provided evidence that certain drawings had been provided to the buyer during negotiations, which would make the object of the contract sufficiently determined. The question before the court was whether this kind of extrinsic evidence was allowed, in spite of the presence of an entire agreement clause. The court affirmed that extrinsic evidence could be used to ascertain the meaning of a term contained in a written contract, and that an entire agreement clause would not prevent that. It must be noted that the UPICC are not mentioned by the court. They were mentioned by the appellants, alongside numerous English and Scottish authorities, but this reference was not followed by the court.

In addition, Unilex mentions another award,[60] without, however, reproducing its full text. According to the abstract, the tribunal held that an Entire Agreement clause simply indicates that there are no binding agreements between the parties other than those contained in the contract but does in no way affect the rules of interpretation established under the applicable law (in the case at hand, Article 1362 of the Italian Civil Code). In reaching this conclusion, the arbitral tribunal expressly referred, along with legal writings, to Article 2.17 (Article 2.1.17 of the 2010 edition) of the UNIDROIT Principles, as well as to the Comments, which state 'the effect of such a clause is not to deprive prior statements or agreements of any relevance: they may still be used as a means of interpreting the written document'.[61]

Finally, Unilex refers to an ICSID award[62] in which the tribunal stated that article 2.1.17 requires that expectations raised during the negotiations must be reflected in the text of the agreement.[63]

The Unilex database, in summary, shows two approaches to Article 2.1.17 of the UPICC: one advocating the primacy of the contract's language, and the other assuming that the UPICC provide for the primacy of the real intention of the parties, which, in turn, may lead to considerably restricting the effect of the entire agreement clause.

Evidently, this is not sufficient to give guidance as to which approach to choose when addressing the conflict between the contract's language and the principle of good faith.

---

[60] Rendered on 28 November 2002 at the Chamber of Arbitration of Milan, www.unilex.info/case.cfm?pid=2&do=case&id=995&step=FullText, last accessed on 19 July 2013.

[61] www.unilex.info/case.cfm?pid=2&do=case&id=995&step=Abstract, last accessed on 19 July 2013.

[62] *Joseph C. Lemire* v. *Ukraine* ICSID case no. Arb/06/18.

[63] www.unilex.info/case.cfm?pid=2&do=case&id=1533&step=FullText, last accessed on 19 July 2013.

This leaves so much room for the discretion of the interpreter that it seems unlikely that Article 2.1.17 of the UPICC can provide for a harmonised regulation of its subject matter.

4.2.2 No waiver

We saw in Chapter 1 that one of the typical boilerplate clauses that often recurs in contract practice is the no waiver clause. According to this clause, failure by one party to exercise a remedy it is entitled to under the contract does not constitute a waiver by that party of that remedy. A literal application of this clause would permit a party entitled to a remedy (for example, the right to terminate the contract) to behave passively, thereby giving the other party the impression that it will not terminate the contract, and then terminating the contract when circumstances make it advantageous for that party. For example, that party could delay the termination until the other party has omitted to enter into other contracts with third parties in reliance on the continuation of this contract, or until prices have changed so much that it will gain by terminating this contract and entering into a corresponding contract with a third party.

As will be seen in Chapter 3, in many civilian systems, this conduct would be considered as being against good faith, as an abuse of the contractual right.

This would also seem to violate the restatements of principles: both the UPICC (Article 1.7) and the PECL (Article 1:201) have a general duty of good faith and specify that it is mandatory. This seems to mean that the duty to act in good faith may not be affected by contract clauses such as the no waiver clause. More recently, the Acquis Principles (Article 7:101) and the DCFR (Article III-1:103), both largely based on the PECL, say that the performance of obligations shall be in accordance with good faith. This entails additional obligations that may be introduced, or even that obligations expressly agreed to by the parties may be modified.[64] Moreover, the Acquis Principles (Article 7:102) and the DCFR (Article III-1:103) say that a right or remedy shall be exercised in accordance with good faith; this means, *inter alia*, that a party may not exercise a right or a remedy that it has according to the contract, if such an exercise violates good faith.

The literal interpretation of the no waiver clause, thus, may, under some circumstances, be contradicted by the restatements of principles. To what extent the restatements may override the contract text will depend on the interpretation of the principle of good faith. As was seen in Section 4.2.1 above with regard to the entire agreement clause, this may create uncertainty in the application of the UPICC and the PECL. This prevents the most important goal of these restatements; namely, that of harmonising the law.

---

[64] See Acquis Principles, Part B, Section 3 ('Explanation') in the comments on Article 7:101.

4.2.3 Subject to contract

We saw in Chapter 1 that one of the purposes of letters of intent is to stipulate that a break-off of the negotiations is permitted and that under no circumstances shall this expose any of the parties to liability. This seems to coincide with the approach taken in English law, as will be explained more in detail in Chapter 3. According to this logic, expecting that a party takes into consideration the needs and expectations of the other party while negotiating a contract runs counter to the very essence of a negotiation, where each of the parties positions itself, opens alternative possibilities, and plays the various possibilities against each other to achieve the best economic result for itself. The lack of a duty to act in good faith during the negotiations permits a party to conduct negotiations even without having the intention of concluding an agreement with the other party (for example, for the sole reason of preventing the other party from negotiating with a third party, or for obtaining business information etc.).

Contrary to this approach, the UPICC and the PECL seem to have adopted the opposite civilian approach. The restatements of principles provide that parties must negotiate according to good faith and fair dealing, impose liability for having negotiated contrary to good faith and affirm a duty of information during the pre-contractual phase. These rules may be found in the UPICC (Articles 1.7 and 2.1.15), the PECL (Articles 1:201, 2:301 and 4:106) and the Acquis Principles (Articles 2:101, 2:103 and 2:201).

The DCFR has a more moderate approach, without, however, avoiding challenges similar to those just mentioned. The DCFR does not state a general duty of good faith; however, it states the duty to negotiate in good faith (Article II-3:301) and to inform during the pre-contractual phase (Article II-3:101). This latter duty is mitigated, in respect of commercial contracts, by a reference to good commercial practice. As Section 7.2 below will show, however, the exception for good commercial practice does not seem to constitute a sufficiently precise regime.

The discrepancy between contract practice and the restatements of principles, as well as the different approach taken in the common law system and in these restatements, does not ensure a uniform interpretation of the standard of good faith, as was seen above.

4.2.4 Early termination

Other examples may be given of contractual mechanisms that, if used literally, may give permitted results under English law, but lead to results that would be considered to be against good faith under some civilian laws and under the restatements of principles.

Under English law, as will be seen in Chapter 3, the parties may regulate in their contract that certain terms are fundamental and that any breach thereof will be treated as a fundamental breach and entitle the other party to termination and reimbursement of the full value of the contract. It is possible to envisage situations where this mechanism may be misused. A contract, for example, may provide that a party has a right to terminate in case of the breach of specific obligations by the other party. If the breach has actually occurred, but only in an immaterial manner, and so that it has no significant consequences, it might be contrary to good faith to invoke this right of termination. The terminating party might wish to take advantage of the right of termination for other reasons, for example, because the market has changed and a new contract would be more profitable than continuing to be bound by the old contract. Depending on the interpretation of the underlying principle of good faith, this would be prohibited under the restatements of principles according to Article 7.3.1 of the UPICC and Article 9:301 of the PECL. The lack of a clear standard of good faith, as seen above, prevents the restatements of principles from harmonising the different legal traditions.

4.3 Digests of principles: Trans-Lex

As seen above, the UPICC and the PECL give a central role to the principle of good faith and fair dealing, in a manner similar to the approach taken by civil law. However, both restatements specify that the principle of good faith has to be understood without reference to any national system of law, and only on the basis of the understanding of good faith in international trade. Neither of these codifications, in other words, is self-sufficient: as the principles are laid down in a quite general (and, according to Lord Mustill's evaluation, as seen in Section 4.1, therefore, useless) manner, they depend on other sources that permit specifying the particular legal effects. According to the restatements, these sources have to be found in international trade.

Assistance in the specification of these general rules might be sought in a highly recognised database on transnational law, organised by the University of Cologne under the direction of Professor Berger: the Trans-Lex Principles Database. The idea behind this database is to enhance the 'creeping codification of the *lex mercatoria*'[65] by creating a comprehensive digest of principles and rules of the transnational commercial law, based on a variety of sources such as 'international arbitral awards, domestic statutes, international conventions, standard contract forms, trade practices and usages, other sample clauses and academic sources'.[66]

It may be interesting here to verify to what extent the use of the Trans-Lex database may succeed in specifying the principle of good faith and thus offer a harmonised standard that is capable of rendering the UPICC and the PECL operative.

The Trans-Lex database lists the principle of good faith and fair dealing as one of the main principles of international contract practice, and refers to various sources

---

[65] The idea was introduced in Berger, *The Creeping Codification of the Lex Mercatoria*.
[66] www.Trans-Lex.de/content.php?what=8, last accessed on 19 July 2013.

upon which the principle is said to rely: legal literature, arbitral awards, court decisions, international instruments, model laws and contract terms.[67]

A brief consideration of these sources follows below:

(i)   The Trans-Lex list of legal literature dealing with the principle of good faith and fair dealing is long and impressive, and it reflects the large variety of positions in respect of the subject, also including those that deny the existence of an international legal standard for good faith and fair dealing.[68] No uniform opinion arises from the doctrine quoted in the Trans-Lex. From this source, therefore, it is not possible to clarify and specify the content of the standard in international trade.

(ii) Among the sixteen arbitral awards listed in the Trans-Lex database in support of the principle, six awards seem to have applied the standard of good faith of a state law,[69] and the remaining awards refer mainly to the principle in general terms, as a moral rule of behaviour. On the basis of these ten awards (of which two are rendered in investment arbitration and are therefore not necessarily relevant, as will be seen in section 5 below), it seems difficult to conclude whether the standard of good faith and fair dealing in international trade is to be interpreted as a moral rule that does not require an active duty of loyalty (such as the standard would be interpreted in common law); as a rule that must ensure that the contract is interpreted and performed accurately (as it would be interpreted in Italian law); as a rule that permits integrating the contract and balancing the interests of the parties (as it would be interpreted in German law); or as a rule that permits correcting the contract and that requires each party to actively take into consideration and also to protect the interest of the other party (as it would be interpreted in Norwegian law), or yet in another way, that is characteristic only of international trade.[70]

(iii) The international conventions mentioned in the Trans-Lex database are the CISG, the UNIDROIT Convention on Factoring of 1988, and the Vienna Convention on the Law of Treaties of 1969. The relevance of these conventions, however, is questionable, as will be seen below.

---

[67] www.trans-lex.org/901000, last accessed on 19 July 2013.

[68] For example, Peter Schlechtriem, *Good Faith in German Law and in International Uniform Laws* (Pace Law School Institute of International Commercial Law, 1997).

[69] ICC award no 5832 of 1988 applies Austrian law, ICC award no 6673 of 1992 applies French law, ICC award no 8908 of 1999 applies Italian law (corroborated by the UNIDROIT Principles), ICC award no 9593 of 1999 applies the law of the Ivory Coast, ICC award no 9839 of 2004 applies US law and CRCICA award no 154/2000 applies Egyptian law.

[70] More extensively, see Giuditta Cordero-Moss, 'International Contracts Between Common Law and Civil Law: Is Non-State Law to be Preferred? The Difficulty of Interpreting Legal Standards such as Good Faith' (2007) 7 *Global Jurist Advances* 1–38. On the different function of the principle of good faith in German and in Italian law, see H.-J. Sonnenberger, 'Treu und Glauben: ein supranationaler Grundsatz?', in *Festschrift für Walter Odersky* (De Gruyter, 1996), pp. 703–21, 705 ff. See also the references made in footnote 42 above.

(a) The CISG is silent on the question of good faith as a duty between the parties or as a correction to the terms of the contract. This silence is not due to carelessness, but is a conscious choice taken during the drafting. Various delegations had, during the drafting of the Convention, repeatedly requested that the text of the Convention expressly included a provision stating a duty for the parties to perform the contract according to good faith. During the negotiation of the Convention, specific proposals were presented on good faith in the pre-contractual phase, as well as general proposals dealing with the requirement of good faith. The specific proposals relating to pre-contractual liability were rejected, and the generic proposals on good faith were incorporated into Article 7. Article 7, however, does not formulate a rule directed to regulate the parties' conduct in the contract; it states a rule instructing the interpreter of the Convention. The Convention shall be interpreted in good faith. Whether this good faith interpretation of the Convention entails a duty for the parties to act in good faith towards each other is an open question.[71] The main arguments against the inclusion of good faith as a duty of the parties were that the concept is too vague to have specific legal effects and that it would be redundant if mention thereof only had the feature of a moral exhortation.[72] The text and the drafting history of the CISG, therefore, do not seem to cast useful light on the question of specifying the legal effect of a general principle of good faith in international trade.

(b) The Factoring Convention contains, unlike the CISG, a rule prescribing good faith between the parties, in addition to the rule on the interpretation

---

[71] For an extensive evaluation on this matter, as well as references to the literature and to the legislative history in this respect, see A. Kritzer, *Pre-contract Formation*, an editorial remark on the Internet database of the Institute of International Commercial Law of the Pace University School of Law, www.cig.law.pace.edu/cisg/biblio/kritzer1.html, pp. 2ff., with extensive references also to the Minority Opinion of M. Bonell, who was representing Italy during the legislative works. According to Bonell, an extensive interpretation of the CISG would justify application of both the concepts of pre-contractual liability and of good faith: see M. Bonell, 'Formation of Contracts and Precontractual Liability under the Vienna Convention on the International Sale of Goods', in ICC (ed.), *Formation of Contracts and Precontractual Liability* (International Chamber of Commerce, 1990), pp. 157–78. Affirming that it is commonly acceptable that Article 7 of the CISG applies also to the interpretation of the contract and the relationship between the parties, Ulrich Magnus, 'Comparative Editorial Remarks on the Provisions Regarding Good Faith in CISG Article 8 (1) and the UNIDROIT Principles Article 1.7', in J. Felemegas, An International Approach to the interpretation of the United Nations Convention on Contracts for the Internatioanl Sale of Goods (1980) as Uniform Sales Law (Cambridge University Press, 2007), pp. 45–8. For a sceptical view, see Goode, Kronke, McKendrick, *Transnational Commercial Law*, pp. 279ff. Schlechtriem and Schwenzer's recognised commentary on the CISG clearly affirms that Article 7 of the CISG only applies to the interpretation of the convention and does not extend to interpretation of contracts nor does it create duties between the parties: I. Schwenzer (ed.), *Schlechtriem Schwenzer Commentary on the UN Convention on the International Sale of Goods (CISG)* 3rd edn, (Oxford University Press, 2010), Article 7, para. 17.

[72] See, extensively on the background for the limited role of good faith in the CISG, Goode, Kronke, McKendrick, *Transnational Commercial Law*, pp. 278ff. and 528.

of the Convention present also in Article 7 of the CISG. Incidentally, the presence of a rule on good faith between the parties in addition to a rule on good faith in the interpretation of the Convention seems indirectly to confirm that the rule contained in Article 7 of the CISG is not sufficient to create a duty of good faith between the parties – otherwise, it would not have been necessary to add this rule in the Factoring Convention. The Factoring Convention regards a very specific kind of contract, and it can be questioned as to what extent its provisions may be extended to all branches of international trade.[73] Even if such an extension was possible, however, the rule on good faith is written in a general way and does not give criteria that could be useful for clarifying its scope.

(c) The Vienna Convention on the Law of Treaties is a convention on how states are supposed to perform the treaties that they have ratified; it does not seem to have direct relevance to the standard between private parties in international commerce.[74]

(iv) Two restatements of state law are listed as references: the Contract Code drawn by the English Law Commission and the Uniform Commercial Code of the United States.[75] Being the expression of the legal tradition in the respective states, these instruments cannot be used to support an autonomous interpretation of the standard in international trade. The Trans-Lex database also mentions various other state laws and court decisions: however, as seen above, these sources have been expressly excluded by the assessment of the standard of good faith and fair dealing under the UPICC or the PECL, as interpretation is to be made autonomously on the basis of sources within international trade. Moreover, the selection of domestic acts and decisions of states that are in favour of an active rule on good faith, and disregarding acts and decisions of states that restrict the rule (or vice versa), would be arbitrary.

(v) The Trans-Lex database lists one model contract: the General Conditions of Contract for the Standard Contracts for the UK Offshore Oil and Gas Industry. One clause is highlighted as the main reference to the general duty to act in good faith: Clause 33 on business ethics. This clause contains a commitment to not engage in undue influence or corrupt activities, and does not, therefore, seem to be helpful in substantiating the content of the general duty of good faith. The

---

[73] At the moment of writing this chapter, twenty-five years after its conclusion, the Convention has been ratified by seven countries (www.unidroit.org/english/conventions/1988factoring/main.htm). Therefore, it cannot be deemed as enjoying a significant scope of application.

[74] On the impossibility of assuming an automatic interchangeability between the fields of public international law and of international commercial law, see Section 5 below.

[75] In earlier editions of the database (see www.Trans-Lex.net/, last accessed on 27 November 2007), these codifications were listed as transnational instruments. In the most recent version of the database, they have been moved to a new category termed 'model laws'.

links to other clauses of the General Conditions (on *force majeure* and liquidated damages) are relevant to other principles of the database, and not to the principle of good faith.

(vi) Five transnational instruments are listed in the Trans-Lex database: the already mentioned UPICC, PECL, Acquis Principles, DCFR and, surprisingly, the principles adopted by arbitral tribunals under the auspices of the Cairo Regional Centre for International Commercial Arbitration – which do not seem to have direct relevance. As has been seen, the listed transnational restatements assume an autonomous interpretation that has to be based on the standard applied in international trade.

When the Trans-Lex refers to the UPICC and the PECL to support a principle of good faith in international trade, it creates a vicious circle, because the UPICC and the PECL, in turn, make reference to international trade practice to substantiate this principle.

In conclusion, digests of principles do not seem to succeed in specifying the content of the principle of good faith in international trade. However, this specification is necessary in order to make restatements such as the UPICC, the PECL or the DCFR operative, as was shown in Section 4.2 above.

4.4 Trade usages

Trade usages are often referred to as an important source of transnational commercial law.[76] Assessing a trade usage might be quite demanding. In respect of the principle of good faith, for example, which the above analysis showed is so important in the interpretation and performance of a contract, there does not seem to be evidence of a uniform usage that might be valid for all types of contracts on an international level or for one single type of contract.

Even evidence that certain conduct is common in a certain branch of the trade does not necessarily mean that there is a binding usage to that effect.[77]

As was seen in Chapter 1, commercial contracts often contain clauses that recur in all types of transactions and present relatively constant language, the so-called boilerplate clauses such as: entire agreement, no waiver, no oral amendments, no reliance, liquidated damages, sole remedy, assignment, representations and warranties and several others. Their main aim is to create a self-sufficient system for the contract. The contract is meant to be interpreted solely on the basis of its terms and

---

[76] Goode, Kronke and McKendrick, *Transnational Commercial Law*, pp. 39ff., convincingly argue that trade usages are not self-validating and require external validation, usually in the form of a reference contained in the governing law.

[77] *Ibid.*, pp. 39ff., referring to *Libyan Arab Foreign Bank* v. *Bankers Trust Co* [1989] QB 728. On the establishment of uncodified usage and the *lex mercatoria*, see Ray Goode, 'Usage and its Reception in Transnational Commercial Law', (1997) 46 *International and Comparative Law Quarterly*, 1–36.

without reference to external elements. The purpose of these clauses is, in other words, to avoid interference by principles such as good faith and fair dealing. While each of these clauses is quite common in commercial contracts, there is no evidence that any of these clauses has specific legal effects that may be considered to be generally recognised on an international level. These terms are typically adopted from common law contract models, and, as will be seen in Chapter 3, can be incompatible with the civil law model based on good faith and fair dealing. Even within English law, and even more so within the common law legal family in general, there is not necessarily one single generally acknowledged interpretation of the scope of each of these clauses.[78] There seems to be no basis, therefore, to assume the existence of a uniform interpretation of these contract terms that could elevate them to the status of trade usages.[79]

Not only are the legal effects of these clauses not uniformly recognised; it also seems that the parties do not always consciously insert those clauses in the contract with the clear intention of obtaining certain effects. As the description of the dynamics of contract drafting made in Chapter 1 Section 3 shows, parties may not even have been aware of the detailed content of the boilerplate clauses, or they may have willingly taken the risk that they would not have had the intended effects under the applicable law. This does not seem to comply with the criteria that need to be met in order to qualify a certain practice as a trade usage; namely, the requirement that the parties are convinced that that conduct is a legal obligation (*opinio juris ac necessitatis*).

4.5 Summing up

General principles, restatements of contract law principles and trade usages in the field of general contract law are not sufficiently specific or systematic to create a harmonised regulation of general principles such as good faith. At the same time, they give the principle of good faith a central role in the interpretation and application of contracts. Since there is no harmonised standard according to which the principle may be applied, application will vary considerably depending on the interpreter's legal tradition, experience and approach. These transnational sources, therefore, are not capable of providing a harmonised frame for international contracts.

---

[78] See Edwin Peel, 'The Common Law Tradition: Application of Boilerplate Clauses', in Giuditta Cordero-Moss (ed.), *Boilerplate Clauses* International Commercial Contracts and the Applicable Law (Cambridge University Press, 2011), pp. 136ff.

[79] One clause that seems to have reached a uniform interpretation, at least in the field of maritime law, is the clause 'time is of the essence', which thus transplants into civilian systems the English law formalistic power to repudiate a contract for a breach that might be immaterial: see § 348 and 375 of the Norwegian maritime code.

5 The difficult task of harmonising legal areas

Generally recognised principles are referred to as sources in a variety of contexts: public international law disputes between states, investment protection disputes between states and foreign investors, commercial disputes between private parties. Sometimes, legal literature and arbitral awards refer to 'principles rooted in the good sense and common practice of the generality of the civilised nations' as one of the applicable sources in commercial arbitration. This wording is taken from Article 38 of the International Court of Justice (ICJ) Statutes regarding sources of public international law to be applied in disputes between states.

The generally acknowledged principles that apply to commercial disputes, however, are not necessarily the same general principles that apply to disputes between states or between foreign investors and the host country. It is necessary to distinguish between international disputes involving public international law and those involving commercial law.

Not only disputes between states, but also between states and foreign investors, are often, if not necessarily always, based on rules or general principles of public international law. Disputes between a foreign investor and the host state are mainly based on an alleged breach by the state of a rule of international law, be it a treaty-based standard of treatment or a customary principle. The point with these allegations is that the host state has used its sovereign powers in a manner that violates rules and principles that are binding on states. This is the only, or the most effective, defence available to a foreign investor against the host country: in the absence of rules and principles of public international law, the state would be free from any restrictions on the use of its public powers because it could pass legislation that renders any abusive or discriminatory act legal within its territory. Public international law is the dimension above national sovereignty that sets fundamental and generally recognised (or agreed to) criteria limiting the national states' otherwise unrestricted use of their respective sovereign powers.

Rules and principles of public international law are not necessarily equivalent to the rules and principles of commercial law, whether international or not. Commercial disputes mainly involve obligations of private law between private parties (or, at least, parties acting as private parties). They do not involve any use of public or sovereign powers, therefore they do not require any dimension superior to the sovereign state to restrict the latter's otherwise unlimited powers. They mainly concern contractual conduct that is restricted by the contract and by the governing law. To illustrate the difference on a quite elementary level, while investment awards need to resort to public international law in order to find criteria against which it is possible to evaluate whether the state's introduction of a new law or use of administrative powers is legal, it suffices for commercial awards to look at the governing law in order to find criteria for the lawfulness of the buyer's refusal to pay the price in full or the seller's invocation of a circumstance limiting liability.

For those who believe strongly in the necessity of avoiding national laws, and advocate that transnational law is better for international contracts, this will be a transnational, but still commercial, law. This latter law is not national, and can therefore improperly be defined as international; however, it is not the same as the international law in the proper sense. Transnational commercial law creates private law obligations and remedies between private parties: the buyer's refusal to pay the full price, the seller's invocation of the limitation of liability. It has nothing to do with the set of rules that bind the states and limit the exercise of their sovereign powers.

The most evident problems in applying public international law to commercial disputes might arise in the legal systems that adhere to the dualistic theory, according to which the rules of public international law bind the state towards other states but do not represent binding sources within that state until they are ratified or otherwise incorporated into the legal system. However, as will be seen below, applying rules that are meant to regulate the relationship among states as sources for commercial relationships may create problems quite irrespective of the traditional divide between the dualistic and the monistic theory, the latter of which considers public international law as a part of the domestic legal system without the necessity of specific legislation.

5.1 Unilateral declarations in public international law

The already mentioned Trans-Lex digest refers to various sources upon which the principle of good faith relies. Of particular relevance here is that, among the court decisions invoked as a source of the principle of good faith for commercial contracts, there are some decisions of the ICJ.

Among the ICJ decisions listed as the source for the principle of good faith in commercial contracts, the digest mentions the decision taken in *Australia* v. *France*.[80] This decision is rendered in connection with Australia's reaction against France carrying out nuclear tests in the South Pacific in spite of having made declarations that it would not do so.

In the part of the decision that the Trans-Lex emphasises as relevant, the ICJ analyses whether unilateral declarations made by a state with the intention of being bound are binding on it. The Court observes that one of the basic principles governing legal obligations is that of good faith, and continues by affirming that 'Just as the very rule of *pacta sunt servanda* in the law of treaties is based on good faith, so also is the binding character of an international obligation assumed by unilateral declaration'.

---

[80] [1974] ICJ Reports 253, 267ff., at www.trans-lex.org/output.php?docid=380700&markid=901000, last accessed on 19 July 2013.

The ICJ decision in *Australia* v. *France* is a decision rendered by a court of public international law and deals with public international law obligations between states. If it extended its relevance to commercial contracts, it would mean that, as a general principle of international law stated by the ICJ, a private party making a commercial offer to another private party is bound by that offer, particularly if the offer is presented as irrevocable. As seen below, this may create some difficulties.

Unilateral declarations do not always have a binding character in contract law. Among other legal systems, English law does not generally consider unilateral promises as enforceable. As will be seen in Chapter 3, Section 6.1, the English law of contract has an additional requirement for considering a promise as enforceable: the requirement for consideration. This requirement can be briefly described as the necessity of both parties having reciprocal benefits and detriments. In the absence of a mutual benefit and detriment, a unilateral promise that gives benefit only to the promisee and detriment only to the promisor would be unenforceable. In most typical contracts, the consideration is identified through the price: in a sale agreement, for example, the seller promises to sell the thing (thereby creating for itself the detriment of depriving itself of the thing, and the benefit for the buyer of taking over the thing), and the buyer promises to pay the price (thereby creating for itself the detriment of paying the price, and for the seller the benefit of the transfer of the money).

Following the above, the English law of contracts does not consider a unilateral offer as binding, not even if the offer, by its own terms, is irrevocable for a certain period: it is necessary to have consideration, otherwise the promise to keep the offer firm is not enforceable.[81]

How can the unenforceability of irrevocable offers in the English law of contracts be reconciled with the ICJ clear statement that unilateral declarations are a sufficient source of binding obligations? Is the English rule of consideration in contrast with the principle of good faith in public international law? Could a case be brought against England in the ICJ because English contract law violates public international law? Or, even more drastically, could a private party be considered liable for a breach of its obligations contained in an irrevocable offer, notwithstanding that the offer is not binding under the (English) law governing it?

It seems quite evident that English contract law does not violate the basic principles of public international law. It simply has a different scope of application. It does not relate to obligations between states or to unilateral declarations by a state not to carry out atmospheric nuclear explosions off the coast of another state. Similarly, the ICJ was not aiming at creating a precedent for the regulation of commercial offers between private parties.

---

[81] *Offord* v. *Davies* [1862] 12 CBNS 748.

That the words 'good faith' or 'binding unilateral declaration' may be used both in public international law and in commercial law does not justify the conclusion that they have the same assumptions, functions and meaning in both spheres. Accordingly, the concepts are not interchangeable.

In summary, generally acknowledged principles of public international law are not necessarily capable of creating obligations between private parties and do not represent, therefore, a source of harmonised transnational commercial law.

6 The difficult task of replacing the governing law

As was mentioned in section 1 above, sometimes voices are raised to advocate that international contracts should not be governed by national law, but by a transnational system of law that does not necessarily emanate from authoritative sources. One of the advantages of the transnational law was said to lie in its spontaneous character: by being based on international business practice rather than on acts or conventions, the transnational law would ensure that it, at any given time, reflected the needs of the parties. Some of the strongest supporters of a spontaneous transnational law seem, over time, to have turned their back on their earlier position and now prefer more structured, semi-legislative instruments. This became apparent in the on-going process of developing a European contract law. In their joint response to the Communication from the Commission of the European Communities that initiated the process on a common European contract law,[82] the academic group defining itself as the Commission on a European Contract Law (the author of the PECL, chaired by the Danish Professor Lando) and its successor, the Study Group on a European Contract Law (the co-author of the DCFR), bluntly dismissed the primary source of transnational law – the spontaneous development by market forces of appropriate regulations and models – as not sufficient to bring about a uniform regulation of private law.[83] Earlier, this was praised as the most adequate source of regulation for international commerce.[84] The PECL, that represent (together with the UPICC) one of the best and most comprehensive codifications of transnational law, are also dismissed, with the observation that, for the moment, such a restatement cannot be reckoned to replace state law: what it lacks – in addition to a more comprehensive and detailed scope – is the legal basis for being considered as binding even when it does not comply with the mandatory rules of state laws. Hence, the joint response proposes that restatements of principles be enacted with binding force,[85] and it proposes

---

[82] 11/7/2001, COM (2001) 398 final.
[83] Response to the Commission Communication by the Commission on European Contract Law and the Study Group on a European Civil Code, ec.europa.eu/consumers/cons_int/safe_shop/fair_bus_pract/cont_law/comments/5.23.pdf, p. 44, p. 26.
[84] See, for example, Lando, 'The *Lex Mercatoria*', and Ole Lando, '*Lex Mercatoria* 1985–1996', *Festskrift til Stig Strömholm*, (Iustus Förlag 1997), pp. 567ff.
[85] Response to the Commission Communication, p. 35.

extending the conflict rules of European private international law so as to permit choosing restatements of principles as a governing law.[86]

The same doubts as to the effectiveness of a free development by market forces as well as to the usefulness of a restatement are expressed by the ICC in its response to the Communication – for numerous decades, one of the most convinced supporters of the transnational law as an efficient alternative to state laws. The ICC's Department of Policy and Business Practices expresses 'concerns as to whether non-binding principles are sufficient',[87] though emphasising the importance of the Principles as a first step towards harmonisation.

If the spontaneous development via market forces as well as a restatement of European law (without enactment or legal basis within private international law) are described as insufficient to replace state law by two of the most transnational law-friendly entities – the authors of the PECL and the ICC – even stronger doubts seem to apply in respect of the other sources of transnational law mentioned earlier, which (apart from the UPICC, that in this respect can be compared to the PECL) do not even have the goals of being comprehensive or of restating the law, but simply provide a regulation of specific types of contract or of specific areas.

The sections below analyse the ability of transnational law to govern a contractual relationship to the exclusion of any national law.

6.1 Private international law

The first question to be addressed is the legal basis for claiming that transnational sources may govern a contract to the exclusion of any other governing law. If they are to replace the governing law, they will not be subject to any mandatory rules or principles of the otherwise applicable law, with the exception of overriding mandatory rules. Additionally, in the case of gaps or a lack of clarity, there will be no governing law to fall back on. If, on the contrary, transnational sources are simply incorporated into the contract and become contract terms, they remain subject to any mandatory rules of the applicable law, and they will be interpreted according to the governing law's underlying principles and will be integrated by the governing law's default rules.

The wording of Article 1.4 of the UPICC seems to suggest the latter alternative: 'Nothing in these Principles shall restrict the application of mandatory rules, whether of national, international or supranational origin, which are applicable in accordance with the relevant rules of private international law.'

In addition, the Rome I Regulation on the Law Applicable to Contractual Obligations excludes that the parties may select, to govern their contract, sets of rules that are not national laws (with an exception for possible future European instruments of

---

[86] Response to the Commission Communication, p. 37.
[87] Document 15 October 2001 AH/dhh Doc. 373/416, p. 3.

contract law).[88] The Rome I Regulation is a conversion of the previous 1980 Rome Convention on the Law Applicable to Contractual Obligations. According to the prevailing opinion, the Rome Convention permitted the parties to choose, as governing law, a national law, but not transnational sources. In connection with its conversion, proposals were made to extend the scope of party autonomy to transnational sources;[89] however, these proposals were not accepted, and the adopted text of the Rome I Regulation has finally clarified that the parties may only choose a national law with which to govern their contract.

Incidentally, an extension of party autonomy would only have provided a partial solution: the parties' choice would have had effect only within the scope of party autonomy, thus leaving unaffected the areas where other conflict rules are applicable. As will be seen in Chapter 4, Section 4, whenever the legal relationship has implications that go beyond the mere contract law, party autonomy does not apply and other conflict rules step in to select the governing law. Thus, if the contract has implications in terms of property law (a pledge as security for a party's obligations), of company law (a shareholder agreement regulating the competence of corporate bodies) or of insolvency law (a loan agreement with an early termination clause that would affect the solvency of the debtor), just to name some very common situations, the law applicable to those aspects will be selected on the basis of specific conflict rules, and not on the basis of the choice made by the parties.

Transnational sources, thus, may be incorporated into the contract by the parties, but may not be selected to govern the contract to the exclusion of any national law, not even in mere contractual matters.[90] In commercial arbitration, on the contrary, arbitration laws[91] and arbitration rules[92] often give the parties the possibility of choosing 'rules of law' to govern the dispute; these words, as opposed to 'law', are interpreted as extending beyond national laws and to also covering transnational sources, as will be explained in Chapter 5, Section 3.5.2 below. Confirming the point

---

[88] Council Regulation No 593/2008, 4/7/2008 OJ L 177/6 Article 3. The Preamble, in item 13, confirms that nothing prevents the parties from incorporating into the contract transnational instruments of soft law; as a consequence of such an incorporation, however, the soft law is given the status of a term of contract, not of governing law. See also Goode, Kronke, McKendrick, *Transnational Commercial Law*, pp. 515ff.

[89] The Green Paper on the conversion of the Rome Convention, COM (2002) 654 final, section 3.2.3, asked whether the rule on party autonomy should be changed so that the parties are allowed to choose an international convention or general principles of law instead of a national law. The original proposal by the Commission, COM (2005) 0650 final, contained a rather restrictive access to do so, but this formulation was deleted in the finally approved text of the Regulation.

[90] It must be noted here that the Hague conference has issued, in 2012, the Draft Hague Principles on the Choice of Law in International Contracts. In Article 3, these principles allow for the possibility that the parties choose transnational sources as a governing law. This is a publication that has the characteristic of soft law, and is thus not intended to be binding. Considering the unclear relationship between arbitration and private international law (see Section 4.5), it seems that this instrument may be useful within international arbitration.

[91] See, for example, the UNCITRAL Model Law, Article 28.

[92] See, for example, the Arbitration Rules of the ICC, Article 17.

of view that the UPICC are simply incorporated into the contract when the dispute is decided by a court, whereas they, under some circumstances, may be chosen as governing law when a dispute is submitted to arbitration, see the UNIDROIT comments on the various Model clauses that the UNIDROIT recommends to write in the contract, if the contract is meant to refer to the UPICC.[93]

This does not necessarily mean that the parties enjoy much more flexibility during arbitration: as Section 4 above showed, transnational law does not have the ability to govern a relationship to the full exclusion of national laws. Therefore, there is little difference between incorporating the transnational law as if it were the terms of the contract, and choosing it as a governing law: ultimately, a national law will necessarily be applicable.

6.2 Sources conflicting with the governing law

In many situations, as described in Section 3 above, transnational sources will be applied as a supplement to the governing law – either because they regulate details that are not regulated by the governing law, or because they regulate matters that are not regulated by the mandatory rules of the governing law. In some situations, transnational sources might conflict with the mandatory rules of the applicable law. The relationship between contractual terms and transnational law on one side, and state law on the other side, then becomes apparent. Below follow some examples where the UCP 600 and the UPICC do not have the ability to deviate from the mandatory rules of the governing law.

6.2.1 The UCP 600

As seen in Section 3.2 above, the UCP 600 are a successful source of soft law regulating letters of credit. In some cases, the mechanism of the letter of credit has been considered to conflict with the rules of the governing law and has been overridden by state law.

In particular, the two aspects mentioned above – the autonomy of the payment obligation and the implication of the roles as the advising or corresponding bank – are uniformly applied in letters of credit, irrespective of the fact that the particular letter of credit may or may not make express reference to the UCP 600.

However, in some cases, these principles of the letters of credit have been considered to conflict with the rules of the governing state law and have been overridden by state law. Some of these cases will be examined below. For the sake of completeness, it must be recognised that the cases discussed below represent the exception rather than the rule. Some of them have implications of a political character and

---

[93] UNIDROIT, Model Clauses for the Use of the UNIDROIT Principles of International Commercial Contracts, www.unidroit.org/english/principles/modelclauses/modelclauses-2013.pdf, Model Clause No 1, General remarks, § 4, pp. 5–6.

others may be criticised for being wrong. The purpose of highlighting these cases is not to question the ability of the UCP 600 to properly regulate letters of credit – a task that the UCP 600 actually carries out egregiously. The purpose is to show that there may sometimes be tension between transnational sources and the governing law; and that, in these cases, the governing law will prevail.

6.2.1.1 Case 1[94]

The beneficiary of a letter of credit presents documents to obtain payment under the letter of credit. The bank refuses payment, because not all of the documents listed in the instruction have been presented. In particular, a 'Receipt signed and proving delivery of the goods' was listed as one of the documents to be presented, and was not presented. The beneficiary claims that payment is due in spite of the lack of these documents, because the delivery can be proven by other means. Is the beneficiary entitled to obtain payment under the letter of credit?

According to the principles that rule documentary credits, as seen above, the obligation of the bank to pay is strictly dependent on the instructions that it has received. If the instructions provide for payment upon presentation of specific documents, then payment has to be effected upon presentation of those documents (irrespective of any supervening circumstance), and only upon presentation of exactly those documents. Payment on presentation of documents different from those listed in the instructions can expose the bank to liability towards the applicant.

In the case described here, the receipt was one of the listed documents, and was not presented.[95] An application of the principles governing the documentary credits, therefore, should lead to the conclusion that payment was not to be effected by the bank. The creditor maintains its claims towards the debtor, but the bank cannot effect a payment in violation of the instructions. The creditor will have to satisfy its claim directly with the debtor.

However, the Swiss Supreme Court, in the analysed case, decided in the opposite way. The reason for deciding that the bank had to effect payment was that, by not effecting payment by invoking the instructions, and in spite of the presence of other documentation showing that payment was due, the bank would abuse its rights. This abuse of rights would be in contrast with Article 2 of the Swiss Code of Obligations, which is mandatory. We have here an example of a conflict between a principle of transnational law (the irrelevance of the underlying obligation to a letter of credit) and the mandatory rules of the national governing law, whereby the state law prevailed.

---

[94] *Société de Banque Suisse* v. *Société Generale Alsacienne de Banque* [1989] BGE 105 II 67.

[95] The inclusion of a signed receipt among the documents to be presented is a rather inefficient means: if the receipt has to be signed by the buyer, who is also supposed to make the payment, it will easily be able to stop any possibility of effecting payment by withholding the signature on the receipt. It is an important principle that the production of none of the listed documents should be in the power of none of the parties. Otherwise, the parties may influence the circumstances that trigger payment, and the neutrality and independence that a letter of credit should provide is seriously undermined.

6.2.1.2 Case 2[96]

A letter of credit is issued by a Ugandan bank. Citibank of New York acts as an advising bank. In 1972, the Ugandan government prohibits the Ugandan bank from making a foreign exchange payment to the Israeli beneficiary. Consequently, the issuing bank instructs the advising bank to cancel the letter of credit. The beneficiary claims payment under the letter of credit from Citibank. Is the beneficiary entitled to payment in accordance with the letter of credit?

As we have seen above, there is a clear distinction between the role of an advising bank and the role of a confirming bank. An advising bank does not assume obligations in its own name; it just acts on behalf of the issuing bank. If the issuing bank instructs the advising bank not to effect payment, the advising bank is obliged not to effect payment. If it nevertheless does, then it will not be in a position to obtain reimbursement from the issuing bank, because it did so in violation of the agreement between them.

In the case mentioned here, Citibank was an advising bank, and it had received instructions from the advising bank not to effect payment; therefore, Citibank was not obliged to effect payment.

However, the Court of Appeal of New York found that the bank had to pay. The reasoning was as follows: New York is the financial capital of the world, and if it wants to maintain this pre-eminent position, it is important that the operators under New York law protect the justified expectations of the parties. The fact that payment had become illegal under Ugandan law does not affect the role that a New York bank should play. This is a situation where a recognised principle of transnational law (the diversity in responsibility between an advising bank and a confirming bank) conflicts not with some mandatory rules of the governing law, but with some policies, which in the eyes of the court must have been so important that they represented public policy and they had to override them.

6.2.1.3 Case 3[97]

DCA has entered into a contract for the supply of certain military equipment to the State of India and has issued a letter of credit as a performance guarantee. The main document to be presented to obtain payment under the letter of credit is a certificate by the State of India stating that DCA is in breach of contract. War breaks out between India and Pakistan, and the US announces an embargo on India. The military equipment is delivered FOB at DCA's plant; DCA alleges that it has performed its obligation to supply the equipment at its plant. The embargo prevents the shipment going abroad, and the State of India presents to the banks a certificate of breach of contract, as provided for under the instructions of the letter of credit, and requests payment under the letter of credit. Is the beneficiary entitled to payment under the letter of credit?

---

[96] *J. Zeevi & Sons* v. *Grindlay's Bank (Uganda)*, 37 N.Y.2d 220, 333 N.E.2d 168, 371 N.Y.S.2d 892.
[97] *Dynamics Corp. of America* v. *Citizens and Southern National Bank* [1973] 356 F.Supp.991.

The principles governing documentary credits, as we have seen, clearly state that payment has to be effected upon presentation of the listed documents, and that the bank shall not be concerned with the underlying transaction. If the State of India has presented a certificate of breach of contract, and this was the document that had to be presented according to the instructions, then payment should be made.

However, the District Court of Georgia resolved to grant a preliminary injunctive relief and a permanent injunction against the bank, protecting the debtor from claims relating to its obligation to effect payment.

The Court first confirmed the known principles governing letters of credit: that payment has to be made by the bank, irrespective of the circumstances of the underlying transactions, if the listed documents have been presented. However, the Court went on by considering the matter of fraud, and affirmed that, in the case of fraud, the bank should nevertheless have the obligation to effect payment to 'innocent third parties', whereas, in cases where the beneficiary is not 'innocent', the bank does not have the obligation, but the option to effect payment. The Court went on by affirming that, in this case, the beneficiary was not an innocent third party, because there was a dispute as to the validity of the certificate of breach of contract presented to the bank for payment. The Court affirmed that the certificate of breach was unspecified (the wording being 'failed to carry out certain obligations of theirs'). The Court affirmed, further, and correctly, that the beneficiary did not have to prove that the breach actually had taken place, since this would be a question relating to the underlying contract, and the court had no jurisdiction on that matter (the contract had chosen arbitration in India for settlement of disputes arising out of the contract). The Court then justified its issuance of the injunction on the basis of its alleged duty to guarantee that the beneficiary does not take 'unconscientious advantage of the situation and run off with plaintiff's money on a pro forma declaration which has obviously no basis in fact'. In this case, therefore, the principles governing documentary credit have been superseded by the governing law's rules on fraud. Several comments are possible on this decision: we will concentrate on the quality of the listed documents and on the question of fact.

When it comes to the quality of the document, the court is concerned with the fact that the certificate was unspecified. This, however, should primarily have been a concern of the parties when they drafted the instructions to the bank. Allowing payment upon presentation of a certificate issued by the beneficiary is not advisable, as it can open up possible abuses. Allowing such a certificate, without specifying its contents, is even less advisable, since it means that there are no parameters that have to be met before the beneficiary issues such a certificate. What surprises one, in this case, is that the court has found it appropriate to override the agreement between the parties, because the list of documents had not been written with the appropriate diligence.

The next comment is a matter of fact, and, as such, does not belong to the dispute upon which the court had jurisdiction. However, the court invites this comment, by mentioning that the beneficiary should not run off with the money with no basis in fact. If the goods had to be delivered FOB, then the responsibility for clearing them for export was with the seller.[98] If the goods could not be exported, the seller had not complied with its obligations, even if the goods were made available at the place of delivery. The goods could not be exported because of an embargo and not because of a lack of diligence by the seller, and therefore it might be questioned as to whether this could amount to a default by the seller. However, the adoption of the term FOB indicates that the risk for not obtaining the export licence is held by the seller, and not the buyer.

6.2.2 The UPICC: irrevocable offer

The case of an offer that purports to be irrevocable for a certain period is an example of the relationship between the UPICC and the mandatory rules of the governing law. As long as the offer is not accepted, there is no contract between the parties. However, a written offer with a promise of irrevocability has legal consequences that are regulated by the contract law of each state. What would the legal consequences be, if the offeror decides to revoke the offer before the term indicated in the firm offer has elapsed?

Firm offers are regulated in Article 2.4 of the UPICC. The article starts by setting forth a general rule, according to which offers can be revoked until they have been accepted. The second paragraph of the article is devoted to irrevocable offers, and reads as follows:

(2) However, an offer cannot be revoked
    (a) if it indicates, whether by stating a fixed time for acceptance or otherwise, that it is irrevocable; or
    (b) ...

The solution provided by the UPICC, therefore, coincides with the solution provided by civil law systems, as will be seen in Chapter 3, Section 6.1. But what if the relationship is subject to English law? As Chapter 3, Section 6.1 will show, English law has a different outcome for this situation, due to the applicability of the doctrine of consideration. The doctrine of consideration is mandatory, and cannot be derogated from by agreement of the parties, or by a non-binding source of transnational law with persuasive authority. If the relationship is subject to English law, therefore, the solution suggested by the UPICC will be overridden by the governing law. As long as the UPICC are incorporated into the contract (as opposed to chosen as a governing law), then they are not able to provide a harmonised solution. As was seen in Chapter 2, Section 6.1, generally, sources of transnational law are deemed to be incorporated into the contract when the dispute is brought before a court. When a dispute is submitted to arbitration, on the contrary, various arbitration laws and

---

[98] Another matter is that the term FOB assumes that the place of delivery is a port, and not the seller's plant, as it apparently had been agreed in the contract.

arbitration rules permit the parties to choose transnational sources as governing law, as Sections 6.1 above and Chapter 5, Section 3.5 explain. The particular situation analysed in this section would receive a harmonised solution if the parties or the arbitral tribunal were empowered to choose the UPICC or the PECL and had done so. On the insufficiency of these sources at providing harmonisation in other respects, see Sections 4 above, Section 6.3 below and Chapter 3, Section 7.

6.3 Gaps in transnational sources

In some situations, transnational sources do not provide a regulation. The doctrine of autonomous interpretation, meant to prevent different interpretations of transnational provisions and described in Chapter 2, Section 4.2 for the UPICC and the PECL, was also developed to permit the filling of gaps without impairing the uniformity of the transnational law. Thus, the CISG aspires to being interpreted in a way that is not affected by the rules and principles of the system within which it is being applied – which would undermine its goal of representing a uniform regulation. Article 7 of the CISG provides for an autonomous interpretation of its provisions:

(1) In the interpretation of this Convention, regard is to be had to its international character and to the need to promote uniformity in its application and the observance of good faith in international trade.

When it comes to lacunas, the CISG ultimately makes reference to the national governing law:

(2) Questions concerning matters governed by this Convention which are not expressly settled in it are to be settled in conformity with the general principles on which it is based or, in the absence of such principles, in conformity with the law applicable by virtue of the rules of private international law.

Similarly, the UPICC (Article 1.6) and the PECL (Article 1:106) contain guidelines for interpretation and application. In their first paragraphs, both articles establish the principle of autonomous interpretation: the restatements of principles shall be interpreted having regard to their international character, and bearing in mind their purpose to promote uniformity in their application. In other words, this paragraph aims to avoid the restatements being interpreted in the light of state laws. The second paragraph of both articles provides that, in the case of lacunas, the interpreter will have to apply, to the extent that is possible, the general principles underlying the restatements. The autonomous interpretation is enhanced by this provision: lacking an express regulation of a certain aspect, the interpreter will first have to look at the principles that inspire this codification, and construe them so as to elaborate a regulation in line with the fundamental ideas upon which the principles are based. It cannot be excluded, however, that even the underlying principles are not sufficient to provide the regulation of a certain aspect. In these cases, lacunas will have to be filled by applying the governing law, as is expressly stated in the PECL, Article 1:106(2).

The ideal of uniformity that inspires the restatements, consequently, might fail, if the solutions provided by state laws differ from state to state.

Below follows an example of failure by the UPICC to provide a uniform regulation where the national laws diverge.

6.3.1 Choice between contracts

Assume that a seller has entered into a plurality of contracts with several buyers for the sale of its products. If a *force majeure* event prevents the production of part of the volume that the seller has committed to its buyers, the position of the seller will vary according to the governing law. As will be seen in more detail in Chapter 3, if the governing law is Norwegian, the seller will be under the obligation to supply, to the fullest possible extent, the first commitment in time, and it will be excused towards the other buyers. If the governing law is Italian or German, the seller will be entitled to reduce the supplies to each buyer pro rata. If the governing law is English, the seller will remain under its full obligations and will not be excused by frustration of the contract assuming the contract does not provide for this eventuality.

One of the most important functions attributed to transnational law is to eliminate discrepancies such as these, and to provide a uniform and reasonable treatment that can be used to govern international contracts in respect of the expectations of the parties. Would the UPICC succeed in giving a harmonised solution? As opposed to the example of the irrevocable offer made in Section 6.2.2 above, the matter of allocation of risk is within the freedom of contract, and therefore is capable of being harmonised by transnational sources. However, the UPICC do not contain an answer to the situation arising in the case of partial impediment and the plurality of creditors. Article 7.1.7 of the UPICC regulates *force majeure* circumstances preventing in total and in part the contractual performance, but it does not regulate the allocation of risk in cases of the plurality of creditors. Article 8:108 of the PECL has similar content.

How can this lacuna be filled? In the case of partial impediment and the plurality of creditors, it does not seem that the interpretation rules contained in Article 1.6, or even the reference to usages of Article 1.9 of the UPICC can offer any specific help. Principles underlying the codification, referred to in Article 1.6, do not seem to be relevant to this particular situation. In 2010, a Chapter 11 was added to the UPICC dealing with the plurality of obligors and of obligees. Article 11.1.9 allocates obligations pro rata among the obligors, when these are jointly and severally liable towards another party. This, however, regulates the situation when a plurality of parties has assumed the same obligation towards another party, or when a plurality of parties is entitled to the performance of the same obligation by another party. This is quite a different situation from the one envisaged here. In our scenario, there is a plurality of discrete bilateral contracts, and none of the buyers has any rights or obligations towards each other. A rule that assumes joint and several liability, as with the provision of Article 11.1.9, therefore, cannot be considered relevant and the underlying principle is of no help. It could be possible to interpret Article 7 on the basis of an analogy with the solution presented by civil law systems. As mentioned above, the civilian solution provides for a corresponding reduction of the performance in case of partial impediment, and is construed to permit a pro rata reduction among the various creditors. However, how could such an interpretation by analogy with the state laws of the civil law system be compatible with the above-mentioned Article 1.6, which wishes to avoid that the UPICC are interpreted in light of state laws? As far as Article 1.9 is concerned, referring to usages and practices, it does not seem easy to determine what generally recognised usages might say in this situation. The principle of *rebus sic stantibus*, which is the expression of the *force majeure* rule in the transnational law, does not seem to have generally recognised rules on partial impediments and the plurality of creditors. Therefore, the consequences of the situation arising in our scenario have to be solved by applying the governing law.

In this situation, in conclusion, transnational law has not achieved its aim of providing a uniform regulation of international contracts.

6.3.2 The CISG as an expression of transnational law

The CISG is taken into such a high level of consideration, that it is sometimes invoked as a source of transnational law, beyond its scope of application as a binding international convention. The genesis of the CISG and the ideals that inspired it, described in section 2.1 above, actually confirm that the goal of the Convention is to provide a 'universal' treatment for the most important type of contract within international trade, thus eliminating the barriers to international business that might arise as a consequence of different national regulations. The actual success of the CISG slightly contradicts the universality of its goals,[99] since the number of states that ratified it (seventy-nine) is not overwhelming, compared to other conventions (the New York Convention on arbitration has been ratified by 149 states), and taking into consideration that a state that is of paramount importance within international trade and international commercial law, the UK, has not ratified it. Moreover, Article 6 of the CISG gives the parties the possibility of excluding the applicability of the Convention. This possibility to be able to opt out of the CISG is taken advantage of quite frequently, especially when one of the parties is from the US.[100]

---

[99] This reservation is expressed by McKendrick, 'Harmonisation of European Contract Law', p. 6.

[100] Lisa Spagnolo, 'Green Eggs and Ham: The CISG, Path Dependence, and the Behavioural Economics of Lawyers' Choices of Law in International Sales Contracts', (2010) 6(2) *Journal of Private International Law*, 417–64 ssrn.com/abstract=1664168. For a thorough analysis of the exclusion of the CISG, see I. Schwenzer, P. Hachem and C. Kee, *Global Sales and Contract Law* (Oxford University Press, 2012), paras. 5.17ff.

There are good reasons for questioning the appropriateness of an approach that extends the applicability of international conventions beyond their scope of applica-tion:[101] a convention is a binding instrument and is the result of careful negotiations that reflect the extent to which the various states are willing to be bound. The negotiations on the text of the convention sometimes result in wording that is so general or unclear that it can be interpreted as permitting each of the conflicting positions to be supported during the negotiations.[102] In other situations, and perhaps more openly admitting the impossibility of reaching an agreement, conventions may be silent on certain aspects of the matter that they regulate.[103] In yet other situations, they may make open reference to the applicable national law for supplementing or regulating specific aspects.[104] Sometimes conventions permit the ratifying states to make reservations against the applicability of certain rules in the convention.[105] Conventions also contain a detailed description of their scope of application, both territorially[106] and in respect of the subject matter.[107]

All these, and many others, are techniques that are used to obtain a commitment by the ratifying states to at least the minimum regulation that is contained in the convention. A state, for example, may be willing to commit to a convention only if its reservation against the application of a certain rule is accepted. If a state is not willing to commit to a convention notwithstanding the possibility to reserve against the

---

[101] See Goode, Kronke, McKendrick, *Transnational Commercial Law*, p. 47, criticising the ICC award no 5713 of 1989, which applied the CISG as if it was a directly applicable source of transnational law, in spite of the circumstance that the convention had not been ratified by any of the states involved and without giving regard to the applicable law.

[102] See, for example, Article 4 of the Rome Convention on the Law Applicable to Contractual Obligations (now replaced by the Rome I Regulation), which was interpreted differently by courts belonging to different legal traditions: see Chapter 4, Section 3.2.1.

[103] An example is the matter of overdue interest that could not be regulated in detail in the CISG; see for an extensive explanation Goode, Kronke, McKendrick, *Transnational Commercial Law*, pp. 528 and 301ff.

[104] For example, the CISG refers in Article 28 to national law to determine whether the remedy of specific performance is applicable.

[105] For example, the CISG allows the ratifying states to make reservations against the application of parts of the Convention. Norway, for example, has excluded applicability of Part II of the Convention, on the formation of contracts (the so-called Article 92 reservation), and the Scandinavian countries have excluded the applicability of the Vienna Convention to inter-Scandinavian contracts (the so-called Article 94 reservation). Several countries (also including Argentina, Chile, China, Russia and the Ukraine) have reserved against the provisions that permit contracts to be created, modified or terminated by other means than in writing (the so-called Article 96 reservation). These and other reservations render the application of the Vienna Convention less uniform than would have been desirable for a uniform law, even among countries that have ratified it (for a full list of the reservations and of the states that have made them, see www.uncitral.org).

[106] For example, the Rome Convention on the Law Applicable to Contractual Obligations (now converted into the Rome I Regulation) is universal and is applied even in relationships where the other party's country has not ratified it, whereas the Lugano Convention on Jurisdiction and Enforcement of Judge-ments in Civil and Commercial Matters assumes that both involved countries have ratified it, at least in the part regarding the enforcement of judgments.

[107] For example, the CISG applies only to contracts of sale, and not to all contracts of sale; its scope of application is specified in Article 2.

application of certain rules, it does not ratify it – and the convention will not become binding for that state. How can all these restrictions be disregarded simply by stating that, by some states ratifying a convention, the principles underlying that convention are to be considered as transnational rules that may be applied beyond their precise scope of application? Would this mean that the whole convention is to be considered as transnational law and therefore binding, notwithstanding that a state has made certain reservations or has decided not to ratify it? What is, then, the effect of making the reservations or not ratifying?

This reasoning applies to conventions that intend to create harmonised legislation, mainly within the area of private law or other areas within the states' power of legislation. The purpose of these conventions is to align the legislation of its signatory states in the relevant area. These conventions, therefore, have effects within the scope of the states' sovereignty, and depend on states' sovereignty to become effective.

The reasoning may be different in respect of conventions that create rights and obligations among the states. Principles of public international law do not necessarily depend on states' sovereignty to become effective, and it cannot be excluded that such principles may be created without the intervention of a particular state.

In addition to these systemic objections to the applicability of a convention beyond its scope, there are situations where the convention – having been drafted for the purpose of regulating a certain specific area – presents lacunas or refers to the national governing law. The CISG refers to national law in a series of respects: validity of the contract and effects of the sale on property (Article 4), gaps in the convention (Article 7), specific performance (Article 28), industrial property claims (Article 42), payment modalities (Article 54), retention's effects towards third parties (Article 71) and calculation of interest (Article 78).

An ICC arbitral award[108] illustrates a case of a lacuna. The dispute was between a Korean seller and a buyer from Jordan. The seller was to issue a performance guarantee, and the buyer was to open a letter of credit for the payment of the goods; the buyer also had to issue a performance guarantee in favour of the final buyer of the goods, an Iraqi buyer. Due to several delays, the delivery was rescheduled and the duration of the letter of credit was extended; a dispute then arose regarding whether the actual delivery was delayed in respect of the extensions, and whether payment was due under the guarantees. The claimant asked the arbitral tribunal to solve the dispute by applying the transnational law, in this case defined as *lex mercatoria*, and affirmed that in that case the *lex mercatoria* was to be deemed equal to the CISG. The arbitral tribunal first noticed that the applicability of the *lex mercatoria* was not undisputed. However, assuming that in that case the *lex mercatoria* could be identi-fied with the CISG, it would have been impossible to solve the dispute on that basis. The tribunal noticed that in that dispute it might be necessary to evaluate situations

---

[108] ICC award made in case no 6149 of 1990, in ICCA, *Yearbook Commercial Arbitration XX* (Kluwer International, 1995), pp. 41ff.

such as the unjust enrichment or limitation of rights, which are not regulated by the CISG. Therefore, the tribunal decided to apply choice-of-law rules for the purpose of identifying the national governing law, and resolved to apply Korean law to the dispute.

6.4 Summing up

Transnational law lacks the detail and exhaustiveness (as well as the formal force of law) necessary to replace national laws.

7 The autonomous contract

As was seen in Chapter 1, international contracts are often drafted without bearing in mind what law will govern the contract. The clause choosing the governing law is often negotiated after the parties have agreed on all the commercial aspects of the transaction, and after the regulation of such commercial content has been drafted. Sometimes, the parties do not reach an agreement on what governing law to choose, and therefore they do not write a choice-of-law clause in their contract. At times, the parties do not attach significant importance to the choice of the governing law, and agree on the proposal of one of the parties without paying attention to the implications of that choice. At other times, the parties do not even think of the question of the governing law. In all these aforementioned situations, the result is that a contract was drafted without the awareness of the legal system that the contract was subject to. In other words, the parties assumed (or deliberately took the risk that the assumption was fallacious) that the contract represented a sufficient regulation of their relationship, that it would be enforceable without any problems in all relevant jurisdictions, and that it would not be affected by rules or principles external to the contract, other than those that the parties may have made reference to.

This may induce one to assume that international commercial contracts are autonomous and not subject to any national law. The autonomous contract would, according to this theory, be detached from domestic law and would have to be interpreted and applied autonomously in the light of its own language, non-state principles and rules of international trade. It will be shown below that this is an erroneous conception.

The theory of the autonomous or detached contract may, to a certain extent, be connected with the doctrine of the internationalisation of contracts entered into between foreign investors and states. These contracts prompt the necessity of restricting the state's role as a sovereign that may introduce new legislation, and thus unilaterally and unduly modify the conditions of the investment. To avoid such abuses, the Washington Convention of 1965 establishing the ICSID arbitration, provides, in Article 42, that the tribunal is to apply (in the absence of a choice of law made by the parties) 'the law of the host countries ... and such rules of international law as may be applicable'. This formulation is usually interpreted to mean that the national law of the host country is to be applied inasmuch as it does not violate international law.[109] Investment agreements formalising oil investments in Libya contained governing law clauses according to this principle; following nation-alisation, three arbitral proceedings were initiated and led to three different results: in the *Liamco* case, the tribunal applied Libyan law, amended with a general principle regarding the necessity of providing compensation if assets are nationalised;[110] in the *BP* case, the tribunal found that there were no principles common to both Libyan and international law, and proceeded to apply general principles of law;[111] and, in the *Texaco* case, the tribunal assumed that the parties had wished to submit the agreement to public international law.[112]

As already seen in Section 5 above, however, principles and doctrines developed in the sphere of investment protection are not necessarily automatically transferrable to the sphere of commercial contracts. In the Libyan cases, the arbitrators could easily apply the well-established public international law principle about compensation on expropriation; in a commercial dispute, in contrast, the arbitrators may need to find sources on quite technical questions, such as the conditions for excluding liability, or the relevance of the negotiations and the subsequent conduct of the parties in the interpretation of the contract. Section 4 above showed that transnational principles are not sufficiently specific and systematic to harmonise the various laws and create a set of general principles that may govern all aspects of general contract law; in section 6 above, it is shown that transnational sources do not have the ability to fully replace a governing law. Hence, and as will be illustrated below, commercial contracts may not be subject to 'internationalisation' and thus be able to escape from the scope of the governing law to the same extent as investment contracts with states may.

7.1 Standard contracts

The European Commission seemed to encourage, albeit for a short period,[113] stand-ard contracts as a tool towards harmonisation of the various state contract laws.[114] It was soon realised, however, that contracts, even if they are standardised, are subject to a governing law and cannot derogate from this law's mandatory rules. Therefore, a standard contract, to be effective across the entire territory of the EU, would

---

[109] See Christoph Schreuer, Lavetta Malintoppi, August Reinisch and Anthony Sinclair, *The ICSID Convention: A Commentary*, 2nd edn (Cambridge University Press, 2009), Article 42, para. 153ff.

[110] *Libyan American Oil Company* v. *The Government of the Libyan Arab Republic* [1982] 62 ILR 140.

[111] *British Petroleum (Libya) Ltd* v. *The Government of the Libyan Arab Republic* [1979] 53 ILR 297.

[112] *Texaco Overseas Petroleum Company, California Asiatic Oil Company* v. *The Government of the Libyan Arab Republic*, award of 9 January 1977, [1978] 17 ILM 3.

[113] First Annual Progress Report on European Contract Law and the Acquis Review, COM(2005) 456 final.

[114] See the Action Plan on a More Coherent European Contract Law, COM (2003) 68 final and European Contract Law and the Revision of the Acquis: The Way Forward, COM (2004) 651 final.

necessarily have to comply with the strictest of the criteria set by the various member states. This, in turn, would have prevented the standard contracts from adopting any more flexible criteria offered in other member states, hence preventing progress in contract practice. This would not have led to a harmonisation that seems desirable.

That a contract, even a standard contract, is subject to a governing law – and that the governing law, even for an international contract, is a national law – has impact, even beyond that law's mandatory rules. As will be shown in Chapter 3, national laws differ from one another in respect of how contracts are to be interpreted, and this may lead to standard contracts being interpreted differently and having different legal effects depending on the governing law. As shown in this chapter, transnational sources do not have the ability to harmonise the general contract law and thus cannot ensure a uniform interpretation of standard contracts.

Standard contracts, therefore, do not seem to be the appropriate tool with which to harmonise commercial contract laws. Moreover, there is an abundance of standard terms issued by a large number of organisations such as the ICC, branch associations such as the ISDA, FIDIC or Orgalime, or even by commercial companies. Standard contracts prepared by FIDIC and Orgalime compete to regulate similar contractual relationships within the same branch of construction; the very fact of this competition speaks against their ability to reflect a harmonised transnational law.

The wealth of documents issued by a disparity of sources creates an additional uncertainty, since it creates the risk of attaching normative value to terms written by organisations or institutions that do not act impartially.[115]

As a tool for harmonising international (in the particular proposal commented upon here, EU) contract law, it has been proposed[116] that standard contracts should be negotiated by organisations representing the involved parties. The democratic selection of the drafting parties would ensure legitimacy, and the collective character of the negotiations would ensure a balanced result that takes into account all of the involved interests.[117] In the proposal, EU enactments should give these documents the force to derogate from mandatory rules of the applicable law, thus avoiding the

---

[115] See Goode, Kronke, McKendrick, *Transnational Commercial Law*, 34ff. and Symeonides, *Party Autonomy and Private-law Making*, p. 6, who wishes a 'check to the unbounded euphoria that seems to permeate much of the literature on the subject' of non-state norms as a source of the new *lex mercatoria*. See also Fabrizio Cafaggi, 'Self-regulation in European Contract Law', in Hugh Collins (ed.), *Standard Contract Terms in Europe: A Basis for and a Challenge to European Contract Law*, (Wolters Kluwer, 2008), pp. 93–139, 137ff.

[116] For a recent suggestion to promote autonomous agreements that are not affected by the differences among the various contract laws, see Hugh Collins, 'The Freedom to Circulate Documents: Regulating Contracts in Europe', (2004) 10 *European Law Journal*, 787–803. For an incisive analysis of how standard contract terms would not be capable of being autonomous because they are subject to, among other things, the governing law's influence in respect of the normative context and the interpretation, see Simon Whittaker, 'On the Development of European Standard Contract Terms', (2006) 1 *European Review of Contract Law*, 51–76.

[117] In a certain sector of Norwegian business, this practice is widespread and successful, and results in standard contracts that are known under the name of 'agreed documents'. These standard contracts have a high degree of persuasive authority, and courts tend to accept the solutions contained therein, even though they would not be acceptable in a contract negotiated between private parties: see Rt. 1994 p. 626.

above-mentioned prospect of having to comply with the strictest of the potentially applicable laws. This regime would indeed solve the problems of legitimacy and of compliance with the law. However, these contracts would not be immune from another major problem affecting transnational sources: the lack of a uniform standard for interpretation, as was seen in this chapter.[118]

7.2 'Good commercial practice'

The Academic DCFR, the Acquis Principles and the CESL mentioned in section 2.2 above seem to indirectly endorse the idea of an autonomous contract. They have a double approach to commercial contracts: as was seen in Section 4.2 above, they extend rules of consumer protection to commercial contracts (including an extensive and mandatory principle of good faith), and then moderate them by reserving for contrary good commercial practice.

As was seen in Section 4 above, the principle of good faith is given a central role in the restatements of principles, but has a content that is difficult to specify in a uniform way. Reference to good commercial practice as the only concretisation of the principle of good faith assumes that the interpreter is in a position to define good commercial practice and to assess its content. For want of better guidelines, it may be assumed that the sources of good commercial practice do not differ significantly from the sources of the transnational commercial law that were analysed above: general principles, soft law and trade usages. As seen in Section 4 above, these sources are not capable of giving a clear and harmonised picture of the transnational law of commercial contracts; hence, they do not give a clear picture of what good commercial practice is. In addition, scholarly works on the convergence of legal systems may be considered as relevant. As Chapter 3, Section 3 will show, little guidance seems to be found there either.

In addition to those sources, contract practice may be given particular attention. As was seen in Chapter 1, contract practice generally adopts contract models prepared on the basis of English law or at least of common law systems, which, according to the traditional conception discussed in Chapter 3, do not contemplate good faith and fair dealing as a standard. Contract practice is, therefore, quite distant from the principles underlying the DCFR and the CESL, as was commented on in Section 4.2 above. Even if, as seen in Chapter 3, Section 3, the system of English law might not always allow for the effects of all contract clauses, common law contract models are clearly drafted on the assumption that the contracts shall be interpreted literally and without influence from principles such as good faith. As a consequence of the broad adoption of this contractual practice, the regulations between the parties move further and further

---

[118] A similar criticism is made by Whittaker, 'On the Development of European Standard Contract Terms', 54ff.

away from the assumption of a standard of good faith and fair dealing, even in countries whose legal systems do recognise the important role of good faith.

This renders it even more difficult to specify the content of the general clause of good faith by reference to the general standard of good commercial practice.

8 Conclusion

The foregoing text shows that transnational instruments are a useful supplement to the governing law for specific and technical aspects of commercial relationships. If they are enacted as binding instruments, they will apply directly; if they are soft law, they will need to be incorporated by the parties unless they reflect trade usages.

The legal effects of a contract do not flow simply from the contract itself, but are a result of the combination between the contract and the governing law. In particular, the governing law influences the interpretation of the contract. In addition, the governing law plays an important role in filling any gaps that the contract might have; moreover, mandatory rules of the governing law will override any regulation to the contrary that the contract might contain. As will be seen in Chapter 3, this means that the wording of one and the same contract may have different legal effects depending on the governing law, and that the transnational law does not manage to overcome these differences and create a harmonised regime.

This does not mean that the transnational law may not regulate international contracts. Contract laws usually do not contain many mandatory rules; therefore, the parties might not even notice that the contract is regulated by a certain governing law. In the absence of mandatory rules (i.e., within the scope of the freedom of contract granted by the governing law), the parties are free to use their contract to develop practical mechanisms to respond to the needs of the specific case. Within this scope, and as long as there are no interpretative challenges, transnational sources thrive: commercial practice and transnational sources provide useful regulations and models, and the parties develop mechanisms for the regulation of their respective interests that do not depend on the governing law and may be used across the borders.

What the contract and the incorporated transnational law might not achieve, however, is to harmonise the general interpretation and application of contracts. These depend on the general contract law, which, in turn, is a result of each system's legal tradition. Unless transnational law is interpreted and applied by a centralised court that, over time, may create a coherent body of jurisprudence, its application will be tainted by the interpreter's own legal tradition, thus impairing the desired harmonisation. Aspirations to create a coherent jurisprudence by avoiding national courts of law and submitting disputes to international commercial arbitration are doomed to fail because of the fragmentation of arbitration, as will be seen in Chapter 3, Section 1.7, as well as the ultimate control of judicial courts over arbitral awards.[119] Commercial arbitration is carried out in a large variety of institutions in all regions of the world, and many proceedings are ad hoc and therefore outside of the framework of any institution; the more or less systematic publication of commercial awards organised by some institutions is not capable of giving any significant harmonisation to such a fragmented picture. A significant number of commercial disputes are decided by arbitrators appointed by private parties according to the most disparate criteria, and awards are written with the sole purpose of solving the particular dispute and with the awareness that they will not be read by anyone else besides the parties involved. Sometimes awards do not even need to state reasons for the decisions. Not only is coherence of arbitration practice not a goal that the commercial tribunals wish to pursue to a particularly high degree; even if it were a goal, it would be impossible to achieve in such a multifaceted system.

---

[119] Courts may not review the awards, either in terms of the merits or in regard of the application of the law. However, if the award disregards particularly important principles of the legal system, it may be deemed, *inter alia*, to violate public policy and thus be ineffective. For an analysis of the matter, see Chapter 5.

The impact of the governing law

As we have seen in Chapter 1, international contracts are often written without regard to the governing law – on the assumption that the terms of the contract are sufficiently clear to exclude the necessity of having to consult the governing law, and with the awareness that there is a risk that some of the clauses may not be enforceable under the governing law. This chapter will analyse the consequences of this attitude, in other words: what happens if a contract is drafted without taking into consideration the governing law?

The governing law may have a significant impact on the interpretation of a contract. In addition, the governing law may have mandatory rules or default rules that regulate the object of the contract. These rules may supplement or replace the contractual provisions.

Assuming that the parties have regulated their transaction in the contract with the intention that the contract should be the only and exhaustive regulation of their relationship, we can envisage the following scenarios: (i) the contract regulates aspects that are already regulated by the governing law, (ii) the contract regulates aspects that are not regulated by the governing law, (iii) the contract does not regulate aspects that are regulated by the governing law, and (iv) neither the contract nor the governing law regulate certain aspects. Each of the scenarios in which the contract overlaps, conflicts with or supplements the governing law, can in turn be divided into two according to whether the relevant rules of the governing law are mandatory or not; that is, if the governing law specifies that those particular rules cannot be derogated from by contract or if the governing law permits the contract to regulate the subject matter in a way that is different from the regulation provided for by law.

Perhaps what is even more important than the contract's compliance or non-compliance with the governing law's provisions (whether mandatory or not), is the question of how the contract will be interpreted. As we will see below, the interpretation of a contract is highly influenced by the principles underlying the applicable contract law.[1]

---

[1] Taking the same position, is Simon Whittaker, 'On the Development of European Standard Contract Terms', (2006), *European Review of Contract Law*, 51–76, 63ff. Whittaker brings further examples of the impact of the legal tradition on the interpretation of contracts, which are not mentioned here, in particular, on exemption clauses and variation clauses.

I will start with a short introduction to the main differences in the common law and the civil law approach to the interpretation of contracts.

This overview will be followed by an analysis of the extent to which common law and civil law may be deemed to converge, and the relevance that this convergence has to the question of the interpretation and application of contracts.

I will then consider the impact of the governing law regarding the interpretation of the contract.

Thereafter, I will analyse what the consequences are of the various scenarios of overlap, conflict and supplementation between the contract and the governing law.

Finally, I will discuss to what extent international arbitration is immune from the difficulties that arise from the influence that legal traditions have on the interpretation of contracts.

1 English law privileges predictability

As was mentioned in the course of Chapters 1 and 2, the common law and the civil law approach to the interpretation of contracts are quite different from each other. Under English law, the interpreter of a contract is expected to establish the mutual intention of the parties on the basis of the document itself. The wording of the provisions has to be understood according to its plain and literal meaning; even if the interpreter attempts to read the provisions in a manner that does not lead to absurdity[2] or inconsistency in terms of the remaining provisions,[3] it will not be possible to construe the contract in a manner that runs against the language. A famous restatement of the principles on interpretation of contracts made by Lord Hoffmann[4] renders the interpretation of contracts more lenient so as to enable adapting the wording to the purpose of the contract by taking into account the factual background of which the parties could reasonably have had knowledge at the moment of entering into the contract (however, excluding the previous negotiations of the parties, their declarations of subjective intent and the subsequent conduct of the parties, which are allowed in the civil law tradition) – the so-called factual matrix of the contract. However, this purposive rather than literalist approach does not go so far as to permit a substitution for the bargain that was actually made by the parties, one which the interpreter deems to be more reasonable or commercially sensible; this is not allowed under the English law on contract interpretation.[5] The importance of the literal interpretation is also strengthened by the interpretation rule according to which reference in the contract to a certain case will exclude that the contract applies to other corresponding cases that have not been expressly mentioned: *expressio unius est exclusio alterius*.[6] In a recent decision, the English Supreme Court has gone far in affirming that the interpretation

---

[2] *Investors Compensation Scheme Ltd* v. *West Bromwich BS* [1998]1 WLR 898 (HL).
[3] *Watson* v. *Haggit* [1928] AC 127.   [4] *Investors Compensation Scheme Ltd* v. *West Bromwich BS*, pp. 912f.
[5] *Charter Reinsurance Co Ltd* v. *Fagan* [1997] AC 313.   [6] *Hare* v. *Horton* [1883] 5 B & Ad 715.

of a contract that is more consistent with the commercial purpose of the contract shall be preferred, but it has been careful to underline that this assumes that that particular construction must be possible on the basis of the wording of the contract.[7]

An English judge does not have access to pre-contractual negotiation or surrounding documentation in order to ascertain the common intention of the parties, nor do the courts hear evidence of the parties as to what their intention was at the time of writing the contract.[8]

In addition to having little access to surrounding circumstances, the English interpreter also has little possibility of filling in the gaps in the contract by assuming implied terms. Some acts have introduced statutory terms that are to be deemed as implied terms of the contracts falling within the scope of those acts (for example, the Sale of Goods Act 1979). In the absence of statutory terms, however, the general rule is that a judge has only to interpret the contract that the parties have made, and is not to make the contract for the parties.[9] The courts do not fill in gaps in the contract, even if it would be reasonable to do so; they fill in gaps where this is necessary to give business efficacy to the contract, or when inclusion of such a term is obvious (which assumes, however, that both parties are satisfied with the implied term, and renders this alternative fairly unviable when the parties have conflicting interests or motives).[10]

This approach finds its historical explanation in the selective borrowing of the Roman law-based doctrines of natural law, which was carried out by the English lawyers who first systemised the law of contracts at the end of the eighteenth century.[11] English lawyers did not borrow the naturalistic doctrines that classified contracts into different types, where each type had its own set of regulations that was deemed to express natural obligations attached to that particular kind of contract. Hence, English law failed to adopt a systematic set of rules for each contract type that could integrate or guide the interpretation of contracts. The judge's respect of the parties' will was not mediated by the existence of a statutory or doctrinal set of rules governing the specific types of transaction. Consent by the parties was conceived not as consent to a type of contract with its immanent rules, but to the very words of the contract. This approach to the interpretation of contracts, opposed to the approach of the civil law systems, is today mitigated by a series of statutory rules that have created implied terms of contract similar to the declaratory rules that civil law systems attach to the various types of contracts. This is particularly true in the field of protection of

---

[7] *Rainy Sky SA et al.* v. *Kookmin Bank* [2010] UKSC 50, particularly at paras. 21–13, 30, 34, 40, 43 and 45.

[8] Whittaker, 'On the Development of European Standard Contract Terms', 64.

[9] *Phillips Electronique, Grand Publique SA* v. *BSB Ltd* [1995] EMLR 472.

[10] See Jack Beatson, Andrew Burrows and John Cartwright, *Anson's Law of Contract*, 29th edn. (Oxford University Press, 2010), pp. 151ff. This has permitted the development of sets of implied terms for various types of contract; see Whittaker, 'On the Development of European Standard Contract Terms', 62f.

[11] See, for more extensive references, J. Gordley, *The Philosophical Origins of Modern Contract Doctrine* (Oxford University Press 1991), pp. 146ff., 159.

the weaker contractual party, this being mainly identified with the consumer. In commercial contracts, statutory implied terms are less frequent.

Not only can the terms of the contract only be integrated to a restricted extent but the extent to which the terms of the contract may be corrected by applying the principle of good faith is also negligible in commercial contracts.[12]

It is not unusual to read English court decisions that give effect to the wording of a contract, while at the same time admitting that they consider the result unsatisfactory. For example, if the parties have stipulated sufficiently clearly in the contract the legal consequences of a default, and if the stipulation does not violate the mandatory rules of law, those consequences will be enforced, even if it may be unfair to do so. In a contract for the lease of a computer, for example, the contract entitled the leasing company, in case of a breach of the obligation to pay the instalments punctually, to recover possession of the computer and to claim payment of the overdue unpaid instalments, as well as payment of all the future instalments that were not yet due and payable at the moment of terminating the contract. The court realised that the contract regulation would lead to the leasing company obtaining the possession of the computer (that was later sold to a third party), as well as the full price for the same computer. The court also realised that this result would have been illegal, if the contract had been worded in such a way that the payment of the full price could be interpreted as being a penalty on the defaulting party. However, the court observed that the terms of the contract were such that the payment of the full price could not be interpreted as a penalty, but as a consequence of a breach of condition and therefore of a repudiation of the contract. Repudiation of the contract entitles, under common law, the innocent party to obtain the full value of the bargain. In spite of the dissatisfaction created by this situation, the court decided that the wording of the contract should be given effect to.[13]

English law maintains to this date the element of consideration; that is, the requirement that a contract, to be enforceable, must contemplate an exchange between the parties. This is based on the elaboration that the natural lawyers made of the Roman *causa* up to the eighteenth century, according to which a contract is enforceable only if it can be justified in philosophical terms by applying the virtues of liberality or commutative justice. This, however, should not lead the observer to the conclusion that English law recognises in the element of the consideration the same significance that the natural lawyers saw in it, and that therefore English law pays attention to ensuring the equitable content of the contracts. Quite the contrary, as the element of the consideration is essential for the existence of an enforceable contract, but the English judge is expected to ascertain the formal existence of the consideration, not to examine the adequacy of the consideration. Evaluating the adequacy of the consideration – that

---

[12] See Whittaker, 'On the Development of European Standard Contract Terms', 65. See also the references in footnote 86.

[13] *Lombard North Central plc v. Butterworth* [1987] 1 All ER 267, Court of Appeal.

is, verifying whether the contract is fair or not – is considered to be paternalistic and not in compliance with the expectations that English lawyers have in respect of their legal system.[14] Even the equitable relief for a so-called unconscionable bargain, which could at first sight be deemed to be equivalent to an assessment of the transaction's reasonableness, is not meant to reinstate the balance between the contractual parties, but is based on its value as evidence that a fraud has taken place. A significant inadequacy of the consideration, in other words, might be considered as one of the elements to prove that a fraud has taken place and might therefore serve to exclude the enforceability of that contract even if the contract is binding at law. The question of ensuring fairness in the exchange, however, is not relevant at all. The attitude of English law towards the risk of being bound by a contract that is not fair is clearly expressed in the formula used by Lord Mansfield in 1778 and that is still often referred to: *caveat emptor*, let the buyer beware.[15] This attitude is usually explained by reference to the central role that maritime and financial transactions have played and still play in the English system. In these highly professionalised settings, the interests of the operators are deemed to be better served by ensuring enforceability of the contracts according to their words rather than by intervening on the agreement between the parties in the name of an unpredictable justice.

The English judge does not have the task of creating an equitable balance between the parties, but has to enforce the deal that the parties have voluntarily entered into. The parties are expected to take care of their own interests, and they expect from the system a predictable possibility of enforcing their respective rights in accordance with the terms of the contract. A correction or integration of these terms would run counter to these expectations, and the English judge does not, consequently, assume that role (unless specific statutory rules require him to do so, which happens mainly in the context of consumer contracts). This is seen as the most appropriate attitude for a system where commercial and financial business flourishes.

2 Civil law systems privilege justice, but to different extents

Civil law systems have developed in quite a different way. Until the eighteenth century, continental Europe elaborated Roman law on the basis of natural law. The natural lawyers justified the legal effects of contracts on the basis of Aristotelian philosophy and its classification of the virtues. During the nineteenth century, the doctrine of natural law was abandoned in favour of a more positivistic–exegetic approach in France, and in favour of an historic–teleological approach in Germany. These two approaches influenced the remaining civil law countries, and against this background, civil law systems are divided into Romanistic (influenced by the French approach) and Germanic (influenced by the German approach) systems.

---

[14] See, for further references, Gordley, *The Philosophical Origins*, pp. 146ff. See also Section 6.1 below.
[15] *Stuart v. Wilkins* [1778] I Dougl. 18, 99 Eng. Rep. 15.

The contract was, in the nineteenth century, deemed to be based on the parties' will, not on some virtues, duties or imperatives naturally stemming from human relations, as the natural lawyers had assumed earlier.

The ideals of the French Code Civil are characteristic for the era in which the Code was conceived. Issued shortly after the French Revolution, the Code Civil is based on the desire to establish a liberalistic order where the individual enjoys the freedom to regulate its interests as he deems fit, where private property is respected and the public system's interferences are reduced to the minimum. Additionally, the ideals of the Enlightenment are clearly present, and the law is seen as a scientific system that consists of abstract rules with a perfect consistency with each other so that there is no need for subjective evaluations. The task of the judge is simply to apply these rules to specific cases, in a mechanical way, without any moral or social evaluation. The lawyer is aware of the possibility that the mechanical application of the law can sometimes bring forth unjust results according to the circumstances of the case, but this consequence of the formal rigidity of the system is gladly accepted in the name of the higher value of the predictability of the legal system.

The only true law is deemed to be positive law; that is, the codified text of the law, and this has to be applied without making any recourse to natural reason or equity.[16]

The drafters of the French Code Civil affirmed clearly that an adult's duty is to contract with prudence, and that the law owes him no protection against his own acts.[17] The legal system's task became one of respecting and enforcing the parties' will, without evaluating it on the basis of equality in exchange or other criteria that had been central in natural doctrines. However, the continental legal systems had already adopted a developed system of regulations relating to the various types of transactions, based on the natural doctrines. Contracts had been classified into types, and to each type belonged a detailed list of natural obligations. These regulations were not abandoned during the nineteenth century, since they had lost their aura of natural law and had become positive law. The respect of the parties' will, therefore, was tempered with the application of the detailed rules on the various types of contract. Hence, continental lawyers interpreted the contracts in the light of the concurring or integrating rules that the legal system had for every type of contract.

In Germany, contract law was codified in 1900 in the Bürgerliches Gesetzbuch (BGB). The object of the codification was the elaboration of the law that had been carried out very actively by German legal doctrine during the preceding two centuries; legal scholars had devoted considerable energy to classifying and systemising primarily Roman law.[18] The BGB thus codified the result of the scientific ideals of the

---

[16] For a historical analysis and further references see Gordley, *The Philosophical Origins*, pp. 220ff.

[17] *Ibid.* p. 201.

[18] On the characteristic features of the German law of contracts see, *inter alia*, Antonio Gambaro and Rodolfo Sacco, *Sistemi giuridici comparati* (Utet Giuridica, 2002), pp. 339ff. and Konrad Zweigert and Hein Kötz, *Einführung in die Rechtsvergleichung* (Mohr Siebeck, 1996), pp. 130ff.

eighteenth and nineteenth centuries: rules were expressed on the highest possible level of abstraction, whereby the internal consistency of the system was the ultimate goal. In addition to the ideal of scientific abstraction and consistency, the BGB was inspired by the ideal of liberalism, according to which each individual should be permitted to regulate their own interests as he/she deemed fit and should be expected to take the responsibility therefor. In addition to the ideal of liberalism, the BGB partially also reflects the sociological engagement of the historic line of thought, as is witnessed by the few so-called general clauses contained therein: not abstract rules that simply require to be applied mechanically by the judge, but rules that contain guidelines (such as the rule on good faith in the performance of contracts in § 242 of the BGB) and require an evaluation by the court of the legal rule's purpose and of the consequences of its application in the specific case. The social situation following the First World War, with dramatic hyperinflation, was the background for the Supreme Court's active application of the general clause on good faith contained in § 242 of the BGB. This was used to revert the BGB's focus on the will of the parties, and to privilege an equitable balance of the parties' interests from a substantive point of view rather than from the formal application of the words of the contract.[19] Since then, the German courts have applied § 242 so often and in so many active ways that a systematisation and classification of court practice requires 1187 paragraphs in the most acknowledged commentary on § 242.[20]

3 Convergence between civil law and common law?

Comparative law research has proven that many of the contradictions that are traditionally held to exist among the various legal systems and, notably, between the common law and the civil law, can be reduced to a common core that is shared by most legal systems.[21]

While this common core may be found at a rather high level of abstraction, differences may persist and have great relevance on a more practical level. That two systems may achieve a certain result may justify the observation that there is a

---

[19] RGZ 107, 18ff. See also, for further references, among others Reinhard Zimmermann and Simon Whittaker (eds.), *Good Faith in European Contract Law* (Cambridge University Press, 2000), pp. 20ff.

[20] J. von Staudinger, *Kommentar zum Bürgerlichen Gesetzbuch mit Einführungsgesetz und Nebengesetzen*, (Sellier de Gruyter, 2009), § 241–3.

[21] Reinhard Zimmermann, *The Law of Obligations: Roman Foundations of the Civilian Tradition* (Oxford University Press, 1996), has largely proven that common law and civil law 'were (and are) not really so radically distinct as is often suggested' (at p. xi). *The Common Core of European Private Law Project* (Kluwer Law International, 2003), under the general editorship of M. Bussani and U. Mattei, is perhaps the most systematic enterprise aiming at assessing the common core within European private law. Among the books published in the frame of this project is Zimmermann and Whittaker (eds.), *Good Faith in European Contract Law*, which has particular relevance to the topic of this book. Pointing out the convergence between common law and civil law, see Annuck de Boeck, and Mark van Hoecke 'The Interpretation of Standard Clauses in European Contract Law', in Hugh Collins (ed.), *Standard Contract Terms in Europe: A Basis for and a Challenge to European Contract Law* (Wolters Kluwer, 2008), p. 244, reducing the persisting difference to a matter of time before the common law adopts the civilian approach (notably, in respect of the principle of good faith).

common core between the two systems; however, if the techniques with which this result may be achieved differ in each of the systems, a contract written in a certain way may meet the requirements of one system but not of the other one. The result, hence, will be achieved only in one of the systems, notwithstanding the theoretical possibility of being able to achieve it in both. Contract drafters may not rely simply on the abstract common core; they should also take into consideration the specific requirements of the regulation in the relevant system.

Traditionally, the common law is held to be concerned with preserving the parties' freedom to contract and to ensure that their contracts are performed accurately according to their precise wording. An English judge is less concerned with providing the means for ensuring a balanced relationship between the parties; the judge's task is rather to enforce the deal that the parties have voluntarily entered into. The parties are expected to take care of their own interests, and they expect, from the system, a predictable possibility for enforcing their respective rights in accordance with the terms of the contract. A correction or integration of these terms would run counter to these expectations, and the English judge does not consequently assume that role (unless specific statutory rules require him to do so, which happens mainly in the context of consumer contracts).

This is traditionally seen as one of the main features that distinguishes the common law and civil law in respect of contracts: the civil judge has more power to evaluate the fairness of the contract and intervene to reinstate the balance of interests between the parties; he or she is more concerned with creating justice in the specific case than with implementing the deal in the most predictable manner. In doing so, the civil judge is guided by general clauses and principles of good faith and fair dealing. The English law of contract does not have a general principle of good faith.

Comparative studies have shown that the absence of a general rule on good faith does not mean that English law cannot achieve, in particular contexts, the same results that can be achieved in other systems applying the rule of good faith. Other legal techniques are applied to obtain results that are, in part, similar to a general duty of good faith. An often quoted decision has expressed this clearly:

> English law has, characteristically, committed itself to no such overriding principle [as the principle of good faith] but has developed piecemeal solutions in response to demonstrated problems of unfairness. Many examples could be given. Thus equity has intervened to strike down unconscionable bargains. Parliament has stepped in to regulate the imposition of exemption clauses and the form of certain hire-purchase agreements. The common law also has made its contribution, by holding that certain classes of contract require the utmost good faith, by treating as irrecoverable what purport to be agreed estimates of damage but are in truth a disguised penalty for breach, and in many other ways.[22]

---

[22] Brimham LJ in *Interfoto Picture Library Ltd* v. *Stiletto Visual Programmes Ltd* [1988] 2 WLR 615.

However, as will be seen in the sections immediately below, these piecemeal solutions do not necessarily always have the same scope of application as a general principle.[23] In spite of the evolution during the last few decades, English courts are said to

> remain very conscious of the need to maintain commercial certainty in their approach to the construction of express terms, a consciousness which can be seen in their remaining degree of discomfort with recourse to 'reasonableness' in argumentation as to one or other competing interpretations of a contract term and their continued rejection of a general principle of good faith in the performance or non-performance of contracts.[24]

It is not always justified to generalise particular rules and elevate them to the status of expressions of a principle underlying the whole system, considering them as symptoms of a general convergence between the common law and the civil law. Admittedly, if the general principle of good faith does not exist in the English law on commercial contracts, it does not necessarily mean that other areas of English law do not operate with a principle of good faith.[25] It does not necessarily mean that the

---

[23] That the English approach is not equivalent to a general clause as known in the civil law is shown by Simon Whittaker, 'Theory and Practice of the "General Clause" in English law: General Norms and the Structuring of Judicial Discretion', in Stefan Grundmann and Denis Mazeaud (eds.), *General Clauses and Standards in European Contract Law*, (Kluwer International, 2006), pp. 57–76, 64ff. and Hugh Collins, 'Social Rights, General Clauses, and the Acquis Communitaire', in Stefan Grundmann and Denis Mazeaud (eds.), *General Clauses and Standards in European Contract Law* (Kluwer International, 2006) pp. 111–40, 117 ff. The same is affirmed also by Jonathan Mance, 'Is Europe Aiming to Civilise the Common Law?' (2007) 18 *European Business Law Review*, 77–99, 94 and footnote 45. See also the references in Chapter 2, footnote 51. On the different approach to the doctrine of good faith and fair dealing in English law and in the civil law jurisdictions see Roy Goode, Herbert Kronke, and Ewan McKendrick, *Transnational Commercial Law – Texts, Cases and Materials* (Oxford University Press, 2007), pp. 527ff., affirming that the UPICC doctrine is used differently according to the legal tradition of the user: where the doctrine is invoked in a common law system, it can be seen as an attempt to introduce it in a legal system that does not have such a principle; where it is invoked in a civil law system, it simply reflects the important role that this principle has in civil law jurisdictions. As was recently observed, under the influence of, particularly, European law, 'good faith may have made its mark on the surface of the law of contract, but it has hardly captured the hearts and minds of English common lawyers': Roger Brownsword, 'Positive, Negative, Neutral: The Reception of Good Faith in English Contract Law', in Roger Brownsword, Norma J. Hird and Geraint Howells, *Good Faith in Contract*, (Ashgate/Dartmouth, 1999), pp. 13–40, 15. The author supports a positive view of good faith, as it permits the judges to avoid what he defines as 'contortions or subterfuges in order to give effect to their sense of the justice of the case' (p. 25). However, the author points out that this view is 'probably shared by no more than a minority of English contract lawyers' (*ibid.*). See, for example, Michael Bridge, 'Good Faith in Commercial Contracts', in Roger Brownsword, Norma J. Hird and Geraint Howells (eds.), *Good Faith in Contract* (Ashgate/Dartmouth, 1999), pp. 139–64, affirming that good faith gives too much power to the individual judges freed from the disciplined tradition of contract law, and pointing out that 'visceral justice was, and remains in my view, an emotional spasm' (p. 140), and that 'law is a discipline, not a reflex' (p. 150).

[24] Whittaker, 'On the Development of European Standard Contract Terms', p. 65.

[25] That relying on a monolithic view of legal systems may be misleading is convincingly argued by Michele Graziadei, 'Variations on the Concept of Contract in a European Perspective: Some Unresolved Issues', in Reiner Schulze (ed.), *New Features in Contract Law* (Sellier European Law Publishers, 2007), pp. 311–24, who shows, on pp. 321ff., that notions of good faith are to be found in English law when looking beyond the narrow borders of contract law, notably in the field of fiduciary obligations. The author underlines, thus, that

principle applied in that context underlies the whole legal system, when in a particular context, a certain result inspired by good faith may be achieved. A principle might not be unknown in a certain area, but this does not automatically mean that it extends to other areas of the law within that system. This is true, for example, in respect of particular rules assuming good faith in English law, rules that do not necessarily extend their scope to have a general validity for commercial contracts.

Many situations that would be covered by a general principle are left out by the specific rules of English law and thus remain unregulated. As such, failure to give to the other party information relevant to that party's evaluation of the risk or the value of the transaction is not penalised under English law, as this conduct is not specifically regulated, and does not violate any duty of loyalty between the parties.[26] Even the doctrine of misrepresentation, which could at first sight be deemed to be equivalent to a duty to exercise good faith during negotiations, does not ensure the same results. False information given to the other party during negotiations gives rise to damages in tort; however, silence is not generally considered to be false information. Withholding relevant information during negotiations, therefore, does not constitute misrepresentation and the parties remain free to adopt such conduct without consequences.[27]

These features, among others, distinguish the common law from civilian traditions and, as was seen in Chapter 2, from various transnational sources as well. It was observed that:

> European law in the sense of the domestic law of other Member States need have no impact on English law, and indeed it is hard to find many instances in which it has done so. . . . The same is true of European law as mediated through 'soft law', such as the Principles of European Contract Law.[28]

The observed trend towards a convergence between the two legal families, moreover, seems to be particularly dependent on a consideration of the common law in its totality; that is, including both its body of law and of equity (as well as the statutory law and default rules), and disregarding the effects that the contract may have on their applicability in the specific case.

The system of justice peculiar to English law that is called equity, originally administered by the Court of Chancery, developed remedies to mitigate the consequences of the strict application of the law that was made by the courts. Today,

---

the absence of a general notion of good faith in the restricted context of contracts (defined as commercial contracts) does not exclude its presence in the wider picture of English law. However, as is argued in this book, this shall not induce one into assuming the converse; i.e., that the presence of the good faith notion in the context of fiduciary obligations entails that the principle is also applicable to commercial contracts.

[26] In some situations, a duty of care arises between the parties; it does not seem, however, that negotiations of commercial contracts are within that number; see, for example, Denning LJ in *Chandler* v. *Crane, Christmas & Co* [1951] 2 KB 164 and see Ackner LJ in *Walford* v. *Miles* [1992] 1 All ER 453, House of Lords.

[27] Hugh Beale (ed.), *Chitty on Contracts: Vol. I, General Principles*, 31st edn (London, 2012), para 6-017ff.

[28] Hugh Beale, 'English Law Reform and the Impact of European Contract Law', in Stefan Vogenauer and Stephen Weatherill (eds.), *The Harmonisation of European Contract Law* (Hart Publishing, 2006), pp. 31–8, 37.

English law consists of two bodies: the body of law, which gives the parties formal rights on the basis of statutory law or of common law, and the body of equity, which gives remedies that, under precise, definite and limited circumstances, prevent one party from exercising the formal rights that it has at law.

The effects of a contract under the common law in its strict meaning, its effects 'at law', seem to differ quite dramatically from the legal conceptions of the civil law; the equitable rules and remedies moderate the harshest effects achievable at law. This is also true of non-mandatory rules at common law; that is, rules that may be derogated from in the contract. Thus, it is mainly equity and non-mandatory rules that permit the convergence between the different legal traditions.

In many instances, however, English law permits the avoidance of the effects achievable in equity or by its non-mandatory rules if sufficiently clear expressions of intention were made by the parties in the contract. Many of the contract clauses that are typical for commercial contracts are specifically written with the purpose of avoiding the remedies or other non-mandatory mechanisms existing in the English system, as was seen in Chapter 1, Section 4. Therefore, these clauses are responsible for annulling the convergence between the common law and the civil law systems. The original intention of the clauses, in other words, is to permit the harsh legal effects that mostly distinguish the common law, in the strict sense, from the civil law. Examples of these clauses were made in Chapter 1 and will be seen in the next section.

As the foregoing observations show, convergence between the legal families may be observed on an abstract level, but this is not necessarily sufficient to avoid divergent results in the specific cases. As was observed, 'there remain very significant differences in the way in which courts in Member States interpret express terms and discover implied terms, itself reflecting wider features of the national laws and of legal principles'.[29]

The impact of the governing law on the interpretation of contracts will be analysed in the next section.

4 The effects of the governing law on the interpretation of contractual terms

The effects of specific contract terms are heavily influenced by the legal system under which the contract is interpreted.[30]

In the following sections, we will examine how the governing law influences the interpretation of the clauses that were examined in the previous chapters: entire agreement, no waiver, no oral amendments, subject to contract and early termination.

In addition, we will discuss representations and warranties.

---

[29] Whittaker, 'On the Development of European Standard Contract Terms', p. 63.

[30] The interaction between the contract and the governing law was the object of a research project that I ran at Oslo University; for more information see www.jus.uio.no/ifp/english/research/projects/anglo/. The project resulted, among other things, in a book: Giuditta Cordero-Moss (ed.), *Boilerplate Clauses, International Commercial Contracts and the Applicable Law* (Cambridge University Press, 2011).

4.1 Boilerplate clauses

We will first turn to the so-called boilerplate clauses – contract language that is inserted in most commercial contracts without particular negotiations, and that is meant to regulate the interpretation and functioning of the contract.

4.1.1 Entire agreement

The purpose of the entire agreement clause is, as seen in Chapter 1, to isolate the contract from any source or element that may be external to the document. The parties' aim is thus to exclude that the contract is affected by terms or obligations that do not appear in the document. The original purpose of the clause was to exclude the application of the exceptions to the parol evidence rule and thus reinstate the strict regime at common law.

The parties are obviously entitled to regulate their interests and to specify the sources of their regulation. Therefore, the entire agreement clause is allowed and implemented according to its terms in most legal systems. However, many legal systems provide for ancillary obligations deriving from the contract type,[31] from a general principle of good faith[32] or from a principle preventing an abuse of rights.[33] This means that a contract would always have to be understood not only on the basis of the obligations that are spelled out in it, but also in combination with the elements that, according to the applicable law, integrate it. The same contract, therefore, risks having different content depending on the governing law: the entire agreement clause is meant to avoid this uncertainty by barring the possibility of invoking extrinsic elements. The entire agreement clause creates an illusion of exhaustiveness in terms of the written obligations.

This is, however, only an illusion: first of all, ancillary obligations created by the operation of law may not be excluded by the contract.[34]

---

[31] See, for France, Xavier Lagarde, David Méheut and Jean-Michel Reversac, 'The Romanistic Tradition: Application of Boilerplate clauses under French law', in Giuditta Cordero-Moss (ed.), *Boilerplate Clauses, International Commercial Contracts and the Applicable Law* (Cambridge University Press, 2011), pp. 210–26, Section 2, for Italy, see Article 1347 of the Civil Code and Giorgio De Nova, 'The Romanistic Tradition: Application of Boilerplate Clauses under Italian Law', in Giuditta Cordero-Moss (ed.), *Boilerplate Clauses, International Commercial Contracts and the Applicable Law* (Cambridge University Press, 2011), pp. 227–32, Section 1, as well as the general considerations on Article 1135 of the Civil Code in section 1; for Denmark, see Peter Møgelvang-Hansen, 'The Nordic Tradition: Application of Boilerplate Clauses under Danish Law', in Giuditta Cordero-Moss (ed.), *Boilerplate Clauses, International Commercial Contracts and the Applicable Law* (Cambridge University Press, 2011), pp. 233–53, Section 1.

[32] See the general principle on good faith in the performance of contracts in § 242 of the German BGB. See Gerhard Dannemann, 'Common Law-based Contracts under German Law', in Giuditta Cordero-Moss (ed.), *Boilerplate Clauses, International Commercial Contracts and the Applicable Law* (Cambridge University Press, 2011), pp. 62–79, Sections 3.2 and 3.3 for examples of its application by the Courts.

[33] See, for Russia, Ivan S. Zykin, 'The East European Tradition: Application of Boilerplate Clauses under Russian Law', in Giuditta Cordero-Moss (ed.), *Boilerplate Clauses, International Commercial Contracts and the Applicable Law* (Cambridge University Press, 2011), pp. 329–43, Section 1.

[34] See, for France and Italy, footnote 31 above. For Finnish law, see Gustaf Möller, 'The Nordic Tradition: Application of Boilerplate Clauses under Finnish Law', in Giuditta Cordero-Moss (ed.), *Boilerplate*

Moreover, some legal systems permit bringing evidence that the parties' agreement creates obligations different from those contained in the contract.[35]

Furthermore, many civil legal systems openly permit the use of pre-contractual material to interpret the terms written in the contract.[36]

Finally, a strict adherence to the clause's wording may, under some circumstances, be looked upon as unsatisfactory, even under English law. English courts, though insisting that a properly drafted entire agreement clause may actually succeed in preventing any extrinsic evidence from being taken into consideration, when faced with such a clause, interpret it so as to avoid unreasonable results. The motivation given by the courts in the decisions may create the impression that a proper drafting may achieve the clause's purpose, but the ingenuity of the court's interpretation gives rise to the suspicion that the drafting would never be found to be proper if the result were deemed to be unfair.[37]

The entire agreement clause is an illustration of a clause by which the parties attempt to isolate the contract from its legal context, which is not completely successful and cannot be fully relied on.

As was seen in Chapter 2, Section 4.2.1, a literal application of this clause seems to contradict the UPICC or the PECL, both of which are based on a strong general principle of good faith, which, furthermore, is specified by an express rule for the entire agreement clause contained in the restatements.

4.1.2 No waiver

As was seen in Chapter 1, the purpose of a no waiver clause is to ensure that the remedies described in the contract may be exercised in accordance with their wording at any time and irrespective of the parties' conduct.

Clauses, International Commercial Contracts and the Applicable Law (Cambridge University Press, 2011), pp. 254–64, Section 2.1.

[35] See, for Germany, § 309 No 12 of the BGB, prohibiting clauses which change the burden of proof to the disadvantage of the other party: see Ulrich Magnus, 'The Germanic Tradition: Application of Boilerplate Clauses under German Law', in Giuditta Cordero-Moss (ed.), *Boilerplate Clauses, International Commercial Contracts and the Applicable Law* (Cambridge University Press, 2011), pp. 179–209, Section 5.1.1.a. Italy, on the contrary, does not allow oral evidence that contradicts a written agreement, see De Nova, 'The Romanistic Tradition under Italian Law', Section 1.

[36] In addition to Germany (see previous footnote), see for France, Lagarde, Méheut, Reversac, 'The Romanistic Tradition under French Law', Section 2; for Italy, De Nova, 'The Romanistic Tradition under Italian Law' Section 4; for Denmark, Møgelvang-Hansen, 'The Nordic Tradition under Danish Law', Section 2.1; for Norway, Hagstrøm, 'The Nordic Tradition under Norwegian Law', Section 3.1; for Russia, Zykin, 'The East European Tradition under Russian Law', Section 2.1. The situation seems to be more uncertain in Sweden, see Lars Gorton, 'The Nordic Tradition: Application of Boilerplate Clauses under Swedish Law', in Giuditta Cordero-Moss (ed.), *Boilerplate Clauses, International Commercial Contracts and the Applicable Law* (Cambridge University Press, 2011), pp. 276–301, section 5.4.2.d, and more restrictive is Finland, see Möller, 'The Nordic Tradition under Finnish Law', Section 2.1.

[37] See Edwin Peel, 'The Common Law Tradition: Application of Boilerplate Clauses under English Law', in Giuditta Cordero-Moss (ed.), *Boilerplate Clauses, International Commercial Contracts and the Applicable Law* (Cambridge University Press, 2011), Section 2.1.

The parties are, of course, at liberty to regulate the effect of their conduct. However, under some circumstances, this regulation could be used by one party for speculative purposes, such as when a party exercises its right to terminate not immediately after the other party's breach that triggers the remedy, but after some time – for example, when it sees that new market conditions make it profitable to terminate the contract. The real reason for the termination is not the other party's old default that was originally the basis for the right of termination, but the change in the market. The no waiver clause, if applied literally, permits this conduct. A literal interpretation of the clause in such a situation is allowed in some systems,[38] but would, in many legal systems, be deemed to contradict principles that cannot be derogated from by contract: the principle of good faith in German law that prevents abuses of rights,[39] the same principle in French law that prevents a party from taking advantage of a behaviour inconsistent with that party's rights[40] and the principle of loyalty in the Nordic countries[41] that prevents interpretations that would lead to an unreasonable result in view of the conduct of the parties.[42] The clause may have the effect of raising the threshold for when a party's conduct may be deemed to be disloyal,[43] but it will not be able to displace the requirement of loyalty in full. As was seen in Chapter 2, Section 4.2.2, a literal application of the clause would also be prevented by the UPICC and by the PECL, both of which assume good faith in the exercise of remedies.[44]

Additionally, in the case of this clause, as seen above in connection with the entire agreement clause, English courts argue as if it were possible for the parties to draft the wording in such a way as to permit results that would be prevented in the civil systems as contrary to good faith or loyalty. The English courts' decisions, however, leave the suspicion that even an extremely clear and detailed wording would not be deemed to be proper if its application would lead to unfair results.[45]

The no waiver clause, thus, promises self-sufficiency in the regime for remedies that may not be relied on.

---

[38] Neither in Hungarian nor in Russian law would the principle of abuse of a right have the effect of depriving a party from its remedy in spite of considerable delay in exercising the remedy: see, respectively, Attila Menyhárd, 'The East European Tradition: Application of Boilerplate Clauses under Hungarian Law', in Giuditta Cordero-Moss (ed.), *Boilerplate Clauses, International Commercial Contracts and the Applicable Law* (Cambridge University Press, 2011), Section 3 and Zykin, 'The East European Tradition under Russian Law', Section 2.2.

[39] See the general clause on good faith in the performance of contracts in § 242 of the BGB. See Magnus, 'The Germanic Tradition under German law', Sections 3.2 and 3.3 for examples of its application by the courts.

[40] See Lagarde, Méheut and Reversac, 'The Romanistic Tradition under French Law', Section 3.

[41] See for Denmark, Møgelvang-Hansen, 'The Nordic Tradition under Danish Law', Section 2.3; for Finland, Möller, 'The Nordic Tradition under Finnish Law', Section 2.2; for Norway, Hagstrøm, 'The Nordic Tradition under Norwegian Law', Section 3.2.

[42] See Møgelvang-Hansen, 'The Nordic Tradition under Danish Law', Section 2.3.

[43] See, for Finland, Möller, 'The Nordic Tradition under Finnish Law', Section 2.2.

[44] See Giuditta Cordero-Moss, 'Does the Use of Common Law Contract Models give Rise to a Tacit Choice of Law or to a Harmonised Transnational Interpretation?', in Giuditta Cordero-Moss (ed.), *Boilerplate Clauses, International Commercial Contracts and the Applicable Law* (Cambridge University Press, 2011), Section 2.4.

[45] See Peel, 'The Common Law Tradition under English Law', Section 2.2.

4.1.3 No oral amendments

As was seen in Chapter 1, the purpose of this clause is to ensure that the contract is implemented at any time according to its wording and irrespective of what the parties may have agreed later, unless recorded in writing.

The clause has a legitimate purpose and the parties are free to agree to it. Under some circumstances, however, the clause could be abused – such as if the parties agree on an oral amendment, and afterwards one party invokes the clause to refuse to perform because it is no longer interested in the contract after the market has changed.

A strict application of the written form requirement is imposed in Russia by mandatory legislation.[46] An application of the clause, even for a speculative purpose, would be acceptable under French law, which has a rule excluding the possibility of bringing oral evidence in contradiction to a written agreement.[47] A similar rule is also present in Italian law, although case law on the matter seems to be unsettled.[48] In German law, the opposite approach applies: German law does not allow excluding evidence that could prove a different agreement by the parties and does not permit terms of the contract that disfavour the other party in an unreasonable way.[49] The Nordic systems would give effect to the wording of the clause by raising the threshold for when it can be considered as proven that an oral amendment was agreed upon. However, once such an oral agreement is proven, it would be considered enforceable out of the principle of *lex posterior*,[50] of loyalty[51] or of good faith.[52]

Even under English law, in spite of the alleged primacy of the contract's wording, it is uncertain whether the clause would be enforced if there was evidence that the parties had agreed to an oral variation.[53]

The no oral amendments clause is yet one more example of a clause that will not necessarily always be applied in strict accordance with its terms.

4.2 Subject to contract

As was seen in Chapter 1, letters of intent often contain a clause excluding liability for the break-off of negotiations. The purpose of this clause is to free the negotiating parties from any liability in case they do not reach a final agreement. This clause protects important interests in international commerce: it must be possible for the parties to wait until they have completed all negotiations before they make a decision on whether to enter into the contract. Often, negotiations are complicated and are

---

[46]   See Zykin, 'The East European Tradition under Russian Law', Section 2.3.
[47]   See Lagarde, Méheut and Reversac, 'The Romanistic Tradition under French Law', Section 4.
[48]   See De Nova, 'The Romanistic Tradition under Italian Law', Section 3.
[49]   See Magnus, 'The Germanic Tradition under German Law', Section 5.1.2.a.
[50]   See, for Denmark, Møgelvang-Hansen, 'The Nordic Tradition under Danish Law', Section 2.2.
[51]   See, for Finland, Möller, 'The Nordic Tradition under Finnish Law', Section 2.3, and for Norway, Hagstrøm, 'The Nordic Tradition under Norwegian Law', Section 3.3.
[52]   See, for Sweden, Gorton, 'The Nordic Tradition under Swedish Law', Section 5.3.2.
[53]   See Peel, 'The Common Law Tradition under English Law', Section 2.3.

carried out in various phases covering different areas of the prospective transaction. In this case, partial agreements on the respective area may be recorded and made 'subject to contract'. When all partial negotiations are concluded, the parties will be able to have a full evaluation and only then will they be in a position finally to accept the terms of the deal.

The parties may freely agree when and under what circumstances they will be bound. However, a literal application of the clause may lead to abusive conduct, such as when one of the parties never really intended to enter into a final agreement and used the negotiations only to prevent the other party from entering into a contract with a third party.

In this case, there is a dichotomy between the common law approach and the civil law approach. English law seems to permit the parties to negate the intention to be bound, without being concerned with the circumstances under which the clause will be applied. A certain sense of unease may be detected in the English courts at permitting parties to go back on a deal, but it seems that a very strong and exceptional context is needed to override the clause.[54] In an often-quoted House of Lords decision, Lord Ackner states that 'the concept of a duty to carry on negotiations in good faith is inherently repugnant to the adversarial position of the parties when involved in negotiations'.[55]

On the contrary, legal systems of the civil law, particularly those influenced by the Germanic tradition, assume that the parties are under a duty of loyalty even during the phase of negotiations of a contract.[56]

Civil law, like the UPICC and the PECL (as was seen in Chapter 2, Section 4.2.3), is concerned with the possibility that such a clause may be abused by a party to enter into or continue negotiations without having a serious intention of finalising the deal. Therefore, such conduct is prevented either by defining the clause as a potestative condition and therefore null[57] or by assuming a duty to act in good faith during the negotiations.[58] Below follow further considerations on the different approaches.[59]

---

[54] *Ibid.*, pp. 154ff.   [55] Ackner LJ in *Walford v. Miles.*

[56] The pre-contractual liability, or *culpa in contrahendo*, was introduced in the German legal system by Rudolf von Jhering, 'Culpa in contrahendo, oder Schadenersatz bei nichtigen oder nicht zur Perfektion galangten Verträgen' (1861) 4 *Jahrbücher für die Dogmatik des heutigen römischen und deutschen Privatrechts* 1ff. The BGB reform of 2002 has now codified it in § 311, but case law had already established, following Jhering, that by starting negotiations, the parties enter into a special relationship creating a duty of loyalty to each other according to § 241.2, the breach of which entitles the other party to reimbursement of damages (in the reformed BGB, according to § 280).

[57] See, for France, Lagarde, Méheut and Reversac, 'The Romanistic Tradition under French Law', pp. 220ff. Potestative conditions are null also under Italian law, see Article 1355 of the Civil Code.

[58] See, for France, Lagarde, Méheut and Reversac, 'The Romanistic Tradition under French Law', pp. 220ff; for Denmark, Møgelvang-Hansen, 'The Nordic Tradition under Danish Law', pp. 242ff.; for Finland, Möller, 'The Nordic Tradition under Finnish Law', pp. 259f; for Norway, Hagstrøm 'The Nordic Tradition under Norwegian Law', pp. 271f.; for Russia, Zykin, 'The East European Tradition under Russian Law', pp. 338f. The duty to act in good faith during the negotiations is spelled out also in § 311 of the German BGB and in Article 1337 of the Italian Civil Code. See, for the UPICC and the PECL, Chapter 3, Section 2.4. For Hungarian law, see Menyhárd, 'The East European Tradition under Hungarian Law', pp. 314ff.

[59] For a more extensive reasoning, see Giuditta Cordero Moss, 'The Function of Letters of Intent and their Recognition in Modern Legal systems', in Reiner Schulze (ed.), *New Features in Contract Law* (Sellier European Law Publishers, 2007), pp. 139–59.

4.2.1 Negotiations in good faith

Would the execution of a letter of intent add to or modify the afore-mentioned approaches to the pre-contractual liability?

The requirement of good faith may be deemed to increase progressively as the parties get closer to each other's position under the negotiations and the expectation that a contract will be concluded become stronger. The execution of a letter of intent, as such, is not an occurrence that has automatic effects in this context; however, depending on its content and on the phase of the negotiations in which the document is signed, and particularly when the letter of intent describes in some detail the final result of the negotiations, it may be considered as evidence of the closeness of the parties' relationship. That the parties negotiated, drafted and executed a document describing their common goals certainly seems to testify for a closer relationship than if only loose contacts had taken place. In itself, the process of drafting and negotiating the letter of intent is likely to have brought the parties closer to each other's position in the aim of formulating the common goals. When the letter of intent contains an extensive description of the deal, it may be considered as evidence of a quite advanced status of the negotiations, and therefore it can be used as a basis for arguing that the duty of good faith owed to each other is enhanced. It would be even more the case if the letter of intent contained a clause referring to negotiations in good faith. The consequences of the breach of such duty will be seen below.

A confirmation of agreement on some points of the deal, which will be included in the contract if the contract is to be finalised, is a combination of commitment and freedom. The parties do not claim to be completely uncommitted; they register that they have agreed on certain terms of the envisaged transaction, and that they agree to insert these terms in the future final contract. The parties, however, do not commit themselves to the final contract or to the other terms of the envisaged transaction. They remain free to negotiate other terms, to introduce new ones, to withdraw yet others or to resolve that they will not enter into the final contract. The direct legal effects consist in the commitment to incorporate the agreed terms in the final contract, if the parties resolve to execute a final contract. Therefore, a party will be in breach of this obligation (and incur a liability for breach of contract) if it insists on executing the final contract without the agreed terms. It does not seem very realistic, however, that a party should openly violate the obligation: if it does not intend to execute the contract, it remains free to do so without violating the obligation to insert the confirmed points, and if it is interested in the final contract but wishes to change the agreed terms, in many situations it will be possible to propose new terms bordering with the already agreed ones that will have the effect of indirectly modifying the agreed terms without directly violating the confirmation of partial agreement. This form of letter of intent, therefore, does not seem to be a very efficient instrument.

Therefore, it is legitimate to investigate whether this form of a letter of intent has some further legal effects, beyond the commitment to incorporate the agreed terms.

These effects could possibly result in an obligation to negotiate the remaining terms of the contract in such a way that they would not contradict or affect the already agreed terms. This would not be an obligation to achieve a certain result, because the parties do not know, prior to the negotiations, what result they will achieve, if they will achieve any at all. It would be an obligation to conduct the negotiations taking into due consideration the terms of the letter of intent, to negotiate in such a way that the terms contained in the letter of intent are not deprived of their intended meaning. This, in other terms, would be an obligation referring not to the result of the negotiations, but to the conduct of the negotiations. It would be an obligation to use the best efforts to reach an agreement incorporating the terms of the letter of intent. Sometimes the letter of intent may contain a clause explicitly regulating a duty to continue negotiations in good faith, which may be considered as equivalent.

Would this obligation have any legal effects? Under English law, it seems that the main means to achieve a pre-contractual liability would be to assume a duty of care between the parties. Where such a duty exists, negotiations must be carried out in good faith. A duty of care in the negotiations normally exists only where there is a relationship of a fiduciary nature, such as in employment contracts, counselling relationships or where a party is performing functions in the public interest within a statutory framework,[60] circumstances that do not normally occur in the context of commercial contracts. Would the execution of a letter of intent create such a duty of care? There is no authority to suggest so; actually, the aversion of English courts to agreements to agree, famously manifested by the House of Lords in *Walford* v. *Miles*, is known:

> A duty to negotiate in good faith is unworkable in practice as it is inherently inconsistent with a position of a negotiating party. . . . [W]hile negotiations are in existence either party is entitled to withdraw from these negotiations, at any time and for any reason. . . . Accordingly, a bare agreement to negotiate has no legal content.[61]

Even if the letter of intent had contained a clause explicitly requiring the parties to negotiate in good faith, therefore, it would not be enforceable. This seems to confirm that a letter of intent is not capable of creating any duty between the parties, even more so if it does not contain any clause on good faith negotiations.

Would a best effort obligation to reach an agreement be enforceable? A best effort obligation differs from a result obligation in that it does not guarantee a result, but it guarantees that measures will be undertaken in order to reach a certain result. If the result is not reached, there is no breach, as long as the measures were properly taken. Best effort obligations are enforceable under English law, as long as the promised

---

[60] *Re Debtors (nos. 449 and 450 of 1998)* 1 All ER (comm.) 149, at p. 158, and see Beale (ed.), *Chitty on Contracts*, para 2–137. See also *Chandler v. Crane, Christmas & Co* [1951] 2 KB 164.

[61] *Walford v. Miles*, 461.

conduct is sufficiently certain. Thus, best effort obligations to obtain an export licence are enforceable (and a breach thereof can be the basis for liability), because it is sufficiently clear what the best efforts would consist of: apply for a licence, comply with the authorities' requirements etc.[62] A best effort obligation to reach an agreement, on the contrary, could be considered as equivalent to an obligation to negotiate in good faith, and would not meet the requirements of certainty:[63] What exactly would be expected of the parties is unclear, given that the parties are not subject to any duty of loyalty or other restrictions during the pre-contractual phase and are free to assess their own interests during the negotiations. Therefore, violation of any such best effort obligation would not be considered as a basis for liability under English law.

In the civil law systems, generally, the obligation to negotiate in good faith arises out of the already mentioned duty of loyalty between the parties. This obligation may be enhanced by the circumstance that the parties have negotiated and executed a letter of intent setting forth the main terms of their negotiations. At a second glance, however, it seems legitimate to question how a violation of this best effort obligation could be established and what would be the consequences of breaching such an obligation.

It seems difficult to find evidence that a negotiation has not been carried out in good faith, or that a party has not used its best effort to reach an agreement, as long as the disagreement regards specific substantial aspects of the transaction. The evaluation of the parties' respective contributions, the organisation of the envisaged activity, the allocation of costs and profits depend on the totality of the envisaged transaction, and on how the transaction fits in each of the parties' business concepts, marketing strategies, procurement arrangements etc. Each party evaluates all of these aspects according to its own criteria and interests, and it might be very difficult to argue that a certain evaluation is not made in good faith.

Should it nevertheless be possible to argue that a party did not use its best efforts to reach an agreement, it seems that the only remedy that would be applicable is the reimbursement of losses incurred by the other party as a consequence of this violation.

The classical civil law remedy for breach of obligation, specific performance, does not seem to be applicable in the case of the obligation to negotiate in good faith. If the object of the obligation had been the result of the negotiations, it could be conceivable to be able obtain the specific performance by considering the final contract as executed. Since the object of the obligation is the process of the negotiations, however, it seems impossible to obtain specific performance by forcing one party to be cooperative. It is possible to imagine a situation where the letters of intent were very detailed and extensive, and one party had then, during further negotiations, presented

---

[62] Beale (ed.), *Chitty on Contracts*, para 2–139 and footnote 707.
[63] *Ibid.* and footnote 708, interpreting *Walford v. Miles*. However, this interpretation is not completely uncontroversial; see, for example, Beatson, Burrows and Cartwright, *Anson's Law of Contract*, pp. 65f., interpreting the same case as if it considered the best endeavours to agree as enforceable.

all the other outstanding terms to the other party; if all of these terms had been accepted in full by the other party, and then the first party had introduced new elements to create a disagreement in the negotiations that was not real, the result of the negotiations might appear to be easier to identify. Even in such an unrealistic case, however, it does not seem possible to obtain specific performance of the obligation to negotiate in good faith by disregarding the last introduction of terms, and considering the contract formed on the basis of the letters of intent and the terms that have been proposed by one party and accepted by the other. Such a specific performance would render the proposal of terms during negotiations as equivalent to an offer that becomes binding if it is accepted. During negotiations, however, the parties are not making offers; they are following the respective strategic lines towards a complex meeting of the minds, and this might well entail a willingness to move closer to the other party on some areas but not on others, introducing new elements for balancing other admissions and so on. It is in the nature of complex negotiations, even if they are carried out in good faith, that the total picture acceptable to each of the parties is not known until the end of the process. A specific performance that crystallises the negotiations prior to the conclusion of the process would not correspond to the function of the negotiations. The only possible remedy seems, therefore, to be the reimbursement of damages. As the terms of the final contract are not determinable, it is not possible to assess the loss incurred by the other party in relation to the expected gains that the negotiated contract would have created if it had been entered into. The reimbursable damages, therefore, would have to be the costs and losses incurred as a consequence of the failed negotiations. This seems to coincide with the regime in the legal systems that regulate the pre-contractual liability.[64]

Even assuming, therefore, that a breach of the obligation to negotiate in good faith may be proven in respect of the substance of the negotiations, which seems to be quite difficult, the letter of intent does not seem to add considerably to the already existing regime of pre-contractual liability.

4.2.2 Exclusion of liability

One of the most important clauses of pre-contractual documents is deemed to be the clause specifying that no party shall be considered as liable for the failure to reach an agreement, and that each party shall bear its own costs and shall not seek compensation from the other party for any losses or damages that it might have incurred as a consequence of the negotiations or their failure. Letters of intent and most other pre-contractual documents are intended to emphasise the parties' full freedom during the negotiations.

As seen above, the freedom to form one's own business evaluation of the envisaged transaction and to decide whether the negotiated terms are acceptable or not does not

---

[64] See Staudinger in *Allgemeiner Teil 4*, §§ 145–56, notes 28 d and 50, with further references.

seem to be restricted by an obligation to negotiate in good faith or a best efforts obligation to reach an agreement, whether they are explicitly contained in a pre-contractual document or implied by the governing law.

It is possible to identify at least two further elements in the desired freedom during the negotiations: freedom in respect of the reasons (beyond the substantial reasons described above) for initiating, continuing or breaking off the negotiations, and freedom in respect of the way in which the negotiations are conducted. In respect of these two elements, the parties might incur liability under many civilian laws, but not under English law. A pre-contractual document is not necessarily capable of excluding this liability; on the contrary, the liability might be enhanced by such a document that seems to be apt to increase the duty of loyalty existing between the parties.

The former element concerns the good faith in the initiation or continuance of negotiations. A party may initiate negotiations knowing from the beginning that it will not enter into the final contract; the negotiations may be started for many reasons, such as, for example, to prevent the other party from entering into a contract with a third party, or to develop its own knowledge about that type of transaction or to have some terms with which to compare the terms of another negotiation that is being carried on in parallel. Alternatively, the negotiations might have started in good faith, but at a certain point in time, one party may have resolved that it will not enter into a contract with that counterparty, and yet might have continued the negotiations, for example, for the reasons just mentioned. The negotiations might then be brought to an end either because the party that did not intend to finalise the contract executed a similar contract with a third party, or because it arranged its business in such a way that the contract was no longer necessary or possible, or because it, for other reasons, lost interest in the real grounds for continuing the negotiations. The break-off of the negotiations may be open or disguised by some substantial impossibility at being able to reach an agreement that has been wilfully created by that party. This conduct does not seem to create liability under English law;[65] it would, though, represent a breach of the obligation to negotiate in good faith existing under many civilian laws.[66]

The latter element would consist, for example, in withholding material information relevant to the other party's evaluation of the negotiated transaction, thus inducing

---

[65] According to the rule expressed by the House of Lord in *Walford* v. *Miles*. See also *Regalian Properties* v. *London Dockland Development Corp.* [1995] WLR 212. A partial remedy against this conduct is represented by the doctrine of restitution; however, restitution aims at recovering a benefit gained by the party that walked away from the negotiations, not at compensating the losses suffered by the other party; see Beale (ed.), *Chitty on Contracts*, para. 29–01ff. In some cases, a restitutionary obligation may arise even if no benefit was gained, but this is mainly if the other party has rendered services at the request of the party breaking off: see Beale (ed.), *Chitty on Contracts*, para. 29–01ff, 29–019ff and Beatson, Burrows and Cartwright, *Anson's Law of Contract*, pp. 68f.

[66] As long as the party breaking off the negotiations has created an expectation in the other party as to the seriousness of the negotiations, there is a breach of the duty of loyalty provided for in § 241.1 BGB; see Staudinger, *Book 2: Vertragsschluss* (De Gruyter, 2005), § 311 notes 109ff.

the other party to continue negotiations that otherwise would have been of no interest. As long as this conduct does not result in giving false information to the other party, it does not seem to be able to create a liability under English law: silence is not deemed to be a misrepresentation.[67] It would represent a violation of the duty to negotiate in good faith existing in many civil law systems.[68]

What would be the remedies for this breach of the duty to negotiate in good faith? As already seen, it does not seem possible to obtain a specific performance in this case, as there is no obligation to conclude a contract and, even if there was one, the terms of the contract would not be determined or determinable with sufficient certainty. The available remedy would be the reimbursement of damages, and the damages would be measured in accordance with the so-called negative interest; that is, the losses connected with having relied on the failed negotiations. A liability in this respect would be an exception to the general principle that each party bears its own costs in connection with negotiations and preparation of contracts, and is based on the theory of *culpa in contrahendo*.

Would a pre-contractual document permit the exclusion of liability for this conduct? As was seen above, a document emphasising that the parties are free to withdraw from the negotiations at any moment and for any reason is certainly sufficient under English law to exclude any liability for, for example, costs incurred by the other party for the specific purpose of preparing the performance of the negotiated contract, since there is no such liability under English law in the first place.[69] The answer is less certain in civil systems. An agreement to exclude liability for gross negligence or wilful misconduct does not seem to be enforceable,[70] therefore the legal effects of the exclusion of pre-contractual liability must be looked for from a different perspective: not as an acknowledgement of one party's possibility of being able to act against good faith, but as an acknowledgement that the other party is aware of the first party's position and that, therefore, conduct in accordance with that position would not be considered to be against good faith. If, for example, a party discloses in the pre-contractual document that it is carrying out parallel negotiations with a third party, failure to finalise the contract because it was concluded with the third party cannot be deemed to be a violation of the duty to negotiate in good faith. Assuming, however, that the pre-contractual document does not mention anything in respect of parallel negotiations, that the negotiations are quite advanced, and that the other party, relying on an imminent conclusion of the final contract, starts to prepare for the performance of the contract by initiating,

---

[67] Beale (ed.), *Chitty on Contracts*, para. 6–017.

[68] Information duties are among the classical duties of loyalty arising out of § 241 BGB; Staudinger, *Book 2: Einleitung zum Schuldrecht, Treu und Glauben* (De Gruyter, 2005), § 241 notes 429ff.; specifically for the pre-contractual phase, see Staudinger, *Book 2: Vertragsschluss*, § 311 note 107.

[69] See footnote 65 above.

[70] In German law, the principle of good faith (*Treu und Glauben*) is contained in § 242 and is considered to be mandatory, see Staudinger, *Book 2: Einleitung zum Schuldrecht, Treu und Glauben*, § 242 notes 107ff.

for example, a costly reorganisation of its activity, if the party that does not intend to conclude the contract does not inform the other party of the uncertainty connected with the finalisation of the contract and silently lets the other party incur these costs, a clause in the pre-contractual document generally excluding liability does not seem to be sufficient.

4.2.3 Conclusion

As the foregoing text shows, awareness of the governing law and of the effects that a letter of intent may have thereunder is necessary to avoid surprises.

Should the letter of intent contain a clause obliging the parties to negotiate in good faith, or to use their best efforts to reach an agreement, that clause would be considered as not enforceable under English law, because it is not sufficiently certain and it would not add considerably to the duty of loyalty already existing in civilian regimes. In neither case would this clause have a considerable impact on the parties' freedom to evaluate the substance of the envisaged transaction and to decide whether or not the negotiated terms were acceptable.

Letters of intent, however, are often written in a way that seems to assume the regime of freedom to negotiate existing under English law: the parties specify that they are not committed to execute the contract, that they are not bound to incorporate in any final contract the terms contained in the letter of intent and that they are not liable for any of their conduct during the negotiations. Under English law, the parties would not really have needed to write all this in the letter of intent, because this freedom would follow by the operation of law. This is not the only example of redundant contractual practice, so it should not be too surprising that the parties spell out in the letter of intent a freedom that they enjoy anyway under the law. Under civil law, the parties might not achieve the described freedom in full; on the contrary, by executing a letter of intent, they run the risk of increasing or specifying the duty of loyalty that in turn reduces their freedom during the negotiations. This is not the only example of contractual practice borrowed from the common law tradition that clashes with principles of the civil law.

4.3 Early termination clauses

As was seen in Chapter 1, contracts may contain a clause defining non-performance of certain obligations as a fundamental breach of contract, thus giving the innocent party the possibility of terminating the contract. The parties define in advance when a fundamental breach is deemed to have occurred, and quite irrespective of the actual consequences that breach may have – unless they insert in the clause wording to that extent, such as 'Upon any *material* breach of a *material* obligation contained in article xx of this contract, the other party shall be entitled to terminate'. The inclusion of this wording may be the object of hard negotiations, and often the final text of the clause ends up without these qualifications. In these cases, the parties actually intend that the early termination clause may be used without having regard to how serious the breach is, and whether termination would be justified in light of the consequences and other circumstances.

It falls within the parties' contractual freedom to regulate their respective interests and to allocate risk and liability between themselves. Among other things, this means that the parties are free to determine the conditions on breach of which the contract may be terminated early. However, a literal interpretation of the clause may lead to unfair results, such as when the breach under the circumstances does not have any consequences for the innocent party, but this party uses the breach as a basis to terminate a contract that it no longer considers as profitable on other grounds – for example, after the market has changed.

If the contract is interpreted in accordance with English law, the contract's language will prevail over considerations of fairness. If it is not possible to avoid unfair results on the basis of the contract language, English courts are inclined to give effect to the clause according to its terms, even though the result under the circumstances may be deemed to be unfair. English courts do so, even if with evident reluctance, to ensure consistency in the law underlying the repudiation and termination of the contract.[71]

The contract-based right of repudiation may be exercised even if the breach did not really have any material impact and is made only for speculative purposes,[72] and even if the particular terms of the contract permit for it to be cumulated with other remedies and the result is unfair.[73]

In this context, therefore, properly drafted language achieves the effects that follow from a literal application of the clause, even if these effects are unfair. Other legal systems, on the contrary, would not allow a literal application of the clause if this had consequences that may be deemed to be unfair, because of the general principle of good faith and loyalty[74] or based on the assumption that the parties would not have intended to achieve such unfair results.[75]

---

[71] See Peel, 'The Common Law Tradition under English Law', pp. 148ff. See also Whittaker, 'On the Development of European Standard Contract Terms', p. 63.

[72] *Moore & Co Ltd* v. *Landauer Co* [1921] 2 KB 519, *Arcos Ltd* v. *Ronaasen* [1933] AC 470. See also the *Union Eagle* case [1997] 2 All ER 215, where an immaterial delay of ten minutes was considered sufficient to rescind the contract. As Lord Hoffmann stated, 'if something happens for which the contract has made express provision, the parties should know with certainty that the terms of the contract will be enforced' (pp. 218ff.) and 'to build an argument on the basis that the purchaser was only "slightly late" would be to encourage litigation about "how late is too late"' (p. 222).

[73] *Lombard North Central plc* v. *Butterworth* [1987] 1 All ER 267, Court of Appeal, that was described in Section 1 above.

[74] See, for Germany, the principle on good faith in the performance contained in §242 of the BGB; for France, Lagarde, Méheut and Reversac, 'The Romanistic Tradition under French Law', pp. 217ff; for Denmark, Møgelvang-Hansen, 'The Nordic Tradition under Danish Law', pp. 239ff; and for Finland, Möller, 'The Nordic Tradition under Finnish Law', pp. 258ff. The same would be obtained under Russian law, based on the principle prohibiting the abuse of rights: see Zykin, 'The East European Tradition under Russian Law', pp. 335ff.

[75] See, for Norway, Hagstrøm, 'The Nordic Tradition under Norwegian Law', pp. 270ff.

This clause is an illustration of contractual regulation that may be applied literally when subject to English law, whereas it has to be applied in combination with the governing law when subject to most civil law systems.

5 Contractual terms contradicting, supplementing or being supplemented by non-mandatory rules of the governing law

Often, no difficulties arise out of contracts that contradict or supplement the governing law, as long as the derogated rules are not mandatory: in the case of a dispute, it is often possible to solve the differences between the parties simply by applying the regulation contained in the contract. Often it will be possible to find a solution to the dispute without having to question the compatibility of the contract with the governing law: if the terms of the contract supplement the governing law, or if they regulate the transaction in a way that is different from a rule contained in the governing law, the contractual terms will prevail, as long as the rule being supplemented or derogated from is not mandatory.

For example, the parties may have agreed on a contractual regulation of the consequences of an impediment to performing the contractual obligations. This is an area that is usually regulated by law, albeit only by way of default rules. In many legal systems, particularly those belonging to the civil law tradition, a party is excused for non-fulfilment of an obligation if performance was prevented by an event beyond that party's control that could not be foreseen or overcome; a so-called *force majeure* event. The parties, however, are free to derogate from these rules. For example, the contract may contain a more detailed regulation than the governing law (the contract may specify how many days the prevented party can wait before it notifies the other party of the *force majeure* circumstance; it may specify how long the *force majeure* circumstance may persist before the contract has to be terminated or renegotiated etc.) or it might contain an allocation of the risk that is different from the one made by the governing law (for example, it may determine that the risk of some impediments, such as not obtaining the export licence from the competent authorities, has to be borne specifically by one party, for example the seller, and cannot be defined as a *force majeure* circumstance). In this area, a sufficiently clear contractual regulation will prevail over the regulation made by the law.

Nevertheless, the governing law may interact with the contractual regulation in various ways. As a result, the same contract clauses may end up having different legal effects depending on the governing law. This may come as a surprise to the parties, who may have spent considerable time and energy on writing detailed formulations in the contract under the illusion that their relationship would be governed fully and only by the text of the contract, but instead have to cope with a result that was affected by the governing law.

Furthermore, if the contract is silent on certain aspects, it does not necessarily mean that no regulation is to be applied. The governing law may contain rules that apply to situations that are not regulated by the contract. However, the regulation implied by law might differ from state to state, so that the contract will be integrated by different regulations, depending on the governing law.

We will consider four examples of clauses that may give rise to different effects depending on the governing law: representations and warranties clauses, liquidated damages clauses, *force majeure* clauses and hardship clauses.

5.1 Representations and warranties clauses

One of the clauses that is often written in contracts sets forth so-called representations and warranties. This clause contains a long list of circumstances that the parties state and guarantee to each other – from the validity of the parties' respective incorporation, to the validity of the obligations assumed in the contract, and the characteristics and specifications of the contract's object. As was seen in Chapter 1, Section 2, the drafting impetus may sometimes reach excesses that are defined as 'nonsensical', even in respect of English law,[76] as when the parties include matters which are outside of the scope of their freedom to dispose (such as the validity of the contract). Most of the circumstances that are represented or warranted, however, relate to specifications or characteristics of the contract's object and have a useful function. These representations and warranties create a liability for the party making them, and, if breached, will either permit the other party to repudiate the contract, or to claim compensation for damages. The clause, therefore, has an important function. The function is particularly important in common law, where the parties are expected to spell out the respective assumptions and obligations in the agreement, and it may be difficult to convince a court to imply specifications or characteristics that were not mentioned in the contract. A party, during contract negotiations, is under no duty to disclose matters relating to the contract's object, and the representations and warranties clause is usually the occasion for the parties to list all of the information that they consider relevant, and where they expect the other party to assume responsibility. Without the representations and warranties clause, there would be no basis for a contractual claim if important information was withheld.

In civil law systems, on the contrary, the parties are under extensive duties to disclose any circumstances that may be of relevance in the other party's appreciation of its interest in the bargain. It is not the party interested in receiving the information that shall request the other party to make a list of specific disclosures; it is the party possessing the information that is under a general duty to disclose matters that are relevant to the other party's assessment of the risk and its interest in the deal. This duty of information exists by operation of law, even if the contract has no representations and warranties clause.

---

[76] See Peel, 'The Common Law Tradition under English Law', footnote 364.

When the parties insert a long and detailed representations and warranties clause, and carefully negotiate its wording, they may be under the impression that this long list exhaustively reflects what they represent and warrant to each other. This impression is in compliance with the effects of the clause under English law, where an accurate wording is crucial for deciding whether a party has a contractual claim or not.[77]

Under civil law, the clause also has effects: if a certain characteristic was expressly represented or warranted in the contract, failure to comply with it will more easily be qualified as a defect in the consent or a breach of contract, without the need to verify whether it had been relied on, whether it was essential, etc. The clause, therefore, creates certainty regarding the consequences of the breach of the representations and warranties that were made.

However, the clause does not have the reverse effect: if a certain characteristic was not included in the representations and warranties, it does not mean that it may not be deemed to be among the matters that the parties have to disclose or bear responsibility for. The parties may have spent considerable energy in negotiating the list and one party may intentionally have omitted certain matters, under the illusion that this would have been sufficient to avoid any liability in that connection. However, if the matter left out is material, the other party may be entitled to claim the nullity of the contract[78] or compensation for damages.[79] The duty of disclosure may not be contracted out[80] and is considered to be such a cornerstone that it applies even to sales that are made 'as is'.[81]

This clause is an example where an accurate drafting may obtain results if the contract is subject to English law, because English law leaves it to the parties to determine the content of their bargain. Civil law, on the contrary, regulates this area extensively, and the drafting by the parties may not affect this regulation, no matter how clear and detailed it is.

5.2 Liquidated damages

As was briefly mentioned in Chapter 1, Section 2, commercial contracts often contain a clause that defines the amount of damages to be paid in case of a breach, such as, for example, the following:

---

[77] See Peel, 'The common law tradition under English law', Section 2.9.

[78] See, for France, Lagarde, Méheut and Reversac 'The Romanistic tradition under French law', Section 12; for Russia, Zykin 'The East European tradition under Russian law', Section 2.8.

[79] See, for Denmark, Møgelvang-Hansen 'The Nordic tradition under Danish law', Section 4.1; for Russia, Zykin, 'The East European Tradition under Russian Law', Section 2.8.

[80] See, for Finland, Möller, 'The Nordic tradition under Finnish law', Section 4.1; for Russia, Zykin, 'The East European Tradition under Russian law', Section 2.8.

[81] Under Norwegian law: see Hagstrøm 'The Nordic tradition under Norwegian law', Section 5.1 – although in the case of a sale 'as is', the duty extends only to what the seller had knowledge of.

> If, due to the fault of the Seller, the goods have not been delivered at dates according to the delivery schedule as provided in this Agreement, the Seller shall be obliged to pay to the buyer liquidated damages for such delayed delivery at the following rates.

This clause quantifies the amount of damages that will be compensated, and has the purpose of creating certainty regarding what payments shall be due in case of a breach of certain obligations. In many civilian systems, this may be achieved by agreeing on contractual penalties. The liquidated damages clause has its origin in the common law, where contractual penalties are not permitted. The main remedy available for breach of contract in common law is compensation by way of damages. In order to achieve certainty in this respect, contracts contain clauses that quantify the damages in advance. As long as the clause makes a genuine estimate of the possible damages, and it is not used as a punitive mechanism, it will be enforceable. The agreed amount will thus be paid irrespective of the size of the actual damage. Due to the influence of English contract drafting on international contract practice, as described in Chapter 1, Section 2, the common law terminology is also adopted in contracts governed by other laws, even when the applicable law permits contractual penalties. In terms of the intention of the parties to these contracts, these clauses are often assumed to work as penalty clauses. This means that they are not necessarily meant to be the only possible compensation for breach of contract or to be paid irrespective of the size of the actual damage. Questions may arise, however, as to the effects of the clause: should they have the same effects as in English law and make the agreed sum payable in spite of the fact that there was no damage at all, or that the damage had a much larger value or that the clause was meant to be cumulated with reimbursement of damages calculated according to the general criteria?

It must first be pointed out that this is one of the clauses that demonstrates the primacy of the contract language in the eyes of English courts. Structuring the clause as liquidated damages rather than as a penalty, permits avoiding the penalty rule under English law. This effect follows appropriate drafting rather than the substance of the regulation. Although the courts have the power to exert control on whether the quantification may be deemed to be a genuine evaluation of the potential damage, they are very cautious in making use of this power, under the assumption that the parties know best how to assess any possible damages.[82] Moreover, the penalty rule applies to sums payable upon breach of contract; appropriate drafting will permit circumventing these limitations by regulating payments as a consequence of events other than a breach, thus excluding the applicability of the penalty rule.[83] This is a good example of how far the appropriate drafting may reach under English law.

In civil law, no matter how clear and detailed the drafting is, there are some principles that may not be excluded by the contract. Thus, the agreed amount of

---

[82] See Peel, 'The Common Law Tradition under English Law', Section 2.7.   [83] *Ibid.*

liquidated damages will be disregarded if it can be proven that the loss actually suffered by the innocent party is much lower[84] or much higher.[85] Contractual penalties may, under certain circumstances, be cumulated with other remedies, also including reimbursement of damages.[86] The English terminology that refers to 'damages' may create a presumption that the parties did not intend to cumulate that payment with other compensation. This may come as a surprise to the parties that used the terminology on the assumption that it is the proper terminology for a contractual penalty; however, if it is possible to prove that the parties intended to regulate a penalty and did not intend to exclude compensation for damages in spite of the terminology they used, the presumption may be rebutted.[87]

Adopting the English legal terminology does not mean that the legal effects that follow from English law shall be applied, as will be seen in Chapter 4, Section 2.2.4. Only if the parties intended those specific effects to happen, will these follow from the contract. In this case, however, the legal effects intended by the parties shall, like any other contract term, comply with the principles of the governing law.

Relying simply on the language of the contract, and particularly if the contract also contains a sole remedy clause, a party could be deemed to be entitled to walk out of the contract if it pays the agreed amount of liquidated damages. The liquidated damages clause could thus be considered as the price that a party has to pay for its default, and as an incentive to commit a default if the agreed amount is lower than the benefit that would have been derived from terminating the contract. In many countries, however, the principle of good faith prevents the defaulting party from invoking the liquidated damages clause if the default was due to that party's gross negligence or wilful misconduct.[88]

The liquidated damages clause is one more example of the different approach to drafting and interpretation in the common law and in the civil law traditions.

---

[84] See, for Germany, Magnus, 'The Germanic Tradition under German Law', Section 5.2.2.a.; for France, Lagarde, Méheut and Reversac, 'The Romanistic Tradition under French law', Section 10; for Denmark, Møgelvang-Hansen, 'The Nordic tradition under Danish law', Section 3.1; for Russia, Zykin, 'The East European Tradition under Russian Law', Section 2.5.

[85] See, for France, Lagarde, Méheut and Reversac, 'The Romanistic Tradition under French Law', Section 10; for Finland, Möller, 'The Nordic tradition under Finnish Law', Section 3.1; for Norway, Hagstrøm, 'The Nordic Tradition under Norwegian Law', Section 4.1; for Russia, Zykin, 'The East European tradition under Russian law', Section 2.5.

[86] See, for Finland, Möller, 'The Nordic Tradition under Finnish Law', Section 3.1; for Norway, Hagstrøm, 'The Nordic Tradition under Norwegian Law', Section 4.1; for Russia, Zykin, 'The East European tradition under Russian law', Section 2.5.

[87] See, for Finland, Möller, 'The Nordic Tradition under Finnish law', Section 3.1; for Norway, Hagstrøm, 'The Nordic Tradition under Norwegian Law', Section 4.1.

[88] See, for France, Lagarde, Méheut and Reversac, 'The Romanistic tradition under French Law', Section 10; for Denmark, Møgelvang-Hansen, 'The Nordic Tradition under Danish Law', Section 3.1; and for Finland, Möller, 'The Nordic Tradition under Finnish law', Section 3.1. The law seems to be unsettled on this matter in Sweden; see Gorton, 'The Nordic Tradition under Swedish Law', Section 6.3.

Whereas the former permits circumventing the law's rules by appropriate drafting, the latter integrates the language of the contract with the law's rules and principles.

5.3 Force majeure

The goals of a provision on exemption from liability for non-performance may be several. In some legal systems, the provision may aim to allocate the risk for supervening unexpected events between the parties according to the system's evaluation of which one of the two parties is closer to bearing that particular risk. This approach assumes a strict liability, triggered irrespective of the conduct of the party that was prevented from performing its obligations.

Alternatively, the provision may aim at rewarding a party who has acted with due diligence, so that a party is not supposed to bear the risk for unexpected events if that party has acted diligently and cannot be blamed for the occurrence of the impediment, even if it would be closer to bearing such a risk in an objective allocation of risk. Finally, the provision may be founded on the aim of avoiding unfair situations in the relationship between the parties.

In many civil law states, a contracting party that fails to perform its obligations is excused, if the failure to perform is due to an impediment that was unforeseen, outside of the control of the prevented party, and the consequences of which could not reasonably have been overcome. Different legal systems have different terminology, but they obtain similar effects. In Germany, for example, the principle of excuse due to the *force majeure* circumstance is contained in § 275 of the Civil Code (BGB), and in Italy, in Articles 1218 and 1463 of the Civil Code (Codice Civile).

According to § 276 BGB, liability for non-performance arises only, in the case of an impediment as described in § 275, if the affected party has acted negligently or with wilful misconduct. According to § 280 ff. BGB, the negligence of the affected party is presumed, and therefore the burden of proof is on the affected party, which has to prove the lack of negligence in its conduct. As long as evidence of lack of negligence is produced, therefore, the affected party is not liable for its non-performance, even if the impediment occurred within the sphere of control of that party.

Article 1218 of the Codice Civile states that a party that does not fulfil its obligations correctly is liable, unless it proves that the non-performance is due to impossibility caused by events that that party is not responsible for. The letter of the rule, therefore, requires that the affected party proves that there has been an external event that has made the performance impossible, and this is a stricter criterion than the proof of lack of negligence provided for by German law. However, Italian courts read this article together with Article 1176 of the Codice Civile, requiring that the debtor must exercise the due diligence of a reasonable person (*bonus pater familias*) in performing its obligations, and affirm that, as long as the affected party has presented evidence that it has acted with due diligence, the exemption provided for in Article 1218 may be applied.[89]

The specific regulation of the *force majeure* circumstance may vary from state to state; however, these regulations have in common the effect of excusing from liability the party that was prevented, if that party acted diligently.

In the common law systems, contractual obligations are deemed to be absolute, and a party would normally not be excused for non-performance, as long as the impediment occurred within that party's sphere of risk and without regard to that party's diligent or negligent conduct. English law has the doctrine of frustration, which could be compared with the civilian principle of *force majeure*. The doctrine of frustration, however, has a narrower scope of application. A contractual obligation is considered, as a starting point, as absolute, and failure to perform will never be excused; however, supervening situations may change the content of the contractual obligations, so that they are not the same obligations that were assumed under the contract. In these situations, the obligor cannot be expected to perform obligations that are different from those that it had assumed, and the contract is frustrated. The so-called 'test of a radical change in the obligation' has been confirmed by the House of Lords, and is deemed to be the prevailing doctrine even now.[90]

Depending on which law supplements the contract, the outcome for the parties may vary.

As an illustration, we can assume a contract without a *force majeure* clause, or with a *force majeure* clause that does not cover certain circumstances that materialised during the performance of the contract. Two scenarios may be assumed:

5.3.1 Supplier's failure

We can assume that a producer of car components enters into a contract for the delivery of certain aluminium components made to the specifications of the buyer, which is a car producer. The seller/producer of components has to procure the aluminium for the production of the components from third parties. After having carried out an extensive process comparing the quality, reliability and conditions offered by the major aluminium suppliers on an international level, the seller enters into a contract for the procurement of aluminium with a recognised supplier, which was offering the best conditions. Due to supervening *force majeure* events, the selected aluminium supplier fails to deliver the proper quality of aluminium according to the time schedule agreed with the producer of the components. As a consequence of the lack of the delivery of aluminium, the seller/producer has to delay

---

[89] C. 86/6404, C. 91/12346.

[90] See, for example, *National Carriers Ltd* v. *Panalpina (Northern) Ltd* [1981] AC 675, and further references in Beatson, Burrows and Cartwright, *Anson's Law of Contract*, pp. 487ff. See Peel, 'The Common Law Tradition under English Law', Section 2.10.

its production, also including the production of the car components for the buyer. Therefore, the seller/producer cannot comply with its obligations towards the buyer.

The question is whether the seller/producer is excused from its non-performance.

The case would be decided differently according to the approach adopted by the legal system. The legal systems that follow the criteria of strict liability and the allocation of risk between the parties according to the respective spheres of control would consider the choice of supplier to be an event falling within the sphere of control of the seller. Certainly this impediment would not fall within the sphere of the buyer and, since all risks have to be allocated between the parties, it follows that it must fall within the sphere of the seller. This is quite understandable from the point of view of the absolute obligations of the parties: the seller has guaranteed that it would sell aluminium components, and the seller has the obligation to obtain the raw material in order to produce the components and deliver them to the buyer in accordance with the agreed terms. Therefore, the impediment could not be considered external to the seller, and the seller would not be excused from liability for non-performance. Under English law, the parties have an absolute obligation to perform the contract accurately. The only situation that may discharge a party from this duty is if a supervening event, without default of that party, makes the performance illegal or impossible. This eventuality is called frustration of the contract, and is applied restrictively, as was shown in the previous section.

This is the same approach to the allocation of liability taken by the CISG. According to Article 79 of the CISG, a party is not liable for failure to perform its obligations if it proves that the failure was due to an impediment beyond its control, that was unforeseeable and that could not reasonably have been overcome.

The CISG does not contain any reference to the diligence of the affected party as a criterion for exempting it from liability; in another context, the convention confirms that diligence is not a criterion for excuse, and Articles 45(1)(b) and 61(1)(b) regulate that each party may exercise contractual remedies for non-performance against the other party without having to prove any fault or negligence or lack of good faith on that party, nor do they mention that any evidence of diligence would relieve the other party from its liability. Additionally, as was seen in Chapter 2, Section 4.3, the CISG does not contain any requirement that the parties act in good faith. The lack of any reference to good faith or diligence in Article 79 also makes it difficult to imply in its rule that the affected party may be exempted on the basis of the criterion of diligence, as it prevails in civil laws.

The Secretariat Commentary[91] (the closest counterpart to an Official Commentary on the CISG) does not address the question of how the criterion of the sphere of control shall be interpreted, whether literally, or as a reference to the actual

---

[91] United Nations Secretariat's Commentary to the UNCITRAL Draft Convention (A/CONF./97/5), available also on the Pace Law School's database, by clicking on the specific convention's articles: www.cisg.law.pace.edu/cisg/text/cisg-toc.html

control and the criterion of responsibility. Bearing in mind that the CISG requires being interpreted autonomously, without reference to domestic legal systems, it seems appropriate to apply the literal interpretation and to see Article 79 as a reference to an objective division of the landscape into two spheres, that of the seller and that of the buyer, without reference to specific actual possibilities for exercising control. This is confirmed by case law and doctrine, which affirm that procurement risk falls within the sphere of the risk of the seller, and that, therefore, failure by the seller's supplier is not deemed to fall outside of the seller's sphere of responsibility (unless the relevant good has disappeared completely from the international market).[92] This is confirmed by the Secretariat Commentary to the second paragraph of Article 79. The provision of the second paragraph applies to failure by sub-contractors, and says that the seller may be excused in case of failure by sub-contractors, only on the condition that the impediment affects both the seller and the sub-contractor. The Secretariat Commentary specifies that this provision does not include suppliers of raw material or of goods to the seller.[93] Failure by the supplier is, therefore, to be distinguished from failure by a sub-contractor, and is subject to the general rule of the first paragraph, which shall be interpreted strictly and without reference to the seller's diligence. However, this is not the only way of understanding the criterion of 'beyond the control'. Article 79 of the CISG may be interpreted differently, depending on the interpreter's legal tradition – something that has been defined as 'troubling'.[94]

German law does not adopt the approach of strict liability and allocation of risk according to the sphere of control. German law moves from the notion of responsibility. If the prevented party is to be blamed for the impediment or its consequences, it cannot be excused from liability. If, however, the prevented party can prove that it has not acted negligently, it will be excused from liability. In the present case, as we have seen, the seller has operated with diligence in the choice of supplier; therefore, it would not be considered liable for non-performance due to failure by the supplier.

According to § 276 BGB, liability for non-performance arises only, in the case of an impediment as described in § 275, if the affected party has acted negligently or with wilful misconduct. According to § 280 ff. BGB, the negligence of the affected party is presumed, and therefore the burden of proof is on the affected party, which has to

---

[92] See D. Flambouras, 'The Doctrines of Impossibility of Performance and *clausula rebus sic stantibus* in the 1980 Vienna Convention on Contracts for the International Sale of Goods and the Principles of European Contract Law: A Comparative Analysis', (2001) 13 *Pace International Law Review*, 261–93, www.cisg.law. pace.edu/cisg/biblio/flambouras1.html, with references to the literature and case law in footnote 20. See also I. Schwenzer (ed.), *Schlechtriem & Schwenzer Commentary on the UN Convention on the International Sale of Goods (CISG)*. 3rd edn (Oxford University Press, 2010), Article 79, paras. 11, 18 and 37, although para. 27 seems to embrace the Germanic tradition.

[93] *Commentary*, p. 172.

[94] Schwenzer (ed.), *Commentary on the UN Convention on the International Sale of Goods (CISG)*, Article 79, para. 11, footnote 28.

prove the lack of negligence in its conduct. As long as evidence of lack of negligence is produced, therefore, the affected party is not liable for its non-performance, even if the impediment occurred within the sphere of control of that party.

The difference in attitude, however, is reduced in respect of what is called in the Germanic tradition generic obligations; that is, the obligation to supply certain goods that are not individually specified and can therefore, in the case of destruction or other impediments in the delivery, easily be substituted with equivalent goods that are readily available on the market. The substance of this distinction, unknown in the common law systems and in the CISG, is that the performance is not deemed to be prevented, even if the goods that were meant to be delivered are destroyed or otherwise cannot be delivered, as long as the goods that were promised are available on the market and the seller is capable of procuring them from another source. As a result, in the Germanic systems, the liability in case of non-performance of a generic obligation is closer to the strict liability of the common law. The distinction between generic obligations and specific obligations, however, does not seem to add anything to a careful interpretation of the concept of impediment: as long as similar goods are available, there is no impediment that prevents delivery. A seller that fails to procure the available goods cannot be deemed to have acted with due diligence, and cannot, therefore, be excused. Also in the Germanic systems, therefore, it would be possible to apply a strict standard of liability without making use of the notion of generic obligations. The category is, therefore, strictly speaking, redundant, and is not present in the new version of the BGB after the 2001 reform, which was inspired by the CISG.

The distinction between common law and civil law in the context of liability for non-performance can be explained with the already mentioned inclination of the English system to privilege predictability for the sake of ensuring that business is carried out smoothly, rather than ensuring that an equitable justice is made in the specific case. Common law (and the CISG) allocate the risk of non-performance between the parties according to where it is most closely to expect that the risk should be borne. This objective rule is not to be defeated by subjective criteria such as a lack of negligence, because it would render the system less predictable. Civil law systems, as already pointed out, privilege (to different degrees) the subjective elements of the specific case in order to ensure that an equitable solution is reached.

An interesting demonstration of the impact of legal tradition on the interpretation of what constitutes an event beyond a party's control is given by Norwegian law.

The CISG was implemented in Norway with an Act on Sale of Goods, that introduced in § 27 the concept of an impediment beyond the control of the prevented party.[95] By introducing this concept, the legislator intended to mitigate the then existing regime, which was based on strict liability.[96]

---

[95] Sale of Goods Act of 13 May 1988 (no 27), § 27.

[96] Ot.prp. nr. 80 (1986–87), pp. 38 ff. and, extensively on the preparatory works in this context, Viggo Hagstrøm, *Obligasjonsrett*, 2nd edn (Universitetsfrolaget, 2011), Section 19.4.2.

As was seen above, in the CISG, the criterion of the sphere of control seems to serve to determine the allocation of risk between the parties, and therefore to represent a border between what abstractly falls within the sphere of the seller and what falls within the sphere of the buyer, irrespective of the factual circumstances of the specific case, the diligence of the parties etc. Interpreting the criterion in the same way would have led to a very strict regulation under Norwegian law; this, however would have contradicted the legislator's intention, as seen above.

Therefore, the criterion of the sphere of control is interpreted by Norwegian legal doctrine[97] not, as in the CISG, as having an *abstract* understanding of each party's sphere of control, since this would have probably rendered the Norwegian regulation as even stricter than prior to the enactment of the Sale of Goods Act. The criterion is interpreted on the basis of the *actual* sphere of control of each party. If one party actually has the possibility of influencing a certain process, then events caused by that process are to be deemed within the sphere of control of that party. Norwegian doctrine also emphasises that, even if a party has started a process, this in itself does not mean that any events occurring in the course of that process are in the sphere of control of that party. The test must be if that party actually had the possibility of being able to influence the part of the process in connection with which those events occurred. Hence, the decision in this case would be opposite to the outcome under the CISG: the seller chose the supplier, and this choice is certainly within the seller's sphere of control (the seller could have chosen another supplier, and then the default would not have happened). However, the seller has no actual possibility of influencing the performance of the supplier, therefore any impediment in connection therewith is to be deemed outside of the seller's sphere of control.[98]

The criterion of the sphere of control, although it is a word-by-word implementation of the CISG, is applied in a significantly different way from the criterion contained in the CISG: not as a way of allocating the risk between the two parties, but as a way of determining whether the affected party had the possibility of being able to control the impediment. The interpretation of this criterion resembles, therefore, the regime that prevails in Germany, where the criterion for exemption from liability is not the sphere of control, but the responsibility of the affected party.[99]

---

[97] *Ibid.* See also Giuditta Cordero Moss, *Lectures on Comparative Law of Contracts* (University of Oslo Institute of Private Law, 2004), pp. 151f.

[98] Hagstrøm, 'The Nordic Tradition under Norwegian Law', Section 5.3. Hagstrøm's interpretation is based on a Supreme Court decision rendered in 1970, long before the implementation of the CISG in the Norwegian system. However, the Supreme Court's decision is still referred to as correctly incorporating Norwegian law after the enactment of the Sales of Goods Act, as the reference made by Hagstrøm confirms. See also Anders Mikelsen, *Hindringsfritak* (Gyldendal, 2011), p. 33.

[99] It must be mentioned here that a recent Supreme Court decision (Rt. 2004 p. 675) affirmed that, in the context of defects of generic goods, the liability is strict, and the test will be whether the defects objectively are within the sphere of control of the seller. In this context, therefore, the Supreme Court has rejected the test of actual control and is more in line with the regulation contained in the CISG.

It is not unlikely that similar discrepancies may occur when the *force majeure* clause of a contract is interpreted.

5.3.2 Choice between contracts

We can assume that the producer of car components has entered into two contracts for the delivery of customised car components to two different car producers. When the seller has nearly completed production for both buyers, an earthquake partially destroys the seller's storage facilities. As a consequence thereof, the seller is capable of delivering the total agreed volume on the agreed delivery date only to one buyer, not to both; alternatively, the seller could deliver on the agreed delivery date only part of the agreed volume to both buyers.

We can assume that the circumstances around the destruction of the storage facility qualify to excuse liability for non-performance; that is, that the facility was built according to the latest standards, all security measures had been properly taken, etc. The question is whether the seller is excused from its partial non-performance, and in what way.

Various legal systems would come to different results. First, not all systems would recognise the situation as a ground for partial excuse of the seller and, second, the systems that would assume a partial exemption provide for different consequences of the excuse.

Some legal systems, such as Italian and German law, would most probably decide the case by excusing the seller from the part of the delivery that has become impossible, and requesting that the impediment is allocated pro rata among the various buyers; that is, that each delivery is reduced proportionally with the reduction in the seller's capacity due to the partial impediment.[100]

Another approach may be found in Norwegian law. Although Norwegian law has no clear rule for this eventuality, an *obiter dictum* in a Supreme Court decision, which has been supported by legal doctrine, seems to indicate that in the present situation the seller would be obliged to perform in full its obligations arising out of the eldest contract, whereas it would be excused from non-performance of the newest contract.[101]

English law would not excuse the seller at all, in accordance with a judicial rule that is being heavily criticised in English legal doctrine.[102] In this case, the affected party had allocated a certain vessel from its fleet for the performance of a particular freight contract, and that vessel afterwards sunk. The performance of the freight contract was prevented, because other vessels of the fleet were allocated to other

---

[100] The eventuality of a partial impossibility and of a corresponding partial excuse is regulated expressly by the Codice Civile in Article 1258, and it can be inferred from the wording of § 275(1) BGB.

[101] Rt. 1970 p. 1059, 1064; see Hagstrøm, *Obligasjonsrett*, Section 12.3.5.

[102] *J. Lauritzen AS* v. *Wijsmuller BV (The Super Servant Two)* [1990] 1 Lloyd's Rep. 1. For the criticism, see Beatson, Burrows and Cartwright, *Anson's Law of Contract*, p. 494f., Edwin Peel, *Treitel on the Law of Contract* 13th edn (Sweet & Maxwell, 2011), para 19–029 and particularly Beale (ed.), *Chitty on Contracts*, para 23–069.

freight contracts and were therefore not available. The court found that the contract could not be deemed to have been frustrated. The real cause of the non-performance was said to be the affected party's election to use that particular vessel for that contract, rather than the sinking of the vessel. Had the affected party elected to use another vessel, the contract could have been performed. The result of this reasoning is that a carrier should regulate an exemption from liability for this eventuality in the contract.[103]

The above shows that situations may be regulated in different ways, according to the governing law, even if the contract is silent. Since some of these regulations may bring forth quite undesirable results, the parties should enquire about the consequences under the governing law of not providing for a contractual regulation of those circumstances, such as, for example, partial impediment and plurality of contractors. If the enquiry shows that the governing law has a regulation that is not deemed appropriate, and if that regulation is not mandatory, the parties should draft in their contract detailed clauses regulating those eventualities.

5.4 Hardship clause

Commercial contracts may contain a so-called hardship clause, for example, as follows:

> Where the performance of a contract becomes more onerous for one of the parties, that party is nevertheless bound to perform its obligations subject to the following provisions on hardship. There is hardship where the occurrence of events fundamentally alters the equilibrium of the contract either because the cost of a party's performance has increased or because the value of the performance a party receives has diminished, and (a) the event was beyond its reasonable control and was one which it could not reasonably have been expected to have taken into account at the time of the conclusion of the contract; and that (b) the event or its consequences could not reasonably be avoided or overcome. If such hardship occurs the parties are bound, within a reasonable time of the invocation of this Clause, to negotiate alternative contractual terms which reasonably allow for the consequences of the event.

This clause regulates, sometimes in detail, under what circumstances, and with what consequences the parties may be entitled to renegotiate their contract because of a supervening and unexpected imbalance in the respective obligations. English law does not provide for any mechanism to suspend or discharge the parties from obligations if the performance, though still possible, becomes more onerous for one party, and neither does French law. Other civilian systems, on the contrary, permit

---

[103] This is the suggestion that is made in the judgment, *The Super Servant Two*, p. 158, which is also repeated by legal doctrine quoted in footnote 102 above.

a party to request a modification of the obligations if changed circumstances seriously affect the balance in the contract.[104] The clause, thus, gives the parties stronger rights than they would have had under English or French law, while at the same time, it may restrict the rights that the affected party would have under other laws. The parties may have introduced a hardship clause in the attempt to take into their own hands the regulation of supervening circumstances and to exclude the application of corresponding rules in the governing law. A clause permitting the affected party to request renegotiations will be enforced in a system where such a right is not recognised by the general law, because it will simply create a new regulation, based on contract but not prohibited by law. The reverse, however, is more problematic: a detailed hardship clause may restrict the right that the affected party has under the applicable law. For example, the clause may contain an intentionally restrictive definition of the events that trigger the remedy, significantly more restrictive than the applicable law's standard of 'more burdensome perform-ance'. Additionally, the clause may regulate that the only possible remedy is the request of renegotiation without suspending the duty to perform, and thus exclude other remedies, such as withholding the performance, which may be permitted by the applicable law.

The parties may actually have written such a restrictive hardship clause with the purpose of limiting the application of the governing law's generous rules. Neverthe-less, the clause may not be understood as the sole regulation in the case of superven-ing imbalance in the contract and may thus be cumulated with the applicable law's rules.[105]

6 Contractual terms contradicting mandatory rules of the governing law

In some cases, the governing law may contain mandatory rules, which cannot be derogated from by the parties, and that are contradicted by the terms of the contract. In these cases, the regulation contained in the contract will have to be overridden by the mandatory rules of the governing law.

Here it is important to notice that some contractual terms that would be compat-ible with certain governing laws would be in contrast with mandatory rules of other governing laws. The same contract, therefore, might be binding or not, according to

---

[104] See, for Denmark, Møgelvang-Hansen, 'The Nordic Tradition under Danish Law', Section 4.2; for Finland, Möller, 'The Nordic Tradition under Finnish Law', Section 4.2; for Norway, Hagstrøm, 'The Nordic Tradition under Norwegian Law', Section 5.2. For Germany, see § 313 of the BGB and for Italy see Articles 1467–1469 of the Codice Civile.

[105] See, for Denmark, Møgelvang-Hansen, 'The Nordic Tradition under Danish Law', Section 4.2; for Finland, Möller, 'The Nordic Tradition under Finnish law', Section 4.2; for Norway, Hagstrøm, 'The Nordic Tradition under Norwegian law', Section 5.2. See, however, German law, that permits the parties to derogate from the statutory regulation in § 313 of the BGB: Magnus, 'The Germanic Tradition under German Law', Section 5.3.2.a.

what law is governing. If the parties had taken into consideration the governing law while drafting, they might have been able to structure the contract in such a way that it would not have contradicted the governing law.

Below we will see some cases that illustrate the relationship between contractual terms and mandatory rules of the governing law.

6.1 Firm offer

We may first look at a situation where one party has sent an irrevocable offer to the other party, without considering the governing law. We can assume that the offer contains the following clause: 'this offer is firm and cannot be revoked by the offeror before 30 days from the date hereof'. The remaining part of the offer is devoted to the specification of the offered goods or services, their price, the timing for performance etc. The offer contains no other clauses, and is signed by the offeror. As long as the offer is not accepted, there is no contract between the parties. However, making a written offer with a promise of irrevocability has legal consequences that are regulated by the contract law of each state. What would be the legal consequences if the offeror decides to revoke the offer, before the term indicated in the firm offer has elapsed? The answer to this question varies, according to what law governs the offer, as well as the structure of the offer.

As an illustration, we can examine two scenarios:

6.1.1 Revocation

A commodity trader receives an irrevocable offer to buy a certain volume of commodity at a certain price. The trader does not accept the offer immediately, but makes contact with other potential sellers to verify whether the offered conditions are competitive. In the meantime, the offeror has found another buyer, who is willing to pay a higher price, and revokes its offer to the trader, before the offer's term elapses.

Under civil law legal systems, the irrevocability clause contained in the offer would be considered as binding,[106] and any revocation of the offer made before the term would not have legal effects. The offeror will continue to be bound by its offer in spite of the revocation, and in case of acceptance by the offeree within the term, the contract comes into place between the parties.

Under the English legal system, on the contrary, the offer would be considered as a unilateral obligation of the offeror, and, as such, not enforceable due to lack of consideration;[107] therefore, the revocation of the offer would have been considered

---

[106] Under German law, for example, § 145 of the BGB specifies that an offer is binding on the offeror, unless by its terms it is revocable.

[107] It is a rule of English law that a promise to keep an offer open needs consideration to make it binding. Consideration is deemed to be given if the offeror gets a benefit or the offeree incurs a detriment in

as valid. If, on the contrary, the offeree had immediately accepted the offer, possibly making the acceptance subject to certain conditions precedent being fulfilled, then the irrevocability clause would be valid and binding on the offeror, as the obligations would be bilateral. Another possibility of making a unilateral offer binding on the offeror is to formalise it as a deed. The doctrine of consideration, therefore, significantly affects the enforceability of the expressed terms contained in the offer.

6.1.2 Revocation and reliance

Let's assume that a construction company intends to participate in a tender relating to the construction of some infrastructure. In order to prepare the bid, the contractor requests irrevocable offers from a series of sub-contractors. On the basis of the sub-contractors' offers, the bid of the contractor wins the tender, and is awarded the construction contract. After the contract is awarded, but before the term contained in the sub-contractors' offers elapses, one of the sub-contractors revokes its offer.

This scenario differs from the previous one especially in one aspect, which is relevant here. In this scenario, the offer has induced an action by the offeree with considerable consequences (the presentation of the bid, the award of the contract); in the previous scenario, the offeree has only made some telephone calls, but has not committed himself towards third parties or engaged in extensive activity as a consequence of the offer. This difference does not have consequences under the civil law tradition, and the revocation of the offer will have no effects in either scenario. Under the common law, however, the difference might have consequences.

A contract that does not have consideration is not enforceable under English law. The English legal system, however, has elaborated certain means to prevent the strict application of the law leading to unreasonable results. These means are available not 'at law', but 'in equity': if the application of the formal requirements of law leads to a result that under the circumstances of the case is inequitable, the affected party will be able to avail himself of some remedies in equity. The equitable remedy applicable in the case described herein is the promissory estoppel, which neutralises the effects of the rule of consideration in many cases.[108] According to this remedy, if parties to a transaction have relied upon a promise that strict legal rights will not be acted upon, they will not be allowed to go back on that assumption if it would be unfair to do so. The equitable remedy of the promissory estoppel, however, is not available in the case described here: a promissory estoppel is available when there is already a cause of action; that is, where the parties were already bound to each other by a contract. English law does not

---

connection with keeping the offer firm. This principle was laid down in the *Stilk Myrick* [1809] 2 Camp 317, and is still prevailing, although with some qualifications: see Beale (ed.), *Chitty on Contracts* para. 3–046ff, particularly 3–051 and 3–052; Beatson, Burrows and Cartwright, *Anson's Law of Contract*, p. 56. On the doctrine of consideration, see Section 1 above.

[108] See, for more details, Beatson, Burrows and Cartwright, *Anson's Law of Contract* pp. 116ff.

consider an irrevocable offer as a cause of action, therefore the equitable remedy is not available and the doctrine of consideration remains applicable.[109]

In the US, on the contrary, the obstacle of the doctrine of consideration has been overcome. The United States Restatement (Second) of Contracts (1981), similarly to English law, maintains that the offer would be considered a unilateral obligation and therefore unenforceable, unless the offer has been accepted by the offeree. However, in this scenario, the offer has induced some action by the offeree, and the Restatement would in this case consider the irrevocability clause as binding (para. 87.2) to the extent necessary to avoid injustice. The Uniform Commercial Code of the United States provides in para. 2–205:

> An offer by a merchant to buy or sell goods in a signed writing which by its terms gives assurance that it will be held open is not revocable, for lack of consideration, during the time stated or if no time is stated for a reasonable time, but in no event may such period of irrevocability exceed three months; but any such term of assurance on a form supplied by the offeree must be separately signed by the offeror.

In conclusion, the offer, drafted as mentioned above, would be binding under civil law systems, and, according to the Uniform Commercial Code, in the US, but not in England. Had the offeree taken into consideration the English governing law, it would have accepted the offer, under certain conditions (for example, under the condition that the offeree is awarded the contract in the tender). Alternatively, the offeree could have requested that the offer provides a space for the offeree's signature and the wording 'for acceptance', or could have sent a separate, written acceptance to the offeror; in this way, the offer would have become binding also under English law.

This shows how important it is to have in mind the governing law while drafting a contract. Knowing the existence of certain rules, such as the rule on consideration in English law, will permit the structuring of the contract in a way that is appropriate to render it enforceable – for example, by providing for acceptance by the offeree.

6.2 Amendments to a contract

A further illustration of the importance of having in mind the governing law while drafting a contract is the situation where two parties decide to amend an existing contract between them. We can assume that, because of a misjudgment of the volume of work required under the contract, the parties enter into an amendment contract according to which the price for the services to be rendered under their contract will have to be increased, whereas all other terms and conditions of the existing contract will remain unchanged.

---

[109] See, for more details, *ibid.*, p. 123.

We can assume that the amendment contract makes reference to the contract that is intended to be amended, and contains a clause according to which 'The parties agree to modify clause XX of the contract, so that the price to be paid to the sub-contractor is 100 instead of 80. All other terms and conditions of the contract remain unchanged'.

Would a contract formalising such an amendment be enforceable? The answer to this question varies according to the law governing the amendment agreement. As an illustration, we can examine two scenarios.

6.2.1 Unilateral obligation

A constructor, engaged in a major project for the construction of various apartments, enters into a contract with a sub-contractor, who is to carry out some specialised carpentry work. They agree on a lump sum for the sub-contract; however, the sub-contractor soon realises that it had underestimated the amount of work required. If the carpenter was to continue performing its obligations under the sub-contract at the originally agreed price, it would not make any profit out of the sub-contract. The sub-contractor invites the constructor to renegotiate the price, and the parties reach an agreement on a price increase. After some time, the constructor finds that the new price is too high, and tries to renege on the amendment contract.

If the amendment contract were regulated by a law belonging to the civil law system, it would be considered as valid and binding. A properly signed document containing an obligation for one of the parties is binding, even if the obligation consists in the amendment of another obligation assumed by those parties under another contract. Traditional grounds for invalidity are if a contract has been entered into as a consequence of duress, error or other similar circumstances that affect the will of one of the parties, or if it contains unfair terms, etc. Otherwise, a contract is valid and binding (apart from situations where one of the parties did not have the authority to enter into the contract, etc., but this is not relevant to our discussion here).

If the amendment contract were subject to the common law, it would not be automatically considered as binding, since it would have to be measured against the doctrine of consideration, which requires a contract to have bilateral obligations, providing for benefits and detriments for both parties to a contract. In the case of a sale agreement, for example, the seller has the benefit of receiving the price, and the detriment of delivering the goods; the buyer will have the benefit of receiving the goods, and the detriment of paying the price. In an amendment contract such as the one envisaged above, however, the sub-contractor would have the benefit of receiving the increased price, but the detriment would consist simply in the performance of the carpentry work that the sub-contractor was already committed to performing anyway under the original contract. There would, therefore, not be a detriment for the sub-contractor as a consequence of the amendment contract. Similarly, the constructor would have the detriment of paying an increased price, but as a benefit, it would only have the performance of the work that it was entitled to obtain anyway under the original contract. There would, therefore, not be a legal benefit for the constructor in entering into the amending contract. The amendment contract lacks consideration, and is therefore not enforceable at common law. An equitable remedy based on the doctrine of promissory estoppel may be applicable. If the parties have agreed to amend a contract, they have created for each other the assumption that they will not insist on applying the original terms of the contract, in spite of the fact that the lack of consideration renders the amendment agreement unenforceable at law. The promissory estoppel would prevent the party making the promise from going back on its promise and insisting on the application of its strict legal rights instead. A promissory estoppel, however, is not always applicable. Among the requirements that have to be met, two might affect the applicability of the remedy to the present case. The effect of going back on the promise and insisting on the strict legal rights must be inequitable. If the amendment of the contract was induced by one party that took advantage of the other party's financial situation, for example, the result of not enforcing the amendment would not be considered as inequitable.[110] Furthermore, the party that is relying on the amendment (the promisee) must have altered its position in reliance on the amendment. The scope of this requirement is not completely clear: it seems, however, that it implies that the promisee must have acted in reliance on the promise in such a way that a revocation of the promise would be detrimental to the promisee.[111] Moreover, a promissory estoppel is not considered to be permanent in its effects: it does not discharge the contractual party from the original obligation (i.e., from the obligation in the terms prior to the amendment), it simply suspends that obligation. This means that the original obligation might be enforceable in the terms prior to the amendment, if the other party serves prior notice to that effect.[112]

6.2.2 Factual benefit

In the same scenario as presented in the previous section, the carpenter realises that a continued performance of the sub-contract at the originally agreed price would mean not only that the sub-contract is not profitable to it, but also that the sub-contractor would face considerable losses. As a consequence of such losses, the sub-contractor might face insolvency and subsequent liquidation; this, in turn, would mean a considerable delay for the constructor, since it would have to replace the sub-contractor and would even run the risk of not finding a new carpenter capable of replacing the specialised skills of the sub-contractor.

---

[110] *D & C Builders Ltd* v. *Rees* [1966] 2 QB 617.
[111] See, for more details, Beatson, Burrows and Cartwright, *Anson's Law of Contract*, p. 120f.
[112] See, for more details, *ibid.*, p.122.

The civilian tradition would have the same approach as in the previous scenario, and would consider the amendment agreement as binding. The common law tradition would have an approach different from the one taken in the previous scenario.

The sub-contractor faces bankruptcy if the original contract is not amended, and this can have negative consequences on the constructor: the sub-contractor will not be in a position to complete its work, the constructor will have to face costs trying to find a substitute contractor to finish the work and the total project will be delayed. Therefore, the constructor has an interest in avoiding the bankruptcy of the sub-contractor. In this case, an evolution of the English doctrine of consideration would make the amendment contract binding and enforceable, since the constructor can be deemed to obtain a benefit from the amendment contract: Not a legal benefit, but a factual benefit, and that is considered as sufficient to qualify as consideration.[113]

The foregoing shows that the governing law may have a considerable impact on the effects of a contract: even if a certain result may, in abstract terms, be obtained in various legal systems, achievement of that result may be prevented in the specific case if the contract does not comply with the requirements set by a certain law – as the case is with the requirement of consideration in English law.

7 Does arbitration ensure a uniform approach to contractual terms?

An observer may be tempted to dismiss the considerations made above about the relevance of national law with a pragmatic comment: most international contracts contain an arbitration clause, and therefore disputes arising in connection with them will be solved by arbitration and not by the courts. International arbitration is a system based on the will of the parties, and arbitrators are expected to abide by the will of the parties and not apply undesired sources that bring unexpected results. Moreover, arbitral awards enjoy broad enforceability and the possibility of courts interfering with them is extremely limited, so that the court's opinion on the legal effects of the contracts becomes irrelevant.[114] While all these observations are correct, they do not necessarily affect the observations made here.

It is true that an arbitral award will be valid and enforceable even though it does not correctly apply the governing law. Not even the wrong application of mandatory rules of law is a sufficient ground to consider an award invalid or unenforceable. Therefore, arbitral tribunals are quite free to interpret contracts and to decide how and if at all these contracts shall interact with the governing law.

---

[113] This was held in *Williams v. Roffey Bros. & Nicholls (Contractors) Ltd* [1991] 1QB 11. See also Beale (ed.), *Chitty on Contracts*, para. 3–053.
[114] On the enforceability of international awards and the scope within which national courts may exercise a certain control, see below, Chapter 5. The grounds for refusing enforcement of an award are listed exhaustively in article V of the 1958 New York Convention on the Recognition and Enforcement of Foreign Arbitral Awards, which has been ratified by about 140 countries.

This, however, will not supply the arbitral tribunal with a satisfactory answer to the question of how to interpret the contract. This is not a mere question of verifying whether mandatory rules have been complied with. It is a deeper and subtler question, and it regards the values upon which the interpretation should be based.

The interpreter's understanding of the relationship between certainty and justice (regarding the function of a contract, the advisability of ensuring a fair balance between the parties' interests, the role of the interpreter in respect of obligations that are not explicitly regulated in the contract, the existence of a duty of the parties to act loyally towards each other and the existence and extent of a general principle of good faith) may lead to an interpretation of the contract that is more literal or more purposive. Some arbitrators may be unaware of the influence that the legal system exercises on them: they may have internalised the legal system's principles in such a way that interpretation based on them feels like the only possible interpretation. Others, and particularly experienced international arbitrators, may have been exposed to a variety of legal systems and thus have acquired a higher degree of awareness that the terms of a contract do not have one natural meaning, but that their legal effects depend on the interaction with the governing law. These aware inter-preters face a dilemma when confronted with a contract drafted with a style extrane-ous to the governing law: on the one hand, they do not want to superimpose on the contract the principles of a law that the parties may not have considered during the negotiations. On the other hand, as was seen in Chapter 2, they have no uniform set of principles permitting them to interpret a contract independently from the governing law. The dilemma is not easy to solve, not even for an arbitrator, particu-larly if one of the parties invokes the governing law to prevent a literal application of the contract (notwithstanding that that party might not have been aware of the governing law during the negotiations). For example, a party may, for the purpose of rebutting the other party's allegations that the contract was breached, argue that a literal interpretation of the text would render the contract invalid under the governing law.

International commercial arbitration is the preferred method for solving disputes arising out of international commercial contracts. There is a diffuse sentiment that international arbitration is more apt in understanding the interests of the parties than national courts are. It is quite unclear, however, what this implies regarding the issue of contract interpretation. Are arbitrators more disposed than national courts to rely on the language of the contract and to disregard possible interference from the principles of national law? Alternatively, do they more readily rely on considerations of good faith, the economic interests that are at stake, trade usages and the like than national courts do? I will argue here that there is no unitary approach within arbitration.

As we have seen in Chapter 1, international contract practice assumes that contracts are self-sufficient and not affected by the governing law. This contract practice may lead to undesired legal effects and is not optimal when looked at from a legal point of view – although, when viewed from a wider perspective, it may turn out to be more advantageous than the alternative, which would mean employing substantial resources in order to ensure legal certainty. The question is whether international arbitration has better means to tackle this divergence than national courts have.

There seems to be no absolute answer to the question of what interpretation better meets the expectations of the parties: a strictly literal interpretation of the terms of the contract, or an integration of the contract with principles of good faith and commercial sense based on law, trade usages, transnational principles or other sources. The former would better reflect the parties' expectations if it is assumed that the parties have consciously intended to achieve specific legal effects with each and every one of the words that they have written in the contract. This, however, does not reflect the reality of how contracts are drafted and negotiated, as was seen in Chapter 1.

As was seen above, the practice of drafting contracts without regard to the governing law does not mean that the parties have opted out of the governing law for the benefit of some transnational set of rules. Just because the parties decided to take the risk of legal uncertainty for some clauses does not mean that the interpreter has to refrain from applying the governing law or that the legal evaluation of these clauses should be made in a less stringent way than for any other clauses. In addition, the fact that some clauses, such as boilerplate clauses, are not negotiated, indicates that giving them excessive importance in the interpretation of the contract would not necessarily result in the interpretation being faithful to the parties' intentions.

The arbitral tribunal is, therefore, expected to understand the dynamics of negotiations in order to properly give effect to the intention of the parties. Blindly applying the wording of the contract without any regard to the principles of the governing law or, to the extent that they are determinable and applicable, of transnational law, would not necessarily reflect the true intention of the parties if the clause that is being applied literally is one of the boilerplate clauses that the parties did not consider carefully. Integrating or correcting a clause with national or transnational principles, on the other hand, might not necessarily reflect the parties' intention either, if the clause that is being interpreted is one of the clauses that the parties carefully negotiated.

7.1 Arbitration as a unitary system?

The question that arises, then, is: does international arbitration ensure such a nuanced interpretation of contracts?

Arbitration is often referred to as an expression of the international business community, thus giving the impression that it is a unitary legal system. What characterises international arbitration, however, is probably the very lack of a unitary system.

The formal framework for arbitration grants it a relative autonomy, which actually gives the appearance of a unitary system. The main instrument upon which arbitration is founded is the 1958 New York Convention on the Recognition and Enforcement of Foreign Arbitral Awards, ratified by 149 countries, that requires that the courts of these countries recognise arbitration agreements, and thus dismiss claims that are covered by an arbitration agreement. The New York Convention also requires the courts to recognise and enforce arbitral awards without any review of the merits or of the application of law – with only a restrictive and exhaustive list of grounds to refuse recognition and enforcement. An important instrument is also the UNCITRAL Model Law on International Commercial Arbitration, issued in 1985 and revised in 2006, which is used as a basis for national arbitration law in sixty-seven countries and has thus contributed to a considerable harmonisation of the areas of arbitration law that are not covered by the New York Convention. The UNCITRAL Model Law is, in turn, based on the same principles as the New York Convention, which means that together these instruments create a harmonised legal framework for arbitration. Both instruments give a central role to the will of the parties. The power of the arbitral tribunal actually derives from the agreement of the parties; therefore, the arbitral tribunal is obliged to follow the parties' instructions in respect of the scope of the dispute, the law to be applied, the remedies to be granted and so forth.

For the sake of completeness, it must be added that both instruments refer to national, non-harmonised legislation in a number of instances, such as the definition of what may be subject to arbitration, when an award is deemed to conflict with public policy, what the criteria are according to which an arbitration agreement is binding on the parties etc.[115] The harmonised framework for arbitration is, therefore, in several significant respects, subject to national law, and this may have an impact on the enforceability of arbitration agreements and of arbitral awards.[116]

The foregoing draws a picture of international arbitration as mainly based on a few international sources giving a central role to the parties' will, and which meets only a few (albeit significant) limits in national law. It is therefore fully understandable that the general impression is that arbitration is a system that reflects the parties' will without being subject to the formalities of a strict application of the law. When applied to the question of the interpretation of contracts, this may lead to the impression that arbitral tribunals are particularly faithful to the wording of the contract and are inclined to follow the parties' will without interference from considerations of law.

---

[115] See Chapter 5. For a more extensive analysis, see Giuditta Cordero-Moss, 'International Arbitration is not only International', in Giuditta Cordero-Moss (ed.), *International Commercial Arbitration: Different Forms and their Features* (Cambridge University Press, 2013).

[116] A research project at the University of Oslo, Arbitration and Party Autonomy ('APA'), analyses the limits that this may impose on party autonomy: www.jus.uio.no/ifp/english/research/projects/choice-of-law/index.html.

This system, however, does not necessarily lead to a predictable and uniform method for the interpretation of contracts. That arbitral tribunals shall follow the parties' instructions means that they shall aim at being faithful to the contract by understanding the business purpose of the contract and the dynamics of drafting and negotiating contracts. This implies that the degree of literal interpretation may vary, depending on the importance that the clauses have for the commercial meaning of the contract as well as the level of awareness that the parties had in respect of the effects of the clauses. As was seen above, an important assumption for a faithful interpretation of the contract lies in understanding the process that leads to the text of the contract: drafting, negotiations, acceptance of legal risk. There is not a clear line between the formalistic and contextual interpretation of contracts: context may be used to cast light on the parties' intentions, particularly when the contract may be interpreted in different ways. There is, however, a difference between a contextual interpretation that is made necessary by a poorly drafted contract and second-guessing what the parties should have written in the contract to comply with principles of fairness or good faith.

This, however, has to fit with the requirement of predictability and objectivity. Particularly when contracts are meant to circulate (for example, because they are assigned to third parties, are used as security or serve as a basis for calculating insurance premiums) it is essential that they are interpreted strictly in accordance with their terms: third parties are not aware of and should not be assumed to take into consideration the relationship between the original parties to the contract, what the original parties may have assumed or intended, or any circumstances that relate to the original parties and that may have had an impact on these parties' interests. It is, therefore, expected that a contract is interpreted primarily, if not exclusively, in light of its terms – without considering matters such as what a fair balance between the parties' interests would be or what one party's expectations might have been. This means, among other things, that an arbitral tribunal that decides a dispute under a law giving great importance to considerations of loyalty between the parties, or of good faith in the negotiations and in the performance of the contract, might be inclined to apply the law flexibly and to give effect to contract arrangements according to their terms in spite of a possible conflict with the governing law, whereas a court might have been more readily disposed to consider the terms as unbalanced or unreasonable, and to interpret them restrictively or extensively to avoid the result that follows from them.

7.2 Various approaches

The observations made above result in the possibility that an arbitral tribunal will adopt a mixed approach to the interpretation of one and the same contract: an approach which is both formalistic and purposive, depending on the clause.

In addition, there is, in the framework of arbitration, a variety of approaches to the interpretation of contracts.

A seminar organised at the University of Oslo in November 2011 in the framework of the research project on APA was devoted to the question of the interpretation of contracts in international arbitration.[117] A panel discussed the parties' expectations when drafting contracts, and confirmed the understanding of the dynamics of contract drafting described in Chapter 1, Section 3: parties do not always expect that each and every one of the contract's clauses will be enforced literally. Often, the parties do not even know whether these clauses are enforceable, and they consider their non-application as a legal risk that they are willing to take.[118]

Sometimes the parties believe that a properly drafted contract, which describes the deal in detail, will make recourse to a governing law or external principles redundant.[119] Sometimes the parties do not bother describing the deal in excessive detail, and they rely on trade usages to integrate the contract.[120] Sometimes a clause with a very technical legal meaning is inserted, without having given consideration to the legal definition and effects that that particular wording assumes.[121]

Another panel in that seminar discussed the arbitrators' approach to the interpretation of contracts and identified a variety of approaches. Some arbitrators affirmed that they apply the governing law accurately if that law was chosen by the parties in the contract,[122] quite irrespective of how considered the choice of law was and how much it influenced the actual drafting of the contract terms. These arbitrators, therefore, will superimpose on the contract terms any principles or rules of the governing law. Another approach was to take into consideration not only the governing law, but also the overriding mandatory rules of third countries, such as, for example, competition rules.[123] According to a slightly less strict approach, arbitrators should take into account, though not necessarily strictly apply, the governing law as well as the rules of third countries.[124] In a similar vein, it was said

---

[117] The programme for the seminar, 'Arbitration and the Not Unlimited Party Autonomy', the list of panel participants and the transcript from the panel discussions are available at www.jus.uio.no/ifp/english/ research/projects/choice-of-law/events/2011/2011-arbitration-and-the-not-unlimited-party-autonomy.html.

[118] See the interventions of David Echenberg, www.jus.uio.no/ifp/english/research/projects/choice-of-law/ events/apa-transcript.pdf, 'Transcript of the APA Seminar ('APA')', pp. 24–6, as well as the interventions of Are Brautaset, pp. 22–4, Petri Taikalkovski, p. 32 and Fredrik Norburg, p. 28.

[119] See the intervention of Brautaset, *APA*, p. 22.

[120] See the intervention of Anders Ryssdal, *APA*, pp. 29–30.

[121] Taikalkoski, *APA*, p. 32, refers to a dispute where the in-house counsel of a company was asked to explain what she intended when she introduced in the contract the distinction between direct and indirect damages. Without giving any consideration to the sophisticated distinctions in this respect contained in her own legal system or in the governing law, she answered: 'Isn't it pretty obvious, direct damage is when money goes out of your pocket, and indirect damages is when money does not come into your pocket'. It is, therefore, not always justified to assume that parties have a high degree of awareness about the legal effects of their contract terms.

[122] See the interventions of Cathrine Kessedjian, *APA*, p. 41 and Gustaf Möller, *APA*, p. 13.

[123] See the intervention of Stephan Jervell, *APA*, pp. 43–4.

[124] See the intervention of Luigi Fumagalli, *APA*, p. 49.

that the governing law should be applied, but not in an overly formalistic way.[125] A different approach was that international contracts should be interpreted in the light of transnational principles.[126] This latter approach would lead to an interpretation of the contract that is not merely based on the contract terms, since transnational principles such as the UPICC or the PECL, as was mentioned in Chapter 2, Section 4.2, contain various expressions of the principle of good faith and fair dealing, which interfere quite heavily with the contract. Conversely, others found that contracts were increasingly being applied literally, without interference from outside principles, whether of law or of soft law.[127] Yet other arbitrators stated that international contracts were not interpreted exclusively on the basis of their own terms, but in light of the parties' interests and trade usages.[128] Taking this line of reasoning even further is another approach, which is more based on a general understanding of the involved interests, rather than on specific sources of law. According to this approach, arbitrators are said to act according to a feeling of what is right,[129] based more on the gut reaction of the individual person than on the legal system to which he belongs.[130] Yet the legal background of the arbitrator is recognised as playing an important role, a sort of imprinting, which will influence the approach taken to, among other things, the interpretation of contracts. Thus, an arbitrator who arbitrates in various languages affirmed that she even thinks differently depending on the language in which she works, and jokingly defined her approach as Freudian; that is, led by her (legal) subconscious.[131] This was echoed by others who spoke about the different 'philosophical' starting point from which lawyers from different legal traditions depart.[132] An extensive international experience was considered to contribute to moderating the strong influence of a national legal background.[133]

If the debate in the above-mentioned seminar may be deemed to be somewhat representative of the approaches that may be met in international commercial arbitration, the picture that results is one of marked diversity in the approach to the interpretation of contracts in international commercial arbitration: contract terms are not necessarily always applied in strict accordance with their terms. There are different degrees of interference and the sources of the interference also vary quite considerably. There is a scale moving from a strict application of the governing law to integrate the contract, via interpretation of the contract terms in the context of transnational soft law principles such as the UPICC and the PECL (which are heavily based on the principle of good faith and may give rise to a substantial possibility of

---

[125] See the intervention of Ivan Zykin, *APA*, p. 17.
[126] See the intervention of Alexander Komarov, *APA*, pp. 45–6.
[127] See the intervention of Taikalkoski, *APA*, p. 37   [128] See the intervention of Ryssdal, *APA*, pp. 29–31.
[129] See the intervention of Michael Schneider, *APA*, p. 57.
[130] See the intervention of Jernej Sekloec, *APA*, pp. 11–12.
[131] See the intervention of Kessedjian, *APA*, p. 40.
[132] See the interventions of Echenberg, *APA*, p. 35; Norburg, *APA*, pp. 27–8 and Schneider, *APA* p. 57.
[133] See the intervention of Brautaset, *APA*, p. 24.

interfering with the contract language), to interpretation of the contract on the basis of its own terms combined with the parties' interests and trade usages, to interpretation of the contract solely on the basis of its own terms. There is also a further approach to interpretation of the contract, which goes under the label of 'splitting the baby'. This Solomonic approach consists in rendering an award in the middle range between the claims of each of the parties. This is not necessarily based on a literal consideration of the contract terms or on an integration of the contract with other sources, but simply on the desire to accommodate both parties.[134] Interestingly, there does not seem to be a uniform perception of the frequency of this approach: a recent empirical study shows that the parties to arbitration perceive that they got a Solomonic award in 18–20 percent of the cases, whereas the arbitrators perceive that they take this kind of equitable decision in only 5 percent of the cases.[135] This, therefore, adds a new variable to the equation of the interpretation of contracts. Not only is it uncertain as to whether the arbitrators will interpret the contract literally, whether they will use sources of law or whether they will apply transnational principles to give a more purposive interpretation; it is also possible that the decision will be influenced by equitable considerations that are not based on the contract or on other legal sources.

   This reveals an important lack of uniformity at two levels: parties' contract drafting is not uniform and arbitrators' contract interpretation is not uniform. In this context, it seems quite illusionary to assume that international commercial arbitration acts as the voice of a unitary international business community.

7.3 The importance of the selection of arbitrators

Given that at least six or seven different approaches to the interpretation of contracts were professed in a discussion involving about eighteen arbitrators, it seems obvious that the outcome of a dispute will depend heavily on who is acting as an arbitrator in the particular dispute. It was even affirmed, rather provocatively, that it is not so much the applicable law that matters for the outcome of the dispute, it is rather the cultural background of the individuals who act as arbitrators.[136]

   The selection of arbitrators has been defined as the ultimate form for forum shopping.[137] The process of selecting arbitrators has undergone tremendous development in the past decades. I remember one of the first arbitrations I was involved in

---

[134] This appears in the 2012 Survey of the School of International Arbitration of Queen Mary, University of London, entitled '2012 International Arbitration Survey: Current and Preferred Practices in the Arbitral Process', Section 7.

[135] 'Queen Mary's Survey', p. 38.

[136] See the intervention of Schneider, APA, p. 57. See also Brautaset, APA p. 24.

[137] These are Cathrine Rogers' words in the Kluwer Arbitration Blog, 'The International Arbitrator Information Project: An idea whose Time has Come', entry posted 09 August 2012 at 10:53 AM, kluwerarbitrationblog.com/

in the mid-1980s as in-house counsel in a multinational company. I made contact with a law firm that specialised in arbitration and said that we were contemplating an arbitration. After just five minutes, I received a telefax with five names of people whom the law firm recommended as potential arbitrators. I had not been asked what type of contract the dispute was based on, who the counterpart was, what kind of expertise the dispute required, let alone whether we were interested in a formalistic or a purposive interpretation of the contract. Today, when parties take into consideration whether they shall appoint a certain arbitrator, they undertake fully fledged research analysing his/her writings and assessing whether he/she has expressed opinions that may be incompatible with the position that they will present in the proceeding, and they even invite him/her to a pre-appointment interview to discuss issues such as availability and conflicts of interest.[138] The relevance of the selection process also appears clearly in the success that a soft law instrument of the International Bar Association has achieved: the IBA Guidelines on Conflict of Interest in International Arbitration.[139] This is an attempt to bring transparent and objective criteria to an area earlier dominated by the recognition of established positions on the basis of reputation and implied criteria. Additionally, arbitral institutions are opening up to a more systematic approach to the criteria for the appointment of arbitrators. The Arbitration Institute of the SCC, for example, has recently published a study on the criteria that it applies in challenges to arbitrators appointed under the SCC rules.[140] The importance of having detailed knowledge of the appointed arbitrators and the environment in which they operate is indirectly confirmed in the revision that was made in 2010 to the UNCITRAL Arbitration Rules: in regulating who should act as an appointing authority in the eventuality that one of the parties does not appoint an arbitrator, it was evaluated whether the Permanent Court of Arbitration (PCA) could carry out this function.[141] It was concluded that a centralised body, even a body of the calibre of the PCA, would not be in a position to properly appreciate all the aspects of the appointment in each of the jurisdictions where appointment might be necessary. Therefore, Article 6.2 of the revised UNCITRAL Arbitration Rules ended up by giving the PCA the task of appointing the appointing authority, who, in turn, would appoint the arbitrator – on the basis of the assumption that a local authority would be in a better position to select the arbitrators.

The development from a list of potential arbitrators quickly scribbled on a fax to a full due diligence process is remarkable, but selection is still made on the basis of

---

[138] The 'Queen Mary's Survey', p. 6 and 7, reports that 86 per cent of the respondents consider it appropriate to conduct pre-appointment interviews.

[139] www.ibanet.org/Publications/publications_IBA_guides_and_free_materials.aspx#conflictsofinterest.

[140] Helena Jung, 'SCC Practice: Challenges to Arbitrators', SCC Board decisions 2005–2007, www.sccinstitute.com/filearchive/2/28190/04-Art32-Jung.pdf, last accessed on 14 February 2013.

[141] Report of Working Group II (Arbitration and Conciliation) on the work of its forty-ninth session (Vienna, 15–19 September 2008), A/CN.9/665, paras 47–50, and Report of the Working Group on Arbitration and Conciliation on the work of its forty-sixth session (New York, 5–9 February 2007), A/CN.9/619, paras. 71–4.

what has been defined as a bizarrely outdated technique mainly based on personal knowledge and hearsay.[142] This is due to the structure of arbitration as a largely private and non-transparent system.[143] Seen from the outside, these features of arbitration may give the impression of a unitary system. As the overview in Chapter 3, Section 7.2 shows, however, there is no basis for assuming that arbitration is a unitary system.

7.4 Conclusion

In conclusion, international arbitration does not have a uniform approach to contract interpretation: it may range from a formalistic application of the contract's wording, to an interpretation of the wording in light of the governing law, to an interpretation of the wording in light of transnational principles of soft law or even of a more equitable character. Even the same arbitral tribunal may adopt more than one approach to the same contract, depending on the tribunal's understanding of the dynamics of negotiations that led to that particular contract's text. This picture certainly contradicts the usual assumption that international commercial arbitration is a harmonised system, uniformly giving expression to the interests of the 'international business community'. Parties have the possibility of influencing the approach to interpretation by selecting arbitrators who represent a certain attitude towards contract interpretation. The process of selection has come a long way in the past decades, but is still unsatisfactorily based on personal experience and anecdotal evidence. This may lead to repeated appointments of the arbitrators who have shown that they represent a certain approach; always appointing the same few people as arbitrators indeed leads to a certain degree of predictability. Most of the arbitral tribunals, however, consist of three arbitrators – usually, one appointed by each of the parties, and the chairperson appointed by the two party appointed arbitrators. If one of the parties has appointed an arbitrator who is known for his formalistic approach and the other an arbitrator known for his purposive approach, the interpretation that the award will depend on is the chairperson's approach, as well as on the deliberations within the tribunal. This, in turn, does not enhance predictability.

8 The drafting style does not achieve self-sufficiency, but has a certain merit

This chapter showed that the terms of a contract are not detached from the governing law: the governing law will influence the interpretation and application of these terms. To what extent the legal effects differ from what a literal application would suggest, varies depending on the governing law.

---

[142] Rogers, 'Kluwer Arbitration Blog'.   [143] *Ibid.* See also the intervention of Kai-Uwe Karl, *APA*, p. 53.

There is, therefore, no reason to rely on a full and literal application of the contract's wording as if it were isolated from the governing law.

If this is so, why do contract parties go on drafting detailed (and sometimes, as seen in Chapter 1, Section 2, nonsensical) clauses without adjusting them to the governing law? Why do they engage in extensive negotiations on specific wording without even having discussed which law will govern the contract?

Each of the parties may repeatedly send numerous delegations consisting of financial, marketing, technical, commercial and legal experts to meet and negotiate specific contractual mechanisms and wording to be inserted in the contract; all of these people may spend hours and days negotiating whether the penalty for a delay in the performance shall be US$ 10,000 or 15,000 a day, or fighting over whether the contract shall include the word 'reasonable' in the clause permitting early termination of the contract in case the other party fails to perform certain obligations. All these negotiations are usually made without even having addressed the question of the governing law. The contract may end up[144] being governed by English law, in which case the clause on penalties will be unenforceable, or by German law, in which case the concept of reasonableness will be part of the contract irrespective of the appearance of the wording. All the efforts in negotiating the amount of the penalty, or in rendering a stricter early termination clause, will have been in vain. Unfortunately, it is not that unusual that the choice-of-law clause is left as the last point in the negotiations, and that it is not given the attention that it deserves.

This does not necessarily mean that the practice of negotiating detailed wording without regard to the governing law is always unreasonable. From a merely legal point of view it makes little sense, but from the overall economic perspective it is more understandable, as was seen in Chapter 1, Section 3.

---

[144] Either because the parties chose it or because the applicable conflict rule pointed to it, as will be seen in Chapter 4.

4

Which state law governs an international contract?

1 Introduction

In the previous chapters, we have shown that international contracts are ultimately subject to a state law, even if the transaction is governed by some transnational sources. The next question that has to be answered is then: which state's law regulates an international transaction? There are rules that have the function of identifying the laws governing international relationships, the so-called conflict rules or choice-of-law rules. The area of law that regulates the choice of the governing law is called private international law (or conflict of laws). What is particularly interesting from the point of view of this book is the role of one of these conflict rules, the most important for contracts: the rule of party autonomy. This rule gives the parties the power to choose which law their contract shall be subject to. This power enhances the impression of self-sufficiency that was described in Chapter 1: if the parties are able to choose the governing law, they may be under the impression that they need not be concerned with any other law but the law of their choice. As this chapter will show, this is a misconception.

The governing law has to be identified by the conflict rules of the state where the court where the action is brought has its venue (the conflict rules of the *lex fori*). Each state has its own conflict rules. Some of the national choice-of-law rules are of international origin as they are contained in supranational regulations applicable in that state or in international conventions that were ratified by that state, such as, for example, the European Regulation on the Law Applicable to Contractual Obligations (Rome I) or The Hague Convention on the Law Applicable to the International Sales of Goods. Some choice-of-law rules are contained in national legislation, such as the Swiss Private International Law Act of 1987, which is a systematic codification, or the Norwegian Act on the Law Applicable to Insurance Agreements of 1992, which is an act regulating choice of law in a specific sector. Other choice-of-law rules are customary or based on judicial precedents, such as most of the Norwegian private international law is. For the purpose of predictability of the governing law, it is highly desirable that the various national conflict rules are harmonised and interpreted, to the highest extent possible, in a uniform way.

If conflict rules differ from country to country, they will determine different laws to govern the same relationship. Depending on where the lawsuit is presented, therefore, a different substantive law may be applicable and the rights and obligations of the parties may be different. Each of the parties will compete in filing a lawsuit in a country with conflict rules that determine a favourable applicable law, even though that country may have only a thin connection with the dispute (so-called forum shopping). This may lead to lawsuits in unpredictable fora, to uncertainty as to the substantive rights and obligations of the parties and even to contradictory court decisions on the same relationship. Harmonisation of the conflict rules contributes to preventing these undesirable effects, because the parties will not be able to speculate on the difference in the applicable law.

In Europe, large parts of the private international law relating to commercial relationships were harmonised by two regulations: the so-called Rome I Regulation on the Law Applicable to Contractual Obligations (593/2008) and the so-called Rome II Regulation on the Law Applicable to Non-contractual Obligations (864/2007). Where there are no harmonised choice-of-law rules, each court will apply the private international law of its own state. In areas such as company law and property, for example, choice-of-law rules are not harmonised, and each country applies its own national conflict rules.

2 The most important conflict rule for contracts: party autonomy

The most important conflict rule for contracts is the rule of party autonomy. Party autonomy gives the parties the power to choose in their contract the law that will govern their relationship. The above-mentioned Rome I Regulation, which constitutes the private international law of all states in the EU (except Denmark, where its predecessor, the Rome Convention, is still applicable), recognises the rule of party autonomy (Article 3), and so do the Swiss Private International Law Act (Section 116) and the Russian Civil Code (Article 1210), just to name some important codifications of conflict rules.

The widespread recognition of party autonomy may enhance the impression that an international contract is a self-sufficient regulation of the underlying transaction, detached from the state laws of the states with which the transaction is connected. Not only may the parties choose the law that will govern their contract, in many systems (such as in all of the above-mentioned systems), they may choose a law that does not have any connection whatsoever with the transaction. The parties may therefore end up with an extremely liberal law that contains very little regulation beyond the regulation made by the parties in their contract.

Party autonomy is recognised as a conflict rule in the vast majority of states participating in international trade and business. However, this does not mean, as some voices enthusiastically maintain,[1] that party autonomy is a universal principle of transnational law, which is generally recognised and therefore not rooted in any specific state law.

---

[1] See, for example, J. D. M. Lew, *Applicable Law in International Commercial Arbitration* (Oceana Publications 1978).

Party autonomy is a conflict rule that is, undeniably, generally recognised; however, the conditions for the exercise of party autonomy may vary according to the rules contained in the private international law of each different state. It goes without saying that a judge has to apply the law of the legal system to which he or she belongs. In disputes having an international character, the private international law of the judge's system (of the *lex fori*) will instruct the judge to apply foreign law, if the conditions for that application, as set forth in the applicable conflict rules, are met. This means that the conditions that have to be met in order to allow the choice of the law made by the party may vary from state to state. For example, some systems permit a choice of law even if the contract is not international, but domestic (for example, English law, assuming that the choice was made in good faith),[2] and others, if there is a foreign element in the transaction (for example, the already mentioned Hague Convention of 1955). Moreover, some systems require that the choice of law be made expressly or appear clearly from the provisions of the contract (for example, the Norwegian Act on the Law Applicable to the International Sale of Goods, Section 3), while others consider it sufficient that the choice of law is clearly demonstrated by the circumstances of the case (for example, the Rome I Regulation, Article 3.1).

The parties do, as a matter of fact, enjoy a large freedom in choosing the governing law. However, this detachment from the connected state laws is not as limitless as it is sometimes perceived to be. The private international law of the *lex fori* might contain, in addition to conditions for the exercise of party autonomy as seen above, considerable limitations to the scope of party autonomy. Below we will look at the scope of party autonomy as well as the most significant elements that restrict it.

2.1 Which law to choose

To ensure predictability and to maintain control on the venue of dispute resolution, it is advisable to include in the contract a clause regulating the governing law and a clause regulating dispute resolution. A variety of choices is available.

Regarding the governing law, it can be chosen from the law of either party or a third law, which does not need to be connected with the contract or the place of dispute resolution.

Regarding the dispute resolution, it can be chosen from ordinary courts and arbitration; the seat of the courts or the arbitration may be chosen, and it does not necessarily have to be connected with the parties or the contract. Regarding arbitration, it can be chosen from ordinary arbitration and fast track arbitration, ad hoc arbitration and institutional arbitration and the seat also has to be chosen. All of these

---

[2] A definition made by Lord Wright in the case *Vita Food Products Inc* v. *Unus Shipping Co* [1939] AC 277 PC is often quoted when describing the requisites of party autonomy. According to this definition, the choice of a foreign law is valid 'provided the intention expressed is bona fide and legal, and provided there is no reason for avoiding the choice on the ground of public policy'.

alternatives will be analysed in this and in the next chapter, to the extent that it is relevant to the question of the parties' influence on the contract's self-sufficiency.

2.1.1 Choice of one of the parties' law

Traditionally, the parties try to avoid the law of the other party governing the contract. Accepting the other party's law is perceived as giving the other party an advantage.

The advantage that one party enjoys if the contract is governed by 'its' law, is, however, overestimated.

If the legal system is transparent and inspired by the rule of law, the nationality of the parties will have no relevance whatsoever to the contents of the governing law (and any system that is not transparent or inspired by the rule of law should be avoided on its own merits, and not merely because it is the law of one party). A pro-nationality bias could possibly be envisaged (more on an unconscious level, though) in the application of the law by the courts or the arbitrators; however, it is fully possible to avoid the other party's country as a seat of the dispute resolution, even if the governing law is from that country. This, therefore, is not necessarily a reason for avoiding the other party's law.

The real advantage is in the knowledge that the other party is assumed to have of the governing law, which is more accurate if it is the law of that party's country. This advantage has limited significance if local law firms are used as advisers to draft the contract or check its compliance with the governing law, and to advise in case of discrepancies in the interpretation or implementation. Admittedly, using an external law firm increases transactional costs; however, for companies that would use a law firm anyway in the process of drafting, it does not make a significant difference if the law firm is from the company's own jurisdiction or from another country.

In conclusion, assuming that the parties come from legal systems inspired by the rule of law and that local legal advisers are used to check the compliance of the documentation, there do not seem to be significant risks in agreeing that the contract will be governed by the other party's law.

As this is perceived to be a material advantage for the party whose law is chosen, and because the real advantage does not need to be so significant, this could be used during the negotiations to obtain other concessions that may be far more substantial, in exchange for accepting the law of the other party.

2.1.2 Criteria for choosing the governing law

Sometimes parties attempt to make a strategic choice of law, and seek advice as to which law is most suited to govern the particular type of contract that they are contemplating. In some cases, it is actually possible to detect a particularly apt law. Some contracts of reinsurance, charter parties as well as some financial contracts, for example, have been developed under English law; it may, therefore, be advisable to choose English law to govern them, rather than a law with principles and a structure alien to those that inspired the contract.

For commercial contracts, generally, however, such as sale, agency, distribution, licence or cooperation agreements, there are no reasons to prefer one law to another one – as long as the chosen law (including the legal literature and case law) is accessible and the legal system to which it belongs is transparent, stable and inspired by the rule of law.

Commercial contracts are rarely subject to mandatory rules of the governing law. Mandatory rules are usually to be found in relationships that affect a third party's rights (such as encumbrances or retention of title), positions that are subject to registration (such as intellectual property rights or matters of corporate law) or where a contractual party is deemed to be weaker than the other (such as labour or agency contracts).

The governing law is still important for contracts that are not subject to mandatory rules – mainly for the impact that it may have on the interpretation of those contracts. It is, however, difficult to predict at the moment of drafting the contract, what kind of differences may arise between the parties in the interpretation and performance of the contract or which position either of the parties will be in during a possible dispute. The interest of either party, therefore, can hardly be useful as a basis for a strategic choice of law.[3]

Nevertheless, it may be possible to make some very general observations.

As was seen in Chapter 3, traditionally, the common law is held to be concerned with preserving the parties' freedom to contract and to ensure that their contracts are performed accurately according to their precise wording. On the contrary, the civil law judge has more power to evaluate the fairness of the contract and intervene to reinstate the balance of interests between the parties; he or she is more concerned with creating justice in the specific case than with implementing the deal in the most predictable manner. In doing so, the civil law judge is guided by general clauses and principles of good faith and fair dealing.

Within the civil law, a further division is possible between the systems that are based on German law (also including the Nordic systems) and those based on French law. The systems based on French law have a more formalistic approach to the interpretation of contracts than the Germanic systems, and are thus closer to the English literal interpretation.

Recent comparative research has started to question whether common law and civil law are as fundamentally different as they are traditionally held to be. However, as was shown in Chapter 3, Section 3, convergence between the systems is not at all complete, and may be seen mainly in areas such as consumer contracts. As long as the field of interest is the interpretation of commercial contracts, the differences persist.

---

[3] For a more extensive argument in the same direction, see Stefan Vogenauer, 'Regulatory Competition through Choice of Contract law and Choice of Forum in Europe: Theory and Evidence' (2013) 21(1) *European Review of Private Law*, 19–22.

2.1.2.1 Literal interpretation: English law

On the basis of the foregoing, as a general guideline it can be said that a contract governed by English law should be very detailed. Among other things, a contract governed by English law should: (i) spell out precisely all the assumptions upon which the contract is based (this is the function of the recitals, which often introduce the contract with a series of 'whereas. . .'); (ii) make express provision for all situations that need regulation; and (iii) specify all effects that are desired as a consequence of the regulation and not leave any gaps to be filled by the interpreter. Without a specific provision, the English contract will not be affected by changes in circumstances, supervening hardships, failed assumptions or considerations relating to the balance of interests between the parties.[4] The mechanisms that are regulated in the contract will be implemented without evaluating whether the circumstances that triggered them were material or whether it is reasonable to assume that the parties intended the mechanism to apply to those circumstances etc.

On a very general level, therefore, it may be said that a party should choose English law to govern a contract that regulates rights upon which the parties may freely dispose, if that party is likely to insist on an accurate performance of the obligations exactly as they are described in the contract. This might be the case if the contract has been drafted by that party in a careful and considered way.

It is important to add, however, that the English law of contracts has principles and rules that are quite unfamiliar to a continental or Nordic lawyer, as was seen in Chapter 3, Sections 5 and 6: the rule on consideration, for example, according to which unilateral promises (such as a firm offer) are not enforceable or the rule that prohibits contractual penalties. The formalistic application of the contract's wording, combined with unexpected effects that may follow from specific legal formulas, may lead to undesirable results.

Therefore, English law should not be chosen as a governing law unless an English lawyer has thoroughly checked the compliance of the contract with English law, as well as the formal reaction to any new circumstances or differences in interpretation between the parties.

2.1.2.2 Purposive interpretation: Germanic law

On the other hand, a contract governed by German or a Germanic law (also including the Nordic laws) does not need to be as detailed and exhaustive as an English contract. The German or Germanic interpreter will: (i) interpret the contract on the basis of the assumptions that comparable parties are reasonably expected to have; (ii) integrate the contract with an implicit duty of loyalty between the parties; (iii) consider all circumstances that may be relevant to the assessment of

---

[4] Unless they trigger frustration of the contract. Frustration has, however, a narrow scope of application and has the effect of 'killing the contract'. See Edwin Peel, *Treitel on the Law of Contract*, 13th edn (Sweet & Maxwell, 2011).

the rights and obligations, even if they are not expressly mentioned in the contract; (iv) fill in any gaps that the contract may have; and (v) excuse a party for non-performance in the case of a change in circumstances that makes the performance excessively burdensome.

On a very general level, therefore, it may be said that a party should choose a Germanic law to govern a contract that regulates rights upon which the parties may freely dispose, if that party is likely to rely on a consideration of the circumstances as a whole, on legitimate expectations and good faith. This might be the case if the contract has been drafted by the other party.

It is important to point out that this may mean that the clear wording of the contract is corrected by the interpreter. This may be particularly relevant to instruments such as letters of intent, which are likely to enhance the duty of good faith and loyalty between the parties if they are governed by a Germanic law, as was seen in Chapter 3, Section 4.2. Thus, even though the letter of intent may contain a clause specifying that no party is liable for failure to reach an agreement, a break-off of negotiations may lead to liability if the negotiations were not started or continued in good faith (for example, because one party intended to prevent the other party from negotiating with others or intended to use the information obtained in the negotiations for other purposes).

Similarly, carefully negotiated clauses containing representations and warranties or remedies for non-performance such as early termination, liquidated damages or hardship clauses, may turn out not to be exclusive of principles contained in the governing law, as was seen in Chapter 3, Sections 4.3, 5.1, 5.2 and 5.4.

2.1.3 Accurate application assumes a thorough understanding of the law

It was seen above that the governing law has an influence on the interpretation of the contract (assuming that the contract is on matters upon which the parties may freely dispose). This assumes that the judge or arbitrator has a thorough understanding of the rules on interpretation and of the role that a judge is expected to have as an interpreter under that law. Generally, this kind of understanding is closely linked to the legal upbringing that a lawyer receives at an early stage of his or her career. A lawyer is not necessarily aware of the role he or she plays in interpreting the contract, and is usually convinced that he or she is interpreting a contract simply according to the natural meaning of its words, without actively interfering as an interpreter. However, as was seen in Chapter 3, the same contract may lead to opposing results just on the basis of the interpretation, and without the interpreter being aware of it. As an example, note the interpretation of the wording on *force majeure* events that is made, respectively, in Article 79 of the CISG and in § 27 of the Norwegian Sales of Goods Act. The wording of these provisions is identical, but they are interpreted differently. The CISG is interpreted as not excusing non-performance due to a supplier's failure, whereas the Norwegian provision is interpreted so as to excuse it; see Chapter 3, Section 5.2.1. As a further example, note an English decision

that interpreted a contract literally:[5] the contract provided that it could be terminated
if the performance had not been completed by 13.00 on a certain day. Completion
took place on the agreed date, but at 13.10. Although the delay did not have any
consequences, the English judge found it obvious that ten minutes delay is a delay
and that the contract could be terminated according to its provision. Any other
decision would have led to the question of how late does it have to be to become a
delay, and this would have been against predictability. A German judge would
probably have considered whether such a slight delay had consequences that would
justify termination. He or she might have, possibly even on an unconscious level,
assumed that the parties must have meant a delay that was more material than ten
minutes.

This is to show that the particular effects of a law depend not only on the
application of that law, but also on the interpreter's attitude. If a German lawyer is
asked to apply English law, the German principles of good faith, loyalty, etc. will
probably unconsciously be superimposed on the English preference for predictability,
and the result will be unlikely to be the same as if an English lawyer had applied the
same law.

Therefore, if a law is applied by a foreign court or an arbitral tribunal where the
arbitrators are not educated in that law, it will be necessary to give a thorough
explanation of that law's principles and, more importantly, of how they are applied.
This will ensure that the governing law will have the effects that are peculiar to it.

2.2 Tacit choice of English law for international contracts?

Assuming that the contract contains a clause choosing a civil law as governing, or,
alternatively, assuming that the contract (lacking an express choice-of-law clause) is
governed by a civil law as a consequence of the applicable conflict rule, shall any
importance be attached to the legal style in which the contract is drafted? As was seen
in Chapter 1, many international commercial contracts are drafted in the English
language and use, as a basis, models that are developed in the English language;
therefore, the contracts reflect the legal terminology and contractual structure typical
of common law systems. Contracts reflecting the common law (particularly, English
law) are drafted quite differently from contracts reflecting the civil law, since each of
them is meant to meet the requirements and fill the gaps of the respective governing
law, and the laws of contract of these two legal families differ quite substantially from
each other. As was seen in Chapter 3, some clauses might not achieve under civil law
the intended effects that can be achieved under the common law; some clauses may
be unenforceable or not have any meaning under a civil law, for example, if they
make reference to legal institutions that do not exist under the civil governing law;

---

[5] *Union Eagle* [1997] 2 All ER 215.

some clauses may be redundant or cover areas that are already regulated in the civilian governing law but in a different way. In these situations, the interpreter has to cope with a lack of coordination between the contract, drafted on the basis of a common law tradition, and the governing law, belonging to the civil law tradition. Should the interpreter disregard the drafting tradition and simply interpret the document on the basis of the governing law? Or should the common law inspiration play a role in the interpretation, in spite of the fact that the governing law is civil?

The first question that should be answered in this context, and that will be analysed here, is a question of private international law: does the use of a common law legal style and contractual structure imply a choice of law? In other words, can the parties be deemed to have tacitly chosen the governing law by having drafted the contract in a way that is typical of the common law? If it is not possible to assume a tacit choice of law because the contract contains an expressed choice of law in favour of a civil law, can the principle of severability allow considering a tacit choice of law only for the clause or part of the contract that otherwise would be unenforceable under the governing civil law? If no tacit choice (total or partial) may be deemed to have taken place, and assuming that the contract does not contain an expressed choice of law, can the contract style have an influence on the application of the conflict rule that usually determines the governing law; that is, the rule according to which a contract is governed by the law with which it has the closest connection? If the use of a certain drafting style may not be deemed to amount to a choice of law, may the interpreter nevertheless attach significance to the legal effects that certain clauses have in the inspiring legal system?

The reasoning made here is based on the rules on tacit choice of law, on severability and on the closest connection contained in the Rome I Regulation, in turn, based on the Rome Convention of 1980 on the Law Applicable to Contractual Obligations.

2.2.1 The use of common law contract models

As was already mentioned in Chapter 1 Section 2, international commercial contracts are written primarily using the model of English or US contracts. This contract practice obviously started because the communication between the parties in international transactions takes place mainly in the English language. It is, therefore, only natural that the contract is also written in English.

Using a certain language does not necessarily mean that the legal system that is expressed in that language is also applied. This is clearly testified to by the numerous contracts written in the English language where the parties have expressly chosen to subject the contract to a governing law that is not expressed in English – be it the law of the state to which one of the parties belongs, the law of the state where the contract will be performed or the law of a third state, which is deemed to be neutral and therefore preferred by both parties. This may lead to choosing the law belonging to a civilian system, and may appear to contradict the circumstance that not only do the drafters of international contracts use the English language, but they are also often inspired by contract models that are developed in England, the US or other common law jurisdictions.

This is a relatively unconscious process. It started several decades ago mainly because of the desire to ensure a proper linguistic result: the numerous publications that commented on or collected English or US model contracts were very useful as a basis for non-native English-speaking lawyers to draft contracts in English properly. Adopting these models, however, also meant adopting the legal structures of the legal system under which the model was developed: separating the proper use of the English language from the adoption of the underlying legal structures would have assumed (i) a thorough knowledge of the English, US or other common law system under which the model had been developed; (ii) an understanding of the function of the various contract clauses in that legal system; (iii) a systematic comparison with the governing legal system; and (iv) an exclusion or correction of the contract clauses that turned out to be tailored to the legal system under which the model was developed and not to the governing legal system. Such an extensive process cannot always be expected in the framework of a commercial case where time and resources are often limited, and as a result, contract models were simply adopted 'as is'. International commercial practice has therefore gradually acknowledged the drafting style that is typical for common law contracts, without really questioning its applicability to civil law systems.

Today, large international commercial contracts are (with only a few exceptions) drafted on the basis of common law models. The sources of these models are often not clearly identifiable and usually not unitary. Every lawyer or law firm will have an archive with texts taken from international branch associations, from international publications, from electronic databases and from previous transactions of various types in which the lawyer or the law firm has been involved in various jurisdictions. Any new draft will be based on a mixture of all these texts, improved with new elements taken from recent experiences, inspired by drafts that had been proposed during the negotiations of a previous deal and added to with clauses that have appeared in yet other deals. In summary, commercial contracts are, with the exception of specific areas where there is a widespread use of recognised standard contracts developed under a specific legal system, a pot-pourri of texts originating from various contract types and different jurisdictions, international documents and personal experience, all of this adopting the common law legal drafting, and without necessarily any particular thought devoted to the compatibility of these models with the governing law.

The power of language is, indeed, considerable: in George Orwell's memorable novel *1984*, the totalitarian system introduced a simplified language, Newspeak, to limit free thought. By prohibiting synonyms, antonyms and words relating to any threatening concepts, the system managed to eradicate alternative thought. Language's ability to influence the content of what is expressed may seem just as significant also in the field of contracts (albeit without the gloomy implications attached to Newspeak), given the close relationship between the definition of a right and its legal effects. If a right is defined in a certain language, it may seem only natural to assume that its effects are those described in the legal system that adopts that language. If this was the case, the use of the English language would imply the creation of rights and obligations corresponding to those existing in English law – just like, in a completely different context and with completely different implications, the use of the Newspeak leads to thoughts that are conforming with the principles of the regime. However, as was seen in Chapters 2 and 3 and as the sections below will show, in the case of contracts the language used to define rights and obligations is not the only parameter for the content of the rights and obligations. In addition to the language of the contract, it is necessary to take into consideration the regulation contained in the contract, and this in turn will have to be interpreted and applied according to the governing law. Unlike the totalitarian regime of *1984*, where no other sources could integrate the language and consequently thought could be moulded by the words that were available to express them, legal concepts do not simply rely on the wording of contract terms.

2.2.2 The governing law

An international commercial contract, more or less consciously inspired by one or more common law systems, as seen above, is generally subject to one single governing law. As will be seen in Section 4 below, a contract is actually governed by more than one law, since conflict rules may render different laws applicable to specific areas, such as the legal capacity of the parties, securities or overriding mandatory rules. The questions of pure contract law, however, such as the rules on interpretation of the contract, general principles on the mutual rights and obligations between the parties, the validity of the contract, the consequences for breach of contract, etc., are generally subject to one single governing law, unless the parties have decided otherwise, as will be seen in Section 2.2.3 below.

The drafters of international commercial contracts often make use of their party autonomy and insert in the contract a clause choosing the governing law. This is permitted by most systems of private international law; in the EU, it is permitted by Article 3 of the Rome I Regulation. Often, the chosen law belongs to a civil system. If the contract contains a choice-of-law clause, or if the parties have afterwards specified what law shall regulate their relationship, there is no doubt that the contract will have to be interpreted in accordance with that law and will have to be subject to the rules of that law (assuming that the choice was valid). This extends to filling in any gaps in the contract with the rules of the chosen law as well as correcting any clauses that might be contrary to the mandatory rules of the governing law. The common law-inspired contract will be, therefore, governed by the chosen civilian law.

If the parties have not chosen the governing law, this will be determined by other conflict rules, based on various connecting factors: as will be seen in Section 3.2

below, in the Rome I Regulation, the connecting factor is generally the habitual residence of the party making the characteristic performance, as regulated in Article 4. If the party making the characteristic performance has its place of business in a country belonging to the civil law family, the contract will be governed by that law, in accordance with Article 4. The common law-inspired contract will be, yet again, governed by a civilian law.

2.2.3 Drafting style as a partial choice of law?

If the contract contains a choice-of-law clause determining that the contract is to be governed by a civilian law, the choice is expressed quite clearly. However, if the contract is written in a common law legal style and contains some clauses that do not make any sense under the chosen law, but have a clear effect under the inspiring law, can the parties be deemed to have made a tacit choice of the inspiring law for that particular part of the contract?

The Rome I Regulation permits, in Article 3, subjecting different parts of the contract to the law of different countries,[6] and the scenario described above would be an example of this principle of severability.

The principle of severability is well known in private international law. The general rule within international contracts is the unitary principle, providing that the governing law shall be applied to the near totality of questions arising out of a contract.[7] In spite of the unitary principle, there is a series of areas where the governing law does not apply: for example, the legal capacity of the parties to the contract,[8] the ability of the agent to bind the principal,[9] the clause choosing the competent courts or the arbitration clause,[10] the validity of the consent of one party under certain circumstances,[11] or any areas where the law of the forum[12] or, under certain circumstances, the law of a third country[13] has mandatory rules of such a nature that they need to be applied in spite of a different governing law (the so-called overriding mandatory rules). Whenever a contract covers any of these areas, it will be subject to severability: the part of the contract falling within each area will be severed from the rest of the contract and will be governed by the law determined on the basis of the relevant conflict rule. The remaining parts of the contract will be subject to the governing law as chosen by the parties or as determined on the basis of the general conflict rule for contracts. In addition, party autonomy does not cover the parts of the relationship that do not fall within contract law, such as the validity of a pledge (which falls within property law) or the validity of a corporate body's resolution

---

[6] 'By their choice the parties can select the law applicable to the whole or a part only of the contract'.

[7] Article 12 of the Rome I Regulation provides that the governing law applies to interpretation, performance, consequences of breach, extinguishing of obligations and consequences of nullity. Article 18 extends the applicability of the governing law to presumptions at law and burden of proof.

[8] Article 1.2(a).   [9] Article 1.2(g).   [10] Article 1.2(e).   [11] Article 10.2.

[12] Article 9.1.   [13] Article 9.3.

(which falls within company law). These aspects will be governed by the law determined by the relevant conflict rule for property or company law.

Thus, Article 3 of the Rome I Regulation has not introduced a principle that is new to private international law. In spite of this, it has been met with some criticism,[14] and its precise effects are not completely uncontroversial.[15] However, in the decades during which this rule has been in force under its predecessor, the Rome Convention, it does not seem to have presented particular problems.[16] The Rome I Regulation has not modified the Rome Convention in this respect. Therefore, the comments that were made in the Report to the Rome Convention are applicable also to the Rome I Regulation.

The Giuliano–Lagarde Report on the Rome Convention specifies that the severability permitted to the parties under Article 3 assumes that the separation of the contract into different parts must be logically consistent.[17] A choice of law according to which the rights of the seller are governed by a certain law, whereas the rights of the buyer are governed by another law, therefore, would not be valid.

Whenever a contract regulates a complex transaction that can be divided into various independent parts, it is possible to sever these parts and subject them to different laws. The most evident example is the arbitration clause, which is independent from the main agreement and sometimes is even regulated in a separate document. Other evident examples are guarantees or other ancillary obligations that may also be regulated in separate documents. Even parts of a transaction that are not usually the object of separate contracts may be logically severable, for example,

---

[14] See Michael Bogdan, '1980 års EC-konvention om tillämping lag på kontraktsrättsliga förpliktelser – synpunkter beträffande den svenska inställningen', (1982) 95 *Tidsskrift for Rettsvitenskap* 14f.; but see the same author's more positive analysis of the matter now that the principle has become part of Swedish law: Michael Bogdan, *Svensk internationell privat- och prosessrätt*, 7th edn (Norstedt Juridik, 2008) pp. 249f.

[15] For example, Kurt Siehr, *Internationales Privatrechts* (C. F. Muller, 2001), p. 125, considers an illogical division of the contract as valid and it leaves it to the parties to suffer the consequences that may arise therefrom, whereas Jan Kropholler, *Internationales Privatrecht* 6th edn (Mohr Siebeck, 2006), p. 462, considers the feasibility of the severability as an assumption of a valid partial choice of law.

[16] The rule of severability in Article 3.1 is often not commented upon particularly at length; see, for example, P. A. Nielsen, *International privat- og procesret* (Jurist- og økonomiforbundets forlag, 1997), p. 500. The Trier Academy of European Law's database on the Rome Convention does not show a particular flourishing of cases on severability; see www.rome-convention.org/cgi-bin/search.cgi. For a reference to some German cases, see Ulrich Magnus, *Staudingers Kommentarzum Bürgerlichen Gesetzbuch mit Einführungsgesetz und Nebegesetzen* (Sellier de Gruyter, 2002), Einleitung zu, §§ 27ff EGBGB, §§ 27–33 EGBGB etc., 2002, § 27, notes 90ff. Severability is a well-known phenomenon within private international law, even beyond the European systems; see, for example, in respect of the US, W. Reese, 'Dépecage: A Common Phenomenon in Choice of Law', (1973) 73 *Columbia Law* Review 58, as well as, emphasising the advisability of avoiding unnecessary splitting of the contract, Eugene Scoles, Peter Hay, Patrick Borchers and Symeon Symeonides, *Conflict of Laws*, 4th edn (Thomson West, 2004), para 18.39.

[17] Mario Giuliano and Paul Lagarde, Report on the Convention on the Law Applicable to Contractual Obligations, 1980 OJ C 282, ('Giuliano–Lagarde Report') pp. 1–50, comment to Article 3, paragraph 4. For an extensive analysis and references, see Martin Windmöller, *Die Vertragsspaltung im internationalen Privatrecht des EGBGB und des EGVVG* (Nomos, 2000).

indexing clauses.[18] For each of these severable parts of the contract, the parties may choose a different governing law. Another matter is whether severing the contract is always meaningful: the choice of a legal system for the liability for breach of contract and of another system for the measure of the reimbursable damages, for example, might lead to the unfortunate combination of a strict liability from one system, with reimbursable damages calculated on the basis of generous criteria from another system. The systems that operate with strict liability usually mitigate the harsh effects of such a wide basis for liability by restricting the reimbursable damages to what is reasonably to be expected according to the normal course of events.[19] The systems that make liability follow negligence, on the contrary, usually extend the reimbursable damages to the actual loss, also including indirect damages.[20] Combining these two systems would result in a very wide (or, as the case may be, very narrow) liability, which is not necessarily a desirable result.

Once it has been established that the parties can, in principle, separate a certain clause or a certain part of the contract and subject it to a different governing law, it must be pointed out that this process may even take place implicitly. If the parties are allowed to exercise their party autonomy for part of the contract, they are allowed to do so in accordance with the form requirements that are generally applicable to party autonomy, and party autonomy may be exercised expressly or tacitly. Therefore, a partial choice of law may also be made both expressly and tacitly. The criteria that must be met in order to have a valid tacit choice of law will be analysed below.

2.2.4 Drafting style as a tacit choice of law?

The previous section considered the situation of a contract containing a choice-of-law clause in favour of a civilian law, but containing one or more clauses obviously inspired by the common law and that do not have legal effects under the chosen civilian law. The question was raised as to whether it may be possible to assume that the parties have made a tacit choice of law for those particular clauses.

The possible relevance of a tacit choice of law becomes even clearer if the contract does not contain any expressed choice of law. Lacking a choice of law by the parties, the general rule is that the governing law is identified on the basis of the applicable default conflict law rule. In respect of contracts, the applicable choice-of-law rule is contained in Article 4 of the Rome I Regulation, and this will be analysed in Section 3.2 below. However, the alternative conflict rule becomes applicable when *a choice*

---

[18] For a list of clauses that have been considered as severable, see J. Kondring, "'Der Vertrag ist das Recht der Parteien' – Zur Verwirklinchung des Parteiwillens durch nachträgliche Teilrechtswahl', (2006) 5 *Praxis des Internationalen Privat- und Verfahrensrechts*, 428.

[19] See, for example, English law: Jack Beatson, Andrew Burrows and John Cartwright, *Anson's Law of Contract*, 29th edn (Oxford University Press, 2010), p. 539f. and Ed Peel, *Treitel on the Law of Contract* 13th edn (Sweet & Maxwell, 2011), para 20–94ff.

[20] See, for example, German law, § 280ff. of the BGB.

made by the parties is lacking, rather than an *expressed* choice made by the parties. The parties are, according to Article 3, first paragraph of the Rome I Regulation, also free to make their choice of law tacitly. Could the circumstance that the parties adopted a common law drafting style be deemed as a tacit choice of law? In other words, can the parties be deemed to have made an implied choice of law in favour of the original law under which the model was developed, rather than being deemed not to have made any choice?

The wording of Article 3 of the Rome I Regulation makes it clear that a tacit choice of law, to be considered as valid, has to appear as an actual choice made by the parties, even if not expressed: 'The choice shall be made expressly or clearly demonstrated by the terms of the contract or the circumstances of the case'. This wording corresponds broadly to the wording of the regulation's predecessor, the Rome Convention, which, in Article 3, said: 'The choice must be expressed or demonstrated with reasonable certainty by the terms of the contract or the circumstances of the case'. The slight change in wording (from 'demonstrated with reasonable certainty' to 'clearly demonstrated') has the effect of enhancing the requirement that the choice must have actually been made by the parties and cannot be inferred out of what could seem to be a reasonable decision on a hypothetical basis. Among other things, this means that the theory of the hypothetical choice of law, that was to be found prior to the Rome Convention, for example, in German private international law, is not applicable any more.[21] It is, therefore, not sufficient to argue that the parties (or reasonable persons under the same conditions as the parties) would have made a certain choice of law if they had considered the question. A hypothetical choice of law may be a reasonable solution to the question of the governing law, but it is not allowed under the wording and the spirit of Article 3, which requires evidence that the parties have actually considered the question and have made a real choice in favour of a specific law. This actual choice of law does not need to be expressed in words and it is sufficient that it is clear from the terms of the contract or other circumstances. Implying from the circumstances a choice of law actually made by the parties, however, is quite different from determining what would be a reasonable choice under those circumstances.

Among the examples of tacit choice that the Giuliano–Lagarde Report on the Rome Convention made is the case of a specific contract form that is known for having been written under a specific governing law, such as the Lloyd's policy of marine insurance developed under English law.[22] By applying this contract form, the parties may be deemed to have tacitly chosen English law.

The case of an identifiable contract form knowingly written under a certain law is quite different from the case of a contract inspired by a more generalised way of

---

[21] See the Giuliano–Lagarde Report, comment on Article 3, paragraph 3, and Magnus, *Staudingers Kommentar*, Article 27, notes 60ff. with further references.
[22] Giuliano–Lagarde Report.

drafting agreements and resulting in a patchwork of a plurality of sources such as international standards, international commercial publications, research databases and experience from previous transactions in a variety of countries etc. As was seen in Section 2.2.1 above, the practice of general commercial contracts such as agency, distribution, sale, commercial cooperation, etc., falls within the latter description. This means, first, that the model upon which the contract is based may be difficult or impossible to determine. Second, even the legal system(s) under which the model was developed cannot be evidently identifiable. While it is clear that these contracts are inspired by the common law, it is usually not at all justified to automatically assume that the original legal system is the English, rather than the US, the Australian or any other system of common law. Even if they belong to the same legal family, there may be considerable differences between the contract laws of, for example, England and the US. If the state law under which the specific contract was developed is not identifiable, or if there is no international usage to subject that specific model to a specific law, the interpreter is left without specific rules on the interpretation of contracts, on contractual remedies and on duties between the parties, etc., that can be applied to the contract. A generic reference to the common law tradition would not be of much help.

A specific state law as a system of origin is usually not identifiable in the commercial contracts drafted as described above, and this would be sufficient to exclude that an actual choice of law may be deemed to have been demonstrated with reasonable certainty, as the Rome Convention requires, and even more so, it would exclude that an actual choice of law is deemed as having been clearly demonstrated, as the Rome I Regulation requires. In addition, the identification of an inspiring system of origin for the contract is usually impossible when inter-national contracts are negotiated by lawyers belonging to different legal systems (neither of which necessarily belongs to the common law family) and on the basis of their own respective international experience and documentation. Even assuming that the first draft presented by one party was developed under a specific legal system (which is not necessarily usual), the origin of that draft is not necessarily known to the other party, and is generally lost during the negotiations, after each of the parties has added to and modified the clauses of the first draft in several rounds. The final text coming out of this process can hardly be said to permit an interpreter to imply with reasonable certainty that the parties actually wanted to choose for their contract the law under which the first draft was originally developed (if any).

The simple fact that the contract is written in English and follows the common law drafting technique, therefore, is not sufficient to identify with certainty the law under which the contract was developed; choosing English or US law as the most representative or well-known laws within that legal family would be totally arbi-trary, and trying to apply a common denominator that is shared by a majority of common law systems would be (very vague and) against the rule of Article 3 of the Rome I Regulation and its predecessor, the Rome Convention, which assume a clear choice of the law of a specific state.[23]

If the parties have inserted in the contract a clause expressly choosing the governing law, it is even more difficult to consider the legal drafting technique as a tacit choice of law. The interpreter would, in this case, deem the parties to have tacitly derogated from an expressed clause that they have willingly inserted in their contract. If at all feasible, such reasoning could be made at best by using the principle of severability of the contract: the expressed choice of law would have to be considered as fully effective and the chosen law would govern the interpretation of the contract, the contractual remedies etc.; to the extent that a specific clause or part of the contract is not capable of having effects under the chosen law, but has effects under the original law of the contract model, the interpreter may see whether it is possible to sever that part of the contract and subject it to the original law. This process, however, would assume that the requirements for a tacit choice are met; therefore, it must be possible to affirm that the parties have intended to render the law of a specific state applicable to that particular part of the contract. The simple fact that part of the contract would not be effective under the expressly chosen law does not seem to be sufficient evidence of an actual will of the parties to (tacitly) choose the other law.

The outcome of the analysis will be different if the contract contains (not choice of, but) specific references to a certain legal system (such as when the scope of liability is defined by reference to a certain statutory provision), or if it applies a standard model that was unequivocally developed under a specific system of law. Standard contracts of this type are applied in specific branches, such as charter parties or marine insurance policies, but are not usual in general commercial practice.

It could be envisaged that the parties to a contract included a clause that had a specific legal effect under a certain law, different from the law governing the contract. The parties may have intended the clause to have the effect that it has under that law. In this case, the clause can be given the effect that it has under that law; however, this is based on the common intention of the parties to obtain that particular result, and not on a tacit choice of law.[24]

---

[23] One of the drafts for the Rome I Regulation, 'Proposal for a Regulation of the European Parliament and the Council on the law applicable to contractual obligations: Rome I', COM (2005) 650 final, permitted a contract to be subject to published restatements of international principles, such as the UNIDROIT Principles of International Commercial Contracts, the Principles of European Contract Law or the Common Frame of Reference currently under preparation. The draft Regulation excluded general principles belonging to the *lex mercatoria* to be chosen as a governing law. The inclusion of international principles contained in the draft Regulation was so controversial that it is not reflected in the final text of the Regulation. General principles belonging to the common law would, in any case, not have qualified for either of these categories, and would therefore not have been allowed according to the draft Regulation.

[24] See Gerhard Dannemann, 'Common Law Based Contracts under German law', in Giuditta Cordero-Moss (ed.), *Boilerplate Clauses, International Commercial Contracts and the Applicable Law* (Cambridge University Press, 2011), pp. 62–79, 69ff.

2.2.5 Drafting style as the closest connection?

If the parties have not expressed a choice of law, the governing law will be chosen applying the connecting factor contained in the applicable conflict rule. In the Rome I Regulation, Article 4 provides a series of connecting factors, one for each contract type, mainly based on the general connecting factor of the habitual residence of the party making the characteristic performance. Paragraph 3 of Article 4 contains an exception: 'Where it is clear from all the circumstances of the case that the contract is manifestly more closely connected with a country other than that indicated in paragraphs 1 or 2, the law of that other country shall apply'. It is, therefore, legitimate to investigate whether the drafting style of the contract may be considered as a circumstance that renders the contract manifestly more closely connected with the country whose law has inspired the drafting.

The answer must be negative. Not only does the style not give sufficiently precise indications to enable the determination of a specific legal system, as mentioned in Section 2.2.4 above, but even the history of Article 4 shows that the criterion of the closest connection must be applied very cautiously. As will be explained more in detail in section 3.2 below, Article 4 of the Rome I Regulation has modified the structure of its predecessor, Article 4 of the Rome Convention. This modification was made with the purpose of clarifying that the choice of law shall be made on the basis of general connecting factors (of which the most important is the residence of the party making the characteristic performance), and that the closest connection represents an exception that must be applied restrictively. The wording used to qualify what circumstances trigger the application of the closest connection shows the exceptionality of the application, in that it requires that the closest connection needs to be 'manifest'. The corresponding wording in Article 4.5 of the Rome Convention was 'if it appears from the circumstances as a whole that the contract is more closely connected'. Permitting the evaluation of such a loose factor as the language of the contract or its legal style would deprive the choice of law of this predictability – particularly considering that these factors are not sufficiently precise to qualify as a tacit choice of law, as was seen in section 2.2.4 above.

In conclusion, the legal style in which the contract is written does not seem to be a relevant criterion in the assessment of which country the contract has its closest connection with.

2.2.6 Conclusion

From the foregoing text it seems possible to conclude that the drafting style, legal technique and language of a contract as such are not sufficient bases for a tacit choice of law (total or partial) or as a circumstance showing the closest connection.

From the point of view of private international law, therefore, an international commercial contract will be governed by and interpreted in accordance with the governing law that is (expressly or tacitly, but with clarity) chosen by the parties, or, when lacking such a choice by the parties, with the law of the country where the party making the characteristic performance has its residence. If the governing law belongs to a civilian system, the contract will be interpreted according to the legal tradition of that law, and its clauses will have the effects that follow from the general principles and rules of that law, even if this may create some discrepancies with the interpretation and effects that the same contract would have if it was governed by a law belonging to the common law tradition.

Discrepancies in the interpretation of the contract may possibly be avoided if a certain contract clause has received a certain interpretation so consistently that the interpretation can be deemed to have become a trade usage: in such cases, however, the discrepancies between the civilian governing law and the common law inspiration will be avoided not because the contract is interpreted according to the common law, but because it is interpreted according to generally recognised trade usages.

2.3 Choosing transnational law?

The parties may choose any foreign law or a plurality of foreign laws to govern their transaction, if the applicable rule of party autonomy permits them to do so. Similarly, the parties may choose to subject their transaction to transnational law, as long as this is within the limit of party autonomy recognised by the private international law of the forum. Choosing transnational law as the governing law may be made in many ways, for instance, by expressly choosing a certain source, such as the already analysed UPICC or the UCP 600. Alternatively, the parties may make reference to no specific source, and simply may refer to generally recognised principles in international trade or some similar language indicating the intention of the parties to exclude the application of a state law.

As seen in Chapter 2, Section 6.1, however, this does not necessarily mean that the chosen transnational law replaces the applicable law in governing the contract. The Rome I Regulation excludes that the parties may select, to govern their contract, sets of rules that are not national laws (with an exception for possible future European instruments of contract law).[25] Thus, transnational sources may be incorporated into the contract by the parties and supplement the governing law, but may not be selected to govern the contract to the exclusion of any national law. The situation appears to be different when the dispute is subject to arbitration: some arbitration laws and rules of arbitration institutions permit the parties to choose 'rules of law' to govern the dispute. As will be seen in Chapter 5,

---

[25] Council Regulation 593/2008, Article 3. The Preamble, in item 13, confirms that nothing prevents the parties from incorporating into the contract transnational instruments of soft law; as a consequence of such incorporation, however, the soft law is given the status of a term of contract, not of governing law. See also Roy Goode, Herbert Kronke and Ewan McKendrick, *Transnational Commercial Law*–Texts, Cases and Materials (Oxford University Press, 2007), pp. 515ff.

Section 3.5.3, the use of these words, as opposed to the power of the arbitral tribunal to choose the 'law' governing the dispute in cases where the parties have not made a choice, is sometimes interpreted so as to permit the parties to choose rules that do not belong to a state law, but to sources that may be defined as transnational.

There is, therefore, an apparent difference in the possibility of choosing the transnational law to govern a contract, depending on whether the dispute is decided by courts of law or by arbitral tribunals. In reality, however, there does not need to be a significant difference. As Chapter 2 Section 4 has shown, it is not unlikely that transnational sources, even though they are formally capable of governing a contract when the dispute is decided in arbitration, in the end will need the support of a national law – because the transnational principles are not sufficiently precise, because of gaps or otherwise.

Moreover, as soon as the scope of party autonomy is restricted by other conflict rules (as we will see in Chapter 4, Section 4), the choice of a transnational law will be affected accordingly.

3 What if the parties have not chosen the governing law?

International contracts very often contain a clause on choice of law, as we have seen above. Sometimes, however, the parties do not exercise their party autonomy. There may be various reasons for the parties' failure to choose the governing law: either the parties have not managed to reach an agreement on what law should be applicable to their contract (for example, because each party insists on the application of its own law), or the contract is very simple and does not contain regulation of matters other than the mere commercial terms, or the parties have forgotten or have not deemed it necessary or desirable to make a choice of law. In this situation, it is not apparent from the face of the contract what law is governing. However, we have seen in Chapters 2 and 3 above that an international contract is always, ultimately, governed by a state law. How can the governing law be determined? The next sections will illustrate the reasoning necessary to identify the governing law.

3.1 First step: determination of the forum

As already mentioned, the governing law is determined by conflict rules; conflict rules may vary from state to state. Therefore, the first step that has to be made in the process of determining the governing law is to find out what conflict rules are applicable. The applicable conflict rules are those of the *lex fori*. Therefore, it will be necessary to determine what the forum is, or what the forum would be, in case of a dispute.

The forum is the court of a state that accepts jurisdiction for the case. In the EU, jurisdiction in civil and commercial matters is determined by the Brussels Council

Regulation on Jurisdiction and the Recognition and Enforcement of Judgements in Civil and Commercial Matters (Brussels I; 44/2001), which replaces the Brussels Convention of 1968 and is directly applicable in the EU, and the parallel Lugano Convention of 2007 (originally of 1988), ratified by the EU, Denmark, Iceland, Norway and Switzerland.[26] As from 2015, the Brussels I Regulation will be replaced by a new version (15/2012), and it is expected that the Lugano Convention will be revised correspondingly.

If there are no conventions or supranational regulations on jurisdiction, the jurisdiction is regulated by the civil procedure law of each state. The rules on jurisdiction, therefore, may vary from state to state: some rules might be very expansive, thus permitting the exercise of jurisdiction on a very slim basis (the so-called exorbitant forum), while other rules are more restrictive and permit the exercise of jurisdiction only if there is a serious connection between the dispute and the state where the legal suit is filed. As a general rule, a court will have jurisdiction if the defendant is resident in that state.[27] However, there might be alternative fora, such as the place where the disputed obligation had to be performed.[28] Additionally, there might be exclusive fora, such as the court of the place where a piece of real estate is registered, if the dispute regards property rights on that estate.[29]

Therefore, there might be more than one potential forum; this means that there might be more potentially applicable conflict rules. In this case, it is advisable to verify the conflict rules of each of the potential fora to see if they point at the same governing law or at different laws. In the latter case, it will be advisable to verify the content of all of the substantive laws that are pointed at by the different conflict rules in the potential fora. One substantive law might be more favourable to a party, and that party might therefore want to file a suit in the state whose *lex fori* contains the conflict rule that points at that governing law. This is called forum shopping, and is a practice that might bring very favourable results to the party that exercises it. This practice has the detrimental general effect of creating uncertainty in the application of the law, because a party may run the risk of being sued in various different states, perhaps even without a real connection with the subject matter. In order to prevent this detrimental result and to facilitate the exercise of cross-border justice, bilateral treaties, regional conventions or international conventions are being drafted and

---

[26] Denmark, as a consequence of its reservations in connection with the Amsterdam Treaty of 1997 on the Union, does not participate in the acts of the European Community based on Title IV of the Treaty. The Brussels Regulation is based on Article 65 of the Treaty, which is contained in Title IV, and therefore the Brussels Regulation does not apply to Denmark: see the preamble of the Regulation, item (21). Following a separate agreement between Denmark and the EU, as per 1 July 2007, the Brussels I Regulation also applies to Denmark. In addition, Great Britain and Ireland do not participate in the acts based on Title IV of the Treaty, but they have the possibility to do so, if they so elect. In the case of the Brussels Regulation, Great Britain and Ireland opted in, and the Regulation is therefore applicable to them: see the preamble, item 20.

[27] See, for example, the Brussels I Regulation and the Lugano Convention, Article 2.

[28] See, for example, the Brussels I Regulation and Lugano Convention, Article 5.1.

[29] See, for example, the Brussels I Regulation and Lugano Convention, Article 22(1).

ratified for the purpose of clarifying which courts have jurisdiction and to exclude the jurisdiction of exorbitant fora. The most notable examples of such instruments are the already mentioned Brussels I Regulation and the Lugano Convention.

To summarise very briefly the rules of Brussels I in respect of the forum for disputes relating to international contracts, we will have to look at Articles 2, 5.1 and 23 of the Convention. Article 2 is the general rule, and provides for jurisdiction of the courts in the state where the defendant is domiciled. Article 5.1 provides for an alternative forum: the forum of the place of performance of the obligation in question (Article 5.1(a) of the Regulation). The Brussels Regulation and the new Lugano Convention define in Article 5.1(b) the place of performance as the place of delivery of goods (if the dispute is based on a sale contract) or the place where the services are to be rendered (if the dispute is based on a service contract). This definition is not exempt from interpretative problems. Article 5.1(c) refers to the general rule of Article 5.1(a), for the eventuality that the rule under 5.1(b) is not applicable (for example, in joint venture agreements there is no delivery of goods or rendering of services, and in licence or agency agreements having a territory that covers more than one state, it might be difficult to choose one particular state) or if the application of 5.1(b) would point to a state that is outside of the EU.

Article 23 permits the parties to agree on the forum that will have jurisdiction (and the choice of forum in the contract is certainly the most preferable alternative to avoid uncertainties).

Often, commercial contracts contain a clause designating the forum for the disputes arising out of the contract. If a contract contains a choice of forum deter-mining the jurisdiction of the courts in a certain country, those courts will have jurisdiction. According to the wording of the choice-of-forum clause, those courts may have exclusive jurisdiction or not. If the clause specifies that the jurisdiction is exclusive, then no other courts may be seized with disputes arising out of the contract (there are some exceptions to this rule, for example, in the case of preliminary measures such as injunctions, as well as in cases where a national law prescribes the exclusive jurisdiction of its courts, for example, for disputes relating to real estate, company matters, privatisation etc.). If the clause does not specify that the chosen forum has exclusive jurisdiction, in some countries, this will mean that a party sued in the chosen court cannot object to that jurisdiction, but neither party is prevented from initiating a proceeding in another court which has jurisdiction according to the applicable private international law. Article 25 of the Brussels I recast, that will enter into force as from 2015, specifies that the choice of forum is deemed to give exclusive jurisdiction to the chosen court.

The main risks of submitting to the jurisdiction of the courts in a foreign country are evident if the local legal system is not founded on the rule of law, is not transparent or stable, or is corrupt. The transaction will be exposed to the effects of a court decision that may have been rendered as a consequence of undue influence, or on the basis of laws that have been retroactively changed or as a consequence of an inaccurate or unfair proceeding.

When considering which court to choose for the disputes arising out of a commercial contract, it is important to have regard to the enforceability of a decision rendered by the chosen court. A decision rendered by a court will be enforceable domestically in accordance with the local legislation, and the losing party will be liable with all its assets that are present on the local territory, also including future assets and future income from business activity. This liability may possibly be restricted by carrying out activity through various separate companies. In principle, each company is a separate legal entity and the assets of one company may not be attached for enforcing a court decision rendered against another company, for example a subsidiary, the parent company or an affiliate belonging to the same group of companies. However, some systems have various criteria for piercing the corporate veil, so that, according to the local rules of civil procedure, the assets of another company in the same group may well be seized to satisfy the credits against the losing party. This possibility is generally excluded in Europe, but it is not unknown in other jurisdictions. A growing trend[30] is to explore the possibilities of holding the parent company responsible (and sue it at its place of business) for its foreign subsidiary's breach of human rights or of environmental legislation: so-called direct foreign liability.[31] The United Nations have established a Special Representative for the Secretary-General on the issue of human rights and transnational corporations and other business enterprises, and adopted, in 2011, the 'Guiding Principles on Business and Human Rights: Implementing the United Nations "Protect, Respect and Remedy" Framework'.[32] The Organization for Security and Co-operation in Europe (OCSE) issued Guidelines for multinational enterprises.[33] Questions of international jurisdiction connected with the matters are addressed in the Guidelines adopted by the International Law Association in 2012.[34]

If a decision was rendered in a local court and the losing party does not have sufficient assets (not even future cash flow) in that country, the winning party may seek to enforce the decision in another country where that company has assets.

Lacking an instrument such as the Brussels I Regulation or the Lugano Convention, enforcement will depend on the civil procedure legislation prevailing in the

---

[30] See Katinka Jesse and Jonathan Verschuuren, 'Litigating against International Business Corporations for their Actions Abroad: Recent Environmental Cases from the Netherlands', (2011) Tilburg Law School Legal Studies Research Paper Series No. 12, papers.ssrn.com/sol3/papers.cfm?abstract_id=1773165

[31] See, for example, the Norwegian Supreme Court decision Rt. 2010 p. 306.

[32] www.ohchr.org/Documents/Publications/GuidingPrinciplesBusinessHR_EN.pdf.

[33] www.oecd.org/daf/internationalinvestment/guidelinesformultinationalenter-prises/oecdguidelinesformulti-nationalenterprises.htm.

[34] International Law Association, Resolution 2012, International civil litigation and the interests of the public, www.ila-hq.org/download.cfm/docid/F784A3AA-7030-433D-96833C48F941FB28. See also the Committee's report: International Law Association, Final Report: International Civil Litigation for Human Rights Violations, (2012), www.ila-hq.org/download.cfm/docid/D7AFA4C8-E599-40FE-B6918B239B949698.

country where enforcement is sought. Some countries enforce foreign court decisions after a relatively easy procedure, similar to the enforcement of arbitral awards described in Chapter 5. Other countries request that their courts review the merits of the foreign decision before it is enforced. Yet other countries do not attach any legal effects to foreign court decisions. In order to assess the enforceability of foreign court decisions in third countries where the losing party has assets (also including income from an activity), it will be necessary to evaluate the civil procedure legislation in each of these countries. The assessment will have to extend to the possibility of piercing the corporate veil, so that the legislation in all countries where the losing party or other companies of the group have assets will have to be considered.

In addition to the internal civil procedure of each country where the losing party and any affiliates have assets or income, it will be necessary to assess whether bilateral or multilateral treaties exist between the country where the court decision was issued and another country where the losing party or any of its affiliates has assets. These treaties may grant to foreign court decisions an enforceability similar to that granted to arbitral awards under the New York Convention, as described in Chapter 5. The most notable treaties of this kind are within the EU and the EFTA area; however, it cannot be excluded that other regions have similar arrangements. It is also quite common to have similar treaties on a bilateral basis. Therefore, a careful assessment of this aspect is necessary.

Finally, it is necessary to mention that in the year 2005, The Hague Convention on Choice of Court Agreements was signed. The Convention has not yet entered into force; when it does enter into force, it will grant, among the countries that will have ratified it, the enforceability of the respective court decisions, if they were rendered on the basis of a choice-of-forum clause made by the parties.

If a contract does not contain a choice-of-forum clause, the question of which courts have jurisdiction will be regulated by the private international law prevailing in each country where a party may try to sue the other party. This may create significant uncertainties, since the private international law may vary from country to country. Generally, a party may always be sued in the country where it is registered or where it carries out its main activity. In the case of a contract between a Norwegian and a Russian company, for example, this means that the courts of Norway would have jurisdiction if the Norwegian company is sued, and the Russian courts would have jurisdiction if the other party is sued. In addition, it is usually possible to sue a contractual party in the country where the main performance is supposed to be undertaken. In addition, the courts of countries that have a certain connection with the transaction may retain jurisdiction. In some cases, courts operate with what is called exorbitant jurisdiction; that is, they accept hearing a dispute, even if the connection with the defendant or the dispute is very distant (for example, if the defendant has one employee in that country, or if it has assets in that country, even if they are of very little value and have no connection to the disputed matter).

In practice, failure to choose the forum is likely to lead to one party suing the other party in its own country. However, it cannot be excluded that a party might have to defend itself in other jurisdictions. In addition, the lack of a choice-of-forum clause might lead to one party filing strategic suits in its own or in other countries to prevent or oppose suits that the other party might have filed against it.

This may create a considerable uncertainty and costly proceedings to ascertain the jurisdiction or to oppose conflicting decisions on the same subject matter.

This is one of the reasons why it is desirable to harmonise conflict rules: if all private international laws of the potential fora have harmonised conflict rules, they will all point to the same governing law. The dispute, therefore, will be decided according to the same law, irrespective of where the suit was filed. This eliminates the most important incentive for forum shopping; namely, the possibility of influencing the selection of the governing law by choosing from among different countries' conflict rules.

3.1.1 Exorbitant jurisdiction

An interesting example of forum shopping and exorbitant jurisdiction is the *Yukos* case. In addition, the *Yukos* case is a good example of an unsuccessful attempt to make public international law relevant even in disputes that apparently do not have a public international law dimension.

Yukos was a Russian oil company which, through active participation in the privatisation process during the 90s, became one of the most important corporations in Russia. In late 2003, Yukos came under investigation for (among other things) tax evasion, and the company's principal owner and chairman, Mikhail Chordorkowskji, was arrested. The media reported extensively on how these measures could be understood as a possible reaction by the Russian President to Chodorkowskji's political ambitions. Be that as it may, the public prosecutor's office submitted detailed accusations against Yukos, the fiscal authorities demanded substantial payments of back taxes, and the courts confirmed these claims and ordered enforcement amounting to several billion euros. The court-ordered auction of Yukos subsidiary Yuganskneftegaz, the company's largest manufacturing company, was announced for 19 December 2004. The national (semi-privatised) company Gasprom planned to participate in the auction with financing from a consortium of banks led by Deutsche Bank. Yuganskneftegaz was auctioned off to a previously unknown buyer, a company called Baikal, for a price Yukos claimed was considerably lower than its value. Shortly thereafter, Baikal was taken over by the state company Rosneft. Yukos maintained that nationalisation took place without sufficient compensation.

Several avenues were taken by Yukos and its shareholders in order to react to the situation.

Various groups of Yukos shareholders initiated investment arbitration proceedings against the Russian Federation on the basis of bilateral investment agreements between their respective home countries and Russia, claiming that their investment had been expropriated illegally and without compensation.[35] The most important proceeding was initiated under the Energy Charter Treaty and is still pending.[36]

Yukos itself (before it was liquidated) brought a claim against the Russian Federation before the European Court of Human Rights. The Court accepted jurisdiction for some claims and dismissed it for others, and resolved that Yukos had been denied fair trial by the Russian authorities. Allegations that the exercise of the state's tax power was not legitimate, but politically motivated, were rejected.[37]

From the point of view of international civil jurisdiction and exorbitant fora, a very interesting aftermath of the *Yukos* case was an action brought before the court of Houston, Texas.

A few days before the scheduled auction of its assets, on 14 December 2004, Yukos sought in Houston, Texas, protection from creditors according to Chapter 11 of the US Bankruptcy Code. This is a measure intended to freeze any actions that any creditors may have against the debtor in order to permit the debtor to reorganise its activity and restructure its debt. The Houston court issued a temporary order[38] preventing any auction regarding Yukos' assets from taking place and any party from financing participation in such auction for ten days (the auction was due five days after the application for protection). Deutsche Bank participated in the proceedings, objecting to the Houston court's jurisdiction in the case. The Russian Federation did not take part in the proceedings.

Yukos did not carry out any business activity in the US. Almost all of its assets and business were located in Russia. The debts that were to be recovered through the auction were matured in Russia in respect of Russian taxes imposed on income generated in Russia. The connection between Yukos and Houston consisted of the fact that the financial director of the company had fled the country and been living in Houston since the dramatic arrest of Yukos's main shareholder, Chodorkowskji, a few days earlier. Moreover, Yukos established a subsidiary in Houston on the same day on which it filed for insolvency protection there. In addition, Yukos opened a bank account in the name of this new US subsidiary just a few hours before filing for insolvency protection, transferring US$ 480,000 from abroad into the account in order to cover lawyers' fees. Yukos later opened an additional bank account in Houston.

As already mentioned, some systems permit their courts to take jurisdiction even on the basis of a very fragile connection: the so-called exorbitant fora. This is detrimental to legal certainty, and has been restricted, for example, by the Brussels and Lugano Conventions and the Brussels I Regulation. The jurisdiction of the Houston court in the Yukos case would without a doubt qualify as an exorbitant forum. Fighting against the jurisdiction of the Houston court, Deutsche Bank argued

---

[35] *Renta 4 SVSA et al.* v. *Russian Federation*, SCC case no. 024/2007; *RosInvest Co UK Ltd* v. *Russian Federation*, SCC case nos 079/2005 and 075/2009. The *RosInvest* award was set aside for lack of jurisdiction by the Stockholm District Court on 9 November 2011 (case no. T 24891-07).

[36] An award on jurisdiction was rendered on 30 November 2009.

[37] Case no 5829/04 of 31 May 2011.   [38] No 04-3952.

that exorbitant fora are restricted by public international law even in the absence of treaty rules specifically addressing the question.

We will consider here the question of the exorbitant jurisdiction in civil cases, particularly the aspect of the possible dimension for public international law.

Court jurisdiction in civil cases is traditionally seen as a question of private international law or of conflict of laws, and it may therefore seem surprising that we focus on its public international law aspects.

We will not analyse the details of the *Yukos* case and we will not delve into the technical aspects of international insolvency law. Our attention is directed solely at the intersection between private and public international law in respect of international court jurisdiction. From the particular perspective taken here, it is possible to generalise the observations made in this insolvency case so as to address the wider question of jurisdiction in civil and commercial cases.

3.1.1.1 The legal question of exorbitant jurisdiction

The obvious question regarding this case is, why Houston?[39] How can a national court be competent for a company's insolvency when virtually all of the company's business, assets and creditors, as well as company headquarters, are located in another state? As this is not an essay on US insolvency law, it is sufficient to refer to the decision rendered by the court in the *Yukos* case: § 109(a) of the United States Bankruptcy Code holds a US court competent when the debtor carries out activity or has assets in the US. Judicial practice has repeatedly affirmed that, in this context, even very small sums are considered as 'assets', and that the existence of a single employee counts as 'activity'. The court therefore had no objections in considering itself territorially competent for Yukos' insolvency, as the company had a bank account with US$ 480,000 for legal costs.[40] The court ultimately dismissed the application, as we will see below, but not for a lack of sufficient connection between the facts of the case and the forum.

This can be seen as an example of the sort of jurisdiction that is deemed exorbitant, because the circumstances of the case have no significant connection with the place of the court.

3.1.1.2 The regulation of international jurisdiction in civil cases

International jurisdiction of a national court is regulated by the court's own national rules of private international law. In certain contexts, such as in Europe, some aspects of international jurisdiction are regulated by conventions or supranational instruments, as was seen above. In the area of insolvency, court jurisdiction is regulated

---

[39] Yukos's goal with the insolvency procedure was above all to prevent the auction in Russia. This would have been the first step towards the commencement of an international arbitration, in which Yukos planned to settle the controversy with the Russian authorities.

[40] Memorandum Opinion, United States Bankruptcy Court for the Southern District of Texas, Houston Division, case no 04-47742-H3-11, 24 February 2005, pp. 20ff.

within the EU by the Council Regulation on Insolvency Proceedings.[41] The scope of this Regulation is limited to the EU; therefore, it does not apply to a case involving a Russian party and a US court. However, the Regulation is representative of how jurisdiction may be regulated in an international setting. Article 3 of the Insolvency Regulation determines that the main insolvency proceedings for a company with cross-border activities are to be conducted in the country where the company has the centre of its main interests (COMI). This connecting factor is also adopted in the UNCITRAL Model Law on Cross-border Insolvency of 1997. The main purpose of the COMI as a connecting factor is to avoid multiple proceedings for the same company, as well as to avoid initiating proceedings in countries with which there is no significant connection. The connecting factor serves, thus, to limit exorbitant jurisdiction. An assumption of jurisdiction as in the *Yukos* case would be impossible under either the Insolvency Regulation or the UNCITRAL Model Law.[42]

As long as international jurisdiction is regulated by national private international law, the danger exists that the respective domestic conflict rules are not coordinated with one another, and that therefore courts in several countries will consider themselves as competent for the same proceeding. This lack of coordination does not necessarily depend on the too extensive scope of exorbitant jurisdiction. It is easy to imagine situations in which several real connecting factors concur; for example, in civil or commercial matters, the place of performance of the obligation and the domicile of the defendant. In these cases, but even more clearly in cases of exorbitant jurisdiction, where there is no real connection between the case and the court, the need for coordinating the respective international jurisdictions becomes evident. For the sake of completeness, it should be mentioned that, while the US is notorious for its inclination towards assuming exorbitant jurisdiction, it is by no means alone in this regard. Exorbitant jurisdiction is found in the Austrian Civil Code[43] as well as in the Norwegian Code,[44] to name just two countries that have found themselves on the blacklists of the Brussels I Regulation and the Lugano Convention. Within Europe, this is limited and coordinated at a supranational level by the above-mentioned instruments. Outside the scope of application of these instruments, however, if no international conventions or supranational instruments exist, exorbitant fora are again applicable. If international *lis pendens* is not regulated by the countries' respective domestic private international law, this can lead to contradictory decisions regarding the same facts.

---

[41] No. 1346/2000.

[42] Another matter is that the connecting factor does not necessarily provide a clear solution, as demonstrated by the *Parmalat Eurofood* case, wherein the main question is whether the main interests of a company are to be determined in respect of the subsidiary or of the parent company: Case C-341/04, www.curia.eu.int/

[43] Article 99 Jurisdiction Norm: A patrimonial claim may be presented in the place where the defendant has some assets.

[44] In the old Civil Procedure Act, Article 32 tvml. In the new version, this basis of jurisdiction is no longer so absolutely expressed.

The only possible reaction to this situation is to refuse the acknowledgement and enforcement of foreign decisions. This is possible because court decisions, in the absence of an international convention or specific domestic regulation, have no legal effects in states other than the state where they were rendered. Thus, a picture emerges in which each country determines its own international jurisdiction, retaining the freedom to refuse the acknowledgement of foreign proceedings and decisions. Transnational cases are thus subject to a number of domestic systems, which are potentially not coordinated with one another.

The question to be answered reads, therefore: what legal remedies are available either to coordinate or to restrict the domestic regulation of international jurisdiction?

3.1.1.3 Restrictions under private international law

The problem of the extraterritorial effect of national laws and decisions has long been recognised, particularly in the field of economic law. This has frequently led to conflicts in the last decades. In the context of competition law, for example, national law is applied, under the *effects doctrine*, to all the effects taking place in the respective country, even if they were caused by activity that was carried out outside of that country. The legislation or decision issued in that country is aimed at preventing the foreign activity that has effects on the issuing country's own territory, but it implies that it also seeks to be applied beyond the issuing country's own national territory. The effects doctrine was developed in the US, but is now recognised in European competition law as well.[45]

This extraterritorial effect can be explained using the categories of private international law. In 1986, the Hamburg Max Planck Institute for Comparative and International Private Law organised a symposium on the extraterritorial application of economic law (*Die extraterritoriale Anwendung von Wirtschatfsrecht*), in which the problem was defined as *Wirtschaftskollisionsrecht* (international economic law)[46] and explained with concepts taken from the private international law doctrine, as *Einseitige Anknüpfung* (unilateral connection)[47] or *Eingriffsnormen* (overriding mandatory rules).[48] Incidentally, Savigny had already recognised the necessity of making an exception to the otherwise completely symmetrical system of private international

---

[45] On the legal position in the EU, see Richard Whish, *Competition Law*, 5th edn, (Lexis Nexis, 2003), pp. 436ff. On national competition legislation based on the effects doctrine, see § 6(1) of Austria's anti-trust code, § 5 of Norway's competition law, § 130(2) of Germany's anti-trust code; for detailed comments and references to the literature and legal practice, see Ulrich Immenga, Ernst Joachim Mestmäcker and Gerhard Dannecker, *GWB Gesetz gegen Wettbewerbsbeschränkungen: Kommentar* (C. H. Beck, 2001) § 130 (2) notes pp. 15ff., 220ff.

[46] Ulrich Drobnig, 'Das Profil des Wirtschaftskollisionsrechts', (1988) 52 *Rabels Zeitschrift für ausländisches und internationales Privatrecht*, 1–7, at 1ff.

[47] Jürgen Basedow, 'Wirtschaftskollisionsrecht', (1988) 52 *Rabels Zeitschrift für ausländisches und internationales Privatrecht*, 8–38, at 8ff.

[48] Kurt Siehr, 'Ausländische Eingriffsnormen im inländischen Wirtschatfskollisionsrecht', (1988) 52 *Rabels Zeitschrift für ausländisches und internationales Privatrecht* 41–102, at 41ff.

law for *zwingendes Recht* (overriding mandatory rules).[49] Under certain circumstances, and if the character of those rules requires it, legal systems may give effect to rules that do not belong to the law that is applicable according to the usual standards of private international law. This is also regulated in the Rome I Regulation, which, in Article 9, allows the application of overriding mandatory rules that belong to a law that is not applicable according to the rules of the Regulation.[50] This is a description of the phenomenon, but it provides no solution to the problems that arise out of this lack of coordination. It retains the integrity of the system of private international law, but does not represent an improvement to its weaknesses.

Mutatis mutandis, the problem of exorbitant jurisdiction can also be described within the system of private international law. Each court may retain jurisdiction under its own applicable domestic private international law, yet its decisions only have legal effect in its own territory, unless there are international instruments or specific legislation attaching legal effects to foreign decisions. In the absence of such a legislative or international 'vehicle' (such as, in respect of extraterritorial substantive law, Article 9 of the Rome I Regulation mentioned above), therefore, court decisions with extraterritorial ambitions do not have legal effects outside their own territory.

This is well understandable in the private international law system: a court decision taken in compliance with the court's own private international law but in violation of other countries' private international law need not have any legal effect in these other countries. However, this may not be enough to meet the interests of the parties involved. If a party, for example, has assets in the territory of the court that retained exorbitant jurisdiction, it is liable with those assets for any violation of that decision, even if the decision is not acknowledged in any other country. In the *Yukos* case, the corresponding scenario would be as follows: had the Houston court finally ruled that the auction in Russia could not take place, the auction could nevertheless have taken place in Russia as planned (as it actually did). A US decision could not be enforced in Russia without the acknowledgement by the Russian system. Should Deutsche Bank have decided to finance Gasprom's purchase in the auction, it would have acted validly in the Russian legal system. However, in this situation, Deutsche Bank would have violated the Houston court decision. This violation would not have had consequences in Russia, but Deutsche Bank would have been liable for it in the US with any assets that it had in the US.

Accordingly, the parties to the *Yukos* case followed different strategies. The Russian Federation applied the previously described private international law approach. Given that the facts fall under the scope of Russian law, it did not take part in the Houston proceedings, ascribing no effect to them. For the Russian Federation, such an attitude was appropriate, because the enforcement of the Houston court's decision against the Russian Federation would be regulated by Russian law on the Russian territory,

---

[49] Friedrich Carl von Savigny, *System des heutigen römischen Rechts* 8 vols. (Veit und Comp. 1849), vol. VIII, p. 33.
[50] See section 4.3.

while enforcement within the US territory of a decision against the Russian Federation did not seem plausible because of the circumstances of the case and the principle of state immunity. Deutsche Bank, on the contrary, participated in the Houston proceedings; it presented every available objection under private international law against the court's jurisdiction. However, such objections can hardly achieve success in a system favouring exorbitant jurisdiction, such as in the US. Deutsche Bank, therefore, supported its argument against the court's jurisdiction using principles found outside of the applicable domestic private international law. It argued for a dimension of public international law, which would restrict those national rules of private international law that permit exorbitant jurisdiction.

3.1.1.4 Restrictions under public international law

There seems to be a general acknowledgement that private international law is a branch of domestic law, and that public international law does not play an important role in shaping the rules of private international law.[51] Within public international law, the principles of territoriality, nationality and protection are generally deemed to constitute the borders for the effects of national law, and, consequently, also for the effects of the rules of private international law. These principles are usually interpreted so extensively that they can hardly be deemed to restrict the shaping of specific private international law rules. Thus, the above-mentioned effects doctrine in competition law could be subsumed under the protection principle, since the anti-competitive activity carried out abroad has effects within the national territory. Exorbitant jurisdiction in the *Yukos* case could be subsumed under the principle of territoriality, because Yukos had assets in the US (although of minor value) and probably performed some business activity within US territory because of its financial director's presence there in the last weeks prior to the application.

From these public international law principles, therefore, it seems difficult to derive a rule that could restrict the domestic regulation of the court's international jurisdiction in civil cases. Are there other sources for such a rule in public international law?

International jurisdiction within the European Community and the European Free Trade Association is regulated by the already mentioned Brussels I Regulation and Lugano Convention. In 1992, The Hague Conference on Private International Law also started working on a convention regarding court jurisdiction, with the aim of proposing an instrument that should be open to the whole world. The Hague Draft Convention was based on the principle that exorbitant jurisdiction is not permitted, and in Article 18, it listed a series of connecting factors that would lead to exorbitant

---

[51] For example, see Kropholler, *Internationales Privatrecht*; Michele Lupoi, *Conflitti transnazionali di giurisdizione* (Giuffrè, 2002), pp. 9ff.; Scoles, Hay, Borcher, and Symeonides, *Conflict of Laws*, p. 2. For a summary of the positions discussed in the mentioned Symposium at the Max Planck Institute, see Christoph Engel, 'Die Bedeutung des Völkerrechts für die Anwendung in- und ausländischen Wirtschaftsrechts', (1988) 52 *Rabels Zeitschrift für ausländisches und internationales Privatrecht* 271–302.

jurisdiction and were therefore excluded as a basis for jurisdiction. Had the Draft been finalised into a convention, many of the problems related to exorbitant jurisdiction would have been resolved for the contracting states. However, in June 2001, it was decided that the Draft would not become a convention, among other reasons, because some states were not willing to waive their access to exorbitant jurisdiction.[52] The Hague Conference's work continued, but its scope was limited to choice of court agreements.[53]

Are the Brussels and Lugano instruments and the failed Hague Draft Convention a sufficient basis to affirm the existence of a general principle of public international law restricting the domestic regulation of international court jurisdiction in civil cases?

The Hague Draft Convention seems to contradict the existence of such a principle. The report on the Draft clearly states that the contracting states remain free to make use of the exorbitant connecting factors, forbidden in the Convention, in cases involving parties from non-contracting states.[54] The Brussels and Lugano instruments are based on the same principle. From these sources, therefore, it seems that, in the absence of an international convention or other public international law instrument to the contrary, the domestic regulation of international court jurisdiction is not restricted. Thus, exorbitant jurisdiction in civil cases is not limited by public international law (beyond the existing instruments), as long as it remains within the extensive scope of the territoriality, nationality and protection principles.

The American Restatement (Third) of Foreign Relations Law contains a guideline for the assumption of international court jurisdiction: that the exercise of jurisdiction is reasonable.[55] What is meant by 'reasonable' is illustrated in § 421(2) with a list of alternative connecting factors.

The scope of this Restatement is not normally understood as being relevant to civil cases.[56] Professor Lowenfeld, however, who worked for a decade on the Restatement,

---

[52] www.hcch.net/index_en.php?act=events.details&year=2001&varevent=29. See also the Hague Conference on Private International Law, 'Some Reflections on the Present State of Negotiations on the Judgements Project in the Context of the Future Work Programme of the Conference', Preliminary document no. 16, February 2002, www.hcch.net/index_en.php?act=progress.listing&cat=5.

[53] The Hague Convention on Choice of Court Agreements was adopted on 30 June 2005.

[54] Peter Nygh and Fausto Pocar, *Report on the Preliminary Draft Convention on Jurisdiction and Foreign Judgments in Civil and Commercial Matters Preliminary Document No 11 of August 2000* (Hague Conference on Private International Law, 2000), pp. 78f., www.hcch.net/index_en.php?act=publications. details&pid=3494&zoek=jurisdiction

[55] § 421(1). Rather than being deemed as a proper rule of public international law, this represents an 'international climate of opinion': Andreas Lowenfeld, *International Litigation and the Quest for Reasonableness: Essays in Private International Law* (Clarendon Press, 1996), p. 60. That it is possible to formulate a principle of public international law according to which a connecting factor should be reasonable is also stated by Fritz A. Mann, *Studies in International Law* (Clarendon Press, 1973), pp. 34ff. This approach has been said to represent the basis for the already mentioned European instruments: Joseph Halpern, 'Exorbitant Jurisdiction and the Brussels Convention: Toward a Theory of Restraint', in Michael Reisman (ed.), *Jurisdiction in International Law* (Ashgate, 1999), pp. 369–87, 378f.

[56] Jurisdiction in civil cases is regulated in American Law Institute, Restatement (Second) of Conflict of Laws (1971), Chapter 3.

stresses that it does not differentiate between civil and public matters.[57] Lowenfeld states detailed arguments for the fact that the criteria of the Third Restatement are also applicable to civil cases. But he also recognises that this does not correspond with general practice and theory in the US.[58] Generally, US courts' reasoning in respect of international jurisdiction in civil cases does not appear to be concerned with the Third Restatement or public international law, but rather with the Constitution and the principle of due process provided in the XIV Amendment.[59] Reasonableness can be used as a criterion, but as a conflict-of-law criterion based not on public international law, but on domestic private international law.[60]

Even if the Third Restatement was applicable to civil cases, this would probably not change much in the above-stated considerations on the interaction between private and public international law: the public international law principles (that is, territoriality, nationality and protection principles) are so broad that they do not significantly restrict the shaping of specific rules of private international law.

Admittedly, some of the connecting factors listed in the second paragraph of § 421 can, if construed restrictively, prevent the exercise of exorbitant jurisdiction; however, if interpreted extensively, they can be used as a basis for exorbitant jurisdiction.[61] In the introductory note to § 421, it is pointed out that it is unclear whether the rules contained therein would be applicable on the basis of public international law or of private international law.[62] A restrictive interpretation would seem not to reflect the existing status of public international law, and would therefore indicate that those criteria apply on the basis of the US's own law, and could therefore not be invoked as a public international law restriction of the US rules on exorbitant jurisdiction.

3.1.1.5 The public international law dimension of the *Yukos* case

In the *Yukos* case, Deutsche Bank submitted a Legal Opinion by the highly respected Oxford professor Alan Vaughan Lowe, arguing for the existence and applicability of a rule of public international law forbidding exorbitant jurisdiction.[63] Here, we are concerned with the main lines of the reasoning and not with the specifics of the case, because

---

[57] Lowenfeld, *International Litigation*, footnote 21, pp. 18ff.   [58] *Ibid.*, p. 53, footnotes 26, 78, 80.
[59] For example, see Scoles, Hay, Borcher, Symeonides, *Conflict of Laws*, footnote 17, pp. 314, 320ff., 336ff., 492ff.
[60] Arthur Taylor von Mehren, 'Adjudicatory Jurisdiction: General Theories Compared and Evaluated', (1983) 63 *Boston University Law Review*, 279–340, describes the development of the US doctrine from a 'power theory' to a 'fairness theory'. The latter finds its basis not in international law's principle of fairness, but rather in a hope for spontaneous cooperation between the states (pp. 238ff).
[61] (i) Business activity in the territory of the state; (j) business activity outside of the territory, but affecting the territory; and (k) the presence of assets in the territory. In all these cases, a connection with the matters in dispute is required.
[62] American Law Institute, Restatement (Third) of Foreign Relations Law of the United States (1989), pp. 304f.
[63] The opinion is published in (2005) 2(3) *Transnational Dispute Management*, www.transnational-dispute-management.com.

our inquiry has to do with the general dimension of court jurisdiction under public international law rather than with the question of the jurisdiction in this specific case.

First, Lowe assesses that no rule of public international law determines jurisdiction in cases of transnational insolvency. Many international instruments move clearly in the direction of a rule based on the COMI, but this should not yet be understood as customary public international law.[64] However, a rule that Lowe considers as generally acknowledged in public international law is the rule that court jurisdiction should be based upon a very close and substantial connection between the forum state and the person, its assets or business activity.[65]

The starting point for arguing that public international law limits exorbitant jurisdiction seems to be the general principle seeking to avoid unreasonable interference with the sovereign authority of other states, which is expressed in § 403 of the Third Restatement. If US insolvency law is construed in such a way that it permits exorbitant jurisdiction to be assumed, it would violate public international law, insofar as it presents interference in foreign affairs. An extensive interpretation of the above-mentioned public international law principles regarding jurisdiction (i.e., the principles of territoriality and nationality) would, however, either exclude or justify such a violation. Such extensive interpretation would, in turn, be incompatible with the just stated public international law principle requiring a very close and substantial connection.[66] The restrictive interpretation of the public international law framework for international jurisdiction would, then, affect the interpretation of the rules under domestic international private law. Thus, the connecting factors are to be interpreted restrictively. The result of this reasoning is that public international law prevents the assumption of exorbitant jurisdiction.[67]

Even if public international law did not restrict the interpretation of national private international law in the way indicated above, according to Lowe, there would be further public international law arguments against exorbitant jurisdiction.

Lowe refers to § 403 of the Third Restatement, which states the principle of comity between nations. This applies in cases in which the exercise of exorbitant jurisdiction is permitted under public international law. In these cases, the exercise of jurisdiction should be made on the basis of a balancing of the involved interests. If the disputed

---

[64] The opinion mentions in paras. 36 to 40 the EU insolvency regulation, the IBA cross-border insolvency concord and rationale and an agreement between the USA and Canada.

[65] *Ibid.*, para. 40. This rule probably derives from the previously mentioned principles of territoriality and nationality, expressed in § 421 of the Third Restatement. As already seen, these principles are so general that they present no real limitation on the shaping of specific rules regarding jurisdiction. However, the list in § 421(2) is formulated in such a way that it could limit their scope; the classification of this section as a rule of customary public international law, however, is not uncontroversial; see above, footnote 62.

[66] If the rule requiring a close and substantial connection is derived from the principles of territoriality and nationality, however, it seems difficult to invoke this same rule as a basis for a restrictive interpretation of the principles.

[67] Paras. 55 and 68. The former paragraph refers to competence to legislate, but is also applicable to judicial decisions (*ibid.*, para. 59).

interests point predominantly to the other state, then jurisdiction should be declined. Lowe points out, however, that it is not uncontroversial as to whether the principle of the 'balancing of interests' corresponds to a mandatory rule of public international law or rather is a rule left to the national laws and to the discretion of the judge.[68]

A further argument, based on the Act-of-State doctrine, applies specifically to this case, and is less relevant to our general perspective and, thus, will not be addressed here.[69]

3.1.1.6 The decision

Yukos responded to these arguments with a Legal Opinion by Professor Barry E. Carter, stating briefly that public international law is not applicable in this case. Carter referred to the recognised US tradition regarding the extraterritorial scope of application of certain legislation, for example, in competition law and in insolvency law. Public international law is relevant only to the extent that the legislation is unclear, which is not the case with insolvency law in the context of the *Yukos* case.

The court, too, does not appear to have devoted particular attention to the arguments of public international law. Not even once do the grounds for the decision refer to the Third Restatement.[70]

The court affirmed that it had jurisdiction from a territorial point of view,[71] but eventually dismissed the application on the basis of a discretionary evaluation of the totality of circumstances.

The court started by affirming that, in the US, jurisdiction is regulated by legislation and in the Constitution. Article 109(a), chapter 11 of the Bankruptcy Code provides that bankruptcy proceedings can be initiated by any person who either resides, or has a domicile, a place of business or property in the US. No restriction of international jurisdiction exists in US law within this framework.[72] Judicial practice has confirmed repeatedly that even a single employee or a very small sum of money in the territory is sufficient for this purpose. As a counterweight, the court enjoys the discretion to decline jurisdiction when the circumstances call for it.

Regarding the question of the principle of comity between nations, the court stated that it did not apply to this case. The judge justified this with the fact that no such precedent exists in the field of voluntary insolvency proceedings. The comity of nations is therefore not a reason in itself for a motion of dismissal. However, it can nonetheless play a role in the court's exercise of its discretion to dismiss the case.

The dismissal of the application was based on the judicial discretion, as regulated in Article 1112(b). This provision contains a list of circumstances that may be

---

[68] Para. 71.
[69] A bankruptcy proceeding in Houston would be a violation of the Act-of-State doctrine, because in the course of the proceedings, the court would have to review the lawfulness of the Russian tax claims and decisions against Yukos. This argument should be seen in the context of Yukos's proposed reorganisation plan, in which it proposed to subordinate the tax claims to the claims of other creditors. The Act-of-State doctrine, however, refers to the merits of the case rather than to the question of jurisdiction.
[70] Memorandum Opinion, referred to in footnote 63.   [71] *Ibid.*, p. 22.   [72] *Ibid.*, p. 21.

considered as grounds for not accepting jurisdiction. The judge found that this list was not exhaustive, and dismissed the application on the basis of the totality of the circumstances.

The circumstances that were considered as grounds for dismissal were the following:

(i)   that Yukos had not acted in good faith (with reference to the circumstances that the real purpose of the proceedings was not a financial reorganisation, that the primary purpose of transferring assets to the US was to attempt to create jurisdiction in the US and that the proceedings were an attempt to substitute Russian law with another legal system);
(ii) that Houston was not the only appropriate forum;
(iii) that the assets were mainly located in Russia, and that any insolvency proceedings had therefore to involve cooperation with the Russian authorities;
(iv) that Yukos' important position in the Russian economy and in oil production made it advisable to conduct the proceedings in a forum where the participation of the Russian Federation was assured.

Based on these arguments, it seems possible to conclude that the proceedings would have been held in Houston if Yukos had played a smaller role in Russia's political and economic situation, and if Yukos had been more longsighted and had established a subsidiary in the US at an earlier date.[73] The practical aspects related to cooperation with the Russian authorities are perhaps more specific to insolvency proceedings than to civil cases in general. Therefore, in other civil cases, this circumstance might not prevent the assumption of jurisdiction.

Let's assume, for the sake of illustration, that the facts were different, and that the court had accepted exercising jurisdiction. We can assume that the Houston court would finally forbid the auction because the company seeking insolvency protection was a small-scale enterprise with limited economic and political significance for the foreign state, which had long had a subsidiary in the US.

Had Deutsche Bank (or an hypothetical equivalent third party in our assumed scenario) had a binding contract with Gasprom (or a hypothetical creditor) for the financing of Gasprom's participation in the auction, it would have faced the choice of either complying with the Houston court's decision and breaching its contract with Gasprom (thus incurring contractual liability), or fulfilling its contract with Gasprom and violating the Houston decision (thus incurring liability, as determined by the US system). This can be seen as a conflict of jurisdiction. Professor Lowe considered this conflict of jurisdiction as a violation of public international law, created by the hypothetical Houston decision.

---

[73] An *a contrario* argument gives no certain results. In US judicial practice, however, there are numerous decisions accepting jurisdiction despite the lack of a real connection (see footnote xx above). This indirectly confirms the result of our *a contrario* interpretation.

The Houston decision could possibly even be seen as a violation of the principle of non-intervention. Admittedly, as long as the decision was not recognised in Russia, no formal interference in foreign affairs would have taken place, because the decision would have no legal effect in Russia. De facto, however, such a decision could have prevented the auction, if, for example, the banks financing the auction were to withdraw for fear of the consequences of the transaction (as actually happened).

3.1.1.7 Consequences of the violation of public international law restrictions on exorbitant jurisdiction

Assuming that public international law contains a rule limiting the scope of extraterritorial effect and the corresponding US rules of private international law on exorbitant jurisdiction, what remedies would exist against a decision issued on the basis of exorbitant jurisdiction and therefore in violation of public international law?

In his Legal Opinion, Lowe mentions the principle of reciprocity, according to which, US enterprises would run the risk of becoming subject to insufficiently grounded insolvency procedures abroad.[74] Such a risk assumes, naturally, that other countries also allow exorbitant jurisdiction in cases of insolvency. Irrespective of how harmful this prospect could prove to US business as a whole, the principle of reciprocity does not appear suitable for the enforcement of Deutsche Bank's own interests. This argument does not appear to grant Deutsche Bank any reimbursement of damages or other relief; it seems rather directed at the court as a reminder of the larger dimension of the case, than useful as a remedy in the specific case.

Lowe suggests that investment arbitration could possibly be initiated under an applicable investment protection treaty.[75] This would have to be an investment treaty between the US and the state of the investor, in this case, most probably Germany.[76] This arbitration procedure could possibly be initiated as a reaction against the enforcement against Deutsche Bank of fines or other sanctions taken against it in the US system as a consequence of Deutsche Bank's disregard of the Houston decision. If the Houston decision proved to be against public international law, a measure taken to penalise its disregard might possibly also be deemed to be illegal under public international law and could be considered as a treatment forbidden by an investment protection treaty (for example, as an illegal expropriation of Deutsche Bank's assets in the territory of the US, or as an unfair and inequitable treatment). Apart from the not obviously satisfied necessity to meet many criteria and the assumption for the admissibility of investment arbitration, their path seems to meet the needs of a private party well. Private parties are interested in remedies which are relatively predictable both in practice and in terms of possible results. Arbitration under an investment treaty fulfils these requirements.

The classic remedy of diplomatic protection under public international law can prove useful in individual cases, but is not generally seen as an effective remedy in a

---

[74] Para. 107f.   [75] Para. 109.
[76] Which do not appear to be in force, see www.worldbank.org/icsid/treaties/treaties.htm.

commercial context.[77] As is known, the investor's home state has discretion as to whether diplomatic protection is granted, and the interests that the state would protect are its own public interests rather than the economic interests of the investor.[78]

This short overview shows that the remedies against the violation of a possible rule of public international law limiting exorbitant jurisdiction are not necessarily appropriate or effective under all circumstances from the perspective of a private party. Pleading the public international law dimensions of exorbitant court jurisdiction might nevertheless be useful to increase the judge's awareness of the potentially extensive political implications of assuming exorbitant jurisdiction.

Raising public international law objections to exorbitant jurisdiction was not openly and directly successful in the *Yukos* case, but it cannot be excluded that it was useful in placing the case into a larger framework.

3.2 Second step: application of the choice-of-law rules of the lex fori

Once the forum has been identified, it will be necessary to look at its private international law. The conflict rules contained therein will determine what state's law governs the contract (and the merits of the dispute). In respect of contracts, we have seen in Section 2 above that the main conflict rule is generally party autonomy. Failing a choice by the parties, the judge will apply the conflict rule set forth in his or her private international law. Until recently, the most common conflict rule was that of the closest connection. The rule according to which, failing a choice of law by the parties, the contract is to be governed by the law with which it has the closest connection, could be found, for example, in the Rome Convention (the predecessor of the Rome I Regulation),[79] and in the Swiss Private International Law Act.[80] As will be seen below, this rule may be interpreted either as a flexible formula that permits considering all elements of a case to find the actual closest connection in the specific case or as a principle underlying fixed connecting factors that apply to the generality of cases for which they are relevant.

The Rome I Regulation has finally clarified that, failing a choice by the parties, the governing law shall be chosen according to fixed connecting factors. The most important connecting factor is the habitual residence of the party making the characteristic performance, which is defined more specifically for various contract types in paragraph 1 of Article 4. The more flexible formula of the closest connection is relegated to the level of an exception that must be applied very restrictively. As the

---

[77] Hanspeter Neuhold, Waldemar Hummer and Christoph Schreuer, *Österreichisches Handbuch des Völkerrechts*, 4th edn (Manz, 2004), p. 499.

[78] Alan Vaughan Lowe, 'Ends and Means in the Settlement of International Disputes over Jurisdiction', (1985) 11 *Review of International Studies* 183–98, at 194ff.

[79] Article 4. Special rules were provided for some types of contracts involving interests that require exceptional protection, such as consumer and labour contracts.

[80] Article 117.

overview below shows, this may be considered as a simple clarification of the status, as it was already under the Rome Convention.[81]

3.2.1 The Rome Convention provided for presumptions

The Giuliano–Lagarde Report on the Rome Convention defined the concept of the closest connection as too vague,[82] and considered it necessary to give it specific form and objectivity by laying down a series of presumptions. The presumption that is of greatest interest here is that contained in Article 4.2: a contract was presumed to have the closest connection with the state in which the party who was to effect the most characteristic performance had its habitual residence or (if a legal entity) its central administration at the time of the conclusion of the contract. If the contract was entered into in the course of that party's business, the criterion of central administration was substituted with that of the principal place of business or with the place of business specified in the agreement.

The performance that was to be considered as characteristic of a contract was the one that determined the social and economic function of that particular legal relationship. Characteristic performance is, for example, the delivery of goods in a sale agreement, the performance of services in a service agreement or the transfer of rights or technology in a licence agreement. The monetary obligation that compensates the party effecting characteristic performance, on the other hand, cannot be considered as being characteristic. If we assume a licence agreement between an Italian licensor and a Norwegian licensee, therefore, the characteristic performance would be that of the Italian licensor; the place of business of the licensor would be in Italy and the licence agreement would be governed by Italian law.

Further presumptions were set forth by Article 4, in subsections 3 and 4, for contracts regarding immovable property and those for the carriage of goods, respectively; however, we will limit our observations to the presumption of the habitual residence contained in Article 4.2.

Article 4.5 permitted the presumption of Article 4.2 to be rebutted in two situations: if the characteristic performance of a contract could not be determined or if all the circumstances of the case showed that the contract had a closer connection with another state than that where the party effecting the characteristic performance resided. If the presumption of Article 4.2 could not be applied, the criterion of the closest connection must be applied.

There were two conflicting interpretations of the relationship between Article 4.2 and Article 4.5 of the Rome Convention.

---

[81] Some consider it as an innovation that restricts the former flexibility of the Rome Convention. A look at the Green Paper on the conversion of the Rome Convention (COM (2002) 6.5.4 final, para. 3.2.5) shows that this is not an innovation, but simply a clarification.

[82] Giuliano–Lagarde Report, p. 21.

3.2.1.1 Loose interpretation: Article 4.2 as a weak presumption

The loose interpretation of the presumption considered the presumption as a pure indication of one of the elements that could be relevant for finding the closest connection. According to this interpretation, the major role would be played by the exception of Article 4.5, which referred to the circumstances of the case as the basis for determining the closest connection.

This loose interpretation seemed to have been applied, for example, by the Danish Supreme Court in 1996 in the context of a construction agreement. In a dispute between a Danish sub-contractor and a German constructor, the Danish Supreme Court applied Danish law, reaching the same result determined by the presumption of Article 4.2. However, the result was based not on the presumption, but on the evaluation of all of the circumstances of the case, which all showed a connection with Denmark (the language of the agreement, the place of conclusion of the agreement, the currency in which the price was invoiced etc.). The Danish Supreme Court, in summary, seemed to have applied the principle of the closest connection rather than the presumption of the habitual residence of the characteristic performer.[83]

3.2.1.2 Strict interpretation: Article 4.2 as a strong presumption

A strict interpretation of the presumption of Article 4.2 saw the presumption as the criterion that is to be applied by the judge as a general rule. Accordingly, the exception provided by Article 4.5 should be interpreted restrictively, as an escape route to be applied only if the criterion set forth in the presumption has no real connecting value in the specific case. This strict interpretation was made, for example, by the Dutch Supreme Court. In a dispute concerning the sale of a paper press by a Dutch company to a French company, the Dutch Supreme Court applied the presumption of Article 4.2 and decided that the governing law was that of the habitual residence of the seller (Dutch law). Dutch law was considered applicable, despite the fact that French law had a closer connection with the contract: the negotiations had been carried out in France in the French language through a French agent, the agreement was written in French and the press was to be delivered and installed in France.[84]

---

[83] UfR 1996, 937; for more extensive comments see J. Lookofsky, *International privatrett på formuerettens område* (Jurist- og Økonomforbundets Forlag, 1997), p. 74; Nielsen, *International privat- og procesret*, pp. 506, 513; Alan Philip, 'First Danish Decisions on the Rome Convention' (1994) *IPRax*, 150f. Other decisions in the same sense can be found in the UK see *Crédit Lyonnais* v. *New Hampshire Insurance Company* [1997] 2 CMLR 610 CA, and *Ferguson Shipbuilders Ltd* v. *Voith Hydro GmbH & Co KG* [2000] SLT 229.

[84] *Société Nouvelle des Papeteries de L'Aa Sa* v. *BV Machinefabriek BOA*, *IPRax* (1994), 243. The Dutch Court operated an anticipatory application of the Rome Convention, which had not yet come into force. See, for extensive comments and further references, W. H. van Lennep, 'Anticipatory Application of a Multilateral Treaty with Uniform Conflict Rules', (1995) 42(2) *Netherlands International law Review*, 259ff. In the same sense, the German Supreme Court (Bundesgerichtshof) also decided similarly; see the decision made on 25 February 1999, *Neue Juristische Wochenschrift* (1999), pp. 2442f.

3.2.1.3 Conclusion

It is obvious that the coexistence of these differing interpretations of the role of Article 4.2 resulted in considerable uncertainty as to the application of the criterion of the closest connection. This undermined the very purpose of the Rome Convention.

To ensure a uniform interpretation, the Rome Convention was accompanied by two protocols establishing an interpretation mechanism by the ECJ that was meant to give an authoritative interpretation of the Convention and a uniform application thereof in all states.[85] After these protocols entered into force, the ECJ was requested to express itself on this matter.[86] The Court, however, did not take the opportunity to clearly endorse one of the two interpretations.

The ECJ was submitted the question as to which interpretation should be embraced, but did not take the opportunity to shed much light on the matter: it simply repeated the wording of Article 4, admittedly specifying that the exception contained in Article 4.2 may be used when the closer connection with another country is 'clear'.

If the Rome Convention was to achieve its purpose of enhancing the predictability of the law, my opinion is that the presumption of Article 4.2 should be interpreted as a strong presumption. What matters mostly is that the parties are in a position to find out which law governs their contract; that the governing law has a close, a closer or the closest connection with the agreement seems to be less important. In so far as it is of particular importance to ensure the applicability of a certain law, for example, because it contains provisions protecting the weaker contractual party, special conflict rules permit the application of the appropriate connecting factors or the direct application of the relevant rules, as will be seen in Section 4. In the other contractual situations, however, where there are no important policies to be taken into account, it may be the same for the parties whether the governing law is that of the seller or that of the buyer. What is crucial is that the parties know which of these laws governs, so that they can assess their own rights and obligations. That a court might prefer an application of its own rather than of a foreign law cannot be deemed as a valid or relevant argument, since it contradicts the very essence of private international law. This approach seems to be in line with the intention of the Rome Convention, as it appears from the Report on the Convention.

---

[85] First and Second Protocols of 19 December 1984.

[86] *Intercontainer Interfrigo SC (ICF) v. Balkenende Oosthuizeb BV and MIC Operations BV* (C-133/08). The decision was based on a request for a preliminary ruling by the Dutch Supreme Court, which basically asked the ECJ to confirm or correct that Court's position on the relationship between the presumption of Article 4.2 and the exception of Article 4.5, as discussed above. The ECJ did little to clarify the matter, and simply repeated the wording of the Rome Convention, albeit adding the requirement that the closer connection shall be 'clear'. It is surprising that the ECJ did not take the opportunity to clarify the question, and even more surprising that the ECJ did not even mention the considerably more restrictive wording of the Rome I Regulation, which, in the meantime, had replaced the Rome Convention. However, the ECJ makes ample reference to the Giuliano–Lagarde Report and its focus on the harmonisation of conflict rules, thus embracing the view that it privileges certainty over flexibility and indirectly supports the interpretation of article 4.2 as a strong presumption.

A loose interpretation of the presumption of Article 4.2, therefore, did not seem to be appropriate; it might serve the purpose of determining a law that has a closer connection than the law of the performer's residence, but it does not serve the even more important purpose of ensuring the predictability of the law, since it leaves too much room for the judge's discretion.

3.2.2 The Rome I Regulation

As already mentioned, the Rome I Regulation clarified that the main rule is that a contract shall, failing a choice by the parties, be governed by the law of the country where the party making the characteristic performance has its habitual residence. This is spelled out in general terms in the second paragraph of Article 4:

> Where the contract is not covered by paragraph 1 or where the elements of the contract would be covered by more than one of points (a) to (h) of paragraph 1, the contract shall be governed by the law of the country where the party required to effect the characteristic performance of the contract has his habitual residence.

To make this even clearer, the first paragraph of Article 4 lays down this rule in specific terms for eight different types of contract, identifying for each of these types who the party is that is making the characteristic performance and mainly designating that law of that party's residence as governing:

(i)   a contract for the sale of goods shall be governed by the law of the country where the seller has his habitual residence;

(ii)   a contract for the provision of services shall be governed by the law of the country where the service provider has his habitual residence;

(iii)   a contract relating to a right *in rem* in immovable property or to a tenancy of immovable property shall be governed by the law of the country where the property is situated;

(iv)   notwithstanding point (iii), a tenancy of immovable property concluded for temporary private use for a period of no more than six consecutive months shall be governed by the law of the country where the landlord has his habitual residence, provided that the tenant is a natural person and has his habitual residence in the same country;

(v)   a franchise contract shall be governed by the law of the country where the franchisee has his habitual residence;

(vi)   a distribution contract shall be governed by the law of the country where the distributor has his habitual residence;

(vii)   a contract for the sale of goods by auction shall be governed by the law of the country where the auction takes place, if such a place can be determined;

(viii) a contract concluded within a multilateral system which brings together or facilitates the bringing together of multiple third-party buying and selling interests in financial instruments, as defined by Article 4(1), point (17) of Directive 2004/39/EC, in accordance with non-discretionary rules and governed by a single law, shall be governed by that law.

In the third and fourth paragraphs, the closest connection is mentioned as an exception:

3. Where it is clear from all the circumstances of the case that the contract is manifestly more closely connected with a country other than that indicated in paragraphs 1 or 2, the law of that other country shall apply.
4. Where the law applicable cannot be determined pursuant to paragraphs 1 or 2, the contract shall be governed by the law of the country with which it is most closely connected.

The wording in paragraph 3, which corresponds to the exception contained in Article 4.5 of the Rome Convention, has a more restrictive scope, since it has added the requirement that it must be 'clear' (and not only that it must 'appear') and that there is a 'manifestly' closer connection (and not simply any closer connection).

4 Are all rules of any other connected laws excluded, once the governing law is chosen?

As Chapter 1 showed, contract drafters have ambitions of self-sufficiency on behalf of the contract (admittedly, these ambitions may be accompanied by the awareness that they may not be fully realised and imply therefore an assumption of legal risk). The possibility of being able to choose the law governing the contract may enhance these ambitions: by choosing which law governs the contract, the parties may be under the impression that they have excluded the applicability of any other laws. The following sections will show that this impression is not correct.

International contracts often contain a choice-of-law clause, and often the law that is chosen does not belong to the country of either party or of the place of performance, but rather is a neutral, third law. In contracts between Norwegian and Russian parties, for example, it is not uncommon that the law chosen is Swedish law. The choice of a neutral governing law is often intended to avoid application of the laws that otherwise might be applicable due to their connection with the legal relationship, be it as the respective law of the parties or the law of the place of performance. Avoiding the application of either party's law, thus preventing the perceived advantageous position that would follow for one party having the contract governed by its own country's law, is sometimes deemed to be advisable. In section 2.1.1 above, we argued that the advantage is not as significant as perceived. More compellingly, it is advisable to avoid the applicability of a law belonging to a legal system which is unstable, not transparent or not subject to the rule of law.

The parties are often convinced that the choice-of-law clause in the contract excludes the applicability of any other country's law to their relationship; even more so, when the contract contains an arbitration clause. Arbitration is based on the will of the parties, and the tribunal is supposed to follow the parties' instructions. Hence, a contract with an arbitration clause apparently enhances the parties' reliance on the choice of law they made in the contract and their impression that any other laws may be disregarded.

Choice-of-law clauses are, however, not always capable of fully achieving the results that are desired by the parties. There are several limits to the effects of these clauses that may depend on various elements:

(i)   the choice-of-law clause may not cover all aspects of the legal relationship regulated in the contract. This is the case, for example, when the contract has implications of company, labour, property or insolvency law or of any area where the party autonomy is restricted by specific private international law rules, such as questions about the legal capacity of the parties;

(ii) certain rules belonging to laws different from the law chosen by the parties may be applicable because of their overriding character, for example, rules of competition law; or

(iii) the law chosen by the parties may give effect to rules belonging to a foreign law, for example, when illegality in the place of performance renders the obligation invalid or unenforceable under the law chosen by the parties.

In these situations, the parties' expectations may be disappointed, as the contract will be subject to rules that they had intended to exclude. In particular, the parties may have drafted a contract that is enforceable under the law chosen by them, yet some of the terms may turn out to be unenforceable because rules belonging to another law are applicable. The arbitration clause does not necessarily prevent the applicability of rules belonging to a law different from the one chosen by the parties. Some of these rules cannot be disregarded even by an international arbitral tribunal and, if they are, the award will be invalid or unenforceable, as will be seen in Chapter 5. Moreover, arbitral tribunals are not immune from the difficulty of interpreting a contract with terms that are not coordinated with the governing law, as was seen in Chapter 3, Section 7.

It is in these situations that the awareness about private international law rules contributes to predictability for international commercial contracts. Rather than being ignored or denied as an element that is foreign to the uniformity aspirations of transnational law, private international law should be appreciated as a useful tool that permits one to understand and predict results that otherwise may come as a nasty surprise.

4.1 The scope of party autonomy: classification and exclusive conflict rules

As mentioned above, very often in international business relationships the parties subject their contract to a governing law of their choice. By so doing, they exercise a power that is granted to them by the vast majority of private international laws – the so-called party autonomy. Party autonomy is the name of a choice-of-law rule, conflict rule or private international law rule – all of these being synonymous definitions of a rule that permits the identification of which country's law governs an international relationship. If the parties do not exercise party autonomy, the applicable law will be determined by other choice-of-law rules.

As was seen in Section 2 above, the conflict rule of party autonomy enjoys extremely widespread recognition in legal systems from all over the world, and is therefore sometimes defined as a 'universal principle' or language to that extent, thus giving the impression that the assumptions and modalities of its exercise, as well as its effects, are uniformly determined and conform to a standard that is independent of any set of conflict rules contained in any applicable private international law. A corollary of this approach is that party autonomy has a presumption of validity and has to be respected in full, particularly by arbitrators. Most arbitration rules and arbitration laws do, as a matter of fact, provide for the tribunal's obligation to follow the choice of law made by the parties, as will be seen in Section 5 below.[87]

Recognition of party autonomy and the judges' and arbitrators' obligation to give effect to it are, certainly, a widely recognised principle that can be deemed to be fundamental in the context of commercial contracts and international arbitration. However, it is not useful and may even be counterproductive to assume that a clause in a contract choosing the governing law is the only basis for its own legal effects, and that it is not subject to limitations of any kind or under any circumstances. Even though party autonomy is a conflict rule that enjoys wide recognition, the scope of the rule is shaped by the private international law that is being applied as a basis for that rule. It may be useful here to give a reminder that private international law, despite its name, is a branch of the national law of each country (the purpose of which is to identify the governing law in an international relationship; hence, the word 'international' in its name). It is highly desirable that private international laws are, to the greatest extent possible, harmonised, and in some regions, the degree of harmonisation that has been reached is considerable – for example, in the EU, private international law is being Europeanised, and outside the EU, international instruments prepared, *inter alia*, by The Hague Conference, aim at harmonising specific areas. However, differences persist among the various conflict rules even among countries that have a uniform regulation, either because some rules fall outside of the scope of the uniform regulation[88] or because uniform rules are interpreted and applied differently.[89] Where there is no uniform regulation to start with, differences in the scope and application of conflict rules are even more likely to occur.

---

[87] See, for example, Article 28(1) of the UNCITRAL Model Law; for non-Model countries, see Section 46(1) of the UK Arbitration Act and Article 187(1) of the Swiss Private International Law Act.
[88] For example, company law and property law are not covered by the Rome I or the Rome II Regulations.
[89] For example, Article 4 of the Rome Convention (the predecessor of the Rome I Regulation) was subject to divergent interpretations, as explained in Section 3.2.1 above.

For party autonomy, as for any choice-of-law rule, the modalities of exercise, the scope of application and the effects are regulated by the private international law to which it belongs. This does not in any way diminish the general principle that the parties shall be permitted to choose the law applicable to their international contract and that judges or arbitrators shall respect and give effect to that choice. As the examples below will show, however, a principle that is expressed so generally needs further specification in order to be operative and such specification is to be found in the applicable private international law. While legislators and interpreters should strive for harmonising the various private international laws, differences still persist that make it impossible to specify the principle in a uniform way and irrespective of the applicable system.

The first aspect that needs to be taken into consideration is the scope of the party autonomy's effects. Traditionally, private international laws permit the parties to choose the law governing contractual obligations. More recently, party autonomy is being extended to other areas of commercial relationships, such as obligations arising out of tort.[90] There are a number of areas of the law, however, where the choice of law is based not on party autonomy, but on other connecting factors set in the relevant conflict rule of the applicable private international law.[91]

Generally, the need to preserve the certainty of title and of the legal relationships towards third parties is the reason for excluding the applicability of party autonomy in these areas. Whenever a contract has implications for the position of third parties (vested rights or legitimate expectations), the choice of a foreign governing law in the contract may affect the third parties' rights, as they are regulated by the law that would otherwise be applicable. It would not be appropriate to permit the contract to affect these third parties' positions by excluding the application of the law that created those rights or expectations. As will be seen below, these considerations are relevant, particularly in areas such as company organisation or capitalisation, legal capacity, winding up or insolvency, property, encumbrances or other securities.

Traditionally, the classification of a subject matter as belonging to one or the other area of the law is made on the basis of the categories as they are defined in the law of the court, the *lex fori*.[92] A judge, thus, will apply the categories of his or her own law to classify the claim as, for example, contractual or based on company law.[93]

---

[90] See Chapter IV of the European Regulation 864/2007 on the law applicable to non-contractual obligations (the so-called Rome II Regulation).

[91] This is indirectly reflected, for example, in Article 1(2) of the Rome I Regulation, listing the areas that fall outside of the scope of application of the regulation's rules. The regulation regulates the law applicable to contractual obligations, and party autonomy is its main rule (Article 3).

[92] There is a considerable amount of literature on the question of classification: see, for example, Kropholler, *Internationales Privatrecht*, pp. 113ff., L. Collins *et al.*, *Dicey, Morris and Collins on the Conflict of Laws*, 15th edn (Sweet & Maxwell, 2012), para 2-001ff.; Scoles, Hay, Borchers and Symeonides, *Conflict of Laws*, para 19.2; Helge Johan Thue, *Internasjonal privatrett* (Gyldendal Academic, 2002), pp. 147ff.

[93] Should the claim be based on a legal institution that is not known in the *lex fori*, it will be necessary to analyse the function of that institution and to classify it according to the category that most closely corresponds to that function.

Thereafter, the judge will apply the conflict rule that, in his or her own private international law, is applicable to that particular area of the law, and the connecting factor contained in that conflict rule will identify the law governing the substance of the claim. As an example, a contract of sale will have contractual obligations between the parties (the quality of the goods, the time of delivery, the price and modalities of payment); these obligations will be subject to the law identified by the conflict rule for contract law, which is party autonomy or, if the parties have not made a choice, the conflict rule for contracts of the court's private international law. The contract will also have some property law implications, primarily regarding the passage of title to the goods. These aspects may have implications for third parties, such as when the seller has sold the same goods to two different buyers. Towards third parties, the question of whether the title to the goods passed to the first or to the second buyer is not decided by the law governing the respective contract, but by the law applicable to property law matters. This law is identified by the conflict rule for property law in the court's private international law (usually, the connecting factor is the location of the goods).

4.2 Classification in arbitration

The foregoing text shows that the classification of a claim is very important for identifying the governing law: a different conflict rule corresponds to each area of law, and to find the applicable conflict rule, it is necessary to classify the claim. If a dispute is decided by a court, the court will classify the claim according to the categories of its own law. In the case of arbitration, it is tempting to resort to the classification made in the law of the place of arbitration, the *lex loci arbitri*. The classification of the subject matter being the first step in the application of a conflict rule, it is reasonable to assume that this classification will be made on the basis of the same legal system to which the conflict rule belongs. In the context that interests us here, this means that the arbitral tribunal will classify the claim and choose the governing law according to what the relevant arbitration rules and arbitration law say on choice of law. The *lex loci arbitri* governs many aspects of the arbitration, such as the powers of the arbitrators relating to production of the evidence, the powers of the judge to order interim measures, the arbitrability of the subject matter, the validity of the arbitral award, etc. Notwithstanding the significance of these matters, and therefore the importance to the proceeding of the law regulating them, the law of the place of arbitration is often frowned upon as not relevant to international arbitration – on the basis of the assumption that the place of arbitration is chosen purely out of practical reasons and is not intended to have any legal implications for the dispute (an assumption that surprises one considerably, given the aforementioned wide range of legal implications determined by the arbitration law of the venue). We will see in Section 5 below that some legal systems have eliminated references to conflict rules in their arbitration laws in order to give effect, albeit partially, to the purported delocalisation of arbitration. Moreover, even many of the systems that have maintained references to the private international law have loosened the link with the private international law of the *lex arbitri*. The classification may, thus, be made according to the *lex loci arbitri*, if the applicable arbitration law instructs the arbitral tribunal to apply the private international law of the place of arbitration.[94] The classification may be made according to another legal system considered by the arbitrator to be more appropriate, if the applicable arbitration law gives the arbitral tribunal the discretion to choose among different systems of private international law.[95] Classification may even be unnecessary if the applicable arbitration law gives the arbitral tribunal the possibility of choosing the governing law without the mediation of private international law (the so-called *voie directe*).[96]

In the context of arbitration, however, it may be useful to advise against giving decisive importance to the taxonomy, and against being too strict in deriving the applicable conflict rule simply from the classification of the subject matter being contractual rather than belonging to the company law or the property law. As will be seen in detail in Chapter 5 below, arbitral awards are subject to control by courts of justice only to a restricted extent, and the wrong application of the law (or the application of the wrong law), let alone the application of the wrong taxonomy, does not cause ineffectiveness of an arbitral award. There are, however, certain instances where failure to apply the proper law may lead to ineffective awards. Therefore, the quest for the criteria determining the proper law in arbitration should be steered by the enforceability of the award rather than by the classification of the dispute according to the *lex arbitri*. If the parties choose a foreign law and the consequent regulation of their legal relationship is enforceable in the relevant jurisdictions, the classification made by the arbitral tribunal and leading to the application of party autonomy will not be reviewed by any courts, and there is no reason for limiting the party autonomy on the basis of a formal classification into one or the other area of the law. If, however, the regulation that follows the law chosen by the parties violates rules that render it ineffective in the jurisdiction where the award should be enforced, then party autonomy is restricted.

The sections immediately below will illustrate some examples of conflict rules that restrict party autonomy and may be relevant in this context. The enforceability of an award giving effect to the choice made by the parties, and thus disregarding the conflict rules for the respective law areas, will be analysed in Chapter 5 below.

4.2.1 Company law

To illustrate how the applicability of company law may remain unaffected by the choice of law made by the parties, a hypothetical case may be presented. Suppose that a

---

[94] Such as the Norwegian Arbitration Act, Section 31.   [95] Such as the UNCITRAL Model Law, Article 28(2).
[96] Such as French law, Article 1511 of the code of civil procedure.

Norwegian and a Russian company enter into various agreements regulating a cooperation between them. In this framework, the Norwegian party buys a minority of the shares of a company owned by the Russian party and by some other investors. This company is registered in the Ukraine, but has its main place of business and its central administration in Russia. To regulate their cooperation, the Norwegian and the Russian party enter into a shareholders' agreement. The shareholders' agreement contains a governing law clause choosing Swedish law and an arbitration clause submitting any disputes arising out of the contract to arbitration under the rules of the SCC.

The shareholders' agreement contains various commitments for each of the parties, such as the obligation not to disclose to third parties specific information, the obligation to meet periodically to ascertain the progress of the cooperation, the obligation to make funds available under certain circumstances, etc.

The shareholders' agreement also contains some obligations regarding the jointly owned company, the operation or competence of its corporate bodies, its capitalisation, etc. For example, the shareholders agree to each appoint a certain number of members to the company's Board of Directors, they specify the areas of competence that each member of the Board shall have and they commit to instruct the Board members appointed by them to vote in the way that the competent Board member has indicated. The shareholders' agreement may further contain rules assessing the value of the respective contributions to the capital of the company and rules for assigning a percentage of the shares in capital increases that corresponds to the agreed assessment. The shareholders' agreement may, finally, contain rules on the transfer of shares to third parties or pre-emptive rights for the existing shareholders.

While the commitments between the parties have a contractual nature and will thus be subject to the chosen Swedish law, the rules of the shareholders' agreement that affect the roles and responsibilities of the members of the Board of Directors, the capitalisation of the company or the transfer of shares have a different nature. Although the parties to the shareholders' agreement have contractually committed themselves to a certain conduct on the Board, to a certain evaluation of the capital contributions and to a certain restriction on the sale of shares, these obligations do not only have a contractual nature. The function of the Board of Directors, the capital of a company and the transferability of its shares (at least under certain circumstances) have a larger significance than the mere balance of interests between the two contracting parties. They affect aspects of the legal personality of an entity that has implications towards third parties, such as the entity's employees, its creditors or the other shareholders.

There are, therefore, reasons for preventing that an agreement between two parties (the shareholders who signed the shareholders' agreement) modifies the position of third parties (such as the position of the other shareholders or of the company's creditors) by changing the governing company law. In other words, party autonomy should not cover matters that may affect third parties' interests; these matters are subject to the law identified on the basis of other connecting factors.

Having established that party autonomy in a shareholders' agreement primarily covers the contractual aspects, however, does not help to identify the law that governs the company law aspects of the relationship. To this end, it is necessary to identify the choice-of-law rule that is applicable for company law.

There is no generally acknowledged rule on what law governs the establishment and organisation of legal entities. Broadly speaking, there are two different approaches: the conflict rule that designates the law of the state where the legal entity is incorporated or registered,[97] in our example, the Ukraine, and the conflict rule that designates the law of the state where the legal entity has its central administration or main place of business (the so-called 'real seat'),[98] in our case, Russia. The rationale for choosing one or the other connecting factor is clear: if the governing law depends on the place of registration, a company is recognised and can operate without having to adapt to company law rules of the countries where it has an establishment. The countries where the company is established, in other words, are ready to accept the criteria and rules of the company's country of origin without questioning their suitability or expecting adjustment to meet with their own standards.

If the governing law depends on the law of the country where the company has its real seat, on the contrary, this country insists on imposing its own standards. The company law's rules on capitalisation, organisation of the corporate bodies, protection of the minority shareholders, etc., are considered to be so important that all companies carrying out their main activity in that country are expected to comply with them, irrespective of where they are registered and of what criteria their company law of origin has.

Traditionally, the place of registration is used as the connecting factor, particularly in the common law countries, whereas conflict rules in many civil law systems, particularly those inspired by German law, are traditionally based on the main place of business.

Within the EU and the EFTA, however, a conflict rule based on the place of business has been deemed to be against the freedom of establishment if it results in imposing restrictions on the possibility of a company registered in one state carrying out its activity in another state.[99] Hence, for companies registered in an EU or EFTA country, another EU or EFTA state where they have their main seat cannot impose its own company law and has to recognise the capitalisation, transferability of shares, limits to the legal personality, etc., as they are determined in the company law of the country of origin. This, however, does not mean that the connecting factor of the

---

[97] Such as English law, see Collins *et al.*, *The Conflict of Laws*, para 30–002ff., US law, see the Restatement, (Second), of Conflict of Laws (1971), para 296 f., Scoles, Hay, Borchers and Symeonides, *Conflict of Laws*, para 23.2ff., the Swiss Private International Law Act, Article 154 and the Italian Private International Law Act, Article 25.

[98] See Kropholler, *Internationales Privatrecht*, pp. 571ff.

[99] See particularly the ECJ decisions in the cases of *Centros* (C-212/97), *Überseering* (C-208/00), *Inspire Art* (C-167/01) and the *National Grid* (C-371/10).

real seat has disappeared from the landscape of European private international law: the ECJ has recently confirmed that companies are creatures of national law, and that it is up to national law to determine the connecting factors that each state requires for a company to be organised or to continue existing under its law.[100] If a state has the real seat as a connecting factor, and a company originally registered in that state moves its real seat to another country, thus losing the basis for the original registration, the country of origin may request that the company is wound up before the real seat is moved (under certain conditions that prevent discrimination).[101]

Thus, a conflict rule based on the real seat will be deemed to violate European law when it restricts a company's freedom of establishment by requesting that the company (duly organised in one member state) complies with requirements of the other member states where the company intends to carry out its main business. However, a conflict rule based on the real seat does not violate European law when it requires that the company (duly organised under that state's law) winds up before it moves its real seat to another state. Using the real seat as a connecting factor, thus, is acceptable under European law, when it regards the question of the valid organisation and existence of a company in the country of origin. On the contrary, the real seat is not an acceptable connecting factor when it restricts the ability to carry out activity in the country of destination, thus limiting the freedom of establishment.

Imposing the conflict rule of the place of registration in regard to the freedom to establish means that all systems have to mutually recognise each other's company laws. This is in compliance with the policy underlying European cooperation and its work towards an internal market: member states are supposed to share the fundamental principles upon which they regulate economic activity, and therefore they should accept each other's company laws without insisting on compliance with their own criteria.

In respect of companies coming from outside of the EU or EFTA area, conflict rules are not affected by the requirement to ensure freedom of establishment, and it is up to each private international law to decide whether to accept any other country's company law, and thus apply the connecting factor of the place of registration, or to consider its own rules as prevailing for companies having their main activity in that country and thus apply the connecting factor of the real seat. If a dispute arises out of the described shareholders' agreement and a court was called upon to decide on it, the judge, when deciding on the company law aspects of the dispute, would disregard the choice of law made in the contract and would apply instead the company law identified by the conflict rules of the *lex fori*.

---

[100] The first decision that moved in this direction was the *Daily Mail* decision by the ECJ (C-81/87), now confirmed by the decision *Cartesio* (C-210/06).
[101] See the *National Grid* (C-371/10).

In Chapter 5, we will see some examples of the relevance that the conflict rule for company law has to arbitration.

4.2.2 Legal capacity

Suppose that the Russian party in the above-mentioned example, by its statutes or the law that governs it, has a requirement that certain types of contract become binding on the company only if they have been signed by two authorised persons – one signature is not sufficient to create obligations. If the contract contains a clause subjecting it to Swedish law (which does not contain the same requirement) and is signed only by one person, which criterion applies to determine whether the company is bound: the criterion set by the chosen Swedish law (one signature, the contract is binding) or that set by the Russian law (two signatures, or the contract is not binding)?

There is no uniform conflict rule to identify which law governs the legal capacity of the party to a contract. The example made above is based on an actual case decided by the Court of Appeal in Stockholm: the court found that the question of legal capacity is subject to the law of the relevant party.[102] In our example, therefore, the applicable law would be Russian law.

In common law states, the legal capacity is sometimes considered a question of the contract, and is therefore governed by the law that governs the contract.[103] More generally, however, the capacity to enter into a contract is regulated by the law governing the company.[104] The Rome I Regulation excludes from its scope of application the choice of law relating to whether an organ may bind a company, which means that within Europe there is no harmonisation of the conflict rule applicable to the legal capacity of the parties, and each state has its own conflict rules to determine the law deciding whether the parties had the competence to enter into a contract.[105] A judge would decide questions of legal capacity on the basis of the law selected by the applicable conflict rule, and would disregard the choice of law contained in the contract. In Chapter 5, we will see that the conflict rule for legal capacity also has great significance in arbitration.

---

[102] Svea Hovrätt, 17 December 2007, T 3108–06, see (2008) 6(5) *ITA Monthly Report, Kluwerarbitration*,

[103] See for the US, Restatement (Second) Conflict of Laws, para 198 and Scoles Hay, Borchers and Symeonides, *Conflict of Laws*, para 18.2. English law has a similar approach, although only in respect of restrictions to the legal capacity, and without taking into consideration the law chosen by the parties: see Collins *et al.*, *The Conflict of Laws*, para 30–021ff.

[104] See, for Germany, Kropholler, *Internationales Privatrecht*, p. 581 and for Switzerland, the Private International Law Act, Article 155(c).

[105] See, however, Article 13 of the Rome I Regulation, according to which, in the event of a contract entered into by persons located in the same state, the foreign party cannot invoke the foreign applicable law on legal capacity to assert his or her own legal incapacity, if that person had legal capacity under the law of the state where the contract was entered into (unless the other party was aware of the incapacity of that party). It is controversial as to whether this can be extended to companies; see Kropholler, *Internationales Privatrecht*, p. 581.

4.2.3 Winding up and insolvency

Suppose that the Russian party and the Norwegian party have a wider cooperation that creates various mutual payment obligations. The agreement provides that each party's payment obligations shall be set off against the other party's payment obligation, so that only the net amount shall be due. If one of the parties becomes insolvent, will its creditors be able to claim payment in full for the outstanding obligations from the other party, or will the set-off agreement be respected so that only the net amount exceeding the other party's claims will have to be paid? Will this be influenced by the law applicable to the various obligations, or will these be irrelevant, in cases where the parties have chosen a different law?

Suppose that the agreement contains a so-called close-out netting arrangement, according to which all obligations of the debtor become immediately due and payable (even prior to their maturity) upon the default by that party of one of its obligations. A variation of this arrangement is the so-called acceleration, particularly widespread for loan agreements, according to which the loan shall be terminated and the whole outstanding amount shall become immediately payable if the borrower 'threatens to become insolvent'. The reason for these mechanisms is evident – the creditor wishes to ensure that the debtor has sufficient means to comply with its obligations. If the financial situation of the debtor is such that there is an imminent risk of becoming insolvent, the repayment of the loan may be affected. Moreover, if the borrower becomes insolvent, the insolvency proceeding will aim at redeeming all of the borrower's liabilities, and there may not be sufficient means to repay the loan in its totality. To avoid this situation, the close-out netting arrangement aims at obtaining payment of all outstanding obligations prior to any financial difficulties that may arise as a consequence of the default and possible subsequent cross-defaults in other contracts, and the loan agreement has a mechanism that provides for repayment of the outstanding amount prior to the initiation of an insolvency proceeding, so that the lender does not have to divide the borrower's assets with the other creditors. Many legal systems have insolvency regulations that aim at preventing these mechanisms, and that permit reversing payments that were made within a certain period prior to the initiation of the insolvency proceeding. Can the lender avoid the application of these rules by submitting the close-out netting arrangement or the loan agreement to a foreign law? If this was possible, the equality of treatment among the creditors, which is a fundamental principle of most insolvency regulations, would be considerably weakened, and the creditors would not be able to assess the assets that are available. This is not a recommendable situation, and for this reason, the choice of law contained in the agreement, while fully effective for the contractual aspects of the legal relationship, may not have full effect for the part that has implications on the winding up or insolvency proceeding.

As a general approach, insolvency proceedings are governed by the law that is applicable to the insolvent company. In the case of companies having activity in more than one state, this raises the question of how to ensure a just and equal treatment for all creditors in respect of assets that may be located in various countries. There are two opposite approaches: territorial and universal. According to the former, a state's law and jurisdiction extends only to the assets that are located in the state's territory. According to the latter, the competent state's law and jurisdiction is to be recognised by foreign states.[106]

To harmonise this area, the EU issued the European Insolvency Regulation (1346/2000), which determines that for a company with cross-border activities, insolvency is governed by the law of the place where the main proceeding is carried out. In turn, the main proceeding is to be conducted in the country where the company has the Centre of main interests ('COMI'). The rebuttable presumption is that the COMI is where the company is registered.[107] However, from the application of this connecting factor, the insolvency regulation carves out a series of situations that involve vested rights by third parties, such as property and security rights, set off and retention of title, and confirms for them the applicability of the governing law determined according to the respective conflict rule (which is not necessarily the law chosen by the parties, as will be seen below). To what extent this will be sufficient to prevent the applicability of the insolvency rule reversing payments or transactions made in the last months or years(s) prior to the insolvency, depends on whether the rule is deemed to override the proper law or not (see Section 4.3 below).

4.2.4 Property

Suppose that an English company transfers to a Russian company the possession of a certain raw material, for example alumina, so that the Russian company may process it and produce aluminium of a certain quality so as to make it available again to the English company against payment of a fee – a so-called tolling agreement. The tolling agreement specifies that title to the material does not pass at any time and that the English company remains the owner of the material even when it is located in the Russian party's premises. The contract contains a choice-of-law clause that selects English law, and under English law, this arrangement is valid. Suppose that the Russian party, while in possession of the material, goes bankrupt. Suppose that the trustee receives claims from various parties in respect of this material: from the English party, that according to the tolling agreement always had title to the material; from a Russian bank, that in the time during which the material was in the possession of the Russian party had granted a loan to this party and obtained a first priority pledge on the material as security; and from a trader that had entered into a contract

---

[106] See Scoles, Hay, Borchers and Symeonides, *Conflict of Laws*, para 23.17, Collins *et al.*, *The Conflict of Laws*, para 30–010ff., Kropholler, *Internationales Privatrecht*, pp. 582f. and the Swiss Private International Law Act, Article 155 (b).

[107] It is to be noted that the same connecting factor is suggested in the UNCITRAL Model Law on Cross-border Insolvency of 1997.

for the purchase of the material on the assumption that the Russian party was the owner and had the right to dispose of it.

There are, thus, potentially four claims on the same volume of material: (i) by the original owner, because the tolling agreement never transferred title; (ii) by the bank, because it registered a legal pledge on the material; (iii) by the purchaser, because it entered into a binding contract of purchase; and (iv) by the generality of the Russian party's creditors, because the material is in the possession of the debtor.

Which of these claims prevails will depend on whether title to the material actually passed. In turn, this will depend on the law governing the passage of title.

The law governing the passage of title is not necessarily the law that the parties chose to govern the contract regulating the transfer. The choice of law made in the contract has effects for the obligations of the parties towards each other, but it does not necessarily have the ability to affect vested rights or legitimate expectations by third parties. In particular, it does not affect the question of who has title to the goods vis-à-vis third parties. For the effects towards third parties, the applicable law is not the law chosen to govern the contract, but the law of the place where the goods are located: the so-called *lex rei sitae*.[108] The material is located in Russia; thus, if Russian law considers the rights of the third parties as valid (assuming, for example, that the third parties were acting in good faith and that the formal requirements are complied with), the bank and the purchaser may have a claim on the material, in spite of the fact that the contract between the English and the Russian party expressly excludes any passage of title as a consequence of the delivery of the material, and notwithstanding that the law chosen by the parties to govern the contract permits such exclusion.

This latter observation deserves being commented upon. If the rights *in rem* by third parties are governed by the law where the goods are located, and if the law chosen by the parties in the contract (English law in our example) is the law of the same place (because the goods were located in England when the contract was entered into), does this mean that the third parties' rights are regulated by English law even after the goods were moved to Russia? The general rule is, as a matter of fact, that the law of the place where the goods were located at the time of entering into the contract governs; however, this rule is limited to the rights between the parties to the contract. Thus, if title to a good was validly retained under the *lex rei sitae*, the obligations between the parties are not affected, even though the goods are transferred to a country where retention of title is not valid. However, towards third parties, it will be the law of the place where the goods are located at any time that governs. Thus, in spite of the circumstance that the title of the material is regulated

---

[108] See, for example, Articles 100 and 104 of the Swiss Private International Law Act and the comments made in H. Honsell, N. P. Vogt, A. K. Schnyder and S. V. Berti (eds.), *Basler Kommentar Internationales Privatrecht*, 2nd edn (Helbing Lichtenhahn Verlag 2007), pp. 648ff.; § 43(1) of the German EGBGB and Kropholler, *Internationales Privatrecht*, pp. 559ff.; for English law, see Collins et al., *The Conflict of Laws*, para 24–029ff.

between the parties by English law, even though the material is on Russian territory, it is Russian law towards third parties that will regulate the possibility of establishing a security right, purchasing goods etc.[109]

In a dispute concerning property rights, a court applies the law selected by the applicable conflict rules, and the choice of law made in the contract is of no effect. In Chapter 5, we will see to what extent these conflict rules are relevant if disputes arising out of the contract are subject to arbitration.

4.2.5 Assignment, security interests and collateral

Suppose that one of the parties assumes an obligation to pay a certain amount of money to the other party. For example, in the case of the tolling agreement made above, the Russian party issues a performance bond guaranteeing the proper performance of its obligations, and the English party requires a security for that payment. The parties agree that the debtor shall secure its obligations by pledging in favour of the creditor, the English party, all future products of the debtor's manufacturing plant in Russia, or the future proceeds that the Russian party will have for the sale of its future products. The parties choose to submit the contract to a law that permits the pledge of future (bulk) things or, as the case may be, of future income. Are the parties justified in relying simply on the chosen law and disregarding the Russian law on pledges? If the pledge of bulk things or the pledge of future things or claims is not allowed under Russian law, is the choice of law made in the pledge sufficient to render the pledge valid between the parties and effective towards third parties?

A further method to create a security interest is to assign to the creditor a claim that the debtor has towards another party (for example, the manufacturer assigns to its raw material supplier, as payment of the raw materials, the claims that the manufacturer will have in the future against the purchasers of the manufacturer's products). To consider the assignment valid in respect of third parties (the manufacturer's clients or the manufacturer's other creditors), is it sufficient to comply with the law chosen by the parties, or is the law governing the assigned claim also relevant?

Another method to create security interests is to deliver to the creditor, as so-called collateral, certain assets (usually cash or securities), providing that the creditor will be entitled to retain them upon default by the debtor of the secured obligation. As the creditor already has the availability of the assets, this arrangement minimises the risk

---

[109] See, for US law, Scoles, Hay, Borchers and Symeonides, *Conflict of Laws*, para 19.11ff.; for German law, see Kropholler, *Internationales Privatrecht*, pp. 560ff.; for English law, see Collins *et al.*, *The Conflict of Laws*, para 24–021. Swiss law makes a compromise in article 102(3) of the Private International Law Act and permits that a retention of title perfected abroad maintains its effect for three months after the goods have entered the Swiss territory; however, not in respect of third parties in good faith. For further comments on the opposed interests in security of title v. security of transaction see Janeen M. Carruthers, *The Transfer of Property in the Conflict of Laws*, (Oxford University Press 2005) pp. 98f. and particularly para 3.59 and 3.67ff.

of loss in the case of default. Will the collateral need to be recognised as such under the law of the place where the assets are located, or is the recognition by the law chosen by the parties sufficient to prevent, for example, that the creditor's creditors attach the assets to satisfy their credit?

An encumbrance on an asset ensures the beneficiary that the proceeds from the sale of that asset will be used to satisfy its claim. Consequently, the encumbrance restricts the availability of that asset for the other creditors, who will be able to apply to their respective credits only that part of the asset's value that remains after the beneficiary has satisfied its claim. The general rule in respect of creditors is that they shall be treated equally, and the priorities that are given via pledges or other encumbrances are an exception regulated by mandatory rules of law and are generally subject to publicity and registration. If a bank is considering giving a loan to a party and requires security, it must be allowed to rely on the formalities and procedures of the applicable law when verifying whether the debtor's assets are already subject to encumbrances in favour of other creditors. If it was possible for a debtor to avoid these requirements by choosing a foreign law for a contract containing an encumbrance, the bank would have to verify the status of the assets in all the world's jurisdictions in order to satisfy itself that the assets are free from encumbrances. This is obviously not a recommendable situation, and this is the reason why the creation of encumbrances or other security rights that may affect the position of third parties is not subject to the choice of law made by the parties in the agreement. The rights and obligations of the parties between each other are regulated by the law that they have chosen, but the enforceability of security rights that may affect third parties is not. Should the encumbrance turn out not to be effective under its proper law, the consequences between the parties will be determined by the law that they chose. While in some systems the debtor may be deemed to be in breach of its contractual commitment towards the creditor, even though the performance of the obligation is illegal or ineffective under its proper law, under other systems, the invalidity of one obligation may affect the validity of the whole contract, thus rendering the encumbrance a nullity even between the parties.

The law governing encumbrances on tangible goods is generally determined by the same conflict rule as the law of property seen above; that is, the connecting factor is the state where the goods are located.[110]

The effects of the assignment between the assignor and the assignee are governed by the law governing the contract of assignment, whereas the law governing the effect of the assignment between the assigned debtor and the assignee is, generally, the law governing the claim that is being assigned – see, for example, Article 14 of the Rome I Regulation. The Rome I Regulation does not regulate the effects of the assignment

---

[110] See, for Swiss law, Article 100 of the Private International Law Act; for English law, Collins *et al.*, *The Conflict of Laws*, para 24–035ff.; for US law, the Uniform Commercial Code, Article 9–103(1); and for Norwegian law, B. E. Konow, *Løsørepant over landegrenser* (Fagbokforlaget, 1999).

towards third parties,[111] but in Article 27, there is a provision for revising the Regulation in this respect. The revision is long overdue, but in 2012 a study was published that will probably be used as a basis for such a revision.[112] The law of the place where the debtor is located is seen as applicable in some private international laws.[113] In other systems, the connecting factor determining the applicable law is the place of the creditor.[114] To harmonise this area, the UNCITRAL has prepared the 2001 Convention on the Assignment of Receivables in International Trade, but the instrument has so far not entered into force.

For the eventuality that the security interest or collateral is created with securities or other financial instruments, specific rules may be recommendable. Therefore, the EU has issued two directives,[115] and various other initiatives are being pursued by international organisations such as The Hague Conference, the UNCITRAL and the UNIDROIT.[116] These conflict rules will be applied instead of the rule of party autonomy when a dispute is decided by a court. To what extent submitting disputes to arbitration may give a broader application of the law chosen in the contract will be seen in Chapter 5.

4.3 Overriding mandatory rules

One of the effects of party autonomy is that the law chosen by the parties applies (within the limits of the scope of party autonomy, as was seen in Section 4.2 above) to the exclusion of any other law. This means that rules of the law that would have been

---

[111] See the opposite applications by the German and Dutch courts of the two parts of Article 12 of the Rome Convention (the predecessor of the Rome I Regulation): BGH 8.12.1998, XI ZR 302/97, *IPRax* (2000), 128f., and *Brandsma g.g.* v. *Hansa Chemie AG*, Hoge Raad, 16 May 1997, *Nederlands Internationaal Privaatrecht* 15 (1997) 254ff. See also *Raiffeisen Zentralbank Oesterreich AG* v. *Five Star General Trading LLC and others* [2001] EWCA Civ 68 (2001) QB 825, following the German approach. Extensively, see Alix Flessner and Hendrik Verhagen, *Assignment in European Private International Law* (Sellier European Law Publishers, 2006). See also Collins *et al.*, *The Conflict of Laws*, para 24–058ff. The corresponding Article 14 in the Rome I Regulation does not seem to contribute with a clarification.

[112] The British Institute for International and Comparative Law Study on the question of the effectiveness of an assignment or subrogation of a claim against third parties, and the priority of the assigned or subrogated claim over a right of another person, ec.europa.eu/justice/civil/document/index_en.htm.

[113] See the US 2001 reform of the Uniform Commercial Code, Article 9–103(3), and Scoles, Hay, Borchers and Symeonides, *Conflict of Laws*, para 19.17ff.

[114] See Article 105 of the Swiss Private International Law Act and the notes on it in Honsell, Vogt, Schnyder and Berti (eds.), *Basler Kommentar*, notes 14ff.

[115] See, for a clear analysis of the implementation of the Collateral Directive 2002/47, the Commission Evaluation, ec.europa.eu/internal_market/financial-markets/collateral/index_en.htm/ and, in particular, the response to the questionnaire to the private sector on the implementation of the Directive written by the ISDA, the branch association for the privately negotiated derivative industry, ec.europa.eu/internal_market/financial-markets/docs/collateral/2006-consultation/isda_en.pdf.

[116] See the 'UNCITRAL, Hague Conference and UNIDROIT Texts on Security Interests: Comparison and Analysis of Major Features of International Instruments relating to Secured Transactions', www.unidroit.org/english/publications/joint/securityinterests-e.pdf.

applicable if the parties had not made a choice, will not apply – not even this law's mandatory rules are applicable. This does not mean, however, that the parties need not concern themselves with other laws that may affect the contractual relationship.

Overriding mandatory rules will be applied notwithstanding the parties' choice of a different governing law, even though there are no specific conflict rules to restrict party autonomy such as those seen in Section 4.2. Overriding mandatory rules apply even when the parties have chosen that their relationship shall not be subject to any state law. As was seen in Chapter 2, Section 6.1, one of the major sources of transnational law, the UPICC, expressly confirms, in Article 1.4, that mandatory rules of law prevail in the case of conflict with the Principles; even more so, this will apply to overriding mandatory rules.

These rules override the choice of law made by the parties and even the choice of law made in accordance with applicable conflict rules. Overriding mandatory rules are directly applicable on the basis of their function and the interests that they represent. It must be emphasised here that not all the rules that are mandatory are also overriding.[117] Where this quality is not given expressly in a statutory rule, it will be a matter of the interpreter's discretion to determine whether a rule is not only mandatory (in which case the choice of another law is sufficient to escape from its scope of application), but also has an overriding character (in which case the rule remains applicable in spite of the choice of a different law). The decision will have to be based on the function of the rule and the policy that underlies the regulation, as well as on the balancing of the various interests that are involved in the specific case.

---

[117] This follows from a systematic interpretation of private international law, see, for example, for US law, Scoles, Hay, Borcher and Symeonides, *Conflict of Laws*, para 18.4(2). For European private international law, this is expressly clarified in the Rome I, Recital No 37. Article 9 of the Rome I Regulation adopts the terminology 'overriding mandatory provisions'; thus clarifying the terminology of its predecessor, the Rome Convention, 'rules that must be applied irrespective of the otherwise applicable law'. Both expressions are an important qualification to the general definition of 'mandatory rules', the latter to be found in Article 3.3 of the Rome I Regulation (and of its predecessor, the Rome Convention), regulating the eventuality that the parties to a domestic (not international) contract have chosen a foreign governing law. For domestic contracts, these instruments allow only a restricted choice of law that shall not affect the applicability of the mandatory rules of the law of the state with which all the elements of the contract are connected. These rules are defined in Article 3.3 as 'mandatory rules', and are described as the rules 'that cannot be derogated from by contract'. In Article 3.3 there is no qualification of these mandatory rules as overriding, as is made in Article 9 of the Rome I Regulation (or as could be found in Article 7 of the Rome Convention, which stated that they should be the kind of mandatory rules that must be applied whatever the governing law). In other words, both the Rome I Regulation (and the Rome Convention) operate with two different concepts of 'mandatory rules': the 'ordinary' mandatory rules, which cannot be derogated from by contract if they belong to the governing law (regulated in Article 3.3), and the 'overriding' mandatory rules, which may be given effect to, even if they do not belong to the chosen law (regulated, respectively, in Articles 9 and 7). In the English version of the Rome Convention, this difference was not immediately apparent; that these two concepts are different, however, was confirmed by the other language versions of the Convention: in the French version, for example, the mandatory rules of Article 3.3 were called *dispositions imperatives* and those of Article 7 were called *lois de police*, whereas in the German version, they were called, respectively, *zwingende Bestimmungen* and *zwingende Vorschriften*.

It is not always easy to determine whether a mandatory rule is overriding or not, and rules that are deemed as overriding in one state might not be overriding in another state. Also, the overriding character of a rule should be evaluated in light of the protection that the same interest enjoys under the chosen law. The private international law gives some guidelines as to the criteria on which the discretion shall be exercised: for example, the necessity of a particularly closed connection with the law in question or to what extent rules belonging to foreign laws may be applied. In the Rome I Regulation, the possibility of applying overriding mandatory rules notwithstanding the governing law is regulated in Article 9.

Not all substantive rules protecting particularly important interests become applicable by overriding the choice of law made by the parties on the basis of the interpreter's discretion. Sometimes the policy upon which a certain rule is based and the connection between the legal relationship and a certain country are such that a general conflict rule is enacted to ensure application of the provision based on that policy. In these cases, the loose approach based on the functional evaluation of the rule and a balancing of the interests involved, which was just described, and that characterises overriding mandatory rules, is replaced with more mechanical rules based on the application of pre-determined connecting factors. Thus, the same interest may be regulated in some systems by rules that are applicable on the basis of specific connecting factors, whereas in other systems, they may be applied directly as overriding rules. Application of a rule on the basis of a connecting factor is by far preferable, in terms of predictability, to application as a consequence of a functional analysis made by the interpreter. The opinion that predictability should be preferred to a case-based functional analysis, however, is not uncontroversial.[118]

One of the interests that is increasingly being considered as particularly important and that could be regulated by overriding mandatory rules is the protection of the weaker contractual party. In the interest of predictability, as seen above, however, specific conflict rules have been created for many areas where a party is deemed to need protection, for example, in fields such as labour law,[119] consumer law,[120]

---

[118] See, for example, Friedrich K. Juenger, *Choice of Law and Multistate Justice* (Martinus Nijhoff Publishers, 1993), G. Kegel, 'The Crisis of Conflict of Laws', (1964) 112 *Recueil des Cours*, 91, and Simeon Symeonides, 'Material Justice and Conflicts Justice in Choice of Law', in P. Borchers and J. Zekoll (eds.), *International Conflict of Laws for the Third Millennium: Essays in Honor of Friedrich K. Juenger* (Transnational Publishers, 2001), pp. 125ff.

[119] The Rome I Regulation provides in Article 8 for an exclusive conflict rule in the event that the law chosen by the parties gives the employee a worse protection than the law that would otherwise have been applicable. In the US private international law, the overriding character of labour law seems to relate particularly to the statutory restrictions to non-competition agreements, see Scoles, Hay, Borcher and Symeonides, *Conflict of Laws*, para 18.5. See, for Norwegian law, the Protection of Employees and Working Environment Act, section 5.

[120] The Rome I Regulation provides in Article 6 for an exclusive conflict rule in the event that the law chosen by the parties gives the consumer a worse protection than the law that would otherwise have been applicable. For US law, see Scoles, Hay, Borcher and Symeonides, *Conflict of Laws*, para 18.4(3).

insurance,[121] carriage[122] or agency.[123] Applicability of these rules is then is based on determined and predictable connecting factors, rather than on the more uncertain functional analysis.

Another overriding interest is the protection of the security of rights and of third parties, such as in the fields of incorporation of legal entities, insolvency and property. These areas are usually outside of the scope of party autonomy, therefore the proper law will be determined on the basis of other connecting factors, as seen in Section 4.2. A direct application of these rules as overriding mandatory rules is not necessary: the consideration that would justify such a direct application is taken care of by the specific conflict rules.

Mandatory rules that override the contractual regulation may also be found in respect of other interests, such as the protection of the national economy (for example, import–export regulations, foreign exchange regulations, securities exchange regulations, competition regulation etc.) or public interest (for example, embargo).

Most of these rules have a public law character and are outside the scope of party autonomy; therefore, it is quite natural that they are not affected by the choice of law contained in the contract. It may, nevertheless, be worthwhile mentioning them here, because they may affect the parties' rights and obligations under the contract. The parties to a contract often tend to rely on the choice of law made by them to such an extent that they expect no interference of any kind by any other laws, including public law rules. They may, therefore, be surprised by the application of these rules.

Some illustrations may show the impact that overriding mandatory rules may have on the choice of law made by the parties.

4.3.1 Competition law

Suppose that two competing manufacturers enter into a contract for the licensing of certain technology, and that the transfer of technology is accompanied by a system for sharing the market between the two competitors, which violates European competition law. The contract contains a choice-of-law clause, according to which

---

[121] The Rome I Regulation provides in Article 7 for exclusive conflict rules in the field of insurance. These are based on several European directives, see especially Directive 88/357 and 90/619. For US law see Scoles, Hay, Borcher and Symeonides, *Conflict of Laws*, para18.5.

[122] The Rome I Regulation provides in Article 5 for some restrictions to the parties' choice of law. This area is regulated by a series of international instruments, such as the so-called Hague Rules of 1924, the Hague–Visby Rules of 1968 and the Hamburg Rules of 1978. See, for Norwegian law, the Maritime Code, section 430 and section 252 combined with section 310.

[123] The EC Directive 1986/653 related to self-employed commercial agency contains a series of rules for the protection of the agent. For Norwegian law, see the Agency Act § 3, based on the European regulation. In US law, the commercial agents do not enjoy a particular statutory protection, but distributors and franchisees do, and these rules are deemed to be overriding: see Scoles, Hay, Borcher and Symeonides, *Conflict of Laws*, para 18.5.

the governing law is a foreign law of a non-EU Member State. If a dispute arises between the two parties, the party that is being claimed against for a contract breach may allege that the contract is null and void because it violates European competition law. The other party will allege that EU competition law is not applicable to the contract, that the choice of the foreign governing law was meant specifically to avoid applicability of EU law and that the will of the parties shall be respected.

The purpose of the EU rules on competition is to ensure that business parties do not distort the market by, for example, sharing it between themselves. Practices such as market sharing have a negative effect on the offer and on the prices, and this negatively affects the buyers. If the parties could avoid the applicability of these rules by subjecting the contract to a third law, their party autonomy would affect the position of the buyers, and this is not desirable. Hence, competition rules will apply to agreements and market practices that have effect on the relevant territory, irrespective of the law that governs the contract.[124]

A court hearing this case will apply EU competition law irrespective of the different choice of law contained in the contract. To what extent an arbitral tribunal will do the same is discussed in Chapter 5.

4.3.2 Labour law

Suppose that a Norwegian company agrees to contribute to the capital of a Russian company following the commitment by the latter to, among other things, within a certain term, reduce the number of its personnel by one third. The contract is subject to Swedish law. Russian mandatory rules of labour law on the protection of employees provide for a lengthy and complicated procedure before the number of employees can be reduced. As a consequence, the Russian party is not able to perform the obligation that it assumed towards the Norwegian party. The Russian party will invoke Russian mandatory rules of labour law as an excuse for the delay in performing its obligations, and the other party will deny the relevance of rules of Russian law because the contract excluded its applicability by choosing Swedish law as governing the contract.

Labour law obviously aims to protect the employees, and a contract between the investor and the employer is not capable of excluding the applicability of the labour protection that the employees enjoy. Assuming that the investor and the employer, aware of this circumstance, had agreed to modify all the employment agreements so that each of the employment agreements contained a choice-of-law clause in favour of Swedish law, would the protection afforded by Russian labour law be excluded? Even a choice-of-law clause in each employment agreement would not be capable of achieving the exclusion of Russian labour law, partly because there is a special conflict rule for labour law, and partly because these rules are typically

---

[124] C-129/97 (*Eco-Swiss*).

considered to have an overriding character and remain applicable in spite of any contrary choice of law made by the parties.

The relevance of these considerations to arbitration will be discussed in Chapter 5.

4.3.3 Agency contracts

Suppose that an Italian producer enters into a contract with a Norwegian agent for the promotion of the producer's products and the development of a market in the Norwegian territory. In the contract, the parties provide that the agreement may be terminated at the discretion of the producer and that no compensation shall be paid to the agent upon such termination. The contract contains a choice-of-law clause determining the law of New York as governing, because this regulation of the parties' interests is allowed under that law. Under Norwegian law, however (as well as under Italian law), the agent is entitled to compensation upon termination of the relationship. Is the choice-of-law clause sufficient to exclude the application of the Norwegian rule on compensation?

The rule on compensation is part of a set of rules designed to protect the agent, which is deemed to be the weaker party in the relationship. An agency assumes that the agent exercises its activity for the benefit of the principal. On termination of the relationship, the results of the agent's activity benefit the principal, who will then enjoy the market and the goodwill developed for it by the agent. The agent, on the other hand, will not have any benefit from the activity carried out for the principal. Hence, the compensation upon termination is meant to balance the parties' interests. The protection regime is deemed to relate to all commercial agents carrying out their activity within the territory, and the circumstance that the parties chose a different law to govern the contract should not exclude its application.[125]

4.3.4 Insurance

Suppose that an English insurance company and a Norwegian ship owner enter into an insurance contract for the liability that the ship may incur towards third parties. The insurance contract contains a pay-to-be-paid clause, affirming that the insurer will make any disbursement only after the insured has reimbursed the damage caused to the third party. The contract contains a clause choosing English law to govern it, and the regulation contained in the contract is in compliance with English law. The pay-to-be-paid clause means, *inter alia*, that if the insured becomes insolvent or goes bankrupt before a reimbursement of damages was made to an injured third party, the insurance company will not be under an obligation to make any disbursement.

Assuming that the injured party is Norwegian, it will have, according to Norwegian mandatory law, a direct action against the insurer. Will the injured party be able to claim payment under the direct action, in spite of the circumstance that, thanks to the

---

[125] See the ECJ decision in *Ingmar* (C-381/98), where the question arose because the principal was located outside Europe.

pay-to-be-paid clause, the insurance company is not obliged to make payment under the insurance contract or under the law chosen to govern the contract?

Contracts of insurance are widely regarded as adhesion contracts, drafted unilaterally by the insurance company and imposed on the insured; the weaker party without any real bargaining power. Therefore, statutes and regulations often contain detailed mandatory rules that the parties may not escape from by subjecting the contract to a foreign law. For special insurance contracts regarding large business activities, the mandatory regulation is less extensive. However, certain rules remain mandatory even in this context – for example, the rule on the direct action in case of insolvency of the insured.[126] In the case described above, the choice of law made in the insurance contract might have been deemed as overridden by the mandatory rule of the direct action. Alternatively, and preferably, it might have been deemed not to be relevant, since the rights exercised by the injured in the direct action are not contractual rights and are thus subject to another conflict rule.[127]

4.3.5 Good faith and fair dealing

Some legal systems, particularly those inspired by German law, base their contract laws on the principle of good faith and fair dealing, as was seen in Chapter 3. This principle may be used to guide the interpretation and performance of the contract so as to create ancillary obligations for the parties that were not expressly provided for in the contract, or even to correct the regulation contained in the contract. Contract clauses that expressly permit an interpretation or a performance violating the principle of good faith and fair dealing (for example, exempting from liability even in cases of gross negligence or wilful misconduct or permitting termination of the contract for capricious reasons) might be deemed to violate the principle of good faith and fair dealing. If the contract is subject to, for example, English law, which, as seen in Chapter 3, Section 3, has no general principle of good faith for commercial contracts, there are no obstacles to a literal implementation of the contract's provisions, as long as their terms are sufficiently clear.

Assuming that a contract contains a choice-of-law clause in favour of English law, and that it would be governed by a civil law, if it was not for the choice made by the parties, would the literal implementation of these clauses be affected by an overriding principle of good faith and fair dealing in the law that would have been applicable

---

[126] Deemed to be overriding in the Norwegian preparatory works to the Act on the Law Applicable to Insurance Contracts, Ot.prp.nr. 72 (1991–92), p. 66.

[127] The EU Regulation 864/2007 (Rome II) on the law applicable to non-contractual obligations allows for two alternative classifications of a claim based on direct action: either as contract right or as a right based on tort; see Article 15. For a comment on a case similar to the one described here, see Giuditta Cordero-Moss, 'Direct Action against the Insurer: A Recent Decision by the Norwegian Supreme Court Illustrates the Norwegian Approach to Private International Law', in Talia Einhorn and Kurt Siehr (eds.), *Intercontinental Cooperation through Private International Law: Essays in Memory of Peter Nygh* (Asser Press, 2002), pp. 55–67.

if the parties had not chosen English law to govern the contract? As was seen in Chapter 3, the principle of good faith and fair dealing is considered to be central in the contract laws of civil law systems; as was seen in Chapter 2, the principle has been transferred from there into various restatements of principles of contract law that have the goal of being applicable to international contracts, such as the UPICC and the PECL, as well as the DCFR. It has also been proposed that many overriding rules based on good faith, which so far have been applicable to consumer protection, should also be extended to commercial contracts.[128] In addition, the proposal for a Regulation that should introduce, as an optional instrument, a CESL[129] extends regulation on consumer protection to commercial contracts, when one of the parties is a small- or medium-sized enterprise. There are some indications that rules express-ing this principle might have an overriding character and thus remain applicable in spite of a different choice of law made by the parties.[130]

However, extreme cautiousness is recommended, as will be seen in Chapter 5 below.

The very fact that the CESL is meant to be an optional instrument, which becomes applicable only if both parties expressly agree on adopting it, speaks against considering its rules as overriding. The quality as overriding is not compatible with the rules of non-applicability if the parties elect not to adopt them. Overriding mandatory rules are those rules that are not only mandatory, but also those that are so important for the public interest of the state that they shall be applicable irrespective of any contrary choice of law. An optional instrument is, by definition, not mandatory; all the more it lacks the impellent character that would be required to consider a mandatory rule as overriding.

4.4 Overriding mandatory rules of third states

Application of the law chosen by the parties may also be limited by overriding mandatory rules belonging to laws different from the *lex fori*. A judge will normally

---

[128] For example, the Principles of EC Contract Law issued by the European Research Group on Existing EC Private Law (the so-called Acquis Principles), extend to commercial contracts various rules based on the protection of the consumer, such as imposing liability for having carried out negotiations in bad faith (Article 2:103), imposing a duty of information in the pre-contractual phase (Article 2:201), imposing performance in good faith (Article 7:101), providing that a right or a remedy shall be exercised in good faith (Article 7:102), providing that the terms of a contract are not binding if they have not been individually negotiated and if they have been incorporated by reference having been made in the contract (Article 6:201). For criticism on this approach, see Giuditta Cordero Moss, 'Consumer Protection except for Good Commercial Practice', in Reiner Schulze (ed.), *CFR and Existing EC Contract Law* (Sellier European Law Publishers, 2008), pp. 78–94. See aslo sections 2.4 and 2.7.2 above.

[129] Common European Sales Law, COM (2011) 635 final.

[130] The preparatory works on the Norwegian Act on Choice of Law in Insurance Contracts, commenting on the act's provision about overriding mandatory rules (a provision modelled on the then prevailing Article 7 of the Rome Convention, since the act is the implementation in Norway of the EC Directive on the same subject matter), affirm that one of the rules of Norwegian law that might be deemed to have an overriding character according to that provision is § 36 of the Norwegian Contracts Act, imposing the principle of good faith and fair dealing on contracts.

apply the overriding mandatory rules of his own law; some systems of private international law recognise the possibility of giving effect to overriding mandatory rules of third states, if there is a sufficiently close connection between the dispute and the third state, for example, Article 19 of the Swiss Private International Law Act. The Rome Convention had a similar provision in Article 7.1. This provision, however, was so controversial that the Rome Convention itself permitted its signatories, in Article 22.1(a), to reserve against the application of this rule. Among others, England and Germany reserved against the application of Article 7.1 of the Rome Convention. The Rome I Regulation has considerably restricted the applicability of overriding mandatory rules of third countries: Article 9.3 says that effect may be given to such rules to the extent that they belong to the law of the country where the contract is to be performed, and only in so far as they render the performance unlawful.

The restricted access for the application of overriding mandatory rules of third states given by Article 9 of the Rome I Regulation does not exceed the scope of other legal mechanisms that were already adopted in various legal systems: the possibility of taking into consideration the overriding mandatory rules of third countries when these render performance impossible or illegal. These will be discussed more in detail below.

4.5 Impossibility of the performance due to a foreign law

As we have seen so far, the choice of the governing law made by the parties does not exclude the application of rules belonging to other laws. In addition, there are situations where the rules of a law that is not governing the contract are not directly applied, but create legal effects that have to be taken into consideration under the governing law. In these cases, the effects of the foreign rules will be considered as facts and will be given the legal effects that the governing law gives to similar facts. The foreign rules will not be applied, but the factual consequences that the foreign rules have created in the foreign state will be taken into consideration when applying the chosen law.

We can assume, for example, that a Norwegian and a Russian company enter into a contract for the purchase by the Norwegian buyer of certain raw materials produced by the Russian seller. The parties agree to have their contract governed by Norwegian law. The export of those raw materials is subject to licensing by the competent Russian authorities; due to reasons outside the control of the seller, the competent authorities do not issue a licence for the export of the sold goods. The goods, therefore, are ready to be delivered, but cannot physically leave the state, because the customs authorities will not allow them to pass the Russian border without the export licence.

The Russian seller invokes the Russian export rules to excuse its own non-performance; the Norwegian buyer does not accept the failure to obtain the export licence as an excuse for non-delivery. The buyer argues that the rules on export licences are rules of Russian law, and the parties have chosen Norwegian law to govern the contract.

The buyer's allegation that Russian law should not be applied is correct; however, this does not mean that a Norwegian judge can completely disregard the existence of the Russian export rule, or, better, the consequences of its existence. The goods have been stopped at customs, and cannot be exported: this is a factual situation preventing the export, which happens to derive from the existence of a licensing system in Russia. Should this impossibility of being able to export be considered differently by the Norwegian judge from impossibility deriving from a flood, fire or other natural event beyond the control of the seller?

The judge will note a supervening impossibility of performing the agreement, and will evaluate, on the basis of the contract's terms and conditions and of the applicable law (Norwegian law, chosen by the parties), what legal consequences are to be attached to this.

Whether the seller will be excused on the basis of the *force majeure* clause in the contract, or will be considered to be in breach of contract for not having complied with all the conditions required to perform its obligations, depends on the examination of the factual circumstances and on the allocation of risk provided for in the contract. Failing a contractual regulation of this eventuality, the judge will decide by applying the *force majeure* rule contained in the governing law (Norwegian law): the exporter will be excused, if the circumstances that led to the refusal to issue the export licence qualify as *force majeure* circumstances under the governing law.

In conclusion, the Russian export rules are not applied, but their application made by Russian authorities can be considered as facts and can be given legal effects under Norwegian law. Accordingly, the buyer's allegation that Russian export rules are inapplicable is correct, but this does not mean that Russian export rules should not be taken into consideration.

4.6 Illegality of the performance under a foreign law

What happens if the contract, valid under the chosen law, violates mandatory rules of other laws, but this violation does not result in a physical impossibility in performing the contract as examined above?

We can assume the case of a Norwegian seller and a Russian buyer, who enter into an agreement for the sale of certain goods. Import of these products is subject to payment of import duties under Russian law. The parties agree to circumvent Russian customs regulations by dividing the invoicing of the price into two parts. One invoice, expressing only part of the value of the goods, would accompany the goods for customs clearance; the balance of the price would be invoiced separately, and paid for not by the Russian importer, but by an offshore company affiliated to the importer. In this way, the Russian importer (illegally) gets to pay lower import duties, since the import duty is a percentage of the invoiced price. The Norwegian manufacturer would properly account for both invoices in its books, and feels therefore that it has not violated any Norwegian law. The Norwegian seller would assume that a violation of Russian law would not be relevant, since the contract contains a governing law clause choosing Norwegian law. The seller feels safe in its opinion that it has not violated any governing law. Is the seller's opinion justified? Does violation of (or assistance in violating) foreign law really have no consequences under the chosen law?

The opinion of the seller is not, at least not always, justified: different states have different approaches to the question of the violation of foreign law, but often it is possible to find in the governing law a rule on illegality; sanctioning behaviours that conflict with foreign laws. Therefore, as in the previous section in respect of the impossibility of performing a contract due to a foreign law, also in the case of the illegality of a contract according to a foreign law, it may be possible to apply the chosen law and yet take into consideration the foreign law.

In the particular case mentioned above, for example, the seller would have contributed to a violation of Russian customs rules; the Norwegian judge would not be in a position to apply Russian customs rules that are outside of his or her jurisdiction, and are not part of the governing law. However, the Norwegian Customs Act contains a rule (Section 16-5) that considers a violation of foreign customs rules as a violation of Norwegian customs rules. Therefore, the behaviour, illegal under the foreign law, also has consequences under the governing law.

A Norwegian Supreme Court decision has applied this principle in a broader area.[131] The Court affirmed that, if a party agrees with another party to violate (in the particular case under consideration) foreign tax laws, it is criminally punishable under the Norwegian rule on receiving proceeds from a crime (Criminal Act, Section 317). In this case, the Norwegian party had agreed to enter into certain simulated transactions so that the Russian party could evade Russian tax law. The reasoning was as follows: if the evaded tax law had been Norwegian, the parties would have violated Norwegian tax law and would have been liable under the relevant legislation. However, the evaded tax law is foreign and a Norwegian judge cannot apply foreign tax law. The Norwegian party made a gain in entering into the arrangement with the other party, and this gain must be considered as the result of an illegal action. Obtaining gains from illegal actions is a crime under Norwegian law, and the fact that the illegality is under a foreign law is not relevant, as long as corresponding actions carried out on the territory of Norway would be illegal under Norwegian law (the requirement of double illegality).

In other legal systems, a choice of governing law leading to the violation of another law might result in a conflict with the governing law's or the *lex fori*'s own sense of justice; therefore, the choice of law may be considered as invalid. The German BGB, for example, contains a rule on *Sittenwidrigkeit* that can be applied in similar circumstances (§ 138).

---

[131] Rt. 1997 p. 1637.

English law has traditionally requested that a choice of law be made in good faith;[132] a choice of law made for the purpose of evading foreign law may be considered not to be in good faith and, therefore, is invalid. However, it might be difficult to ascertain whether the choice of law was made in bad faith so as to evade the otherwise governing law, or whether there were other reasons for making the choice. In both examples mentioned above, for example, the choice of Norwegian law to govern the contract is a perfectly natural choice, with Norway being the state of the seller.

Other systems might adopt concepts such as that of comity of nations, whereby recognition of a fraudulent choice of law would result in a hostile act towards the state issuing the violated laws. Some English decisions have this approach, particularly when recognition of the contract would lead to carrying out illegal action in the foreign state.[133]

As already mentioned, Article 9.3 of the Rome I Regulation permits giving effect to foreign rules if these belong to the country where the performance should be made and make such performance unlawful. This is, however, not automatic, and the court is directed to consider the nature and purpose of the provisions, as well as the consequence of applying or not applying them.

Finally, there is always the last resort of the *ordre public* clause: a judge will not accept a choice-of-law clause if the effects of that choice conflict with fundamental principles in the judge's legal system. The application and interpretation of the *ordre public* clause should be restrictive and narrow, as we will briefly see in the next section, but can most probably be justified in cases of contracts violating fundamental policies of another state, particularly when these policies are common to the *lex fori*. Contracts violating foreign laws in respect of smuggling, corruption and entry into a contract under duress, for example, are traditionally considered to violate the *lex fori*'s *ordre public*.[134]

In conclusion, choice of a governing law different from the law that is being violated may not always permit the parties to escape the consequences of their violation.

4.7 Violation of the ordre public of the lex fori

A general principle of private international law is that a judge will not apply a foreign law if application thereof will result in an intolerable violation of the basic principles on which the *lex fori*'s system is based (*ordre public* or public policy).

---

[132] The requirement that the choice of law must be made *bona fide*, mentioned by Lord Wright in the case *Vita Food*, [1939] AC 277 PC, is often quoted in English literature.

[133] See Trevor C. Hartley, 'Mandatory Rules in International Contracts: The Common Law Approach', *Recueil des Cours* vol. 266 (The Hague Academy of International Law, 1997), 341ff. and 389ff.

[134] James Fawcett, Janeen M. Carruthers and Peter North, *Cheshire, North & Fawcett Private International Law*, 14th edn (Oxford University Press 2008), pp. 139ff.

The Rome I Regulation contains the same regulation in Article 21, and so do the Swiss Private International Law Act in Article 17 and the Russian Civil Code in Article 1193.

These regulations have one feature in common that is essential to the proper interpretation of the *ordre public* clause: they have a very narrow scope.[135] The *ordre public* clause is not intended to be used simply on the basis that there is a discrepancy between the foreign governing law and the legal system of the forum. The clause is to be used only under exceptional circumstances, when the result to which the judge would come to by applying the rule of the foreign governing law would conflict with the basic principles upon which the society of the forum is based. A simple difference between a foreign rule and a mandatory rule of the forum, or even an overriding mandatory rule of the forum, therefore, would not in itself qualify as a violation of the *ordre public* of the forum. More on the scope of *ordre public* will be presented in Chapter 5 below.

5 Private international law and arbitration

Questions may be raised about the relevance of private international law to arbitration.[136] Many modern codifications are keen to do away with choice-of-law rules in arbitration, mainly for the purpose of ensuring that the law may be chosen without the interference of formal rules that may be unknown to the parties and thus may lead to surprising results. These codifications support the so-called *voie directe*: direct access to the governing law, without having to be concerned with the criteria for choice of law contained in private international law. We will show here that this eagerness to enhance a direct approach to the law does not necessarily lead to more predictable results.

The ICC Rules of Arbitration were described as a landmark when they, in 1998, deleted any reference to private international law,[137] and are followed now by other arbitration rules.[138] Under Article 21 of the ICC Rules of Arbitration, if the parties

---

[135] See the Giuliano-Lagarde Report and the references made in Giuditta Cordero-Moss, *International Commercial Arbitration – Party Autonomy and Mandatory Rules* (Tano Ascehoug 1999), footnote 222ff.

[136] See the International Commercial Arbitration Committee, 'International Law Association Report Ascertaining the Contents of the Applicable Law in International Commercial Arbitration' (paper presented at the International Law Association Conference, Rio de Janeiro, 2008), pp. 4, 12. That arbitrators are not bound to apply the principles of private international law that are applicable to courts is considered to be an uncontested point by Emmanuel Gaillard and John Savage (eds.), *Fouchard, Gaillard and Goldman on International Commercial Arbitration* (Kluwer Law International, 2004), p. 849. At the same time, arbitrators are said to be under no public duty to enforce state laws: see International Commercial Arbitration Committee, p. 20. See also Luca Radicati Di Brozolo, 'Arbitration and Competition Law: The Position of the Courts and of Arbitrators', (2011) 27 *Arbitration International*, 1–25, 16f.

[137] See Yves Derains and Eric Schwartz *Guide to the ICC Rules of Arbitration*, 2nd edn (Kluwer Law International, 2005), p. 233.

[138] The rules of the LCIA, of the Arbitration Institute of the SCC and the revised UNCITRAL Arbitration Rules give the arbitral tribunal the authority to directly apply the substantive law that it deems appropriate, without going through the mediation of a choice of law rule.

have not made a choice, the arbitral tribunal may freely choose the applicable rules of law directly and without applying any conflict rules. When they choose to submit a dispute to arbitration under the ICC Rules, thus, the parties agree that the arbitral tribunal is not bound to apply any private international law.

The latest, most notable introduction of the *voie directe* was made in 2010, when the UNCITRAL modified its 1976 Arbitration Rules. The Arbitration Rules are not meant to be a model for a convention or for an arbitration law, but are a model contractual document that the parties may decide to adopt to regulate the procedural aspects of their dispute. The Arbitration Rules are thus meant to integrate the parties' agreement, and are subject to the applicable arbitration law. Among other things, the UNCITRAL modified the second sentence of Article 35 (former Article 33) regarding the arbitral tribunal's choice of the applicable law in cases where the parties have not made a choice themselves. While the original version instructed the tribunal to choose the governing law by applying conflict rules of the private international law that they deemed applicable, the revised version does not mention conflict rules or private international law. The arbitral tribunal seems to be completely free to determine on what basis the applicable law shall be selected. This change is meant to enhance flexibility under the Arbitration Rules. The parties should be free to decide on whatever rules they want to see applied to their dispute, and the arbitral tribunal should be free to decide on whatever law it wants to apply, subject only to a contrary will of the parties.

However, the Arbitration Rules are not in a position to create such an unrestricted flexibility regarding the applicable law. The validity and enforceability of the award depend on the applicable law and on the New York Convention. National arbitration law (also including the UNCITRAL Model Law [articles 34 and 36], which has been enacted in over 60 countries) and the New York Convention (Article V) contain restrictions on the possibility of the parties and of the tribunal choosing the applicable law. To name the most important choice-of-law rules contained in these UNCITRAL instruments, an award is invalid or unenforceable: (i) if one party to the arbitration agreement was under some incapacity *under its law*; (ii) if the arbitration agreement was invalid under the law specifically chosen by the parties or, failing a choice (which is the most common scenario, see Chapter 5, Section 2.1.3), *under the law of the place where the award is rendered*; (iii) if the arbitral procedure was not in accordance with *the law of the place where the award is rendered;* (iv) if the award is on a matter that is not arbitrable *under the court's law*; or (v) if the award conflicts with *the court's* public policy. Notwithstanding the strong signals of the revised Article 35, the law of each of the parties, the *lex arbitri* and the law of the court should be taken into consideration regarding legal capacity, validity of the arbitration agreement, arbitral procedure, arbitrability and public policy. Moreover, as will be seen in Chapter 5, case law shows that disregard of the applicable law in areas such as competition regulation, insolvency, corporate matters, agency or distribution may affect the validity and enforceability of an award. Additionally, disregard of the applicable law in the areas of property or labour protection may have similar consequences.

Therefore, the parties and the arbitral tribunal are not completely free to choose the applicable law.

Article 35 of the UNCITRAL Arbitration Rules has the unfortunate effect of enhancing, albeit on a fallacious ground, the impression of self-sufficiency that was described in chapter 1. An impression that, as has just been seen, may turn out to be quite illusionary. Article 1.3 of the Arbitration Rules contains a general reservation stating that the Arbitration Rules may not derogate from mandatory rules of the law at the place of arbitration. Even assuming that a party had understood the relevance of this rule in the context of the choice of law, Article 1.3 is not necessarily sufficient to warn against the ineffectiveness of the award that may follow a free choice of the applicable law. This is because Article 1.3 only reserves against mandatory rules of the law of the place of arbitration, whereas enforceability of the award is determined by the law of the place of enforcement. Both of these laws, moreover, refer to the law of each of the parties when it comes to the validity of the arbitration agreement.

In spite of the strong desire to enhance party autonomy, therefore, rules on choice of law also remain highly relevant in the context of arbitration.

5.1 The relevance of private international law in arbitration

Leaving aside the obvious situation where the parties have not chosen the governing law and it is for the arbitral tribunal to find which law is applicable, we will focus on situations where the parties have made a choice of law, and we will show that conflict rules are relevant even then. The sources applicable to arbitration all confirm that the arbitral tribunal shall apply the law chosen by the parties, as will be seen in Chapter 5, Section 3.1.3. Other rules of choice of law are mentioned, if at all, only to a restricted extent in the sources applicable to arbitration.[139] This does not mean, however, that private international law is totally irrelevant to arbitration.

As was seen in Section 4.2 above, the choice of law made by the parties in the contract has effects only for the contractual aspects of the relationship. A legal relationship, however, may have implications in other areas of the law, such as company, labour, property or insolvency law. Even the simplest contract of sale has implications regarding property law: whether title to the goods has passed to the buyer or not is not a question that is subject to the law chosen in the contract – it shall be decided under the law applicable to property matters. As was seen in Section 4

---

[139] For the eventuality that the parties have not made a choice of the applicable law, arbitral tribunals are supposed to choose the law that is applicable according to the conflict rules that the tribunal considers applicable (see, for example, Article 28(2) of the UNCITRAL Model Law and Section 46(3) of the English Arbitration Act), or the law that has the closest connection with the disputed matter (see, for example, Article 187 of the Swiss Private International Law Act) or the law that the tribunal deems applicable (see, for example, Article 1496 of the French Civil Procedure Code).

above, private international law creates predictability as to which law's rules shall be applicable in these instances.

The arbitration clause does not necessarily prevent the applicability of rules belonging to a law different from the one chosen by the parties: as will be seen in Chapter 5, some of these rules cannot be disregarded even by an international arbitral tribunal and, if they are, the award will be invalid or unenforceable. In case of dispute, one party will invoke these rules, whereas the other party will insist on the application of the chosen law.

Ignoring or denying the mechanisms for choice of law does not contribute to predictability.

Section 4 above showed the main restrictions to party autonomy. Although the provisions containing restrictions to party autonomy do not, as a general rule, have relevance to arbitration, they may give guidance to the arbitral tribunal when the arbitral tribunal has to restrict the choice of law made in the contract in order to avoid conflict with the applicable public policy, or when a party invokes one of these rules as a defence against the allegation of breach of contract. As will be seen in Chapter 5, Section 2, disregard of the applicable law may, under some circumstances, render the award invalid or unenforceable. It is important for the arbitral tribunal to be aware of these criteria and, thus, to have an understanding of the relevant conflict rules. On the other hand, the arbitral tribunal's duty is primarily to follow the will of the parties, also including the choice of law contained in the contract. Understanding the proper scope of party autonomy will give the arbitral tribunal useful guidelines as to the effects of the choice-of-law clause contained in the contract. This, in turn, will be relevant to the question of what power the arbitral tribunal has, which again has an impact on the validity and enforceability of the award. This will be discussed in Chapter 5, Section 3.

Within the framework provided by the applicable rules on the validity and enforceability of awards, therefore, private international law may become relevant to arbitration and may be used as guidance by the arbitral tribunal in determining the extent to which the parties' choice of law may be restricted. Indeed, it is desirable in this context to apply private international law principles, because they enhance predictability in such a crucial area as the choice of the applicable law.[140]

In particular, private international law contains rules on the scope of party autonomy and on restrictions to party autonomy by overriding mandatory rules. These criteria permit the determination as to what extent rules different from those chosen by the parties may be applied – provided, however, that they are relevant to the validity or enforceability of the award.

---

[140] For a more extensive analysis see Giuditta Cordero-Moss, 'Arbitration and private international law', (2008) 11 *International Arbitration Law Review*, 153–64, and Giuditta Cordero-Moss, 'Revision of the UNCITRAL Arbitration Rules: Further Steps', (2010) 1 *International Arbitration Law Review*, 96–9.

5.2 *Which private international law is applicable?*

We have seen in the previous section that a choice of law made by the parties in a contract that contains an arbitration clause is not totally independent from the applicable private international law. The next question is, therefore, how to determine which private international law is applicable in international commercial arbitration.

The overview made in Section 4 above showed that it is in no way indifferent as to which private international law is applied. Conflict rules vary from system to system and, consequently, the law designated as applicable varies depending on which country's conflict rules are applied. Therefore, it is necessary but not sufficient to refer to private international law as a tool to avoid surprises in respect of the enforceability of the award. In addition, it is also necessary to specify which private international law the arbitral tribunal shall use in order to assess the party autonomy's borders and the applicability of other laws in specific areas of the legal relationship in dispute.

In respect of courts of law, it is generally recognised that judges always apply the private international law of their own country to designate the applicable substantive law. In respect of international commercial arbitration, there is not a corresponding automatic and absolute reference to the private international law of the place where the arbitral tribunal has its venue. The arbitration law of the place of arbitration has, as a matter of fact, a considerable significance for the arbitration proceeding, in that it governs important aspects such as the arbitrability of the dispute, the regularity of the arbitral procedure, the powers of the arbitrators, the possibility of the courts in assisting the proceeding, for example, by issuing interim measures or challenging the arbitrators, the validity of the award and the fundamental principles of public policy. Therefore, it seems only natural to also look to the law of the place of arbitration when it comes to finding the applicable conflict rules. However, the eagerness to enhance the international character of international arbitration has led various legislatures and arbitral institutions to loosen the link between the place of arbitration and the applicable private international law. Hence, there is no uniform answer to the question of which private international law is applicable to an arbitral dispute. The various arbitration laws and rules of institutional arbitrations present a series of solutions, ranging from the application of the private international law of the place of arbitration,[141] to the application of the private international law that the arbitral tribunal deems most appropriate,[142] the application of conflict rules

---

[141] This is the traditional approach that is still followed in some modern arbitration legislation, for example, Article 31 of the 2004 Norwegian Arbitration Act.

[142] This approach is followed, among others, by the UNCITRAL Model Law (Article 28.2) and the English Arbitration Act (Section 46.3), and it can result in the application of the private international law of the country where the arbitral tribunal has its venue, of another law that seems to be more appropriate or even of no specific law (often, arbitrators compare the choice-of-law rules of all laws that might be relevant and apply a minimum common denominator).

specifically designed for arbitration[143] or the direct application of a substantive law without considering choice-of-law rules.[144]

If the applicable arbitration law or arbitration rules do not give precise guide-lines as to which private international law is applicable to the arbitration, it will be up to the tribunal to decide. The various solutions outlined above give a sliding scale from the most predictable (and thus preferable) regime, where the applicable private international law is determined in advance, via the mixed solutions, where the identification of the applicable private international law is left to the discretion of the tribunal or is only implicitly mentioned by stating a conflict rule, to the least predictable regime that does not mention private inter-national law at all. It is not unusual that arbitral tribunals exercise their discretion so as to enhance predictability and look to the private international law of the place of arbitration. However, in the systems that do not make express reference to the applicability of the conflict rules of the *lex loci arbitri*, this depends on the tribunal's discretion and it cannot be excluded that the tribunal decides to apply other conflict rules.

The Hague Conference on Private International Law, an international organisation existing since 1893 with the purpose of harmonising the private international law, is working on non-binding principles for choice of law in international contracts.[145] These principles are meant to be a source of soft law. While it is unlikely that they will be adopted by courts of law unless the court's private international law is unclear or needs supplementing, they may be an inspiration for arbitral tribunals when the applicable arbitration law does not give clear guidelines as to which private international law shall be applied.

The above-described uncertainty as to the applicable private international law has a negative effect on the predictability of the applicable law, which, in turn, may be decisive for the outcome of the dispute. As long as a private international law is in the picture, however, the interpreter will have, in any case, to choose the proper law by applying a conflict rule; the determination of the law, in other words, will be based on the application of a connecting factor. While the *a priori* identification of the applicable private international law is preferable because it permits the creation of certainty as to which connecting factor will be used (for example, in the case of a company, the law, the place of registration or the seat), a discretionary choice of which private international law is applicable will at least ensure that the proper

---

[143] For example, the Swiss arbitration law (Article 187) contains a choice-of-law rule that designates as applicable the law of the country with which the subject matter of the dispute has the closest connection.

[144] French arbitration law (Article 1496 of the Code of Civil Procedure), as well as the rules of the ICC, of the LCIA, of the Arbitration Institute of the SCC as well as the revised UNCITRAL Arbitration Rules, give the arbitral tribunal the authority to directly apply the substantive law that it deems more appropriate, without going through the mediation of a choice-of-law rule.

[145] The text of the latest draft, as well as the status of the work in progress may be found at www.hcch.net/index_en.php?act=text.display&tid=49.

law will be chosen on the basis of a connecting factor. In the absence of any reference to a private international law, there is no indication that the tribunal will apply a conflict rule to identify the proper law; it may identify the proper law on the basis of completely different criteria, such as, for example, the law that the members of the tribunal happen to know best. This is certainly not a recommendable solution from the point of view of predictability.

5

Does arbitration ensure a self-sufficient contract?

Commercial arbitration, whether domestic or international, is an alternative method of dispute resolution. This means that it is an alternative to the courts of law: if the parties so elect, and if the governing law permits submitting the relevant kind of disputes to arbitration, the parties may decide to exclude the jurisdiction of ordinary courts and to subject their dispute to arbitration instead. It is very common to see an arbitration clause in a commercial agreement specifying that disputes arising out of the contract are to be submitted to arbitration.

Let's assume a contract with a clause subjecting it to a certain law, and let's assume that the contract violates the law that would be applicable if it was not for the choice-of-law clause: for example, a shareholders' agreement between a Norwegian and a Russian party regarding a company that they jointly own in Russia. The shareholders' agreement has a clause choosing Swedish law to govern the contract and the content of the agreement violates Russian company law (for example, because it provides for a division of competence between the various corporate bodies that is not in compliance with Russian law). Russian law could have been invoked by one of the parties as a defence to rebut the other party's allegations of breach of contract: the first party would allege that it could not comply with its obligations under the contract because performance of that obligation would have been illegal under the law of the place where the performance was to be made. If the contract contains an arbitration clause, does the arbitral tribunal have the power to disregard the choice of Swedish law made by the parties in the contract and apply Russian law instead? And what if none of the parties invokes Russian law: could the arbitral tribunal nevertheless take it into consideration on its own motion – to avoid rendering an award that would violate mandatory rules in the place where it most probably would be enforced?

If the dispute was litigated in court, the judge would apply the private international law of its own country to assess the borders of party autonomy; that is, to assess to what extent the choice of law made by the parties would also cover matters of company law. As was seen in Chapter 4, Section 4.2.1 above, the court would find that the contract's choice of law does not extend to company law, and therefore there would be no obstacles to taking Russian law into consideration.

It is often assumed that the considerations made in the previous chapters are not generally relevant when the contract has a clause that submits any disputes arising out of the contract to international arbitration. The reasoning is as follows: as opposed to national courts, which belong to a specific national system of law, international arbitration is, by its very nature, international, and is not subject to any state law. Moreover, the arbitral tribunal is dependent on the will of the parties, and therefore cannot decide a dispute by applying national rules that the contract has not made reference to, or even may have intended to exclude.

To verify the correctness of this reasoning, we have to look at the two assumptions that it is based on: is international arbitration really international? In other words, is there no link between international arbitration and national systems of law? And, is international arbitration really completely and solely dependent on the will of the parties? In other words, is there no possibility for national courts to control the activity of international arbitral tribunals and thus create a framework for the arbitral tribunal's duty to follow the parties' instructions?

Arbitration is mostly based on the will of the parties, and the applicable sources of law confirm the central role of the parties' will. The tribunal is bound to follow the parties' instructions, because it does not have any powers outside of the parties' agreement. Therefore, tribunals are generally, and correctly, very reluctant to deviate from the instructions of the parties.

However, the primacy of the parties' agreement needs to be coordinated with applicable rules on validity and enforceability of the arbitral award.[1] It is possible that the parties' instructions contradict the applicable arbitration law's requirements for the award's validity, or the New York Convention's requirements for the award's enforceability. In this situation, if the arbitral tribunal follows the will of the parties, it may face the prospect of rendering an award that is invalid or cannot be enforced. To avoid these undesirable results, the arbitral tribunal may be tempted to disregard the parties' instructions, including their choice of law. This, however, may be done only under limited circumstances and according to restrictive criteria in order to avoid exposing the award to the risk of being annulled or refused enforcement based on the arbitral tribunal exceeding the scope of the power that the parties had conferred on it.

We will verify these aspects in the following sections. Before doing that, however, it might be useful to give a short presentation of arbitration as a method for solving disputes.

In the following sections I will first briefly present arbitration as a method to settle commercial disputes (Section 1); then, I will turn to the question of the effects that an

---

[1] See, for a more extensive reasoning, Giuditta Cordero-Moss, 'Arbitration and Private International Law', (2008) 11 *International Arbitration Law Review* 153. For a similar reasoning see Alan Redfern, Martin Hunter, Nigel Blackaby and Constantine Partasides, *Redfern and Hunter on International Arbitration* (Oxford University Press, 2009), para 3.102, adding also, as the only additional basis with which to restrict the parties' choice, that the parties' choice must have been made *bona fide*. See also the International Commercial Arbitration Committee, p. 21, affirming that the only restriction to parties' choice is the public policy exception. See also Ulla Liukkunen, '*Lex Mercatoria* in International Arbitration', in Jan Klabbers and Touko Piiparinen (eds.), *Normative Pluralism and International Law: Exploring Global Governance* (Cambridge University Press, 2013), pp. 201–28.

award may have if it disregards the law that would have been applicable in the absence of the parties' choice (Section 2). Finally, we will enquire as to what extent an arbitral tribunal has the power to disregard the choice of law made by the parties in the contract and, at the request of one party or on its own initiative, apply a different law (Section 3).

1 Briefly on commercial arbitration

The jurisdiction of an arbitral tribunal on a certain dispute is based, for international arbitration, on the already mentioned 1958 New York Convention on the Recognition and Enforcement of Foreign Arbitral Awards.[2] In Article II, the Convention provides that:

> Each Contracting State shall recognise an agreement in writing under which the parties undertake to submit to arbitration all or any differences which have arisen or which may arise between them in respect of a defined legal relationship, whether contractual or not, concerning a subject matter capable of settlement by arbitration.

An arbitration agreement has two important consequences: first, a valid arbitration agreement excludes the jurisdiction of the ordinary courts of law over disputes covered by the arbitration agreement; and second, the validity of the arbitration agreement is a prerequisite for enforcing the arbitral award rendered in the dispute covered by the arbitration agreement. In international disputes, the award is generally enforced in a country other than where it was rendered, so the New York Convention is applicable. Article V of the New York Convention sets forth the only grounds that can be used to refuse enforcement of a foreign arbitral award. They include the following (Article V(1)(a)): 'The . . . agreement referred to in article II . . . is not valid under the law to which the parties have subjected it or, failing any indication thereon, under the law of the country where the award was made'. Article II makes reference to the arbitration agreement.

An arbitration agreement is usually contained in a simple clause of the contract regulating the commercial relationship between the parties. If the contract does not contain an arbitration clause, the parties might elect to enter into a separate arbitration agreement, perhaps after the conclusion of the commercial contract, or even after the dispute has arisen between the parties. It is, however, usually difficult for the parties to agree on anything once a dispute has arisen between them; therefore, it is advisable to enter into the arbitration agreement or write the arbitration clause at the time of closing the contract, rather than waiting until a dispute has arisen.

---

[2] The New York Convention has been ratified by 149 states. The text of the convention can be found at www.uncitral.org/pdf/english/texts/arbitration/NY-conv/XXII_1_e.pdf. The list of states that ratified it can be found at www.uncitral.org/uncitral/en/uncitral_texts/arbitration/NYConvention_status.html.

1.1 Different forms of arbitration

Arbitral disputes may be carried out under a variety of forms. The considerations made in the following sections on the relevance of national law, control by the courts, the power of the arbitral tribunal, etc. apply to arbitration generally, irrespective of the variety of forms that are available with which to organise arbitral proceedings.

The most important distinction is between ad hoc arbitration and institutional arbitration.

Arbitration is ad hoc when it is constituted purely on the basis of the agreement of the parties. The parties decide to submit the dispute to a panel of arbitrators, they decide how the members of that panel shall be appointed, where the venue of the tribunal shall be what rules of procedure the tribunal shall apply, etc. The regulation of all aspects of the procedure is highly recommendable to avoid deadlocks in case one party is not cooperative during the dispute. However, regulating all aspects of the procedure is a lengthy and complicated matter. In practice, most ad hoc arbitration clauses do not contain any details on the procedure or any reference to arbitration rules. As an alternative to regulating all these aspects in their arbitration agreement, the parties may elect to make reference to a set of arbitration rules that is already available. These rules are meant to integrate the contract between the parties and, once incorporated by reference, they become a part thereof. The UNCITRAL, for example, produced the UNCITRAL Arbitration Rules in 1976; a set of procedural rules that regulate all the aspects of the conduct of an arbitral proceeding (revised in 2010).[3]

If the parties have not regulated the arbitration procedure in the arbitration agreement, and if they have not made reference to a set of arbitration rules, the arbitrators will decide the procedural aspects according to their discretion, subject to the applicable arbitration law.

Ad hoc arbitration is regulated by the arbitration law of the state where the arbitral tribunal has its venue. Arbitration law is usually not very detailed and does not give sufficient guidance in respect of the procedural details that arise during a dispute.

Ad hoc arbitration may, as seen above, be very flexible and ensure that the procedure is fully tailored to the specific disputes, thus avoiding excessive costs due to unnecessary infrastructure or too lengthy a procedure. However, this assumes cooperative parties and professional arbitrators.

If one party is not cooperative, it may considerably delay the procedure by not appointing the arbitrator, by not agreeing on terms, by appointing an arbitrator who is not impartial and who resigns just before the award is rendered, etc. The proceeding may also be disrupted if one of the arbitrators is not diligent or even not impartial.

---

[3] The text can be found at www.uncitral.org/uncitral/en/uncitral_texts/arbitration/2010Arbitration_rules.html.

In this case, institutional arbitration is preferable to ad hoc arbitration, even if the parties made reference to the UNCITRAL Rules for the procedure of the dispute – this is because an institution will give the support of an infrastructure, for example, for appointments of arbitrators if one party has not complied with the terms for appointment and for challenge to the arbitrators, etc. In ad hoc arbitration, these functions are fulfilled by the so-called appointing authority, usually a court at the place of arbitration. This proceeding, however, is time consuming and may become cumbersome if the court acting as appointing authority does not have a high degree of familiarity with the technicalities of arbitration.

Arbitration is institutional if the parties have made reference in the arbitration agreement to a certain arbitration institution. Arbitration institutions are organised, for example, within the ICC, within national Chambers of Commerce, such as in Stockholm, in Oslo or in Milan, within branch associations, such as the London Metal Exchange, or independently, such as the LCIA.

The chosen arbitration institution will administer the arbitral proceeding, applying its infrastructure and the arbitration rules that it has produced. The institution's arbitration rules are deemed to be incorporated into the parties' arbitration agreement. Having made reference to arbitration within a certain institution, the rules of that institution will be applied automatically to the proceeding and the parties do not need to provide for extensive regulation in their agreement.

Most institutional arbitration rules provide for default rules that enable avoiding delays in the procedure due to an uncooperative party. In addition, institutional arbitration, like ad hoc arbitration, is subject to the arbitration law of the place where the arbitral tribunal has its seat.

In conclusion, institutional arbitration is preferable, unless there is certainty that both parties will act cooperatively and in good faith throughout the proceeding.

For arbitration carried out in Europe, there is a variety of institutions that offer widely recognised services.[4] Among those that are most relevant to international contracts are the following:

1.1.1 *International Chamber of Commerce* www.iccwbo.org/court/arbitration/

The ICC is an international private organisation with a seat in Paris and offices in most countries of the world. The ICC has, among other things, been administering arbitration for many decades and has developed a sophisticated infrastructure in connection with this activity.

ICC arbitration does not necessarily have to take place in Paris; as a matter of fact, a large number of ICC arbitrations have their seat in Switzerland, particularly in Zurich.

---

[4] For a thorough analysis of the various forms of arbitration see Giuditta Cordero-Moss (ed.), *International Commercial Arbitration: Different Forms and their Features* (Cambridge University Press, 2013).

When ICC arbitration is chosen, the parties subject the procedure to the ICC Arbitration Rules and involve, in addition to the arbitral tribunal that they appoint, the ICC Secretariat and the International Court of Arbitration, a permanent body that scrutinises all draft awards before they are rendered, thus ensuring a high degree of quality. The ICC Arbitration Rules provide for a procedure that is particularly appropriate for extensive and complex disputes.

The complexity of the procedure and the size of the infrastructure ensure a high-quality result, but require a commitment of resources and time that may be excessive for small or medium-size claims.

1.1.2 *London Court of International Arbitration* www.lcia.org

The LCIA is a widely known institution. Generally, however, arbitration in England may become more time consuming and costly than expected, because the English Arbitration Act allows for the possibility of challenging, before English courts, the validity of arbitral awards rendered in England to a larger extent than the arbitration law of other countries does.

1.1.3 *Arbitration in Switzerland* www.swissarbitration.ch/index.php

Switzerland is a widely recognised venue for international arbitration. Often, arbitration in Switzerland is administered under the ICC Rules or as ad hoc arbitration under the UNCITRAL Rules.

Arbitration in Switzerland may also be organised in the frame of a Chamber of Commerce, for example, in Zürich or Geneva. The Swiss Chambers of Commerce apply Arbitration Rules that are arbitration-friendly and comply with modern standards.

Swiss courts have a high expertise in respect of arbitration and are generally arbitration-friendly when they are requested to verify the award's validity.

1.1.4 *International Arbitral Centre in Vienna* wko.at/arbitration/

The International Arbitral Centre of the Austrian Federal Economic Chamber has an established tradition of resolving disputes involving Central and Eastern European parties.

Austria has a new Arbitration Act, which is broadly aligned with the modern arbitration-friendly standard. The Austrian courts, however, have occasionally set aside arbitral awards on rather formalistic reasons.

1.1.5 *Stockholm Chamber of Commerce* www.sccinstitute.se/

The Arbitration Institute of the SCC has been, since the 1970s, the preferred venue for so-called East–West arbitration involving Western and East European or Soviet parties, thanks to the neutral status of Sweden. The Arbitration Institute of the SCC was recommended in 1977 as the venue for resolving disputes between US and USSR parties by the American Arbitration Association and the USSR Chamber of Commerce. Stockholm continues to be a preferred arbitration venue for East–West disputes, even following the changed political situation and the decreased importance of considerations regarding political neutrality.[5] In addition to maintaining its presence in East–West arbitration even after the collapse of the Soviet Union, the SCC has expanded its scope and a considerable percentage of the disputes administered by it involve European or Asian parties.

The SCC rules provide for very effective procedures and focus on providing proceedings that are speedy and not as costly as those administered by other arbitration institutions.

The Swedish courts are generally arbitration-friendly and very restrictive in interfering with the awards, even though they are frequently requested by losing parties to set aside arbitral awards that are alleged to be invalid.

1.2 The relevance of national law to international arbitration

An international arbitral award is an enforceable decision on the basis of the New York Convention. This means that, if the losing party does not comply with the award voluntarily, the winning party may present the award to the enforcement court of any state where the losing party has some assets and where the New York Convention is in force, and the court will have to enforce the award after having carried out a rather restricted, mainly formal review of its enforceability. The grounds for refusing to enforce an award are set forth in Article V of the New York Convention.

In the following sections, we will verify whether our previous observations on the relationship between the contract, state law and transnational law are relevant to the enforceability of an international arbitral award.

1.3 Is there a difference between international arbitration and domestic arbitration?

When the terminology 'international arbitration' is used, the term international usually refers not to the arbitration, but to the dispute that is being arbitrated. Some special arbitrations, particularly investment arbitration, take place in the framework of international conventions, and are therefore international themselves. The ICSID arbitration on investment disputes between foreign companies and host states, for example, is based on the Washington Convention of 1965 on the Settlement of Investment Disputes between States and Nationals of Other States. The legal regime to which an ICSID arbitration is subject is international; therefore, an ICSID arbitration can

---

[5] See, for example, the text of the 1992 Optional Arbitration clause for use in contracts in US–Russian trade and investment, prepared by the American Arbitration Association and the Chamber of Commerce and Industry of the Russian Federation, recommending arbitration in Sweden under the UNCITRAL Rules, in A. J. van den Berg (ed.), *Yearbook Commercial Arbitration XIX* (Kluwer International, 1994), pp. 279–82. The Optional clause is still operative today; see www.sccinstitute.com/?id=&newsid=45358 last accessed 15 August 2013.

be defined as international. Most of the commercial arbitration disputes, on the contrary, are subject to the legal regime of a state law, even if they are defined as international. Generally, an arbitration will be subject to the arbitration law of the state where the arbitral tribunal has its venue, unless the parties have chosen a different law to govern the proceeding.[6] If a dispute between a Norwegian and a Russian party, for example, is submitted to arbitration in Stockholm, the arbitration will be Swedish. The dispute is international, but the arbitration is subject to Swedish arbitration law. The award rendered will be considered as a Swedish arbitral award, and will be enforceable in Sweden according to Swedish enforcement rules, and in other states according to the respective rules on enforcement of foreign (Swedish) arbitrations. The vast majority of states have ratified the 1958 New York Convention on the Recognition and Enforcement of Foreign Arbitral Awards. The New York Convention will therefore be the basis for enforcing the Swedish award in these states, including Norway and Russia.

The term 'international', therefore, may be misleading. We are, generally, in the presence of a *national* arbitration that deals with an international dispute, and it can be enforced abroad as a foreign award. Some national arbitration laws have different legal regimes for arbitrations taking place on their territories, according to whether the dispute is domestic or international,[7] while others have the same regime.[8] A widely recognised model for state laws on international arbitration is the 1985 UNCITRAL Model Law on International Commercial Arbitration, revised in 2006.[9] This Model Law has been adopted in over sixty states,[10] and has been largely followed or used as a term of reference in a series of other states. The Model Law, originally designed for arbitrations solving international disputes, is also often used for arbitrations solving domestic disputes. In Norway, for example, the Arbitration Act, based on the Model Law, does not differentiate between arbitrations regarding international or domestic disputes.

An arbitral tribunal resolving an international dispute, however, might feel less bound to state law than a tribunal resolving a national dispute. We have seen in Chapter 4 Section 5 above, for example, that some arbitration laws and arbitration

---

[6] Some national arbitration laws permit that the parties to an arbitration located on their territory choose the procedural law of another state to govern the arbitral proceeding. It is, however, a rare occurrence and it is not advisable that the parties choose an arbitration law that is different from the arbitration law of the place where the tribunal has its seat. They may choose arbitration rules (such as the UNCITRAL Rules, the ICC Rules or other rules), but this does not exclude the applicability of the arbitration law. The parties very often choose the law that the arbitral tribunal shall apply to the dispute, but that is the substantive governing law, and it does not also extend to cover the procedural aspects of the arbitration.

[7] For example, the Swedish Arbitration Act, Section 51, the Swiss Private International Law Act, Article 192, and the Belgian Civil Procedure Code, Article 1717.

[8] Norway has the same regime for domestic and international arbitration, based on the UNCITRAL Model Law. See also the Dutch Arbitration Act and the German arbitration law after the reform of 1997.

[9] The text of the Model Law can be found at www.uncitral.org/pdf/english/texts/arbitration/ml-arb/07-86998_Ebook.pdf.

[10] The list of states that have adopted the Model Law can be found at www.uncitral.org/uncitral/en/uncitral_texts/arbitration/1985Model_arbitration_status.html.

rules do not impose application of the private international law of the state where the arbitral tribunal has its seat. International tribunals might also feel that they owe more obedience to the parties that have appointed them, than to a national legal system of which they are not a permanent body. Hence, sometimes it is possible to encounter the already mentioned opinion according to which state law is not as relevant to international contracts if the dispute is submitted to international arbitration as it would be if the dispute were submitted to a national court of law. In the following sections, we will analyse to what extent this opinion is justified.

1.4 When does state law become relevant to international arbitration?

As is known, international arbitration is an alternative method of settling contractual disputes, which is based on the consensus of the parties. If the parties agree to submit disputes between them to arbitration, then the ordinary courts will have to decline jurisdiction on those disputes, and the only possible mechanism to solve the dispute will be the arbitration that has been chosen by the parties. If, on the contrary, the parties have not entered into an arbitration agreement, disputes between them will have to be solved by the national court that has jurisdiction (according to international treaties, regional regulations or national civil procedure law, as was seen in Chapter 4, Section 3.1). An arbitral tribunal, in other words, bases its existence upon the agreement by the parties. Moreover, the parties determine the composition of the arbitral tribunal, the procedural rules that have to be followed by the arbitral tribunal, the scope of the tribunal's competence and its power. The arbitral tribunal is bound to follow the instructions of the parties; otherwise, it exceeds the power that the parties have conferred on it. If the arbitral tribunal exceeds its power, neither its jurisdiction nor its award are founded on the parties' agreement, and there is, consequently, no legal basis for any of the two. We will revert in Chapter 5, Section 3 below, in the context of the control that the courts may exercise on arbitration, to what consequences it has for an award when it was not based on the parties' instructions.

Arbitration's dependence on the parties' will, which is so uniformly recognised, is an important factor strengthening the opinion that arbitration is a private matter between the parties, and that national courts or state laws have no possibility of interfering with the parties' will. This opinion is certainly confirmed by the observation that the vast majority of arbitral awards are complied with voluntarily by the losing party. The parties agree to submit the dispute to arbitration, then they instruct the arbitral tribunal as to the scope of the dispute, the rules to be applied, etc., then the losing party recognises the arbitration's result and complies voluntarily with the award. In situations such as this one, the totality of the arbitration takes place in the private sphere of the parties. There is no point of contact between the national courts and the arbitration. Consequently, there will be no national judge that decides to override the parties' contract or expectations by considering an agreement invalid because it violates EU competition law,[11] or a firm offer as not binding because it does not comply with some formal requirements set by the chosen law.[12] The arbitrators may or may not decide to apply these rules, but, as long as the losing party accepts the result of the arbitration, there will be no possibility for any judge to verify the arbitrator's decision. In these cases, therefore, the considerations made in the previous chapters are relevant only to the extent that the arbitral tribunal is requested by the parties or elects to apply state law to the dispute.

When the losing party does not voluntarily comply with the award, the courts will intervene. In these cases, the considerations made in the previous chapters may become relevant, as the following sections will show.

1.4.1 International arbitration and the state law of the place of arbitration

A statement that is often to be met, in respect of international arbitration, is that arbitration is detached from national laws. According to an opinion that was quite influential, especially some decades ago, arbitration is international, and, as such, it does not even have a forum.[13] Particularly, no importance should be attached to the legal system of the place of arbitration: this opinion assumed that the mere circumstance that an international arbitration happens to have its seat in a certain state should not create any link with the legal system of that state. The choice of the place of arbitration, according to this opinion, is based on considerations of practical convenience, such as the relative vicinity to the states of both parties, the possibility of having convenient flight connections or the availability of modern and efficient meeting facilities.

As a matter of fact, the place of arbitration has a significant impact that may affect the validity and enforceability of the arbitral award, and the venue should therefore be chosen first of all out of legal considerations.[14] This will be seen more in detail in the following sections.

---

[11] Violation of EU competition law is, according to a controversial ECJ decision, to be deemed as a violation of *ordre public* (*Eco Swiss China Time Ltd* v. *Benetton International NV*, C-126/97). See Chapter 4 sections 4.3.1 and Chapter 5, Section 2.6.4.4.

[12] See Chapter 3, section 6.1.

[13] See, for example, Marc Blessing, 'Choice of Substantive Law in International Arbitration', (1997) 14(2) *Journal of International Arbitration*, 39–65; Marc Blessing, 'Keynotes on Arbitral Decision-Making: The New 1998 ICC Rules of Arbitration', (1997) *The ICC International Court of Arbitration Bulletin* Special Supplement, 44ff.; Lando, 'The *Lex Mercatoria* in International Commercial Arbitration' (1985) 34 *International and Comparative Law Quarterly*, 765ff.; Jan Paulsson, 'Arbitration Unbound: Award Detached from the Law of its State of Origin', (1981) 30 *International and Comparative Law Quarterly*, 358–87, 358ff., 362ff. and 381; Jan Paulsson, 'Delocalisation of International Commercial Arbitration: When and Why it Matters', (1983) 32(1) *International and Comparative Law Quarterly*, 53–61.

[14] Not only the law of the place of arbitration, but also other national laws may have an impact on arbitration, and this is quite irrespective of whether the parties have chosen them to apply or have even decided that they shall not apply: the law of the place of enforcement and, to a certain extent, the law applicable to the substance of the dispute. See, more extensively, Giuditta Cordero-Moss, 'International Arbitration is Not Only International', in Giuditta Cordero-Moss (ed.), *International Commercial Arbitration: Different Forms and their Features* (Cambridge University Press, 2013), pp. 7–39.

Personally, I have never experienced that the parties, when drafting the arbitration clause in a contract, pay attention to the above mentioned practical aspects of the venue. On the contrary, there is either a struggle to locate the venue in each party's own state or a state having a similar legal system, or a consensus on locating the venue in a legal system generally known as neutral and having extensive experience with that kind of arbitration. For example, in contracts between Western parties and Russian or former Soviet parties, it is very common to see an Arbitration clause locating the venue of arbitration in Stockholm. Sweden has traditionally been considered as a neutral state, and the Arbitration Institute of the SCC has developed a considerable expertise in this field.

1.4.1.1 The relevance of the *lex arbitri* to the procedure of the arbitral proceeding

Generally, arbitration is governed by the arbitration law of the place where the tribunal has its venue (the territoriality principle). The territoriality principle is affirmed, for example, in the Swedish Arbitration Act, Section 46, the Swiss Private International Law Act, Section 176, the English Arbitration Act, Section 2, the Italian Code of Civil Procedure, Section 816.1 and the UNCITRAL Model Law, Section 1.2. The territoriality principle applies only to the law governing the arbitral procedure, and does not extend to cover also the law governing the merits of the dispute. The law governing the merits of the dispute is the law chosen by the parties or, failing such choice, the law applicable according to the conflict rules that the tribunal considers applicable (for example, UNCITRAL Model Law, Section 28.2, the English Arbitration Act, Section 46.3), or the law that has the closest connection with the disputed matter (for example, the Swiss Private International Law Act, Section 187.1) or the rules of law that the tribunal deems applicable (for example, the French Civil Procedure Code, Section 1511). Some states have also opened up the possibility of the parties choosing the law governing the arbitral procedure. Therefore, in these states, the parties may derogate from the territoriality principle in respect of the arbitral procedure: see, for example, the Swiss Private International Law Act, Section 182.1. A clause in the commercial contract specifying which law shall govern the contract, however, is not sufficient to choose the law governing the arbitration – not even if the arbitration agreement is made in the form of a clause contained in the same commercial contract. If the parties wish the arbitral proceeding to be regulated by a law different from the law of the place where the arbitral tribunal is seated, they have to make a specific choice of law expressly for the arbitral procedure (assuming that the arbitration law of the place of arbitration permits making such a choice).

In England, a High Court decision commented that, in theory, it would be possible to submit arbitration to a procedural law different from the law of the state where the arbitral tribunal has its venue, but the result would be highly unsatisfactory or absurd.[15]

---

[15] [1993] 3 Lloyd's Rep., 48. On the adequacy of considering that the law governing the arbitral agreement is the law of the state where the tribunal is seated, see Fritz A. Mann, 'Lex facit arbitrum', in Pieter Saunders (ed.) *Liber Amicorum for Martin Domke* (Martinus Nijhoff 1967), pp. 157ff., 164ff.

Irrespective of whether the parties have chosen to submit their dispute to an ad hoc or an institutional arbitration, the arbitral proceeding will thus generally be subject to the arbitration law of the state where the arbitral tribunal has its venue. If the parties have provided for arbitration rules (either directly in the agreement or by reference to arbitration rules such as the UNCITRAL, or indirectly via the choice of an institutional arbitration), these rules will apply to their proceeding and will prevail over the rules contained in the national arbitration law, if the latter is allowed to be derogated from by the agreement of the parties. In the case of mandatory provisions of the national arbitration law, however, the arbitration law will override the arbitration rules chosen by the parties. An example of a mandatory provision is the rule that defines which claims are arbitrable; other examples are the rules ensuring due process of law, such as the necessity to give both parties the possibility of being heard.[16]

In addition, the law of the place of arbitration contains rules on the powers of the arbitrators to issue interim measures, to summon witnesses and to request assistance from the local courts in such operations. In addition, this law contains rules on the role of courts, for example, in the case of a challenge to the impartiality of the arbitral tribunal.

Arbitration laws are, usually, quite liberal in their regulation of arbitration. The parties wish to have as much flexibility as possible in the organisation of this mechanism for dispute resolution as it is chosen precisely because it leaves ample room for private determination. If state law started to regulate arbitration in detail, this method of dispute resolution would probably lose much of its appeal to commercial parties. However, if there were no regulation at all, the parties might fear that fundamental principles of process might be neglected. Therefore, a successful arbitration law is an instrument that manages to ensure a high degree of flexibility, but one which provides certain rules to protect the principle of due process.

1.4.1.2 The relevance of the *lex arbitri* to the challenge of an arbitral award

The assumption that the legal system of the seat of arbitration (*lex arbitri*) has no link with the arbitration itself is not correct in further respects. As mentioned above, the losing party may, in most jurisdictions, challenge before the national courts the validity of an arbitral award that has been rendered in that state. This means that the courts of the state of arbitration have the possibility of controlling the validity of the award; and this is definitely an important link between international arbitration and the forum. The judicial control on arbitral awards in the phase of a challenge is regulated by national arbitration law. This means that the arbitration law of the *lex arbitri* determines whether the award is valid or not. The already mentioned UNCITRAL Model Law has created a certain harmonisation in numerous national arbitration laws; and the Model Law provides, in article 34, a list of grounds upon

---

[16] The UNCITRAL Model Law contains provisions to this extent, for example, in Articles 18, 23.1, 24.2 and 24.3.

which a national court may set aside an arbitral award rendered in that state. However, since national arbitration laws belong to each national legal system, it will always be necessary to verify the state law of the state of the seat in order to ascertain what possibilities the judge has in terms of annulling an award.

In some states, awards rendered in disputes without any contact with that state enjoy a certain detachment from the system of the forum. In French law,[17] a reform of the arbitration law made in 2011 permits the parties to agree on a waiver of their right to recourse against any arbitral award rendered in France in an international dispute. Additionally, Swiss[18] and Belgian[19] law permit the parties to enter into an exclusion agreement, thus excluding the court's jurisdiction to challenge the validity of the award. However, an exclusion agreement may be entered into only for awards rendered in disputes where neither party was resident in the country where the award was rendered. Also, Swedish law[20] permits the parties to exclude the control by Swedish courts on arbitral awards rendered in Sweden in disputes where neither party is a resident of Sweden, but only in respect of the so-called relative invalidity grounds; that is, grounds that have to be invoked by one of the parties. Exclusion agreements are not allowed by Swedish law in respect of absolute invalidity grounds, upon which the judge can act on his or her own motion. In most other states, as well as under the UNCITRAL Model Law, the control of the courts cannot be excluded.

The list of grounds upon which a court may declare an award invalid varies, as mentioned, from state to state. In some states, as in England, the judge has relatively wide powers. Among others things, an English judge may verify the arbitral tribunal's application of law, although the possibility of setting aside an award for an error in law has been significantly restricted in the English Arbitration Act of 1996. In most other European states, the list of invalidity grounds can be broadly said to coincide with the list contained in Article 34 of the UNCITRAL Model Law, which, in turn, coincides with the list of grounds upon which an award may be refused enforcement under the New York Convention. These grounds may be summarised as referring to invalidity or irregularity in the following areas: the arbitration agreement, the composition of the arbitral tribunal, the procedure of the arbitration and the scope of power exercised by the tribunal. In addition, the award can be declared invalid if there is a contrast with that state's *ordre public* or with that state's rule on arbitrability. Sections 2 and 3 below examine the grounds for invalidity that are relevant to the question of how self-sufficient an international contract may be.

1.4.1.3 The relevance of the *lex arbitri* to the enforcement of an arbitral award

The *lex arbitri* is also relevant in the context of the enforcement of an award. If the award is sought to be enforced in the same country where it was rendered,

---

[17] French Code of Civil Procedure Article 1522.   [18] Swiss Private International Law Act Article 192.
[19] Belgian Judicial Code Article 1717(4).   [20] Swedish Arbitration Act Article 51.

the *lex arbitri* will coincide with the law of the place of enforcement, which is discussed in Section 1.4.2 below. Even if the award is sought to be enforced in another country, the *lex arbitri* may be relevant. In Article V.1.(e), the New York Convention considers it as a sufficient ground to refuse enforcement of an award, if the award has been set aside by a competent authority in the state where the award was made. The New York Convention, however, does not specify on what grounds an award may be set aside; this is for the arbitration law of the court of challenge to determine. Therefore, even if enforcement is uniformly regulated by the New York Convention, reference to the annulment of an award opens a channel between the enforcement of an award and the non-harmonised grounds for annulment of the *lex arbitri*. Usually, an award that has been annulled in its state of origin is considered as no longer having any legal effect; however, French courts enforce awards that have been set aside,[21] and there are also some precedents – albeit not undisputed – in other countries, such as the US.[22] Recently, a Dutch court[23] decided to enforce an award despite its annulment in the country of origin: Russia. This decision, however, cannot directly be compared to an enforcement decision in a usual commercial case, based as it was on considerations of impartiality and independence of the Russian courts, as this was a case involving the interests of the Russian state. The award had been rendered in a dispute on investment protection regarding breaches by the Russian Federation of its public international law obligations following what the arbitral tribunal had found was an unlawful treatment of the oil company Yukos.

Disregarding an annulment made in the award's country of origin is, however, the exception rather than the rule, and it is certainly not uncontroversial.[24]

1.4.2 International arbitration and the state law of the place(s) of enforcement

As already mentioned, if the losing party refuses to abide by the award, the winning party will have to seek enforcement with the courts of a state where the losing party has some assets. The enforcement of foreign arbitral awards is regulated uniformly by the New York Convention, which provides a simple and arbitration-friendly procedure. The only grounds that a court may invoke to refuse enforcement of an arbitral award are listed in Article V of the New York Convention. These grounds correspond to those contained in the UNCITRAL Model Law in respect of a challenge of the validity (Article 34), as well as in respect of enforcement (Article 36). Therefore, the enforcement of an arbitral award can be refused in case of invalidity or irregularities

---

[21] The most well-known example is *Hilmarton*, reported in *Yearbook Commercial Arbitration XX*, pp. 663–5 and *XXII*, (Kluwer International, 1997), pp. 696–8. See also the *Chromalloy* decision, reported in *Yearbook Commercial Arbitration XXXI*, (Kluwer International, 2007), pp. 629ff.

[22] For references, see Gary Born, *International Commercial Arbitration* (Kluwer International, 2009), pp. 2677–91.

[23] Decision of the Amsterdam Court of Appeal of 28 April 2009.

[24] For an overview of the literature on this matter see Born, *International Commercial Arbitration*, pp. 2672ff.

relating to the arbitration agreement, the composition of the arbitral tribunal and the arbitral procedure, as well as an excess of power, conflict with the *ordre public* of the state of enforcement and conflict with the arbitrability rule of the state of enforcement. In addition, as seen above, an award may be refused enforcement if it has been set aside in the state of origin. Sections 2 and 3 below analyse the grounds for refusing enforcement that are relevant to the question discussed in this book.

1.5 Specific criteria for invalidity or unenforceability of arbitral awards: is an international award really detached from state law?

Arbitration is, as known, an out-of-court method of dispute resolution that is mostly based on the will of the parties. The tribunal is bound to follow the parties' instructions, because it does not have any powers outside of the parties' agreement. Tribunals are, therefore, and correctly, very reluctant to deviate from the instructions of the parties. In some situations, however, the arbitral tribunal may consider whether it should disregard the choice of law made by the parties in the contract. One party could invoke rules of the law that would be applicable if they did not contain a choice of a different law – for example, one party may contest the other party's claim for breach of contract, alleging that there was no breach, because the non-performed obligation was invalid under that law. An arbitral tribunal may even consider disregarding the contract's choice of law if following the contract's choice of law would result in an award that is invalid or cannot be enforced because it violates certain principles of the country where the arbitral tribunal has its seat or of the country where enforcement will be sought. To avoid rendering invalid or unenforceable awards, the arbitral tribunal may be tempted to disregard the parties' instructions, also including the contract's choice of law. This, however, exposes the award to the risk of being annulled or refused enforcement on the basis of another ground; namely, that the arbitral tribunal went beyond the scope of the power that the parties had conferred on it.

As was seen above, as long as arbitral awards are complied with voluntarily by the losing party, there is no contact between the national courts and the arbitration.

If the losing party does not voluntarily accept the award, there are two possibilities of obtaining judicial control on an award: (i) the losing party may challenge the validity of an arbitral award before the courts of the place where the award was rendered; and (ii) the losing party may abstain from carrying out the award, so inducing the winning party to seek enforcement of an arbitral award by the courts of the country (or countries) where the losing party has assets.

1.5.1 Challenge to the validity

The validity of an award may be challenged before the courts of the place where the award was rendered. As the challenge is regulated by national arbitration law, and may differ from country to country, it is impossible to carry out an analysis in general terms regarding validity. We will here look at the discipline contained in the already mentioned UNCITRAL Model Law on International Commercial Arbitration, which is acknowledged as embodying a general consensus in the matter of arbitration, is adopted more or less literally in sixty-nine countries and is used as a term of reference even in many countries that have not formally adopted it.[25]

The grounds that may be invoked under Article 34 of the UNCITRAL Model Law to make an award invalid are the same grounds that may be invoked under Article 36 of the Model Law as defences against the enforcement of an award. These are, in turn, the same grounds that are listed in the New York Convention on the Recognition and Enforcement of Foreign Arbitral Awards as the only possible defences against the enforcement of an award.

1.5.2 Enforcement

Enforcement of an arbitral award is regulated, in the 149 countries that have ratified it, by the already mentioned 1958 New York Convention on the Recognition and Enforcement of Foreign Arbitral Awards.

In Article V, the New York Convention contains an exhaustive list of the grounds that may be invoked to prevent the enforcement of an award.

2 Grounds for refusing enforcement or for invalidity of the award

We will analyse here the grounds for refusing enforcement or setting aside an arbitral award that are relevant to questions of governing law. As was seen above, enforceability is regulated uniformly by the New York Convention. Challenge to the validity, on the contrary, is regulated by national law. National arbitration laws are not harmonised, and it is therefore impossible to make statements having general validity in this respect. We will focus here on the UNCITRAL Model Law on International Commercial Arbitration. The Model Law was intended as a source of harmonisation in international arbitration. To this end, and to ensure continuity, it was deliberately aligned with the New York Convention.[26] In the interests of harmonisation, both instruments shall be interpreted autonomously. An autonomous interpretation aims at construing and applying a rule in a uniform way that is common to all countries that have adopted or ratified the instrument. It assumes that a court avoids special interpretations due to peculiarities of its specific national system, and it requires that a court takes into consideration the construction and application of the instrument in other countries as a parameter for its own interpretation. As the criteria for

---

[25] For example, Sweden and England have Arbitration Acts that follow their respective legislative tradition and cannot be considered as having adopted the Model Law. However, the Model Law has consistently been taken into consideration in the drafting work.

[26] See the Explanatory Note by the UNCITRAL Secretariat on the Model Law on International Commercial Arbitration, www.uncitral.org/uncitral/en/uncitral_texts/arbitration/1985Model_arbitration.html.

challenging the validity and resisting the enforcement of an award are identical in all these provisions, the interpretation or application of Articles 34 and 36 of the UNCITRAL Model Law, as well as of Article V of the New York Convention, are relevant to each other. Therefore, we will deal with the grounds for invalidity and the grounds for unenforceability jointly, and the comments made on the Model Law will be applicable also to the New York Convention, and vice versa.

It is, however, important to bear in mind that, as mentioned above, invalidity of an arbitral award is regulated by the various national laws, and that there may be further grounds for invalidity in the countries that have not adopted the UNCITRAL Model Law.

There is a strong consensus on the opportunity to restrictively interpret the provisions on the invalidity and unenforceability of arbitral awards; that is, to restrict the scope of judicial control.[27] Nothing in the wording of Articles 34 and 36 of the UNCITRAL Model Law or Article V of the New York Convention suggests that the courts have the authority to review the merits of the arbitral decision, either in respect of the evaluation of the facts or in respect of the application of the law.[28] Judicial control under the UNCITRAL Model Law and under the New York Convention, in other words, may not be used as a vehicle for the court to act upon an error in law incurred by the arbitral tribunal, no matter how evident the error is. The impossibility of being able to control the arbitral award in terms of the merits, also including the application of the law, is generally acknowledged both in theory and in judicial practice.[29]

As we will see below, this restriction in the scope of judicial control is of the utmost significance for the question that we are analysing here; that is, to what extent the arbitral tribunal may interpret and apply the contract without any reference to the applicable law.

2.1 Invalidity of the arbitration agreement

Article V(1)(a) of the New York Convention, regulating the enforcement of an arbitral award, states that enforcement may be refused if '[t]he . . . agreement referred to in article II . . . is not valid under the law to which the parties have subjected it or,

---

[27] Born, *International Commercial Arbitration*, vol. II, pp. 2714ff., and Redfern, Hunter, Blackaby and Partasides, *Redfern and Hunter on International Arbitration*, paras. 11.56–11.60.

[28] See Born, *International Commercial Arbitration*, pp. 2865ff., Redfern, Hunter, Blackaby and Partasides, *Redfern and Hunter on International Arbitration*, para. 11.56.

[29] In common law, there is a tradition of permitting a certain control over an error in law during the phase of a challenge to the validity of an award, although it has been considerably restricted in modern legislation (see, for example, Section 69 of the English Arbitration Act). This, however, does not affect the enforceability of a foreign award that is governed by the New York Convention. See Gary Born, *International Commercial Arbitration: Commentary and Materials*, 2nd edn (Kluwer Law International, 2001), p. 181, with references to the US doctrine of manifest disregard of the law, which may be used as a defence against enforcement of a US award, but not of a foreign award.

failing any indication thereon, under the law of the country where the award was made'. Articles 34 and 36 of the UNCITRAL Model Law contain similar wording.

Arbitration agreements are usually in the form of an Arbitration clause contained in the contract regulating the commercial relationship between the parties. Based on the ambitions of self-sufficiency described in Chapter 1, the parties may be under the impression that their agreement to arbitrate relies exclusively on the contract and is, under any scenario, effective according to its terms. The validity of an arbitration agreement, however, depends on the applicable law – and the law applicable to an arbitration agreement is not necessarily the law applicable to the commercial contract. The applicable law will affect the scope and the form requirements for the arbitration agreement. Chapter 1 showed how the drafting of Arbitration clauses evolved to specify which disputes are referred to arbitration; Section 2.7 will discuss how the applicable law affects which disputes are deemed to be arbitrable. Sections 2.1.1–2.1.8 will analyse the impact of the applicable law on the formal validity of an arbitration agreement.

2.1.1 National arbitration laws on the validity of arbitration agreements

According to Article V(1)(a) of the New York Convention, the validity of the arbitration agreement is governed by the law to which the parties have subjected that agreement (which is not the same as the law that the parties have chosen to govern their contractual relationship) or, failing any choice in this respect, the law of the country where the award was made. The latter – the *lex arbitri* – is more commonly used, as parties rarely specify the law governing their arbitration agreement. Neither do model Arbitration clauses recommended by arbitration institutions[30] or (for ad hoc arbitration) by the UNCITRAL[31] contain a choice of law specific for arbitration. The Model clauses may suggest adding which law governs the contract, but this applies to the merits of the dispute, not to the procedural aspects of the arbitration, as is confirmed by the wording suggested by the LCIA ('The governing law of the contract shall be the *substantive* law of []') and by the SCC ('This contract shall be governed by the *substantive* law of [...]'). Article V(1)(a) of the New York Convention therefore generally leads to the application of the law of the country where the arbitral tribunal is seated to determine whether the arbitration agreement is valid. National laws may vary considerably in the formal requirements that they lay down for arbitration agreements. Some lay down strict criteria, while others are less demanding or lay down no formal requirements at all. Article 178(1) of the Swiss Private International Law Act requires the arbitration agreement to be in writing, which is said to include an exchange of telegrams, faxes or other means of

---

[30] See, for example, the model clauses recommended by the ICC (www.iccwbo.org/Products-and-Services/ Arbitration-and-ADR/Arbitration/Standard-ICC-Arbitration-Clauses/), the LCIA (www.lcia.org/Dispute_ Resolution_Services/LCIA_Recommended_Clauses.aspx) or the SCC (www.sccinstitute.com/english-14. aspx#arbitration).

[31] Contained as an annex to the Arbitration Rules, see www.uncitral.org/pdf/english/texts/arbitration/arb-rules-revised/arb-rules-revised-2010-e.pdf.

telecommunication that provide a record of the agreement.[32] Similar criteria are found in Article 1031 of the German Code of Civil Procedure, which, in addition, specifies that the writing requirement will be deemed to have been met if the arbitration agreement is contained in a document sent to one party and if such a party has not raised any objections in good time.[33] Section 5 of the English Arbitration Act requires that the arbitration agreement be in writing, which is explained as meaning that it has been made or evidenced in writing or is contained in an exchange in writing.[34] However, Section 5 goes on to qualify as written agreements, those that are also made other than in writing, as long as they refer to terms that are in writing and agreements that have been recorded in writing only by one party. It also specifies that reference to anything being written or in writing includes its being recorded by any means. Even more liberal is the Swedish Arbitration Act, Article 1 of which recognises any arbitration agreement, provided it has been agreed by the parties, without laying down any particular form for that agreement.[35] A similar provision is found in the Norwegian Arbitration Act.[36]

---

[32] Article 178(1) of the Swiss Private International Law Act reads: 'The arbitration agreement has to be made in writing, by telegram, telex, telefax or other means of telecommunication which provide a record of the agreement'.

[33] German Code of Civil Procedure Article 1031 reads:

'(1) The arbitration agreement shall be contained either in a document signed by the parties or in an exchange of letters, telefaxes, telegrams or other means of telecommunication which provide a record of the agreement.

(2) The form requirement of subsection 1 shall be deemed to have been complied with if the arbitration agreement is contained in a document transmitted from one party to the other party or by a third party to both parties and – if no objection was raised in good time – the contents of such document are considered to be part of the contract in accordance with common usage'.

[34] English Arbitration Act Section 5 reads:

'(1) The provisions of this Part apply only when the arbitration agreement is in writing, and any other agreement between the parties as to any matter is effective for the purpose of this Part only if in writing. The expressions 'agreement', 'agree' and 'agreed' shall be construed accordingly.

(2) There is an agreement in writing –
   (a) if the agreement is made in writing (whether or not it is signed by the parties),
   (b) if the agreement is made by exchange of communications in writing, or
   (c) if the agreement is evidenced in writing.

(3) Where parties agree otherwise than in writing by reference to terms which are in writing, they make an agreement in writing.

(4) An agreement is evidenced in writing if an agreement made otherwise than in writing is recorded by one of the parties, or by a third party, with the authority of the parties to the agreement.

(5) An exchange of written submissions in arbitral or legal proceedings in which the existence of an agreement otherwise than in writing is alleged by one party against another party and not denied by the other party in his response constitutes as between those parties an agreement in writing to the effect alleged.

(6) References in this Part to anything being written or in writing include its being recorded by any means'.

[35] Article 1 of the Swedish Arbitration Act reads:

'Disputes concerning matters in respect of which the parties may reach a settlement may, by agreement, be referred to one or several arbitrators for resolution'.

[36] Section 3–10 of the Norwegian Arbitration Act reads:

'(1) The parties may agree to submit to arbitration disputes which have arisen, as well as all or certain disputes which may arise in respect of a defined legal relationship'.

An arbitration agreement that is entered into by reference, tacitly or even orally, would satisfy the applicable formal requirements only if the applicable law is liberal in its requirements or lays down no formal requirements at all. On the other hand, an arbitration agreement entered into electronically would be valid not only where the applicable law is liberal in its requirements or lays down no formal requirements, but also where there is a written requirement, since this requirement may be construed as including exchanges by various means of telecommunication. The same construction is also possible for Article II of the New York Convention, as will be discussed below in Section 2.1.3.

2.1.2 UNCITRAL Model Law on the validity of arbitration agreements

Article 7(2) of the Model Law originally defined the scope of the writing requirement for arbitration agreements as follows: 'An agreement is in writing if it is contained in a document signed by the parties or in an exchange of letters, telex, telegrams or other means of telecommunication which provide a record of the agreement'.

The Model Law followed the New York Convention in requiring arbitration agreements to be in writing. It clarified this requirement so as to cover technological developments that were known at the time it was drafted, while at the same time allowing for future technological developments, so long as they provide a record of the agreement.

The original spirit of these instruments was to give effect to arbitration agreements made using the technological means of communication commonly employed in business practice. In other words, the wording of the instruments was not to become a burden on the parties, preventing them from making use of developments in technology that did not yet exist at the time the instruments were drafted. Hence, the original version of the Model Law could be construed as allowing arbitration agreements made electronically, even though electronic communication did not exist at the time of drafting the Model Law. This could be used as an argument in support of a similar interpretation of the New York Convention.

The Model Law was amended on 7 July 2006 at UNCITRAL's 39th session, and the amendments were recommended by the General Assembly at its 61st session.[37] This was the culmination of a process that had begun in 1999 when the UNCITRAL Working Group on Arbitration took up the issue of the writing requirement for arbitration agreements.[38]

With regard to qualifying an agreement made electronically as an agreement in writing, the Working Group emphasised that the clarification resulting from

---

[37] General Assembly Resolution A/RES/61/32 of 2006. The full text of the amended Model Law can be found at www.uncitral.org/pdf/english/texts/arbitration/ml-arb/MLARB-english_revised%2006.pdf. See also the Explanatory Note to the amended version of the Model Law, with further references: www.uncitral.org/pdf/english/texts/arbitration/ml-arb/MLARB_explanatory_note.pdf.

[38] Official records of the General Assembly, fifty-fourth session, supplement no. 17 (A/54/17), paras. 344–50

the amendment did not alter the existing liberal interpretation of the Model Law, but simply confirmed that interpretation.[39]

The 2006 amendments to the Model Law included two options for Article 7 on the writing requirement. One option maintained the original structure of Article 7 and specified what was to be understood by writing in new subsections: 3 and 4. In this first option,[40] Article 7(3) explained that the writing requirement is a question of proof of the agreement, and not a prerequisite for its existence. Article 7(4) then laid down how the writing requirement is to be understood. In doing so, it largely followed Article 6(1) of the UNCITRAL Model Law on Electronic Commerce. Thus, the writing requirement is met by an electronic communication if its content is accessible so as to be usable for subsequent reference. There then follows a non-exhaustive list of examples, including electronic data interchange, electronic mail, telegram, telex and telecopy.

The debate within the UNCITRAL Working Group on Arbitration and the first option in the Article 7 amendments can be seen as confirmation that the writing requirement should not exclude those means of communication commonly used by businesses.

This is not to say, however, that the writing requirement is on the verge of being totally abandoned. While the original text of the Model Law permits arbitration agreements entered into tacitly (in an exchange of statements of claim and defence where the alleged existence of the arbitration agreement is not denied) or by reference, and while some state laws have already done away with formal requirements, as seen in Section 2.1.1 above, no consensus reigned over whether the Model Law should follow the initiative taken by those states. This can be seen from reactions to the second option in the Article 7 amendments.[41] In this option, there was no reference to any formal requirements, and therefore no need to spell out that electronic communications complied with the writing requirement or that agreements entered into tacitly or by reference were permissible. The comments made by governments

---

[39] See A/CN.9/WG.II/WP.118, para. 11.

[40] The text of the amended Article 7, option I, reads as follows: '(1) [not amended: arbitration agreement]. (2) The arbitration agreement shall be in writing. (3) An arbitration agreement is in writing if its content is recorded in any form, whether or not the arbitration agreement or contract has been concluded orally, by conduct, or by other means. (4) The requirement that an arbitration agreement be in writing is met by an electronic communication if the information contained therein is accessible so as to be useable for subsequent reference: "electronic communication" means any communication that the parties make by means of data messages; "data message" means information generated, received, sent or stored by electronic, magnetic, optical or similar means, including, but not limited to, electronic data interchange (EDI), electronic mail, telegram, telex or telecopy. (5) Furthermore, an arbitration agreement is in writing if [wording as in the original article 7(2): exchange of statements of claim and defence]. (6) [agreement by reference to another contract as in the original Article 7(2), amended in that the contract referred to does not need to be in writing]'.

[41] Option II of the amended Article 7 reads: '"Arbitration agreement" is an agreement by the parties to submit to arbitration all or certain disputes which have arisen or which may arise between them in respect of a defined legal relationship, whether contractual or not'.

suggest that this option did not enjoy their full and unanimous support.[42] It was nevertheless adopted as an alternative to the first option.

As a consequence, states that adopt the UNCITRAL Model Law on International Commercial Arbitration will, in the future, have to choose between the first option requiring that the arbitration agreement be in writing, where it will be necessary to clarify that any electronic communication meets that requirement, and the second option, where there are no formal requirements at all.

While the first option does not appear incompatible with the New York Convention, as will be seen below, the complete absence of formal requirements in the second option might create some problems.

2.1.3 Article II of the New York Convention on the validity of arbitration agreements

Article II of the New York Convention requires states to recognise arbitration agreements that have been entered into in writing (amongst certain other criteria). Article II (2) specifies: 'The term "agreement in writing" shall include an Arbitral clause in a contract or an arbitration agreement, signed by the parties or contained in an exchange of letters or telegrams'. Whether or not this definition also covers agreements entered into electronically depends on the interpretation made of Article II(2).

There is no explicit reference to electronic telecommunication in the wording of Article II. This is hardly surprising, as no one could have imagined in 1958, when the Convention was drafted, that technological developments would lead to electronic exchanges between opposite ends of the world and that such exchanges would be part of daily life for international business.

The wording of the New York Convention needs to be interpreted in light of the technological context in which the Convention was drafted. The reference to 'an exchange of letters or telegrams' must be seen as a reference to the most modern means of telecommunication that were known at the time. The intention of the Convention was therefore to recognise arbitration agreements that were entered into by absent parties using the means of communication that they generally employed in the course of their business. In 1958, these means were letters and telegrams. Technological development subsequently led to the telex. Exchanges by telex were not expressly referred to in Article II(2) of the New York Convention, yet court decisions in various countries stated that Article II(2) must be construed to cover exchanges by telex, too.[43] Further technological development made way for the fax

---

[42] See, particularly, the comments by Italy (A/CN.9/609), Belgium (A/CN.9/609/Add.3), France (A/CN.9/609/Add.5) and Austria (A/CN.9/609/Add.6). Germany, on the other hand, favoured the second option (A/CN.9/609/Add.2).

[43] See, for example, the Austrian decision published in *Yearbook Commercial Arbitration I* (Kluwer International, 1976), p. 183, and the Swiss decisions published in *Yearbook Commercial Arbitration XII* (Kluwer International, 1987), p. 502 and *XXI* (Kluwer International, 1996), p. 681. For further references, see the note by the UNCITRAL Secretariat contained in A/CN.9/WG.II/WP.139 for the 44th session of the

and, again, although there is no explicit reference to faxes in Article II(2) of the New York Convention, courts have construed the Convention as covering arbitration agreements entered into by fax.[44]

Technological development has continued and today it allows for communication by electronic means. It seems only natural to extend the interpretation of Article II(2) once again, so as to cover the most modern means of communication that are widely used for concluding contracts. To do otherwise would be contrary to the spirit of the Convention, which was aimed at recognising arbitration agreements, provided that they were concluded in a form that was generally adopted for the conclusion of contracts.

This interpretation is not only a natural continuation of the construction that the courts have made of Article II(2) whenever new means of telecommunication have become commonly adopted (i.e., first telex, then fax, and now electronic communication), but it is also confirmed in the wording chosen by the UNCITRAL to define the writing requirement for arbitration agreements in the original 1985 Model Law on International Commercial Arbitration and in the 2006 amendments to the Model Law, as seen above. Although the Model Law does not formally constitute a basis for interpreting the New York Convention, it is natural to construe the latter in light of the former, as they are linked by a common path of development.[45]

Such an interpretation is not, however, uncontroversial, and clarification has been sought[46] to prevent different courts from construing the New York Convention in different ways and thereby undermining the uniformity of interpretation, which is one of the most valuable assets of the New York Convention.

To this end, the UNCITRAL General Assembly adopted a 'Recommendation regarding the interpretation of Article II(2) and Article VII, paragraph 1, of the Convention on the Recognition and Enforcement of Foreign Arbitral Awards, done in New York, 10 June 1958, adopted by the United Nations Commission on International Trade Law on 7 July 2006 at its thirty-ninth session'.[47] The adoption of this document followed intensive debate within the Working Group on how best to

---

Working Group on Arbitration (January 2006), regarding the preparation of uniform provisions on the written form for arbitration agreements, para. 22 and footnote 52: www.uncitral.org/uncitral/en/commission/working_groups/2Arbitration.html.

[44] See, for example, the Swiss decision published in *Yearbook Commercial Arbitration XXI*, p. 685 and, for further references, the UNCITRAL Secretariat note A/CN.9/WG.II/WP.139, footnote 53.

[45] The Swiss Supreme Court has expressly stated that Article II(2) must be read in light of Article 7(2) of the UNCITRAL Model Law on International Commercial Arbitration, see A. J. van den Berg, 'The Application of the New York Convention by the Courts' in A. J. van den Berg (ed.), *Improving the Efficiency of Arbitration Agreements and Awards: 40 Years of Application of the New York Convention*, ICCA Congress Series No. 9 (The Hague: Kluwer Law International, 1999), p. 32.

[46] See the general observations and the discussion within the UNCITRAL Working Group on Arbitration, particularly in the report of its 32nd session in 2000, A/CN.9/468, paras. 88–106: daccessdds.un.org/doc/UNDOC/GEN/V00/530/64/PDF/V0053064.pdf?OpenElement. For an overview of court interpretation of Article II(2), see the UNCITRAL Secretariat note A/CN.9/WG.II/WP.139, footnote 57.

[47] A/RES/61/33, www.uncitral.org/pdf/english/texts/arbitration/NY-conv/A2E.pdf.

approach the need for clarification of the New York Convention. An interpretative instrument capable of encouraging a uniform interpretation in accordance with current practice was seen as the most effective means.

To endorse its authority, the Recommendation recalls, in the preamble, the UNCITRAL's responsibility in contributing to the progressive harmonisation and unification of international trade law and achieving a consensus between the world's legal, social and economic systems. The preamble also recalls how important a uniform interpretation of the Convention is for promoting international trade, points out the diversity of legal practices relating to the form of the arbitration agreement, and refers to the Convention's aim of allowing recognition and enforcement of arbitral awards to the largest possible extent. The Recommendation also refers to subsequent legal instruments, such as the UNCITRAL Model Law on International Commercial Arbitration and the UNCITRAL Model Law on Electronic Commerce. On this basis, Article 1 of the Recommendation calls for Article II(2) of the New York Convention to be interpreted in such a way that the circumstances described therein are not exhaustive.[48] This therefore means that the exchange of letters or telegrams mentioned in Article II(2) should be considered only as an illustration, which can be supplemented with exchanges made by other means of communication.

A Recommendation by UNCITRAL does not have any binding effect on governments, and even less so on national judges interpreting the New York Convention. It is even doubtful whether such an instrument could be truly considered as an authoritative interpretation of the Convention, since the UNCITRAL can hardly be regarded as the issuing or enacting body (the UNCITRAL was established in 1966). However, it would, without any doubt, have the authority of an official view from the United Nations' body responsible for coordinating UN legal activities in the field of international trade law, covering the principal economic and legal system of the world in both developed and developing countries.

There is therefore every reason to give the UNCITRAL's position considerable weight when construing the New York Convention. However, it remains to be seen whether a Recommendation is a sufficient instrument on which to base an interpretation of Article II(2) that might differ considerably from the interpretation currently made in some countries.

Interpreting Article II(2) as covering arbitration agreements entered into electronically would not appear to overstep the limits of customary broad interpretation. As mentioned earlier, this has already been done in the past in respect of previous technological developments. The UNCITRAL Recommendation is thus simply adding its authoritative voice to confirm the correctness of such a construction.

---

[48] Article 1 of the Recommendation reads: 'Recommends that article II, paragraph 2, of the Convention on Recognition and Enforcement of Foreign Arbitral Awards, done in New York, 10 June 1958, be applied recognising that the circumstances described therein are not exhaustive'.

The situation is different, however, with respect to arbitration agreements entered into tacitly or orally. Neither the UNCITRAL Recommendation nor Article II(2) of the New York Convention would appear to provide in their wording such a clear basis for interpretation. A construction permitting such agreements would be quite detached from a literal interpretation of Article II(2).

To summarise, the New York Convention appears to accommodate the situation created by technological progress easily and, in particular, electronic communication. However, extending the writing requirement to new means of communication does not necessarily open the way to recognising arbitration agreements that are not in the written form. In this latter respect, the New York Convention does not match the more progressive regulations found in some national laws and in the second option of the 2006 amendments to the UNCITRAL Model Law on International Commercial Arbitration. Some consequences of this lack of coordination are analysed below.

2.1.4 Competition between state law and Article II of the New York Convention

As seen above, the formal requirements for arbitration agreements differ considerably from one country to another, and even the uniform regulation contained in the New York Convention is under some strain caused by the need to cover new technological developments. The range of requirements relating to form vary from none at all (as in Swedish and Norwegian law) to strict conditions (as in English law). The debate over the 2006 amendments to the UNCITRAL Model Law on International Commercial Arbitration shows a lack of consensus on eliminating the writing requirement.

As already mentioned, the validity of an arbitration agreement has important consequences at two stages: first, when the jurisdiction of the arbitral tribunal is being established, and then if, and when, the arbitral award has to be enforced. If an arbitration agreement is deemed invalid at the first stage, the arbitral tribunal will have no jurisdiction, so the dispute will have to be submitted to the ordinary courts of law. If an arbitration agreement is held to be invalid at the stage of enforcement, this will prevent the arbitral award from being enforced.

It is legitimate to enquire whether an arbitration agreement could be deemed invalid at the enforcement stage (thus preventing enforcement of the award), while having been considered valid in the initial phase (thus preventing ordinary courts from having jurisdiction over the dispute). Such a lack of coordination would obviously be detrimental to the winning party, which could neither enforce its award nor have the case tried in the ordinary courts. To ascertain whether such a risk really exists, it is necessary to look at the parameters for evaluating the validity of the arbitration agreement at each stage.

Article V(1)(a) of the New York Convention regulates the enforcement of an arbitral award and states that enforcement may be refused if '[t]he ... agreement referred to in article II ... is not valid under the law to which the parties have subjected it or, failing any indication thereon, under the law of the country where the award was made'. In spite of this wording, which refers the evaluation of the validity of the arbitration agreement to national law, judicial practice has traditionally considered Article II(2) to contain the applicable criteria.[49] It is only in Italy that some court decisions have been rendered in which different parameters were held to apply at the two stages, with Article II not applying at the enforcement stage.[50]

The reason for considering Article II(2) as solely applicable stems from the fact that for fifty years (and especially in the early decades of its existence) the New York Convention represented an internationally uniform standard, which was, more often than not, simpler and less cumbersome than the provisions of national arbitration laws. The preference given to Article II(2), therefore, reflected a desire to apply a more arbitration-friendly system than that offered by national laws.

However, the standard of what is considered as arbitration-friendly has shifted during recent years as a result of reforms in national arbitration laws.[51] Whereas it would have been relatively uncontroversial some decades ago to state that '[t]he meaning of the uniform rule character of Art. II(2) [is] that it constitutes both a maximum and a minimum requirement, thereby prevailing over either more or less demanding requirements of municipal law',[52] the uniform rule character of Article II(2) is now being increasingly challenged as a minimum requirement.

When national laws are more arbitration-friendly than the New York Convention, doubts may be expressed over the appropriateness of continuing to apply the Article II(2) criteria, rather than the more liberal criteria of national laws. The preference given to national law might be questionable at the initial stage of the arbitration, where the application of national law may be thought to violate the wording of Article II(2),[53] but it would certainly seem appropriate at the enforcement stage, where it is rather the application of the standard contained in Article II(2) that violates Article V(1)(a). The reason for not applying Article V(1)(a) literally disappears if the applicable national law is more arbitration-friendly than Article II(2).

The arbitration-friendly character of some national laws is therefore biting into the character of Article II(2) as a uniform rule, at least at the stage of enforcing an award.

---

[49] See UNCITRAL Secretariat note A/CN.9/WG.II/WP.139, paras. 12–15.

[50] See, for example, Supreme Court decision no. 637, 20 January 1995, *Rivista dell'Arbitrato* (Giuffrè 1995), p. 449 and *Yearbook Commercial Arbitration XXI*, pp. 602f.

[51] Formal requirements for arbitration agreements have been liberalised over recent years in the laws of England (Arbitration Act 1996), Germany (Civil Procedure Code 1997), Sweden (Arbitration Act 1999) and Norway (2004). Switzerland anticipated this trend by modifying its arbitration legislation in 1987. The UNCITRAL Model Law on International Commercial Arbitration is even earlier, dating from 1985.

[52] Van den Berg, 'The Application of the New York Convention by the Courts', p. 31.

[53] See, however, the German Supreme Court decisions in *Yearbook Commercial Arbitration II* (Kluwer International, 1977), pp. 242f. and *Yearbook Commercial Arbitration XX*, pp. 666ff., affirming that Article II(2) allows national law to be applied, commented on in van den Berg, 'The Application of the New York Convention by the Courts', p. 32.

2.1.5 May the more-favourable-law provision of Article VII assist?

Article VII of the New York Convention, containing the so-called more-favourable-law provision, states that the provisions of the Convention shall not 'deprive any interested party of any right he may have to avail himself of an arbitral award in the manner and to the extent allowed by the law or the treaties of the country where such award is sought to be relied upon'. Thus, a national law favourable to enforcement can be applied instead of the criteria of the New York Convention. The UNCITRAL has pointed out the possible importance of this article in permitting the application of state laws that are more favourable than the New York Convention. It also mentions the advisability of extending this article to arbitration agreements.[54] Hence, the above-mentioned Recommendation interpreting the New York Convention included an Article 2 stating that Article VII of the Convention should be read as allowing for the applicability of the law where the arbitration agreement is sought to be relied upon.[55]

Article VII of the Convention and the UNCITRAL Recommendation do not, however, answer all of the problems that might arise from conflicting requirements in relation to the form of the arbitration agreement.

According to the UNCITRAL Recommendation, Article VII is of assistance only where the more favourable standard is contained in the law of the country where the arbitration agreement is sought to be relied upon. In the case of enforcement, this would need to be the law of the country where enforcement is sought (for which the validity of the arbitration agreement is a prerequisite). However, if the more favourable standard is in the law of the country where the arbitration took place, Article VII will be of no avail, not even after the UNCITRAL Recommendation. Article VII therefore only offers assistance if the law of the place of enforcement is more liberal in its formal requirements for the arbitration agreement than the New York Convention.

In practice, the liberal law upon which the parties may have relied when entering into an arbitration agreement that does not comply with strict formal criteria is more frequently the law governing the arbitration agreement; that is, it is usually the law of the place of arbitration. It is unlikely that, when entering into an arbitration agreement, parties would rely on the flexibility offered by the law of the place of enforcement, since that place may vary depending on who is the loser and there could indeed be several places of enforcement if a party has assets in various countries. So, reliance on such law would lead to unpredictability over the validity of the arbitration

---

[54] See the UNCITRAL Secretariat note, paras. 24–34, with an extensive analysis of court practice.

[55] Article 2 of the Recommendation reads: 'Recommends also that article VII, paragraph 1, of the Convention on Recognition and Enforcement of Foreign Arbitral Awards, done in New York, 10 June 1958, should be applied to allow any interested party to avail itself of rights it may have, under the law or treaties of the country where an arbitration agreement is sought to be relied upon, to seek recognition of the validity of such an arbitration agreement'.

agreement. Parties are more likely to rely on the flexibility offered by the law governing the arbitration, since they have chosen this law.

In this case, however, Article VII would be of no assistance, unless the court of enforcement were to construe it so broadly as covering the law of the place of arbitration or the law chosen by the parties to govern the arbitration agreement. Yet such an interpretation would exceed the UNCITRAL Recommendation.

2.1.6 Is the procedural requirement of Article IV an obstacle?

Article IV of the New York Convention contains what could represent an obstacle to the enforcement of an award based on an oral arbitration agreement.

It is generally thought that the New York Convention requires an award to be enforced unless one of the grounds for refusing enforcement listed in Article V applies. Whilst an oral arbitration agreement would be valid under Article V(1)(a) if governed by Swedish or Norwegian law,[56] it could be suggested that enforcement under the New York Convention would be denied, as it would be impossible to provide the court with '[t]he original agreement referred to in Article II or a duly certified copy thereof', as stated in Article IV. Yet, this obstacle is not insurmountable if one considers the hierarchy between Articles IV and V of the Convention. Article V can be regarded as the central pillar of the Convention, containing the grounds for refusing enforcement of an award. It could be argued that if the conditions for validity mentioned in Article V(1)(a) are met, then Article IV should not add further conditions for validity, and that its provisions are merely procedural rules and cannot deprive a party of the benefit of Article V. However, this would then disregard one of the only two procedural conditions contained in the Convention.[57]

The UNCITRAL's 2006 amendments to the Model Law on International Commercial Arbitration included a change to Article 35, which corresponds in substance to Article IV of the New York Convention. In the new wording of Article 35, the requirement that the party seeking enforcement provide 'the original agreement referred to in article 7 or a duly certified copy thereof' has disappeared.

Interestingly, although the 2006 UNCITRAL Recommendation regarding the interpretation of Article II of the New York Convention mentioned that Article VII should be extended to arbitration agreements, it did not clarify that Article IV cannot be used to create additional grounds for refusing enforcement. This may possibly be explained by the continuing existence of the writing requirement in Article II. Even though the Recommendation encourages an extensive interpretation of Article II, the agreement must still be in writing according to Article II. Hence, Article IV's

---

[56] Assuming one does not follow the generally accepted practice, described in Section 3 above, of reading Article V(1)(a) as containing an internal reference to Article II(2) (requiring a written agreement).

[57] A Norwegian Court of Appeal has in the past refused enforcement of an award on the basis of a violation of Article IV of the New York Convention: Halogaland Court of Appeal, 16 August 1999, *Stockholm Arbitration Report*, 1999 at pp. 121ff., with observations by G. Nerdrum. See also Giuditta Cordero-Moss, 'Tvangsfullbyrdelse av utenlandske voldgiftsavgjørelser', (2000) 1 *Nytt i Privatretten* 15–16.

requirement that a copy of the arbitration agreement be supplied when seeking enforcement of the award does not create an additional criterion, but simply extrapolates from the criterion already existing in Article II.

Article IV would, on the other hand, create an additional criterion if a strict interpretation of Article V(1)(a) led to the application of a national law that did not require the arbitration agreement to be in writing. In the above example of an award based on an oral arbitration agreement governed by Swedish law (and therefore valid under Article V(1)(a)), a strict interpretation of Article IV might lead a court to refuse enforcement because the provision contained in Article IV cannot be complied with.

That obstacle could, however, be removed if enforcement is sought in a country whose liberal legislation is made applicable through the more-favourable-law provision of Article VII (assuming that a similar adaptation to accommodate the absence of formal requirements for arbitration agreements has been made as in Article 35 of the UNCITRAL Model Law on International Commercial Arbitration).

However, the winning party is not always able to choose the country where the award is enforced, as this depends on where the losing party has sufficient assets. If enforcement is sought in a country with formal requirements for the arbitration agreement, Article VII will be of no help, as was seen above. The enforcement court will therefore have to decide whether the impossibility of being able to comply with Article IV is a ground for refusing enforcement additional to the grounds exhaustively listed in Article V, or whether it can disregard the procedural requirement laid down in Article IV.

2.1.7 Conclusion

If courts of enforcement follow the customary interpretation of Article V(1)(a) of the New York Convention – that is, they refer to Article II(2) to determine the validity of the arbitration agreement – they will refuse enforcement of an award if the arbitration agreement does not satisfy the formal requirements laid down in Article II(2). Arbitration agreements entered into electronically easily satisfy those requirements, especially in light of the UNCITRAL Recommendation. This is not the case, however, with oral arbitration agreements, even though they may be valid under some state laws and according to the second option of the UNCITRAL's 2006 amendment to Article 7 of the Model Law on International Commercial Arbitration.

If a winning party finds it impossible to obtain the enforcement of an award in its favour, it might wish to file a suit before an ordinary court of law, with a view to obtaining an enforceable judgment in preference to an unenforceable arbitral award. However, depending on the country in which the suit is brought, the court might decline jurisdiction on the ground that the dispute is covered by an arbitration agreement which, albeit oral, is valid under the law of that country.

Thus, it could be said that the liberal position taken on the form of arbitration agreements in some recent legislation and in the second option of the UNCITRAL's

2006 amendment to Article 7 of the Model Law might have the opposite effect of that intended. Rather than facilitating arbitration, it might complicate the application of such a useful instrument as the New York Convention.

The texts adopted by the UNCITRAL in 2006 help to reinforce the arbitration-friendly approach underlying the New York Convention. This is particularly relevant to arbitration agreements entered into electronically. However, the fact that it has been impossible to agree on the complete removal of any formal requirements for arbitration agreements shows that parties still need to be cautious where non-written arbitration agreements are concerned and that they should not blindly rely on the most advanced and arbitration-friendly systems.

From the New York Convention follows that an arbitration agreement has to be recognised as a sufficient basis for the jurisdiction of an arbitral tribunal, as long as the matter is deemed arbitrable. Arbitrability is regulated by the law of the state whose courts are supposed to recognise the arbitration agreement. We will come back to the scope of the rule on arbitrability in Section 2.7. For the moment, it may suffice to note that a dispute is usually deemed to be arbitrable if it regards a subject matter that is within the free disposal of the parties.

2.2 Legal capacity

As was seen in Chapter 1, it seems to be quite a widespread attitude among practitioners to rely fully and solely on the law chosen by the parties and to disregard any other laws – on the basis that an international arbitral tribunal will be obliged to follow the will of the parties. It may therefore come as a surprise that the law chosen by the parties to govern the contract does not decide whether the parties had the legal capacity to enter into the contract. This matter is usually decided by the law applicable to each of the parties.

The relevance of each party's own law in this connection is confirmed by the two most fundamental international sources in respect of arbitration: the 1985 UNCITRAL Model Law on International Commercial Arbitration (as amended in 2006) and the 1958 New York Convention on the Recognition and Enforcement of Foreign Arbitral Awards.

The New York Convention says in Article V(1)(a) that one of the grounds for refusing the recognition or enforcement of an award is that one of the parties to the arbitration agreement was under some incapacity under its own law.

The UNCITRAL Model Law has used this article of the New York Convention as a basis for its own rules on annulment of awards and on the possibility of refusing recognition or enforcement, respectively, in Articles 34(2)(a)(i) and 36(1)(a)(i).

The relevance of private international law to the question of legal capacity in arbitration is illustrated by a Swedish Court of Appeal decision that set aside an arbitral award rendered under the rules of the SCC. The Court of Appeal affirmed, among other things, that the law of Ukraine is applicable to the question of the legal capacity of the Ukrainian party, notwithstanding that the contract contained a governing-law clause choosing Swedish law.[58]

The decision was based on the old Swedish Arbitration Act. The new Arbitration Act from 1999, however, does not present changes that would lead the court to take a different position regarding the specific question of the law applicable to the capacity of a party to enter into the arbitration agreement and the invalidity of the award if such a law had been violated.[59]

The factual circumstances of the case are quite complicated and it is not relevant here to refer to them in full. The essence is that a shareholders' agreement, containing also an arbitration clause, was signed by two officers of the Ukrainian defendant, who put their names beside the signature line, which was left empty for the signature of the defendant's Chairman. The Chairman never signed, and the defendant contested that the Agreement had become binding on it. The shareholders' agreement contained a choice-of-law clause that determined Swedish law as the governing law. The Court affirmed repeatedly that Ukrainian law is applicable to the question of the capacity of a person to sign an agreement with binding effects for a Ukrainian entity. The Court examined the authority of the two officers under Ukrainian law and concluded that one of them had the authority to bind the defendant, whereas the other one did not. The Court then examined what formal requirements Ukrainian law has for the effectiveness of the signatures placed under the agreement, and it concluded that, under Ukrainian law, the shareholders' agreement would have required two signatures, whereas the arbitration agreement contained in the arbitration clause could become binding with only one signature. Thanks to the doctrine of severability, this could have been sufficient to consider the arbitration agreement binding on the defendant, as a matter of Ukrainian law. However, the Court examined the location of the signatures beside the signature line and established, on the basis of witness evidence, that the two signatures were not meant as binding signatures, but as an endorsement, placed on the document by the administration for the benefit of the Chairman, who would thus know that the document was ready to be executed. The Court found that, as a matter of Ukrainian law and practice, such a visa did not correspond to the execution of a contract and that a proper signature was necessary. The Chairman never signed the agreement, and therefore the Court found that the arbitration agreement never came into effect for the defendant. According to Article 20(1) of the old Swedish

---

[58] *State of Ukraine* v. *Norsk Hydro ASA*, Svea Hovrätt, 17 December 2007, T 3108–06, see ITA Monthly Report, Kluwerarbitration, May 2008, Volume VI, Issue 5.

[59] The legal incapacity to enter into the arbitration agreement is a ground for invalidity of the award according to Article 34(1) of the 1999 Swedish Arbitration Act, see the preparatory works: SOU 1994:81 p. 77 and prop. 1998/99:35 p. 48, as well as L. Heuman and S. Jarvin, *The Swedish Arbitration Act of 1999, Five Years On: A Critical Review of Strengths and Weaknesses*, (JurisNet, 2006) pp. 237f. In the new act, the invalidity is no longer 'absolute', which means that it must be raised by the interested party as a defence within a certain term: see prop 1998/99:35 p. 138f.

Arbitration Act, the award rendered on the basis of that arbitration agreement was declared null by the Court of Appeal. Had the decision been taken according to the new Swedish Arbitration Act, the award would have been set aside on the basis of Article 34(1).[60]

The Svea Court of Appeal, thus, considered first the legal capacity to enter into an agreement with binding effects for the represented party, and affirmed that it is governed by the law applicable to that party – irrespective of what law the parties agreed on to govern the contract. The Court proceeded to investigate whether the signatories made use of the authority to bind the principal – an investigation that was also based on the law and practice prevailing in the jurisdiction of the party in question, and not on the law governing the contract.

For the sake of completeness, it should be mentioned that the Svea Court of Appeal decision was presented to the Supreme Court for appeal, but the Swedish Supreme Court denied leave to appeal.[61] Thus, the Svea decision is final, and the Court of Appeal's position that the legal capacity of a party is governed by the law applicable to that party is indirectly confirmed by the Supreme Court.

The Swedish decision finds a basis in international instruments on arbitration, as is shown by the reference made at the beginning of this section to Article V(1)(a) of the New York Convention and the similar Articles 34 and 36 of the UNCITRAL Model Law.

It must be pointed out that Sweden has not adopted the Model Law. However, Sweden used the Model Law as a reference when it reformed its arbitration law. As a result, the grounds for invalidity that are being examined here are common both to annulment and to the enforcement of awards in the countries that adopted the Model Law, as well as in Sweden.

This illustrates that the consideration of private international law is relevant even when an international contract contains an arbitration clause. The question of whether the contract was signed by someone having the capacity to bind the respective party is not decided on the basis of the law chosen by the parties, but on the basis of the law applicable to each of the parties. This law, in turn, is identified by applying private international law rules, as was seen in Chapter 4 Section 4.2.2.

2.3 Constitution of the arbitral tribunal

Another group of grounds for invalidity or unenforceability of an award is connected with the proper constitution of the arbitral tribunal, either because the parties'

---

[60] Assuming that the defence had been raised within the term. In the specific case, the defence had been raised well after the term had lapsed. Under the old Arbitration Act, incapacity to enter into the arbitration agreement was considered as an absolute ground for voidness; i.e., the award became void automatically, and the voidness could not be affected by the lapse of time.

[61] Decision dated 2 June 2008, case no. T 339-08

instructions were not followed, or because the tribunal turned out not to have been impartial or independent or because the rules on the constitution of the tribunal were not complied with.

These grounds, important as they are for the principle of due process, have less relevance to the question that interests us here; that is, to what extent national law may have an impact on the effectiveness of an award.

2.4 Excess of power

Article V(1)(c) of the New York Convention states that an award may be refused enforcement if it decides on matters beyond the scope of the arbitral tribunal's power. Articles 34 and 36 of the UNCITRAL Model Law contain similar provisions.

This ground for invalidity and unenforcement can be relevant to the question discussed in our book, from the opposite point of view to what has been seen so far. So far, we have mainly examined the question of the effectiveness of an award that supports the ambitions of the self-sufficiency of the contract: would an award that merely applies the law chosen by the parties and disregards the applicable law be valid and enforceable? The rule on excess of power is relevant from the opposite perspective: assuming that the arbitral tribunal wishes to apply the governing law on its own motion, or even notwithstanding a different choice of law made in the contract, would the tribunal exceed its power? The analysis on this aspect will be carried out in section 3.3 below.

2.5 Irregularity of procedure

The defence of procedural irregularity adds one parameter to the evaluation of the arbitral award: not only does it permit us to measure the arbitral procedure against the parties' instructions contained in the arbitral agreement, it also makes reference to the arbitration law of the place of arbitration.[62]

The defence of procedural irregularity is seldom applied in the context of choice of law. Generally, this defence concerns the composition of the arbitral tribunal, the respect of confidentiality and strictly procedural matters.[63] However, as will be seen in Section 3.5 below, this rule may become relevant if the arbitral tribunal applies, on its own motion, a law that is different from the law selected in the contract.

---

[62] The wording is, in the UNCITRAL Model Law: 'the composition of the arbitral tribunal or the arbitral procedure was not in accordance with the agreement of the parties, unless such agreement was in conflict with a provision of this Law from which the parties cannot derogate, or, failing such agreement, was not in accordance with this Law'; and, in the New York Convention: 'The composition of the arbitral authority or the arbitral procedure was not in accordance with the agreement of the parties, or, failing such agreement, was not in accordance with the law of the country where the arbitration took place.'

[63] See Born, *International Commercial Arbitration*, p. 2770. See also Redfern, Hunter, Blackaby and Partasides, *Redfern and Hunter on International Arbitration*, paras.11.80–11.84.

2.6 Ordre public *conflict*

Conflict with the *ordre public*, or public policy, is a ground for ineffectiveness that may be applied *ex officio* by the courts and does not require that a party invokes it or proves it.

The rule of public policy has a very narrow scope, as will be seen in Sections 2.6.3 and 2.6.4, and shall be applied only in exceptional cases. This rule permits the court to set aside or refuse enforcement of an arbitral award if the result of recognising or enforcing the award would violate fundamental principles in the court's system.

What is worth noticing in respect of the rule of public policy (and this also applies to the rule of arbitrability that will be dealt with in Section 2.7), is that it refers to the criteria set in the legal system of the court that is at any time competent. By contrast, the other grounds for invalidity/unenforceability relate to the rules of a specified law: the invalidity of the arbitration agreement is determined by the law of the place of arbitration; the legal capacity of the parties is determined by the law of each of the parties; and the regularity of the procedure is determined by the law of the place of arbitration. This means that those particular laws will be applicable irrespective of which court is competent; thus, the validity of the arbitration agreement, the legal capacity of the parties and the regularity of the procedure will be governed by the same law both if the award is challenged before the courts of the place of arbitration and if the award is sought to be enforced before the courts of another country. The rule on public policy, however, relates to the law of the court that, at any time, is dealing with the award. This means that the award will be evaluated according to the public policy of the place of arbitration if it is challenged before the courts of that place, and according to the public policy of the place of enforcement if it is sought to be enforced before the courts of another state.

2.6.1 International *ordre public* as a corrective to positive *ordre public*

Sometimes the term 'international *ordre public*' is encountered, and sometimes the term 'truly international *ordre public*'. The former term does not designate a category of public policy different from the one that will be explained in Sections 2.6.3 and 2.6.4 below, but simply follows a different use of the terminology; the latter term, on the contrary, refers to a different concept. We can briefly analyse the two terms.

International public policy is usually deemed to refer to those principles in a legal system that are so fundamental that they should be respected even if the context of the dispute is international. In other words, the principles should have such an importance for that legal system that they should be considered as basic, irrespective of the existence of a close link between the legal system and the disputed matter.[64]

---

[64] Another way of defining this is through the concepts of relative *ordre public* or the territoriality of the *ordre public*. Both concepts aim at showing that *ordre public* should be given a narrow scope in international contexts: the weaker the connection between the subject matter and a certain legal system, the narrower

The judge who is to determine the validity or enforceability of an award cannot be expected to run counter to these principles, not even if the award does not have any link with the judge's legal system. This concept of international *ordre public* does not differ considerably from the restrictive concept that will be described in Sections 2.6.3 and 2.6.4. The notion of international public policy, like the narrow notion of public policy that is described in these sections, assumes that it is only fundamental principles, and not rules (not even overriding mandatory rules) that constitute the *ordre public*. Then why is one category defined as 'international', whereas the other one is not? This is primarily a question of terminology. In some systems, the term *ordre public*, used in a domestic context, is deemed to have a wider scope than the one that we mentioned above.[65] It is deemed to extend to also cover the overriding mandatory rules of that legal system, those rule that are applied irrespective of the international character of the relationship, and that were described in Chapter 4 Section 4.3. The extensive concept of *ordre public* is also known as 'positive *ordre public*'. This is because *ordre public*, in the extensive sense, has a wider function than the narrow notion described in these sections. *Ordre public* in the narrow sense has the function of excluding an interference with the basic principles of the legal system; it is a barrier against the introduction into the system of incompatible foreign elements. Hence, *ordre public* in the narrow sense is also defined as 'negative *ordre public*'. The wider *ordre public* also has the function of ensuring the application of the legal system's overriding mandatory rules: positive public policy, therefore, is a vehicle for actively applying certain rules of the judge's legal system. Since this is in contrast with the policies underlying the recognition and enforcement of foreign awards (as well as the application of foreign law under private international law as described in Chapter 4 Section 4.7), the positive *ordre public* has to be adapted when operating in an international context. The extensive concept is therefore restricted, by adding the qualification of 'international'. The meaning of international is not – in this context – that the *ordre public* stems from international sources: it is to distinguish it from the domestic context that operates with a positive *ordre public*. In the international context, *ordre public* is negative and limited to those principles that are fundamental and that the judge cannot disregard even if the disputed matter has an international character.

If the concept of *ordre public* is used with the narrow scope described in Sections 2.6.3 and 2.6.4 below, it is not necessary to add the qualification 'international' to restrict it. The narrow concept, also known as negative *ordre public*, enjoys the wider recognition in international legal doctrine, judicial practice and legislation. It is defined as negative, because its function is to prevent the recognition or enforcement of an award (or the application of a foreign law),

---

that system's *ordre public* should be construed. For a clear analysis of the origin of the various approaches, see Helge Johan Thue, *Internasjonal Privatrett* (Gyldendal Academic, 2002) pp. 179f.

[65] For further references, see Giuditta Cordero-Moss, *International Commercial Arbitration: Party Autonomy and Mandatory Rules* (Tano Aschehoug, 1999), footnote 248 and the accompanying text.

if the result of such recognition, enforcement or application would violate fundamental principles of the judge's legal system.

2.6.2 Truly international *ordre public* as a transnational phenomenon

While the discrepancy between '*ordre public*' in its restrictive sense and 'international
ordre public' turns out to be simply a question of terminology, whereby in the
substance there is no significant difference, the term 'truly international *ordre public*'
designates a different concept.

In this case, the qualification 'international' does not refer to the context of the
disputed matter, but to the sources from which the public policy stems. The idea is
that the truly international *ordre public* does not originate from one single legal
system: only if a principle is recognised as fundamental in a plurality of legal systems
can it be considered to be the expression of a policy that is truly international. Truly
international public policy is a concept that is primarily recognised in some academic
circles[66] that consider it to be more appropriate for international transactions and
international arbitration than the national *ordre public* is, even in its restrictive sense.

The usefulness of this concept may be questioned. The concept aims at preventing that
legal systems use their own fundamental principles to declare a foreign award invalid or
to refuse its enforcement (or to restrict the application of the governing foreign law),
if such principles are particular to that specific legal system and do not enjoy recognition
internationally. In such a situation, the peculiarity of that legal system is held to undermine the ideals of international uniformity that inspire international commercial law
and international arbitration. The aim of the theory underlying the truly international
ordre public, therefore, is to disregard the fundamental principles that are proper only in
one legal system, even if they represent the basic values upon which that society relies.
Instead, that legal system should look at those basic principles that are recognised on
a more international level, and prefer those principles to its own. It seems too ambitious
to me, however, to expect that a state waives the application of its own fundamental
principles in the name of an ideal of harmonisation in international commerce. As long
as the validity of an arbitral award is regulated by national arbitration laws, and
the enforceability of an award is regulated by the New York Convention, which, in turn,
makes reference to the national law, the standard of reference will be the fundamental
principles of the *lex fori* (though in the narrow, 'negative' sense described above).[67]

---

[66] For further references see Cordero Moss, *International Commercial Arbitration: Party Autonomy*, footnote
774 and the accompanying text. See Pierre Lalive, 'L'ordre public transnational et l'arbitre international', in
S. Bariatti and G. Venturini (eds) *Liber Fausto Pocar* (Giuffre, 2009), pp. 599–611.

[67] See, confirming the position taken here, the ILA Final Report on Public Policy, Recommendation 1(b),
particularly para. 11, Recommendation 1(c), particularly para. 20ff., Recommendations 2(a) and 2(b),
particularly para. 43; see also the ILA Interim Report on Public Policy for more details. See also
A. Sheppard, 'Public Policy and the Enforcement of Arbitral Awards: Should There be a Global Standard?'
(2004) 1(1) *Transnational Dispute Management*, 7f., commenting on the work on public policy made in the
frame of the International Law Association, International Commercial Arbitration Committee.

2.6.3 Conflict with principles, not with rules

The rule of the *ordre public* is, in the context of international arbitration, unanimously interpreted very narrowly. The rule of the *ordre public* is not meant to permit a judge to refuse enforcement or annul an international award on the basis of any difference between the result of the award and the result to which the judge would have come to by applying his or her own law. Such an extensive use of the *ordre public* rule would run counter to the spirit of the New York Convention, of the UNCITRAL Model Law, of all practice that is generally recognised and of legal doctrine on the international scale.[68]

In particular, the rule of the *ordre public* does not have the same function as ensuring full compliance with rules and principles of the judge's legal system; public policy is usually defined by reference not to specific legal provisions, but to basic notions of morality and justice,[69] features essential to the moral, political or economic order of the country[70] or to most fundamental notions of morality and justice.[71] In a similar vein, the ECJ found, regarding the applicability of the public-policy exception contained in the then-applicable Brussels Convention on Jurisdiction and Enforcement of Judgements, that a court cannot refuse enforcement of a judgement 'solely on the ground that it considers that national or Community law was misapplied in that decision.'[72] The ECJ found that the fact that an alleged error in applying the law concerns rules of Community law does not alter the conditions for being able to rely on the clause on public policy.[73] In particular, a court cannot review the accuracy of the findings of law made in the judgment when the enforcement of that judgment is being sought.[74] Moreover, the judgment must be at variance, to an unacceptable degree, with the legal order of the enforcing state in as much as it infringes a fundamental principle, and the infringement must constitute a manifest breach of a rule of law regarded as essential or of a right recognised as being fundamental.[75]

---

[68] See Born, *International Commercial Arbitration*, pp. 284 ff., with extensive references, and Redfern, Hunter, Blackaby and Partasides, *Redfern and Hunter on International Arbitration*, para. 11.110. See also, for a confirmation of this approach and further references, the International Commercial Arbitration Committee, 'International Law Association Final Report on Public Policy as a Bar to Enforcement of International Arbitral Awards' (paper presented at the International Law Association Conference, New Delhi, 2002). See also the International Commercial Arbitration Committee, 'International Law Association Interim Report on Public Policy as a Bar to Enforcement of International Arbitral Awards' (paper presented at the International Law Association Conference, London, 2000). This is often defined as the 'pro-enforcement bias' of the New York Convention, which, in turn, is considered to constitute a principle of public policy: see Redfern, Hunter, Blackaby and Partasides, *Redfern and Hunter on International Arbitration*, para. 11.105.

[69] Redfern, Hunter, Blackaby and Partasides *Redfern and Hunter on International Arbitration*, paras. 11.109, 11.111 and 11.112.

[70] Dirk Otto and Omaia Elwan, 'Article V(2)', in Herbert Kronke, Patricia Nacimiento, Dirk Otto and Nicola Christine Port (eds.), *Recognition and Enforcement of Foreign Arbitral Awards: A Global Commentary on the New York Convention* (Kluwer Law International, 2010), p. 365.

[71] Otto and Elwan, Article V(2) p. 366.   [72] C-38/98 (*Renault*), para. 33.

[73] *Ibid.*, para. 32.   [74] *Ibid.*, para. 29.   [75] *Ibid.*, para. 30.

This ECJ decision, and the numerous decisions that confirm it,[76] are not rendered under the New York Convention, but there is no reason why the reasoning made in respect of public policy as a ground for refusing recognition and enforcement of judgments under the Brussels Convention (or its successor, the Brussels I Regulation) should not also apply to public policy as a ground for refusing recognition and enforcement of awards under the New York Convention or as a ground to set aside an award under the UNCITRAL Model Law.

Another restriction to the applicability of the *ordre public* exception lies in the requirement that the violation of the fundamental principles must be actual and specific, as opposed to an abstract incompatibility. An award must lead to results that actually violate fundamental principles; it is not sufficient that the award gives effect to a provision that potentially, under other circumstances, could violate the *ordre public*. Thus, a court decision ordering payment of punitive damages for breach of contract has not been deemed to violate the *ordre public* in England. Even though the court affirmed that punitive damages in an abstract sense could be considered to breach fundamental principles of English law, the size of the damages in the specific case was not deemed to do so.[77] This reasoning was made in regard of a court decision, but it may be extended to arbitral awards.

2.6.4 Fundamental principles

We have established that it is not the national rules that must be applied through the public-policy clause, but it is their inspiring principles that may be given effect to. It remains to attempt to define what inspiring principles can be deemed to be of a public-policy nature. Not every principle inspiring a mandatory rule can be considered as a public policy principle. Not even every principle inspiring an overriding mandatory rule (i.e., one of those mandatory rules described in Chapter 4 Section 4.3 and that are deemed to be so important that they shall be applied even in international situations and without taking into consideration the general choice-of-law rules, also known as the *lois de police*) can be considered as being of public policy.[78] It is only the fundamental principles – those that constitute the basis of society – that can be deemed as public policy principles. But how can these principles be identified?

---

[76] Numerous ECJ decisions confirmed that the *ordre public* is violated only in case of incompatibility with fundamental principles: C-7/98 (*Krombach*), C-394/07 (*Gambazzi*), C-145/86 (*Hoffmann*), C-414/92 (*Solo Kleinmotoren*), C-420/07 (*Apostolides*) and C-619/10 (*Trade Agency*).

[77] *Travellers Casualty and Surety Company of Canada (UK) Limited* [2002] EWHC 1704 (Comm).

[78] Radicati Di Brozolo, 'Arbitration and Competition Law: The Position of the Courts and of Arbitrators' (2011) 27(1) *Arbitration International*, p. 6. See also Born, *International Commercial Arbitration*, pp. 2843ff. See also Cordero-Moss, *International Commercial Arbitration: Party Autonomy*, Section 2.6.

There is no absolute rule to determine public policy principles: what is fundamental may vary from state to state, and, even within the same state, the conceptions develop, and what was once deemed a matter of public policy, may not be so a decade later.[79]

Court decisions in the various states annulling an award or refusing to enforce it because the award is in conflict with the court's public policy are reported in the ICCA *Yearbook Commercial Arbitration*, also available at www.kluwerarbitration. com. The UNCITRAL collects court decisions on the Model Law and on the New York Convention in the CLOUT database,[80] which can be searched, among other things, by provision. In addition, the UNCITRAL has recently launched a webpage collecting court decisions on the New York Convention.[81] Moreover, a digest of court cases on the Model Law has been published by the UNCITRAL in 2012.[82] A survey of these decisions shows that awards are not often set aside or refused enforcement. A decision that originated a wide debate in the legal literature was rendered by the EU Court of Justice in the *Eco Swiss* case:[83] here, the Court affirmed that European rules of competition law must be considered as belonging to public policy.

Another situation where arbitral awards are traditionally deemed to conflict with public policy is where the award gives effect to an agreement that violates applicable rules on bribery.[84]

The question that is relevant in this book is whether arbitration may contribute to the self-sufficiency of the contract described in Chapter 1. As described in Chapter 4 Section 4, courts would apply the private international law and restrict the parties' choice of law when this extends to areas where other conflict rules are applicable. Arbitration is commonly believed to obey the parties' instructions to a larger extent. Nevertheless, arbitral awards rendered in commercial disputes may run the risk of conflicting with public policy where contracts are legal under the law chosen by the parties, but violate, in certain areas, the law that would be applicable if the parties had not made a choice of law. If the violated rules were meant to protect third parties' interests or to ensure the proper functioning of systems such

---

[79] The example of swap agreements and other financial-derivative instruments is quite descriptive: this kind of contract developed into a recognised financial activity in the course of the 1980s, and is not considered as being against fundamental principles today. However, until as late as the 1980s, courts in Germany and in Austria were considering them against the basic moral principles of the system that forbid gambling (the so-called *Differenzeinwand*). See, for example, the decision of the Austrian Supreme Court no. 3 Ob 30/83 of 1983, and of the German Supreme Court (Bundesgerichtshof) of 15 June 1987. Shortly thereafter, the Bundesgerichtshof did not consider these agreements as violating any fundamental principles of the German legal system; see, for example, the decision dated 26 February 1991, XI ZR 349/89.

[80] www.uncitral.org/clout/showSearchDocument.do?lf=898&lng=en.   [81] newyorkconvention1958.org/.

[82] www.uncitral.org/uncitral/en/case_law/digests/mal2012.html.

[83] *Eco Swiss China Time Ltd* v. *Benetton International NV* C-126/97.

[84] For a recent critical review of the relationship between bribery and public policy in international arbitration see James Barratt and Hayley Ichilcik, 'Bribery', *The European and Middle Eastern Arbitration Review* (Global Abrbitration Review, 2011).

as banking and financing, an award giving effect to those agreements may have implications in terms of public policy.

Below, I will analyse some areas of law where an international contract may have implications and where it may become necessary to consider conformity with public policy.

2.6.4.1 Company law

We can make reference to the example mentioned in Chapter 4, Section 4.2.2: a shareholders' agreement between the Norwegian and the Russian shareholders of a Ukrainian company with its main place of business in Russia. The shareholders' agreement contains a choice-of-law clause subjecting the contract to Swedish law, and an arbitration clause referring disputes to arbitration under the Arbitration Rules of the SCC.

As was seen in Chapter 4, Section 4.2.2, the commitments between the parties have a contractual nature and will be subject to the chosen Swedish law. However, the rules of the shareholders' agreement that affect the roles and responsibilities of the members of the Board of Directors, the capitalisation of the company or the transfer of shares have a different nature. Although the parties to the shareholders' agreement have contractually committed themselves to a certain conduct in the Board, to a certain evaluation of the capital contributions and to a certain restriction in the sale of shares, these obligations do not only have a contractual nature. As known, the function of the Board of Directors, the capital of a company and the transferability of its shares (at least under certain circumstances) have a larger significance than the mere balance of interests between the two contracting parties: they affect aspects of the legal personality of an entity that has implications towards third parties, such as the entity's employees, its creditors or the other shareholders.

There are, therefore, reasons for preventing that an agreement between two parties (the shareholders who signed the shareholders' agreement) modifies third parties' position by changing the governing company law. This is the reason why, in private international law, party autonomy does not extend to matters that may affect third parties' interests; these matters are subject to the law identified on the basis of other connecting factors.

Depending on the applicable conflict rule, the matters of company law in this case would be decided according to the law of the Ukraine (place of registration) or of Russia (real seat), but not according to the law of Sweden (chosen in the contract).

In our assumption, the dispute between the parties is submitted to arbitration. The dispute may regard one of the company law aspects of the shareholders' agreement. For example, the Norwegian party may claim damages for breach of contract by the Russian party for failure to instruct the Board members appointed by it to vote in accordance with the shareholders' agreement. The Norwegian party may even request the arbitral tribunal to declare the Board resolution invalid, because it conflicts with the shareholders' agreement. The Russian party may respond that following those instructions would have violated the company law of the Ukraine. The Norwegian party would rebut that

Ukrainian law is irrelevant, because the shareholders' agreement contains a clause selecting Swedish law, and no other law shall be taken into consideration.

Assuming that the arbitral award gives effect to the choice of law made in the contract, thus violating the applicable company law, will the award be valid and enforceable in the country to which the applicable company law belongs?

The nature of the public policy rule prevents making general assertions as to the quality of public policy for a whole area of the law. Some rules of company law may protect interests that are deemed to be so fundamental that their disregard may contradict public policy, but it will depend on the circumstances of the case as to what extent the result of a specific violation actually is in conflict with such fundamental principles. On a general basis, however, it seems legitimate to affirm that the policy upon which various rules of company law are based may be deemed so strong that a serious breach of those rules may represent a violation of public policy.[85]

Thus, an award disregarding the applicable company law to give effect to the parties' agreement may run the risk of being ineffective, if it is challenged or sought to be enforced before the courts of the place to which the disregarded company law belongs.[86]

2.6.4.2 Insolvency

Suppose that an English and a Norwegian party have a cooperation that also involves the parties' affiliated companies and creates various mutual payment obligations. The agreement provides that each party's payment obligations shall be set off against the other party's payment obligation, also including the affiliates of that party. If the English party becomes insolvent, its creditors will expect to be able to claim, from the Norwegian party, payment in full of the outstanding obligations. The obligations of the Norwegian party towards the insolvent English party, however, are set off against obligations that some of the English party's affiliates have towards it. Let's assume that the Norwegian party obtained an arbitral award that, on the basis of the set-off agreement, declares all debts by the Norwegian party to be set off against its credits towards the affiliates of the insolvent party, and in addition, orders the English party to pay an excess amount that could not be set off. The Norwegian party will try to enforce this award. If the award is recognised, the claim based thereon will be considered as one of the credits to be satisfied out of the estate. In practice, enforcement of this award would mean that the

---

[85] This matter has been the object of research in a project that I run at the University of Oslo on Arbitration and Party Autonomy (APA), www.jus.uio.no/ifp/english/research/projects/choice-of-law/).

[86] See, for example, the decision of 31 December 2006 by the Federal Commercial Court of West Siberia regarding an arbitral award on a shareholders' agreement between, among others, OAO Telecominvest, Sonera Holding BV, Telia International AB, Avenue Ltd, Santel Ltd, Janao Properties Ltd and IPOC International Growth Fund Ltd. The Court affirmed that the parties to a shareholders' agreement may not choose a foreign law (in that case, Swedish law) to govern the status of a legal entity, its legal capacity, the function of its corporate bodies, or the relationship to and between its shareholders. These matters are, according to the Court, governed by mandatory rules of the law of the place of registration (in that case, Russian law). Violation of these Russian rules was defined as a violation of Russian public policy.

Norwegian party circumvented English insolvency rules on the equality of treatment of the creditors: the Norwegian party would not have to pay to the estate the sums that it owed to the insolvent party and that were set off against the debts of the affiliates. Would this be in compliance with public policy?

As was seen in Chapter 4 Section 4.2.3, matters regarding the protection of the creditors in insolvency situations are outside the scope of party autonomy.

Do the same reasons for considering matters relating to insolvency as not subject to the law chosen by the parties constitute a sufficient basis for invoking the defence of public policy to set aside or refuse enforcement of an award that gives effect to the parties' agreement and thus violates the applicable insolvency law?

The question was answered affirmatively in the United States in a case regarding the enforcement of an arbitral award rendered in London that ordered a Swedish party to effect a certain payment. The debtor was subject to insolvency proceedings in Sweden, and the Court of Appeal found that 'in light of Salen's bankruptcy, [the] enforcement would conflict with the public policy of ensuring equitable and orderly distribution of local assets of a foreign bankrupt'.[87] The court balanced, on one hand, the interest in ensuring the enforcement of international awards, and, on the other hand, the interest in ensuring an equal treatment of the creditors when an insolvency procedure has been opened. The court resolved not to enforce the award, thus preventing one creditor gaining preferential treatment to the detriment of the others. Similarly, a recent French Supreme Court decision refused enforcement of an award that had been rendered against a company that was under insolvency proceedings. The court affirmed that insolvency rules are designed to ensure equal standing between creditors and allow the liquidator to work out an adequate plan for the distribution of the assets. Granting enforcement of an award would allow one creditor to obtain a preferential position over the other creditors, and this would be against internal and international public policy.[88]

Other court decisions have enforced awards in spite of pending bankruptcy proceedings, because the circumstances of the cases did not make enforcement incompatible with the principles underlying the bankruptcy proceedings.[89]

2.6.4.3 Property and encumbrances
Another area where third-party interests may be relevant is that of property and encumbrances. The choice of law made in the contract does not extend to questions of title and security interests, as was seen in Chapter 4, Section 4.2.5.

---

[87] *Salen Dry Cargo AB* v. *Victrix Steamship Co*, in (1990) *Yearbook Commercial Arbitration XV* (Kluwer International, 1990), pp. 534ff., 825 F.2d 709 (2nd Cir 1987).

[88] French Supreme Court, Civil Chamber, 6 May 2009, no. 08–10.281.

[89] *State Property Fund of Ukraine* v. *TMR Energy Limited*, United States Court of Appeals, District of Columbia Circuit, 17 June 2005, 2005 U.S. App. Lexis 11540, in *Yearbook Commercial Arbitration XXX* (Kluwer International, 2005), pp. 1178ff., where the award was not directed at the party that was the object of bankruptcy proceedings. See also, German Court of Appeal, Brandenburg, 2 September 1999, in *Yearbook Commercial Arbitration XXIX* (Kluwer International, 2004), pp. 696ff., where the enforcement was deemed not to be an execution proceeding, but merely a preliminary measure without executory effect.

Would an award that disregards these conflict rules and applies instead the law chosen by the parties be valid and enforceable? Due to a lack of any specific case law on the effectiveness of arbitral awards that give effect to the parties' agreement and violate applicable law on property, encumbrances or security interests, it seems advisable to refer to the reasoning made above in respect of company law and insolvency proceedings, which respond to the same logic.[90]

2.6.4.4 Competition law

In the already mentioned *Eco-Swiss* case, the ECJ determined that European competition rules have to be considered as a part of public policy.[91] The European Court was acting upon a reference made by the Dutch Supreme Court in a case for the annulment of an arbitral award. The award had given effect to the agreement between the parties that violated the provision on competition of the Article 85 of the Treaty of Rome. The Dutch Supreme Court had affirmed that an award violating Dutch competition rules would not be deemed to be against Dutch public policy, and requested a decision by the European Court as to whether European competition policy could be treated in the same way or not. The ECJ ruled that the rule on competition contained in the then Article 85 of the Treaty of Rome is a fundamental provision that is essential for the accomplishment of the tasks entrusted to the Community and, in particular, for the functioning of the internal market. Based on this, the Court explicitly affirmed: 'The provisions of article 85 of the Treaty may be regarded as a matter of public policy within the meaning of the New York Convention'.[92]

The ECJ decision in *Eco Swiss* means, therefore, that the arbitral tribunal risks rendering an award that will be deemed invalid and refused enforcement by European courts if the award gives effect to the choice of law made by the parties in the contract, and this leads to violating the otherwise applicable European competition law: the award will be deemed to conflict with European public policy.[93] This, in turn, is a ground for setting aside the award if the award was rendered in a European country and was challenged before the court of that place, and a ground for refusing enforcement if this is sought before a European court.

That the ECJ has defined European competition law as public policy does not mean that the arbitral tribunal's assessment will necessarily be reviewed by the courts.

The wide debate that followed this decision related, among other things, to the scope and effects of the Court's findings.[94] In judicial practice, at least two approaches have been taken to the question of the courts' power regarding arbitral awards: the so-called maximalist and minimalist approaches. According to the former approach,

---

[90] This matter is currently the object of the already mentioned APA research in a project at the University of Oslo.

[91] *Eco Swiss China Time Ltd* v. *Benetton International NV* C-126/97.   [92] *Ibid.*, para. 39.

[93] This matter has been the object of the already mentioned APA research project.

[94] For an overview and a summary of the debate so far, see Radicati di Brozolo, 'Arbitration and competition law'.

the court has the power to make, in addition to the evaluation made by the arbitral tribunal, an independent evaluation of the application of the competition law in order to ensure the accurate application of competition law. This approach is criticised and is deemed not to express the mainstream position on the subject.[95] The minimalist approach is held to prevail in court practice both in the US[96] and in Europe, and the legal literature affirms that the courts shall not make a full review of the arbitral tribunal's application of competition law but shall accept the arbitral tribunal's evaluation.[97] That the ECJ has defined European competition law as part of public policy does not mean that any violation of every European competition rule will be a breach of public policy. It is only the most serious violations that qualify, and the breach must be concrete and effective, so that it truly jeopardises the goals of competition policy.[98]

That the ECJ has defined European competition law as public policy does not mean that other systems outside of Europe will do the same. In the US, for example, a Court of Appeal enforced an award that gave effect to a market allocation agreement on the basis that the compatibility with US competition law had already been evaluated by the arbitral tribunal and the court could not review such an evaluation.[99]

2.6.4.5 Agency

As was seen in Chapter 4, Section 4.3.3, the ECJ decided that EU law rules protecting commercial agents are essential for the accomplishment of the tasks entrusted to the Community and, in particular, for the functioning of the internal market.[100] In the *Eco-Swiss* case, this expression accompanied the Court's conclusion that violation of those rules (completion law rules in the *Eco-Swiss* case) is in conflict with European public policy.[101]

Let's assume that an agency agreement between an Italian principal and a Norwegian agent has a choice of law selecting Italian law. If a dispute arises between the parties, the Norwegian agent may invoke the conflict rule in the Norwegian Agency Act, which defines the provisions protecting the agent as an overriding mandatory rule and that therefore restricts party autonomy. The Norwegian agent insists on the application of Norwegian law, notwithstanding the choice of Italian law made in the contract. If the arbitral tribunal follows the contract's choice and applies Italian law, it violates the Norwegian conflict rule. Violation of conflict rules in itself does not constitute violation of the *ordre public*, but would an award that disregards the

---

[95] *Ibid.*, p. 10.
[96] *Baxter Int'l* v. *Abbott Laboratories*, 315 F. 3rd 829 (7th Cir. 2003) and *American Central Eastern Texas Gas Co* v. *Union Pacific Resources Group*, 2004 US App. Lexis 1216 (5th Cir. 2004).
[97] Radicati Di Brozolo, 'Arbitration and Competition Law', 9f.   [98] *Ibid.*, pp. 6 and 11.
[99] United States Court of Appeals, Seventh Circuit, 16 January 2003, 315 Federal Reporter, Third Series (7th Cir. 2003), pp. 829ff, in *Yearbook Commercial Arbitration XXVIII* (Kluwer International, 2003), pp. 1153 ff., but see the dissenting opinion by CJ Cudahy, pp. 1159ff.
[100] *Ingmar* (C-381/98), para. 24.   [101] *Eco-Swiss* (C-126/97).

applicable agency law run the risk of being invalid or unenforceable on the basis of the principle laid down in the *Ingmar* decision?

That an award disregards the technicalities of the applicable agency law does not, in itself, mean that its result violates public policy, as was seen in Section 2.6.3 above. In this case, the award applies another country's agency law; both laws have implemented the EU Directive on commercial agents and may be assumed to be based on the same principles. A discrepancy in the technicalities implementing those principles may not be deemed to conflict with the *ordre public*.

Suppose that the agency agreement contained a clause according to which the principal may terminate the contract at any time, at its own discretion, with immediate effect and without having to pay any compensation: the contract regulation would be based on principles dramatically different from the EU regulation protecting commercial agents. The contract could contain a choice-of-law clause selecting the law of New York, which permits this kind of regulation. If a dispute arises and the Norwegian agent claims compensation according to Norwegian law, the principal will respond that Norwegian law is not applicable due to the contract's choice of law. If the arbitral tribunal follows the choice of law contained in the contract, it will rule that termination is valid and no compensation is due. In such a scenario, the principle of protection of the agent is bluntly violated; if the court follows the *Ingmar* principle and considers protection of the agent as a matter of public policy, the validity and enforceability of the award may be affected. Whether the award actually violates the *ordre public*, however, will depend on the specific result in the particular case. As was seen in Section 2.6.3 above, it is not sufficient that the applied rules in abstract terms may lead to unreasonable results; it must be a specific result.

2.6.4.6 Labour law; insurance

Other areas where European directives provide for mandatory rules that protect weaker contractual parties and therefore are deemed to override the otherwise applicable law are the areas of insurance and labour law.[102] For want of specific case law on these rules, it may be useful to refer to the rationale of the above-mentioned *Eco Swiss* and *Ingmar* decisions: to the extent that the mandatory rules of labour law and of insurance law may be deemed to be essential for the functioning of the internal market (including the freedom of establishment and of movement), an award that gives effect to the parties' agreement and thus violates these rules might run the risk of being ineffective if it is presented to a court within the European Community or the EFTA.

2.6.4.7 Good faith and fair dealing

As was seen in Chapter 3, some legal systems, particularly those inspired by German law, base their contract laws on the principle of good faith and fair dealing. This

---

[102] See Chapter 4 Sections 4.3.2 and 4.3.4.

principle may be used to guide the interpretation of the contract, its performance, to create ancillary obligations for the parties (in spite of their not being expressly provided for in the contract) or even to correct the regulation contained in the contract. Contract clauses that expressly permit an interpretation or a performance that violate the principle of good faith and fair dealing might be deemed to violate the principle of good faith and fair dealing. Clauses exempting from liability, even in cases of gross negligence or wilful misconduct, or clauses permitting the termination of the contract for capricious reasons may serve as an example. If the contract is subject to, for example, English law, which has no general principle of good faith for commercial contracts, there are no obstacles to a literal implementation of the contract's provisions, as long as they are sufficiently clear.[103]

Would the literal implementation of these clauses be affected by an overriding principle of good faith and fair dealing in the law that would have been applicable if the parties had not chosen English law to govern the contract (particularly if that is the law of the court that is involved with the award)? As was seen in Chapter 3, the principle of good faith and fair dealing is considered to be central in the contract laws of civil law systems. As was seen in Chapter 2, the principle of good faith has been transferred from there into various restatements of principles of contract law that have the goal of being applicable to international contracts, such as the UPICC and the PECL, as well as into the work towards a common European contract law, such as the DCFR and the CESL. As was seen in Chapter 4, Section 4.3.5, extending the overriding rules based on good faith (which have so far been applicable to consumer protection) to commercial contracts has even been proposed.

The principle of good faith and fair dealing is the basis for many provisions of the EU Directive 93/13 on unfair consumer terms. In the *Claro* case,[104] the ECJ ruled on the question as to whether Article 6 of the Directive represents public policy and thus can be a basis for setting aside an arbitral award. Article 6 of the Directive provides that contract terms that are defined as unfair under the Directive shall not be binding on the consumer.

The ECJ found that:

> as the aim of the Directive is to strengthen consumer protection, it constitutes, according to Article 3(1)(t) EC, a measure which is essential to the accomplishment of the tasks entrusted to the Community and, in particular, to raising the standard of living and the quality of life in its territory.[105]

The ECJ thus concluded that the rule on unfair contract terms is to be deemed as public policy.

The *Claro* decision was rendered in a case involving a consumer and its rationale is based on consumer protection. It is, therefore, quite doubtful whether corresponding rules may be deemed to be public policy when the award regards a commercial dispute.

---

[103] See Chapter 3, Sections 1 and 4.3.   [104] C-168/05.   [105] *Ibid.*, para. 37.

Chapters 2 and 3 argued that the principle of good faith is difficult to apply in commercial contract practice. It does not exist as a general principle in English law, which inspires international contracts. It is given a central role in the transnational restatements of principles such as the UPICC and the PECL, but, as was seen in Chapter 2, Sections 4.2 and 4.3, it is difficult to substantiate the content of a transnational principle of good faith. This speaks against considering the principle of good faith as a principle of public policy. Chapter 4, Section 4.3.5 explained why the latest proposal in the field of European contract law, the CESL, although adopting a central role for good faith that can be found in the PECL, implicitly excludes that the principle is overriding. If the principle does not constitute a basis for overriding mandatory rules, then it is even less likely to be upheld as a public-policy principle (public policy having a narrower scope than overriding mandatory rules).

Case law supports the restrictive approach recommended here.[106]

2.6.4.8 Embargo

Rules that would at first sight seem to be of public policy, such as the embargo rule, have, in several cases, not been considered as such, under the consideration that, even if embargoes are important from a foreign policy point of view, they cannot be considered as being of public policy.[107]

2.6.5 Conclusion

The definition of *ordre public* is relative; it may vary from state to state and, within the same state, with the passing of time. What remains firm is that the exception of the *ordre public* has to be applied restrictively; in particular, the simple violation of a rule is in itself not sufficient to trigger applicability of the public policy clause, not even if the violated rule is mandatory or an overriding mandatory rule. The *ordre public* can be considered as affected first if the result of that violation conflicts with the most fundamental principles of the society.

---

[106] See a US court decision, affirming that it did not have the power to review whether the arbitral tribunal had correctly applied the Illinois Beer Industry Fair Dealing Act: United States District Court, Northern District of Illinois, Eastern Division, 29 September 2004, 2004 US Dist. Lexis 19728, in *Yearbook Commercial Arbitration XXX*, pp. 922ff. The Supreme Court of Canada, Province of Prince Edward Island, 23 March 2001, in *Yearbook Commercial Arbitration XXX*, pp. 459ff., dismissed (albeit on an evaluation of the specific circumstances of the case) that it would be against public policy to give effect to certain agreements entered into by a franchisee because of the unequal bargaining power of the parties. A German Court dismissed that the size of a fee requested for certain services was excessive and against good morals: Hamburg Court of Appeal, 12 March 1998, IPRspr 1999 No. 178, in *Yearbook Commercial Arbitration XXIX*, pp. 663ff. See, however, an Austrian decision considering an interest rate that was too high and was therefore in conflict with public policy: Supreme Court of Austria, 26 January 2005, in *Yearbook Commercial Arbitration XXX*, pp. 420ff.

[107] *National Oil Corporation (Libya) v. Libyan Nun Oil Company* [1990] 733 F.Supp. 800, and *Belship Navigation Inc v. Sealift Inc* [1995], in *Yearbook Commercial Arbitration XXII*, pp. 789ff.

This means that parties do enjoy more leeway if their contract contains an arbitration clause than if disputes are to be decided by courts. However, this leeway is not unlimited.

2.7 Conflict with the arbitrability rule

Another defence that may be invoked to obtain annulment or prevent enforcement of an award is that the dispute was not arbitrable. Below, we will verify the scope of the arbitrability clause, and whether it could be applied to an award rendered on a dispute that was submitted to arbitration in the contract, but where one of the parties or the court holds that arbitration is not admissible under the applicable law.

There are various rules of state law that restrict the ability of the parties to submit to arbitration disputes between themselves. One of the main effects of submitting a dispute to arbitration is, as known, that the parties exclude the jurisdiction of courts of law on the same dispute. The other important effect of arbitration is that the winning party can present the award for enforcement to any court in a state where the losing party has assets. Arbitration enjoys such a significant recognition as long as the disputed matters concern areas that national legal systems consider suitable for self-regulation by private parties. As soon as matters of public policy or of special economic or social interest are touched on, however, it can seem less appropriate for a state to waive jurisdiction or to lend its courts' authority to enforce private awards. In such areas with important policy implications, states wish to preserve the jurisdiction of their own courts of law: this preference is based on the assumption that an arbitral tribunal would not be able or willing to apply the law as accurately as a judicial court would.

The above does not mean, however, that an arbitral tribunal does not have the jurisdiction to apply or take into consideration mandatory rules or even overriding mandatory rules. An arbitral tribunal is empowered to apply, in its totality, the law that governs the dispute, as long as this application remains within the sphere of the private law. It does not matter if a provision of the governing law is mandatory, such as the provision on the limitation of rights, or overriding mandatory rules, such as the provision on unfair contract terms. As long as these provisions regulate the private law consequences of a dispute, and the dispute has been submitted to arbitration, the tribunal is empowered to apply them. This circumstance has been the object of debate, especially in connection with disputes involving questions of competition law.[108] Competition law contains, as is known, overriding mandatory provisions; moreover, special bodies have the authority to impose fines and otherwise sanction the violation of these provisions. Hence, the question has been debated as to whether an arbitral tribunal has jurisdiction on disputes involving matters of

---

[108] See the comments made in the preparatory works to the Norwegian Arbitration Bill (NOU 2001:33, pp. 51ff.) and to the Swedish Arbitration Act (SOU 1994:81, p. 86).

competition law. A commercial arbitral tribunal is not a competition law authority with powers of public law. Therefore, if one party to a licence agreement requests an arbitral tribunal to impose a fine on the other party because the licence agreement or that party's actions violate competition law, the arbitral tribunal must decline jurisdiction. However, if that party requests the arbitral tribunal to rule on the contractual consequences of that violation, the arbitral tribunal has jurisdiction: the tribunal may evaluate whether competition law has been violated and may decide on the consequences that that violation has for the parties. For example, it may decide that a certain contractual clause is invalid due to its conflict with competition law, and that therefore non-compliance therewith by one party does not constitute default under the contract. Similarly, an arbitral tribunal may not rule on the validity of a patent, because this decision is under the exclusive jurisdiction of the competent patent authorities. However, an arbitral tribunal may take into consideration patent legislation to determine whether the patent has been violated, and what consequences this violation has for the parties. In such a case, the arbitral tribunal assumes that a valid patent exists and is valid.[109]

In order to avoid any doubts on the jurisdiction of an arbitral tribunal on the contractual and private law aspects of the dispute, even if the dispute also involves matters that are regulated by overriding mandatory rules, some modern arbitration laws have expressly confirmed this circumstance. The Norwegian Arbitration Act, Section 9.2, expressly specifies this circumstance in respect of competition law: a dispute would be arbitrable under Norwegian law even if it relates to competition law, as long as the tribunal is requested to decide on the civil law effects of the competition law. The same rule is also to be found in the Swedish Arbitration Act, Section 1.3. One might wonder whether the legislators have intended to exclude the arbitrability of the civil effects of any other regulatory provision such as patent law, since they have expressly mentioned only the civil law effects of competition law. The report on the Norwegian bill, however, specifies that there was no intention of excluding the arbitrability of the civil law consequences of other rules, rather a desire to confirm that aspect specifically for competition rules, which have often been the subject of disputes internationally.[110]

In the past, a clear trend could be observed towards reducing the areas in which disputes were not deemed as arbitrable. In the past decades, for example, the US legal system has undergone a clear shift from an expressed suspicion against arbitration, to an arbitration-friendly attitude;[111] the same evolution can be observed in other

---

[109] Some Norwegian Supreme Court decisions have confirmed this approach: Rt. 1979 p. 1117, and Rt. 1977 p. 577.
[110] Report on the Bill on Arbitration, NOU 2001:33, comment on section 2–1(2) (which became Section 9.2 in the Act).
[111] The first Supreme Court judgment recognising the arbitrability of matters that previously were deemed to be for the exclusive competence of courts of law was *Scherk* v. *Alberto-Culver* [1974] 417 US 506. See, for further references, P. D. Carrington, P. H. Hagen, 'Contract and Jurisdiction', (1997) 8 *The Supreme Court Review*, 331ff., 362f. and J. R. Sternlight, 'Panacea or Corporate Tool? Debunking the Supreme Court's Preference for Binding Arbitration', (1996) 74(3) *Washington University Law Quarterly*, 637ff. and 652.

legal systems, such as, for example, the Swedish system.[112] Notwithstanding this trend in favour of arbitrability, however, various areas of law are still deemed to be for the exclusive competence of courts of law. The areas where arbitrability is excluded vary from state to state: as a general rule, arbitration is usually permitted in all matters that fall within the boundaries of private law. This would exclude from the scope of arbitration matters such as taxation, import and export regulations, concession of rights by administrative authorities, bankruptcy and the protection of intellectual property. These matters are mostly regulated by mandatory rules from which the parties cannot derogate. Disputes concerning aspects of commercial transactions falling within the scope of the freedom to contract, as seen above, should be arbitrable even if the solution of the dispute assumes that the tribunal takes into consideration these mandatory rules. As long as the tribunal is requested to decide upon the private law consequences of these rules' existence, and is not required to apply or enforce any of these rules, there should be no obstacles to arbitrability.

Recently, the arbitrability exception is being used more frequently, particularly in disputes involving the mandatory EU regulation protecting commercial agents, when the dispute would have been heard in the court of an EU member state if it had not been for the arbitration clause.[113]

Since the arbitrability rule may have a different scope according to the law it belongs to, it is necessary to find out which law determines whether the subject of the dispute was arbitrable or not. The answer to this question differs according to whether the question is asked during the phase of the challenge to the award's validity or during the phase of enforcement.

2.7.1 The law governing arbitrability in the phase of the challenge to an award

Assume that a US oil company has entered into a contract with the Russian government for the exploration, development and production of oil on the territory of Russia. The transaction is in the form of a Production Sharing Agreement (PSA), a type of contract that assumes that the oil company and the government of the host state enter into a contract that regulates all major aspects of the relationship, including also, in particular, the amount of taxes that the investor is supposed to pay out of the income generated in connection with the transaction. The PSA also contains a so-called grandfathering clause, providing for certain compensation to be paid to the investor if certain taxes are increased during the term of the contract. PSAs are

---

[112] See, for example, the evolution regarding the validity of arbitration clauses entered into in the framework of the general conditions of contracts, as it appears from the comparison of three Swedish Supreme Court decisions rendered in 1949, 1969 and 1980: Lars Heuman, *Current Issues in Swedish Arbitration*, (Kluwer, 1990), pp. 22ff.

[113] See *Accentuate Ltd* v. *Asigra Inc* [2009] EWHC 2655 QB regarding a distribution agreement. See also, in Belgium, Cass., 16 November 06; in Germany, OLG München, 17 May 06; in England, High Court 30 October 09.

regulated in Russia by a specific statute on PSAs, specifying in Article 22 that disputes arising out of the contract may be arbitrated, also in states other than Russia, as long as they arise in connection with rights and obligations which have a private law nature. The PSA statute also specifies that the contracts shall be governed by Russian law.

We can assume that the PSA between the US investor and the Russian government contains an arbitration clause submitting disputes to the Arbitration Institute of the SCC, and we can assume that a dispute arises between the parties in connection with the introduction of some new taxes on oil activity in Russia. We are assuming here a commercial dispute on the interpretation of the grandfathering clause in the contract, not an investment dispute based on public international law principles of investment protection. The Russian government claims that the arbitral tribunal has no jurisdiction, because the dispute regards the introduction of taxes by the Russian government, which is not an arbitrable matter under Russian law (Russian law being the law governing the merits of the dispute). The US oil company claims that the arbitral tribunal has jurisdiction, because the lack of arbitrability under Russian law does not affect the Swedish arbitral tribunal. We can further assume that the arbitral tribunal concludes that it has jurisdiction, and renders an award.

We can imagine two scenarios:

(i)   The arbitral tribunal interprets the Grandfathering clause contained in the PSA and determines what compensation the Russian government shall pay to the investor under the contract as a consequence of the introduction of the new tax; and

(ii) The arbitral tribunal determines that the introduction of the new tax is against the contractual obligations undertaken by the Russian government and rules that the new tax is not applicable to the US investor.

We can assume that the Russian government, in both scenarios, challenges the validity of the arbitral award before the Swedish courts, claiming that the dispute was not arbitrable under Russian law governing the PSA and, therefore, the merits of the dispute. The question is: What law should determine whether the dispute is arbitrable or not, and, consequently, whether the award is invalid or not?

The Swedish court would apply Swedish arbitration law (the Arbitration Act of 1999), which, in Article 33.1, designates the law of the arbitral seat for the purpose of determining the arbitrability of the dispute. In addition to the law of the arbitral seat, the question of arbitrability may also be proven under the law applicable to the arbitration agreement (Article 34.1):[114] this would be the law chosen by the parties to govern the arbitration agreement or the law of the arbitral seat. Therefore, in the case of an oil dispute submitted to Swedish arbitration, the Swedish court deciding on the

---

[114] See Lars Heuman, *Skiljemannarätt* (Norstedts juridik, 1999) p. 702.

validity of the award shall determine the arbitrability of the dispute on the basis of the *lex arbitri* (Swedish law) and not on the basis of the law governing the merits (Russian law).

The law of the arbitral seat is also expressly designated by Article 34.2.(b)(i) of the UNCITRAL Model Law. If the question of arbitrability is deemed to also affect the validity of the arbitration agreement, then the arbitrability of the dispute also has to be verified in respect of the law chosen by the parties to govern (not the dispute, but) the arbitration agreement. If the parties have not chosen the law applicable to the arbitration agreement (which, as seen in Section 2.1.1 above, is not a choice that is usually made), then the law of the state where the award was made will be applicable to the validity of the arbitration agreement.

Other state laws do not expressly mention what law is applicable to the question of arbitrability. Sometimes, it is possible to designate the law of the arbitral seat by way of a systematic construction of each arbitration law. For example, the Swiss Private International Law Act defines in Article 177 what disputes are arbitrable, and determines in Article 176 that Swiss arbitration law is applicable to any arbitration that take place in Switzerland. The law that governs the merits of the dispute is not mentioned in any of these arbitration laws and is therefore not relevant when the court verifies the validity of an arbitral award.

2.7.2 The law governing arbitrability in the phase of enforcement of an award

Lack of arbitrability is also mentioned by the New York Convention as a ground for refusing enforcement of an award. The New York Convention clearly determines the law governing arbitrability: enforcement by a court of an award may be refused if 'the subject matter of the difference is not capable of settlement by arbitration under the law of that state'. It is the law of the enforcement court that governs whether the dispute was arbitrable or not. In respect of the New York Convention, it is rather controversial whether arbitrability might also fall under the scope of Article V.1.(a) of the New York Convention, which provides that invalidity of the arbitration agreement is one of the grounds that may justify a refusal to enforce the award.[115] If this view is accepted, then arbitrability of the dispute has to be verified not only in respect of the law of the enforcement court, but also in respect of the law governing the arbitration agreement. The New York Convention determines the law governing the arbitration agreement as the law chosen by the parties to specifically govern the arbitration agreement (and not, generally, the dispute) or, failing a choice by the

---

[115] The most authoritative commentator on the New York Convention excludes the fact that the question of arbitrability can be considered as also falling within the scope of the validity of the arbitration agreement: see A. J. van den Berg, *The New York Arbitration Convention of 1958* (Deventer, 1981), pp. 288f. See also Born, *International Commercial Arbitration*, p. 2863.

parties, the law of the state where the award was made. As was seen in Section 2.1.1 above, this usually leads to the application of the law of the seat of arbitration.

Additionally, the New York Convention, as with the national arbitration laws seen above, does not mention the law governing the merits of the dispute as relevant to the question of arbitrability. Therefore, in the case of enforcement of the Swedish award rendered in the oil dispute, the enforcement court shall determine the arbitrability of the dispute on the basis of its own law, and not on the basis of the *lex arbitri* (Swedish law) or of the law governing the merits (Russian law).

2.7.3 The law governing the dispute is irrelevant

The lack of arbitrability may lead to annulment or refusal to enforce the award only if the dispute was not arbitrable according to the law of the arbitral seat, or the law of the enforcement court or the law chosen by the parties to govern the arbitration agreement. The law that governs the merits of the dispute, on the contrary, is not applicable to the question of arbitrability.

In our example of the Swedish arbitral award rendered on a dispute concerning a PSA governed by Russian law, this means that Russian rules on arbitrability may affect the validity of the award only in the following two cases: (i) if the award is sought to be enforced in the territory of Russia, or (ii) if the parties have subjected the arbitration agreement to Russian law.

In respect of the former case, it may be sufficient to mention that an arbitral award does not necessarily have to be enforced in the state where the losing party has its residence or main place of business; the New York Convention permits the enforcement of an award in any state where the losing party has some assets.

In respect of the latter case, it must be mentioned that, as noted in Section 2.1.1 above, it is very seldom that arbitration agreements contain a choice-of-law clause, and the choice-of-law clause made in the contract that regulates the commercial relationship between the parties does not extend to the arbitration agreement. It is extremely unusual and not recommendable to subject an arbitration agreement to a law different from the law of the state where the arbitration will take place. It is important to have a neutral and independent arbitration in cases where the relationship between the contractual parties is not balanced. When one of the parties is the government of the host state, for example, modifying the legislation or pressing the competent authorities may influence the outcome of the dispute to which it is a party. In this context, it is important that arbitration is geographically placed in a third state, but what is even more important is that the arbitration has an independent legal framework. Therefore, the choice of the arbitral seat and the choice of the arbitral seat's arbitration law should go hand in hand. The arbitration procedure and the arbitration agreement are governed by the law of the arbitral seat, unless the parties decide otherwise. And I would like to remind you here that a choice by the parties of a certain law to govern the commercial agreement and the merits of the dispute does not imply that the parties have also chosen that law to govern the arbitration agreement.

2.7.4 Arbitrability is equal to the *ordre public* in international disputes without a connection to the *lex fori*

In our example of the Swedish arbitral award rendered in a dispute concerning a PSA, therefore, the losing party may claim (for example, in the phase of the challenge to the award's validity) that the award is invalid because it violates the arbitrability rule contained in Swedish law. The Swedish Arbitration Act (Article 1) only permits the arbitration of disputes on matters where the parties enjoy contractual freedom; therefore, matters of public law are not arbitrable.[116] Would an award rendered in Stockholm on a dispute between the US oil company and the Russian state, arising out of a PSA, be deemed as invalid by a Swedish court on the ground that the disputed matter was not arbitrable under Swedish law?

To answer the question, it may be useful to be reminded of the rationale of the arbitrability rule: the arbitrability rule is meant to preserve the jurisdiction of the courts of law in certain areas of law that are deemed to deserve a particularly accurate application of the law. This particularly affects areas of law with public-policy implications where the public interest is deemed to prevail over the freedom of the parties to regulate their own interests. The legal system does not consider private mechanisms of dispute resolution as sufficiently reliable in this context, and wishes to maintain the jurisdiction of its own national courts of law. How does this rationale apply to our US–Russian arbitration in Stockholm? The dispute concerns the application by the Russian authorities of tax law. Disputes regarding taxation are not arbitrable under Swedish law; the Swedish legal system does not intend to waive the jurisdiction of Swedish courts of law in favour of private arbitration. Assuming that the Swedish court set aside the Swedish arbitral award on the ground that the dispute was not arbitrable, would that mean that Swedish courts of law have jurisdiction on the dispute? Of course not: Swedish courts have no jurisdiction and no interest in exercising jurisdiction on that dispute, because the subject matter has no connection with Sweden and is not subject to Swedish law. The rationale of the arbitrability rule, in short, is not applicable if the dispute has no connection to the state where the arbitration takes place. Then why should the arbitrability rule be applicable?

If a dispute has no connection with the legal system of the arbitral seat, the arbitrability rule should be applicable to set aside an award only if the annulment of the award is necessary to avoid an unacceptable result to which the arbitral tribunal has come.[117]

---

[116] For more extensive comments on the scope of the arbitrability rule under Swedish law, see Lars Heuman, *Arbitration Law of Sweden: Practice and Procedure* (JurisNet, 2003), pp. 156ff.

[117] For a more extensive analysis of the matter see van den Berg, *The New York Arbitration Convention*, pp. 360, 368ff., III-5.1 and footnote 337, who considers the arbitrability rule as a sub-concept of the *ordre public* rule, and therefore superfluous. Partially along the same lines, within Swedish law, see Heuman, *Arbitration Law of Sweden*, p. 70, who states that a dispute that would not be deemed arbitrable if it was domestic, may still be arbitrated if it has an international character. Implying that the arbitrability rule of domestic law coincides with the international public policy of the seat of arbitration, see B. Hanotiau, 'The Law Applicable to Arbitrability', in Albert van den Berg (ed.) *40 Years of Application of the New York*

In itself, the fact that the arbitral tribunal has resolved a dispute that is not arbitrable under the law of the arbitral seat would not be unacceptable: the courts of the arbitral seat would have neither the interest nor the competence to apply their own law to that dispute. What would be unacceptable is a decision made in a specific case, for example, because it has given effect to an agreement that violated a UN embargo. In short, what should be an annulment ground in this situation is not the fact that the tribunal has exercised jurisdiction on the dispute, but the fact that the result of the decision conflicts with the fundamental principles of the court's law. In situations where the dispute does not have any links with the legal system of the arbitral seat, therefore, the arbitrability clause would overlap with the *ordre public* clause. The evaluation of the award's validity, in other words, cannot be made in advance by automatically applying an abstract measure of arbitrability. The evaluation of the award's validity has to be made on the basis of the specific decision rendered in the particular case, and by measuring the actual decision against fundamental principles of the court's law.

Consequently, the court of challenge should conclude, in the second scenario described above, that the award runs against the fundamental principles of the court's legal system, because it decided on matters clearly belonging to the sphere of sovereignty of the host state (in our example, Russian law). An award deciding that the investor is not subject to paying certain taxes introduced by Russian law would be an award that decides on matters that belong to the sphere of Russian sovereignty. A court of challenge may consider this award as running against the principles of comity between nations; therefore, the award may be set aside because it violates the principle of comity in the court's legal system.

In the first described scenario, however, the court of challenge should conclude that the award is valid, even if it decided on matters that are not arbitrable under the court's law. An award deciding that the investor is entitled to a certain amount of compensation as a consequence of modifications to Russian taxation law would be an award that decides on matters relating to taxation; therefore, it is not arbitrable. However, the award would be aimed not at restricting the sphere of sovereignty of the Russian state, but at reinstating the balance of interests in the contract between the investor and the state. Even if the dispute is not arbitrable under the court's law, the award may still be deemed valid. Violation of the arbitrability rule is not, in itself, sufficient to annul an award (when the court has no jurisdiction on the dispute); as long as the award does not violate other fundamental principles of the court's legal system, the award is valid.

2.7.5 Conclusion

The arbitrability rule, in conclusion, does not always present an independent obstacle to the effectiveness of international arbitral awards for two reasons. First, the scope

Convention, The Hague etc. (ICCA Congress Series no. 9, 1999), pp.146–67, 158. For a more extensive discussion, as well as references to some judicial decisions confirming this theory, see Cordero-Moss, *International Commercial Arbitration: Party Autonomy*, pp. 293f.

of what is deemed by state laws as not arbitrable is relatively reduced. Second, if the dispute has no points of contact with the *lex fori*, so that the courts do not obtain jurisdiction by excluding the admissibility of the arbitration clause, then the courts have no interest in enforcing the arbitrability rule. In this situation, the grounds for considering an award as invalid or not enforceable will have to be based on the award's violation of the court's *ordre public*, rather than on the simple fact that the award concerns a dispute belonging to the list of non-arbitrable areas.

Where the court's law is applicable to the dispute, however, it is not unusual that courts make use of the arbitrability exception in order to exercise jurisdiction and ensure an accurate application of the law, if it contains rules with an overriding character.[118]

3 The power of the arbitral tribunal in respect of the parties' pleadings

The scope of the arbitral tribunal's authority is determined by the parties. The primary source establishing the arbitral jurisdiction and the scope of the dispute is the arbitration agreement. In their statements of claim or of defence and their requests for relief, the parties introduce the facts that are in dispute, the evidence that shall prove them, the claims, the legal sources and the legal arguments that shall be the basis for the award. The parties' pleadings determine, therefore, the borders of the dispute upon which the tribunal is called on to decide. The arbitral tribunal is not supposed to exceed these limits.

The self-sufficiency of the contract described in Chapter 1 is meant to be enhanced when disputes are submitted to arbitration, because the arbitral tribunal is expected to rely solely on the contract and on the parties' pleadings. If the arbitral tribunal has the power to look beyond these borders, the self-sufficiency of the contract is challenged. Therefore, it is relevant here to analyse the arbitral tribunal's power.

As seen in Section 2 above, in some situations, the arbitral tribunal may see the necessity of taking into consideration a law different from the law chosen in the parties' contract.

In other situations, an arbitral tribunal may be forced to render the award without having received sufficient instructions or arguments by one or even all of the parties. If one of the parties does not participate in the proceeding, it deprives the process of the contribution of its factual and legal arguments. Even if both parties participate in the proceeding, the arguments presented by one or both of them may not be convincing or not sufficiently developed. In these cases of insufficient instructions or pleadings by the parties, how shall the tribunal decide?

Shall it assume the role of an umpire that passively listens to the presented arguments and decides which of the opposing arguments deserves to win? Shall this umpire role be taken to its extreme, so that, in the case of the failure by one

---

[118] See *Accentuate Ltd v. Asigra Inc* [2009] EWHC 2655 QB.

party to participate in the proceedings, the other party automatically wins, even if its arguments are not convincing?

Or shall the arbitral tribunal take an active role, investigate the relevance and correctness of the produced evidence and develop arguments that were not presented by the parties? Shall this active role go so far as to deciding on the basis of legal sources that were not at all pleaded by the parties? Shall it allow for granting relief that the parties have not requested?

We will analyse these questions below. Two levels of regulation are relevant in this context: rules on the conduct of the arbitral tribunal and rules on the validity and enforceability of the award. As we will see, the tribunal is bound in respect of the factual scope of the dispute, but enjoys considerable freedom in respect of the inferences that it draws from the evidence and in respect of the legal consequences of the proven facts.

3.1 The procedural rules

The arbitral tribunal must comply with the procedural role determined by the applicable regulation. The applicable regulation consists mainly of: (i) the arbitration agreement; (ii) the rules of the relevant arbitral institution in case of institutional arbitration, or the arbitration rules chosen by the parties (if any) in case of ad hoc arbitration; and (iii) the rules in the applicable arbitration law in case of commercial arbitration or in the relevant convention in case of treaty-based arbitration, such as investment arbitration. All of these may determine the tribunal's role and will be examined below.

3.1.1 Arbitration agreements

Arbitration agreements sometimes specify that the arbitral tribunal shall be empowered only to decide on a certain relief, for example, the reimbursement of damages, and not on others, for example, the termination of the contract. In such cases, some of the questions asked here are readily answered: the tribunal would clearly exceed its power if it ordered a relief that the parties have excluded in the arbitration agreement.

The question of the authority of the arbitral tribunal, however, has to be distinguished from the question of the proper interpretation by the tribunal of the contract between the parties, as well as from the question of the proper application of the law. In a contract regulating that the defaulting party shall be liable only for indemnifying direct losses and not also consequential damages, the exclusion of consequential damages is regulated as an obligation between the parties and it is not a restriction on the tribunal's jurisdiction (unless this restriction is reflected in the arbitration clause). If the arbitral tribunal determines that the defaulting party has to reimburse consequential damages, it may have based its decision on a wrong interpretation of the contract or on a wrong application of the law's definition of direct and consequential losses. However, this will not mean that the tribunal has exceeded its authority.[119] The award, therefore, is wrong in terms of the merits, but is not rendered without jurisdiction. In terms of the consequences for the effectiveness of the award, this means that the award is valid and enforceable.[120] If, however, the exclusion of consequential losses had been regulated as a limit to the arbitral tribunal's authority, the award would be invalid and unenforceable.[121] Generally, arbitration agreements do not contain limitations on the tribunal's authority,[122] and they remain silent on the question of the arbitral tribunal's power beyond the pleadings of the parties.

Arbitration agreements, however, often contain instructions in respect of the applicable law. These instructions may be considered as a delimitation of the tribunal's authority.[123] Also here, excess of authority has to be distinguished from error in the interpretation of the contract (its choice-of-law clause) and error in the application of the law (the applicable choice-of-law rules, for which the rules may be applied to restrict or override the choice of law made by the parties). In the latter cases, the courts will not have the jurisdiction to control the award, and the error will not have any consequences for the effectiveness of the award.[124]

---

[119] For similar observations see, in respect of Swedish law, Heuman, *Arbitration Law of Sweden*, pp. 610ff. and 737, and in respect of English law, R. Merkin, *Arbitration Law* (Laforma Law, 2004), pp. 714f. For a US decision applying the same principle, see *Fertilizer Company of India*, Southern District of Ohio, 517 F.Supp 948 (1981) and *ICCA Yearbook Commercial Arbitration VII* (Kluwer International, 1982), pp. 381ff.

[120] As was seen in Section 2 above, the judicial control over the award does not extend to a review of the merits.

[121] On the consequence of an excess of power, see Section 3.2 below.

[122] As an illustration, no limitations to the arbitral tribunal's authority are mentioned in the Model Arbitration clauses recommended by, for example, the Arbitration Institute of the SCC ('Any dispute, controversy or claim arising out of or in connection with this contract, or the breach, termination or invalidity thereof, shall be finally settled by arbitration in accordance with the Rules of the Arbitration Institute of the Stockholm Chamber of Commerce'), the ICC ('All disputes arising out of or in connection with the present contract shall be finally settled under the Rules of Arbitration of the ICC by one or more arbitrators appointed in accordance with the said Rules') or the LCIA ('Any dispute arising out of or in connection with this contract, including any question regarding its existence, validity or termination, shall be referred to and finally resolved by arbitration under the LCIA Rules, which Rules are deemed to be incorporated by reference into this clause'). These standard clauses are sometimes accompanied by a recommendation to specifically regulate the number of arbitrators, the venue of the tribunal and the language of the proceeding; no mention is made of regulating the scope of authority of the tribunal. Often, these standard clauses are applied as a model to Arbitration clauses that are individually drafted; the number of clauses that contain specific limits to the tribunal's authority, therefore, is rather low. The ICC Rules assume that the parties shall, at the beginning of the dispute, agree on Terms of References, specifying the questions that are submitted to the tribunal. These are often drafted as a positive list of questions to be solved, rather than as a list of items that are excluded from the scope of the dispute.

[123] See Redfern, Hunter, Blackaby and Partasides, *Redfern and Hunter on International Arbitration*, para. 3.96f. See also the Committee, 'International Law Association Report', formulating, under the heading Conclusions and Recommendations (p. 19), the following General Principle: '*First*, the principal task of arbitrators in a commercial case is to decide the dispute within the mandate defined by the arbitration clause. Arbitration is a creature of contract. The parties can agree to its scope. That agreement is binding on the arbitrators'.

[124] The courts do not have the power to review the merits of the award; see Section 2 above. For a criticism of a recent decision by the Swedish Court of Appeal confirming this approach in the context of investment arbitration, see below, section 3.1.3(i).

3.1.2 Arbitration rules

Arbitration rules are issued by arbitration institutions such as the Arbitration Institute of the SCC, the ICC and the LCIA, they are chosen by the parties to be used in ad hoc arbitration (such as the UNCITRAL Arbitration Rules of 1976, revised in 2010) or they are issued in connection with treaty-based arbitration (such as the ICSID Rules). Generally, the extent to which the arbitral tribunal is bound by the parties' pleadings and legal arguments is not specifically regulated in the arbitration rules. There are, however, several rules that could be deemed relevant to the subject matter:

3.1.2.1 Party's default

Many arbitration rules provide that the arbitral proceeding may be initiated and may continue in spite of the failure by one party to participate.[125] Once the arbitral jurisdiction is established,[126] a party may not, by failing to contribute to it, prevent an arbitral proceeding and the award from being rendered.

This rule clarifies that it is not necessary to receive the pleadings from all parties to the dispute in order to proceed with the arbitration. However, it does not clarify what role the tribunal shall have in respect of the pleadings: shall the arbitral tribunal accept all the evidence produced and arguments and requests made by the participating party, or shall it evaluate them critically and independently?

3.1.2.2 Adverse inferences

Some rules specify that failure by one party to appear shall not be seen as an admission of the other party's assertions.[127] Most arbitration rules, however, are silent on the matter.[128] This does not usually prevent the tribunal

---

[125] SCC Rules Article 30, ICC Rules Articles 5(2), 23(3) and 26(2), LCIA Rules Article 15(8), UNCITRAL Rules Article 30, ICSID Rules Article 42.

[126] In a commercial dispute, the jurisdiction is established by the arbitral agreement; see the 1958 New York Convention on the Recognition and Enforcement of Foreign Arbitral Awards, Article II. In investment arbitration, the arbitral agreement is, generally, based on the applicable bilateral or multilateral investment treaty, which is deemed to contain an offer to arbitrate by the host state, which is deemed as accepted by the foreign investor by initiating the arbitration: see, for example, Article 26(5) of the Energy Charter Treaty. More generally, see J. Paulsson, 'Arbitration without Privity', (1995) 10 *ICSID Review, Foreign Investment Law Journal*, 232.

[127] See the ICSID Arbitration Rules Article 42(3). This principle does not apply only to investment arbitration: the same principle may be found in modern codifications of commercial arbitration law, such as German law (Code of Civil Procedure, (ZPO) § 1048(2)); see, for example, M. Martinek, 'Die Mitwirkungsverweigerung des Schiedsbeklagten', in G. Lüke, T. Mikami, and H. Prütting, (eds.) *Festschrift für Akira Ishikawa zum 70. Geburtstag* (De Gruyter, 2001), pp. 269ff., X, and Swedish law, see Heuman, *Arbitration Law of Sweden*, pp. 396f. and 405. See also Noah Rubins, '"Observation" in Connection with *Swembalt v. Republic of Latvia'*, *Stockholm Arbitration Report* (SCC Arbitration Institute, 2004–2), 123ff.

[128] For example, the ICC Rules. However, a highly authoritative commentary on Article 21(2) of the previous ICC Rules, which corresponds to Article 26 in the 2012 ICC Rules currently in force, considers it to be a widely accepted principle that failure by one party to appear does not mean admission of the arguments

from drawing adverse inferences regarding the defaulting party, if this is deemed appropriate under the circumstances.[129]

This does not finally clarify the role of the tribunal in respect of the pleadings: that the tribunal may not consider a failure to appear as an admission does not prevent it from accepting the participating party's pleadings as they were presented if it is convinced of their soundness. Conversely, that the tribunal may draw adverse inferences does not mean that the tribunal has to accept the presented pleadings if it is convinced that they are not sufficiently founded.

Both rules, therefore, seem to assume that the tribunal is free to independently evaluate the pleadings of the participating party. The former rule assumes a duty to evaluate independently, whereas the latter only assumes the power to proceed to an independent evaluation. That a tribunal shall not make use of this power, however, and shall blindly accept the pleadings of the participating party, does not seem to comply with the expectations of justice connected with the institute of arbitration.

The ALI/UNIDROIT Principles of Transnational Civil Procedure, a text issued in 2004 by the American Law Institute and the International Institute for the Unification of Private Law and aiming at providing a standard set of principles for transnational disputes as a basis for future initiatives in reforming civil procedure, and aspiring at also being applicable to arbitration,[130] contain some guidelines in respect of the eventuality that a default judgment is to be rendered. These principles are not binding rules, but they may be considered to reflect a certain international consensus on the main aspects of some procedural questions. Article 15.3 requests the court that is rendering a default judgement to determine on its own initiative the following aspects: its jurisdiction, compliance with notice provisions, and that the claim is reasonably supported by available facts and evidence and is legally sufficient. In connection with the latter duty of the court, it is specified that the court is not expected to carry out a full inquiry, but it has to critically analyse the evidence supporting the statement of claims. This does not prevent the tribunal from drawing

---

made by the other party: Yves Derains and Eric Schwartz, *A Guide to the New ICC Rules of Arbitration* (Kluwer Law International, 1998), p. 266.

[129] See the International Bar Association (IBA) Rules on the Taking of Evidence in International Commercial Arbitration of 2010, affirming in Articles 9(5) and 9(6) that the tribunal may draw inferences that are adverse to the defaulting party in case of failure to produce a piece of evidence that was requested by the other party and ordered by the tribunal. See also the commentary on the ICC Rules by Derains and Schwarz, *A Guide to the New ICC Rules of Arbitration*, Article 20(5), footnote 593 and Section 21(2), p. 266: negative inferences are possible, but the tribunal should be cautions in drawing them. This provision was not amended in the 2012 version of the ICC Rules; therefore, the comments may be deemed to be still applicable. Also in the systems expressly excluding that failure to appear is an admission, the tribunal may evaluate the attitude of the parties and draw adverse inferences, if it deems them to be appropriate under the circumstances; see, for Swedish law, Heuman, *Arbitration Law of Sweden*, pp. 397, 405. See also Rubins, '"Observation" in connection with *Swembalt v. Republic of Latvia*', pp. 124ff.

[130] See the introduction to the Principles text, www.unidroit.org/english/principles/civilprocedure/main.htm; see also 'ALI/UNIDROIT Principles of Transnational Civil Procedure' (2004-4) 9 *Uniform Law Review*, 758ff. and 'Comment P-E' on the Introductory Article on Scope and Implementation, 759.

adverse inferences from a party's failure to advance the proceeding or respond as required, in accordance with Article 17.3.[131]

From the foregoing, it seems possible to conclude that an arbitral tribunal is not bound to automatically accept any pleading made by one party in case of failure by the other party to contest it. The question that remains open is how far the tribunal can go in its independent evaluation of a party's pleadings.

3.1.2.3 Additional information

Many arbitration rules permit the tribunal to request that the parties present additional documentation and clarification, to take the initiative to appoint an expert and to proceed to inspections etc.[132]

This possibility of being able to request additional clarification is consistent with the tribunal's independent evaluation of the participating party's pleadings as described in the previous section. However, the access to requesting additional clarification is not limited to the situations where one party fails to appear and the tribunal needs further information to evaluate the other party's pleadings. This access applies in general, even if both parties participate in the proceedings and have presented their respective cases in full.

The possibility of being able to request additional information, therefore, may be used by the tribunal to introduce new elements that were not at all or not sufficiently pleaded by the parties. It is, however, not clear how far the tribunal may go in introducing new elements: may the tribunal ask for additional documentation and clarification in order to better convince itself of the correctness or relevance of the statements made by the parties, or also to investigate facts that were not mentioned by the parties, to apply sources that the parties had not invoked or to order remedies that the parties have not requested?

3.1.2.4 Burden of proof

Some rules expressly state the principle of burden of proof, a principle generally valid in most procedural systems: each party shall have the burden of proving the facts that it relies on.[133]

This principle may appear to contradict the two rules mentioned under the sections on Party's default and adverse inferences above: if the party having the burden of proof does not present sufficient evidence (because it fails to appear, or otherwise), the facts that it invokes may not be considered as proven. The tribunal shall not take over and discharge that party's burden. This, however, does not necessarily mean that the

---

[131] See 'Comment P-17B', (2004-4) 9 *Uniform Law Review*, 792.
[132] For example, the Arbitration Rules of the SCC Article 24(3), ICC Rules Article 25(5), LCIA Rules 21(1), 22 (1)(c) and 22(1)(e), UNCITRAL Rules Article 27(3) and ICSID Rules Articles 34(2) and 42(4). The same is true for the ALI/UNIDROIT Principles, see the 'Comment P-15D' on Article 15.3.3, (2004-4) 9 *Uniform Law Review*, 785f.
[133] UNCITRAL Rules Article 27(1).

pleadings made by the other party are sufficiently proven or substantiated: the party failing to provide sufficient evidence for its case will lose only if the other party has presented pleadings that are sufficiently substantiated. Otherwise, the arbitral tribunal has the possibility of investigating the matter on its own initiative. However, it is not completely clear how far a tribunal can go in its own investigation before it takes over the burden of proof of the defaulting party, thus violating the corresponding principle. That the tribunal shall not, on its own motion, procure evidence without involving the parties seems to be understood;[134] but how far may the tribunal go in requesting additional evidence in accordance with the section on additional information above?

3.1.2.5 Impartiality

Many arbitration rules specify that the arbitral tribunal shall act impartially.[135] This is a fundamental principle of due process that must be deemed to apply even if the arbitration rules do not express it.[136]

It could be questioned as to whether the tribunal acts impartially when it, on its own initiative, verifies the soundness of one party's pleadings or requests additional information as described in the sections on adverse inferences and additional information above. It could be argued that the tribunal, by so doing, acts on behalf of the party that did not appear or that failed to properly contest the pleadings, and that it therefore is in breach of (the rule on burden of proof, and) its duty to act impartially. However, it seems legitimate to affirm that the tribunal, by acting *ex officio* as described, does not act on behalf of the defaulting party, and rather acts in order to achieve a logical and objective result. It is, however, not completely clear as to what extent the tribunal may stretch its role as investigator before it, in effect, takes over the role of the defaulting party and violates the principle of impartiality.

3.1.2.6 Fair hearing

Many arbitration rules provide that the arbitral tribunal shall grant a fair hearing to all parties;[137] this assumes that all parties shall have been given equal and real opportunities to present their respective cases and to respond to the arguments made by the other party. In addition, this principle is a fundamental part of the due process.[138]

If the tribunal's own evaluation has deprived one or more parties of the chance to respond on certain matters, so that the tribunal decides on the basis of elements

---

[134] See, for example, Heuman, *Arbitration Law of Sweden*, p. 397.
[135] SCC Rules Article 19(2), ICC Rules Article 22(4), LCIA Rules Article 14(1), UNCITRAL Rules Article 11 and ICSID Rules Article 6.
[136] The principle is to be found in arbitration laws (see, for example, the UNCITRAL Model Law Article 18 and the Swedish Arbitration Act Articles 8 and 21).
[137] SCC Rules Article 19(2), ICC Rules Article 22(4), LCIA Rules 14(1)(i) and UNCITRAL Rules 17(1) and 27(3).
[138] See the UNCITRAL Model Law Article 34(2)(a)(ii) and the Swedish Arbitration Act Article 24. The principle is also expressly referred to in the New York Convention article V(1)(b)

for which the parties had no chance of being able to present their views, the adversary principle may be deemed as violated. Does the parties' right to be heard relate only to the facts that substantiate the various claims, or does it also extend to the interpretation of these facts and the factual inferences therefrom made by the tribunal?[139] Does the right to be heard also extend to the points of law and to the tribunal's assessment of the legal consequences of the facts in dispute? In certain systems it is uncontroversial that the tribunal enjoys the freedom to assess and apply the law on its own initiative.[140] To what extent this *iura novit curia* approach may collide with the adversary principle is not clarified in the arbitration rules.

3.1.3 Arbitration law

Arbitration law is quite heterogeneous, since it extends from the uniform regulation contained in international conventions (of which the most notable is, for commercial arbitration, the 1958 New York Convention on the Recognition and Enforcement of Foreign Arbitral Awards and, for investment arbitration, the 1966 Washington Convention – the ICSID), via the harmonising, but not binding 1985 UNCITRAL Model Law on International Commercial Arbitration (revised in 2006) to the arbitration law prevailing in each country.

Arbitration law does not, as a general rule, contain a specific regulation on the procedure to be followed in an arbitral proceeding, beyond principles corresponding to those mentioned above in Section 3.1.2 above.

Two rules are often encountered, however, that might have relevance here: the rule preventing the tribunal from deciding the merits as an *amiable compositeur*, unless it has been empowered by the parties to do so, and the rule on the arbitrability of a dispute. These represent limits to the tribunal's discretion in evaluating the pleadings by the parties.

As will be seen in Section 3.5, violation of the former rule may render the award invalid and unenforceable under, respectively, Article 34(2)(a)(iv) of the UNCITRAL Model Law and Article V(1)(d) of the New York Convention on procedural irregularity, combined with a corresponding provision in the arbitration law of the country of origin of the award.[141] As was seen in Section 2.7, violation of the rule on arbitrability renders the award invalid and unenforceable under, respectively, Article 34(2)(b)(i) of the UNCITRAL Model Law and Article V(2)(a) of the New York

---

[139] Case law in common law distinguishes between the fact-finding process, where the parties have a right to be heard, and the drawing of inferences from the evidence, where there is no need for the tribunal to get back to the parties and present its inferences, even if they were not anticipated during the proceeding: Merkin, *Arbitration Law*, pp. 592f.

[140] For a more extensive treatment, see Section 3.3.

[141] As it would be a violation of the rule contained in applicable arbitration law and determining the powers of the tribunal. A rule limiting the tribunal's power to decide *ex bono et aequo* unless empowered to do so by the parties is generally present in arbitration laws (see the UNCITRAL Model Law Article 28(3)), but not without exception: the Swedish Arbitration Act, for example, does not contain it.

Convention, combined with a corresponding provision in the arbitration law of the enforcement court. Additionally, Section 33(1) of the Swedish Arbitration Act contains a similar rule.

3.1.4 Particularly on investment arbitration

Investment arbitration concerns disputes between a foreign investor and the host state, and is carried out in the framework of a BIT between the host state and the investor's state or of a multilateral treaty such as the NAFTA or the Energy Charter Treaty. Awards rendered in investment disputes are subject to the control regime determined by the relevant treaty; this may consist in a special control mechanism.[142] To the extent that investment treaties also open up the possibility for investment arbitration under rules of commercial arbitration, such as the SCC Rules, an award rendered under these rules will be subject to judicial control under the relevant arbitration law in the same way as an award rendered in commercial arbitration. Therefore, it is useful here to verify whether the law establishing investment arbitration (i.e., the relevant multilateral or bilateral investment treaty) contains any rules that may be relevant to our topic.

The treaty establishing arbitration may limit the jurisdiction of the tribunal. For example, arbitral jurisdiction may be limited to claims relating to violations of the treaty or it may also extend to claims relating to a breach of contract.[143] Sometimes, investment treaties refer to arbitration claims that relate only to some of the obligations arising out of the treaty. The treaty between the UK and the Russian Federation, for example, refers to arbitration-only disputes in terms of the quantification of the compensation that has to be paid in case of unlawful expropriation by the host state of the foreign investor's investment. Disputes concerning whether there has been an unlawful expropriation where compensation is due, on the contrary, fall outside of the arbitral tribunal's jurisdiction, according to the treaty. An investment award rendered by an arbitral tribunal organised under the rules of the SCC retained jurisdiction when an investor who had acquired some shares in Yukos claimed that the Russian Federation had breached its obligations under the treaty. The award applied the most favoured nation clause contained in the treaty, and thus extended broader jurisdiction clauses that may be found in other treaties ratified by the Russian Federation to that particular case. The District Court of Stockholm found that a most favoured nation clause may not be used to extend the scope of arbitral jurisdiction determined in the treaty, and set aside the award.[144]

---

[142] In particular, the ad hoc Committee regulated by the ICSID Convention, Article 52.

[143] For more in general on the distinction between contract claims and treaty claims see Christoph Schreuer, 'Investment Treaty Arbitration and Jurisdiction over Contract Claims: The Vivendi I Case Considered', in T. Weiler (ed.), *Leading Cases from the ICSID, NAFTA, Bilateral Treaties and Customary International Law* (Cameron May, 2005), p. 299.

[144] Case no T 24891–07 of 9 November 2011.

Furthermore, the treaty establishing arbitration may contain instructions in respect of the law to be applied by the tribunal to the merits of the dispute.[145]

In the case of a violation of such treaty provisions, it is not appropriate to apply the general principle that an award may not be reviewed for an error in law or for an error in the interpretation of the contract. This is because the error in question would be made in connection not with the decision on the merits (which is beyond the scope of control that a court may exercise on an award), but with the establishment of the tribunal's duties in the conduct of the proceedings, as determined by the applicable arbitration law or investment treaty (which is within the scope of judicial control). The reasoning is the same as for the rules on arbitrability and on the power to render an award *ex bono et aequo* mentioned immediately above.

A criticism of a recent decision by the Svea Court of Appeal in Sweden[146] illustrates this point. The decision was rendered in connection with the challenge to an SCC award issued in an investment arbitration based on the BIT between the Netherlands and the Czech Republic. One of the questions that the Court was called on to decide was whether the arbitral tribunal had disregarded the rule on the governing law contained in the BIT. The Court relied on the principle that an error in the interpretation or application of the law cannot be judicially reviewed, and limited itself to verifying *prima facie* whether the tribunal seemed to have applied a law at all. The Court seemed to consider any more detailed an examination of the matter to be beyond the scope of its own jurisdiction. This approach does not seem to be fully justified, and particularly not in the context of investment arbitration. Even if the award had been rendered in a commercial dispute, the Court would have had the jurisdiction to verify whether the law applied by the tribunal had been selected as a consequence of the tribunal's error in interpreting the contract or in applying rules of private international law (in either case, the Court would not have had jurisdiction to set aside the award) or if it was the result of the tribunal bluntly disregarding the choice of law made by the parties (in which case, the Court would have had the jurisdiction to set aside the award for excess of power).[147] In the case of investment arbitration, however, the matter is even clearer: the applicable law is determined in the Treaty that constitutes the very basis of the tribunal's jurisdiction. A violation of such a rule would not be an error in interpreting the law; it would be a procedural irregularity, and quite a serious one, when considering the important public-policy reasons that underlie a state's acceptance to regulate, in a treaty, its own submission to arbitration.

---

[145] More extensively, in respect of the law applicable in ICSID Arbitration, see Christoph Schreuer, Lovetta Malintoppi, August Reinisch and Antony Sinlcair, *The ICSID Convention: A Commentary*, 2nd edn (Cambridge University Press, 2009), pp. 545ff.

[146] *CME* v. *Czech Republic*, T 8735–01, RH 2003:55 (published in English in the *Stockholm Arbitration Report* [2003–2], pp. 167ff.).

[147] See Section 3.3.1.2 above.

According to Article 34(6) of the Swedish Arbitration Act, a procedural irregularity can be sanctioned through the invalidity of the award if it has probably influenced the outcome of the case. In order to verify whether Article 34(6) of the Swedish Arbitration Act was applicable, the Court should have examined more accurately whether the tribunal's application of the law was in accordance with the rule on choice of law contained in the BIT.[148]

3.2 The ultimate borders: excess of power, the adversarial principle, procedural irregularity

While the arbitral procedure is not regulated in detail by arbitration law, the validity and enforceability of arbitral awards are. Some of the principles that we have seen in Section 3.1.2 above are so fundamental to arbitration that arbitration law sanctions their violation. The sanctions will be the annulment of the award by the courts in the country of origin of the award (regulated by the respective state arbitration act; in the case of ICSID arbitration, the annulment is regulated by the ICSID Convention)[149] and the possibility of being able to refuse the recognition or enforcement of the award by the courts in the enforcement country (uniformly regulated by the New York Convention; in the case of ICSID arbitration, enforcement is regulated by the ICSID Convention).

To the extent that the applicable arbitration rules leave a certain amount of room for the tribunal to choose its own role between the two extremes of a passive umpire and an active inquisitor, the ultimate border is given by the remedies that may affect the validity or enforceability of the award. The grounds for setting aside or refusing to enforce an award are usually interpreted restrictively. In particular, as was seen in Section 2 above, the courts do not have the jurisdiction to review the award in terms of the merits. This means that an error in the tribunal's interpretation of the contract,

---

[148] Criticising the Court's decision, see also the 'Observations' by S. Soltysinski, M. Olechowski, in the *Stockholm Arbitration Report* (SCC Arbitration Institute, 2003–2), 224ff. and 240, and T. Wiwen-Nilsson, in the *Stockholm Arbitration Report* (SCC Arbitration Institute 2003–2), 254f. In favour of the decision, see the 'Observations' by N. Rubins, in the *Stockholm Arbitration Report* (SCC Arbitration Institute 2003–2), 208f., and Bagner, H., in the *Stockholm Arbitration Report* (SCC Arbitration Institute 2003–2), 250. More extensively on the matter, see Christoph Schreuer, 'Failure to Apply the Governing Law in International Investment Arbitration' (2002) 7, *Austrian Review of International and European Law*, 147ff., www.univie. ac.at/intlaw/wordpress/pdf/70_cspubl_70.pdf, last accessed 23 August 2013, criticising the decision commented on here at 182ff. and Schreuer, Malintoppi, Reinisch and Sinlcair, *The ICSID Convention*, Article 52, paras. 191–270 (defining the failure to apply the proper law as an excess of power).

[149] If the investment arbitration is subject to the annulment mechanism regulated in Article 52 of the ICSID Convention, several of the annulment grounds will be similar to those that are generally to be found in national arbitration law: for example, irregularity in the constitution of the arbitral tribunal, excess of power or procedural irregularity. In the interest of predictability and harmonisation of arbitration law, it is desirable that these standards are, to the greatest extent possible, interpreted according to the same criteria, irrespective of the legal framework in which they operate.

evaluation of the evidence or application of the law may not lead to invalidity[150] or unenforceability of the award.[151]

Taking duly into account the mentioned restricted scope of application, the following remedies seem to be relevant to the question of the arbitral tribunal's power.

3.2.1 Excess of power

If the award goes beyond the factual scope of the dispute as agreed upon by the parties, it exceeds the power granted to the tribunal. An award that is rendered beyond the scope of authority of the tribunal is invalid according to the UNCITRAL Model Law Article 34(2)(a)(iii)[152] and unenforceable according to the New York Convention article V(1)(c).[153]

It is generally recognised that the rule, as contained in the New York Convention and the UNCITRAL Model Law, is to be applied restrictively. Thus, the rule is deemed to apply to the factual scope of the dispute, and not also to the arguments made by the parties.[154] This remedy is generally interpreted so restrictively that it is, as a rule, considered not relevant to questions relating to the application of the law. As will be seen in Section 3.3 below, however, it may not be excluded that the remedy is applied in the case of disregard by the arbitral tribunal of the parties' choice of law.

The normal scope of application of the exception of excess of power relates not to the choice of the applicable law, but to the object of the dispute.[155]

We can assume, for example, that a contract for the sale of certain production equipment contains an arbitration clause. At a certain point in time, a dispute arises between the parties, and the arbitral tribunal is requested to decide whether the buyer has to pay the full price for the delivered equipment or a reduced price because of certain alleged defects of the equipment. The arbitral tribunal comes to the

---

[150] The validity of an award is regulated by national arbitration law; the fact that some countries provide for a review of the merits cannot therefore be excluded. In the UNCITRAL Model Law, the exhaustive list of grounds for invalidity is contained in Article 34 and does not include an error in the merits or in the application of the law; the same is true for Swedish law (Arbitration Act, Articles 33 and 34) and English law (Arbitration Act, Sections 67 and 68: the possibility of an English court being able to review an award for an error in (English) law has been significantly limited since the Arbitration Act of 1979).

[151] The exhaustive list of grounds for refusing enforcement is set forth in article V of the New York Convention, which does not contain an error in fact or in law as grounds.

[152] And may therefore be set aside by the courts of the country of origin. See also the Swedish Arbitration Act Article 34(2).The same rule applies to the annulment of ICSID awards; see the ICSID Convention Article 52(1)(b).

[153] Enforcement of ICSID awards is subject to the same rules of enforcement that apply to final court decisions of that state (ICSID Convention Article 54(1)).

[154] Albert Jan van den Berg, 'Consolidated Commentary on the New York Convention', *ICCA Yearbook commercial arbitration XXVIII* (Kluwer International, 2003), p. 512c. See also Born, *International Commercial Arbitration*, p. 2798.

[155] See, for example, G. Kaufmann-Kohler, 'The Arbitrator and the Law: Does He/she Know It? Apply It? How? And a Few More Questions', (2005) 21(4) *Arbitration International* 21(4) (2005), 634f.

conclusion that the price has to be paid in full, but resolves to set off part of that price against a claim that the buyer has against the seller under a different contract, for example, for the sale of some of the buyer's products. According to the UNCITRAL Model Law and the New York Convention, the arbitral award is ineffective (at least for the part determining the set-off) because of excess of power. The mandate that the tribunal had received through the arbitration clause was to decide whether the price was to be paid in full or in part because of defects in the delivery. Any decision regarding counterclaims deriving out of other contracts was not part of the dispute submitted to that arbitral tribunal with the arbitration clause, and could not be decided upon by that award.

3.2.2 Fair hearing

Both parties must have been given the chance to present their cases, otherwise the award is invalid according to the UNCITRAL Model Law Article 34(2)(a)(ii)[156] and unenforceable according to the New York Convention Article V(1)(b).

The adversary principle is fundamental in arbitration; however, this rule is also interpreted restrictively, so as to cover only fundamental principles of due process, such as failure to notify of the arbitral proceeding.[157]

In the systems that do not have a specific ground for annulment of the award relating to the inability of one party to present its case, such a serious violation of due process will be covered by the rule on the *ordre public* or procedural irregularity.[158]

As will be seen in Section 3.4, an active role by the arbitral tribunal in choosing the applicable law or developing its own arguments may challenge the adversary principle.

3.2.3 Procedural irregularity

The procedure followed by the tribunal must respect the fundamental principles of due process and the mandatory rules of the applicable arbitration law (or investment treaty), otherwise the award is invalid according to the UNCITRAL Model Law Article 34(2)(a)(iv)[159] and unenforceable according to the New York Convention Article V(1)(d).

---

[156] And may therefore be set aside by the courts of the country of origin. See also the Swedish Arbitration Act Article 34(6). The same rule applies to the annulment of ICSID awards; see the ICSID Convention Article 52(1)(d).

[157] See van den Berg, 'Consolidated Commentary', pp. 508 1 and 511 4. See also Born, *International Commercial Arbitration*, p. 2737ff.

[158] For example, the Swedish Arbitration Act Article 34(6), and the ICSID Convention Article 52(1)(d); see Schreuer, Malintoppi, Reinisch and Sinlcair, *The ICSID Convention* Article 52, para. 280ff.

[159] And may therefore be set aside by the courts of the country of origin. See also the Swedish Arbitration Act Article 34(6). The same rule applies to the annulment of ICSID awards, see the ICSID Convention Article 52(1)(d).

Procedural irregularity may lead to invalidity or unenforceability of an award if it seriously affects the respect for due process. This rule may cover the disregard of the mandatory rules on the applicable procedural law, but also situations where the tribunal has not acted impartially; however, its interpretation is very restrictive.[160]

As will be seen in Section 3.5, mandatory procedural rules of the *lex arbitri* may, under some circumstances, restrict the arbitral tribunal's possibility of being able to apply transnational sources or to develop its own arguments.

3.3 The tribunal: an umpire or an inquisitor?

Within the range of the principles mentioned in Section 3.2 above, there does not seem to be a generally acknowledged understanding of how active a role the tribunal may assume: commentators' views range from the encouragement of an active role for the arbitral tribunal,[161] to scepticism towards such a role[162] to a near exclusion thereof.[163]

It is not unusual that legal doctrine on international commercial arbitration focuses its attention on the consensual character of arbitration and emphasises that the arbitral procedure should be left totally to the parties. Party autonomy is, and rightly so, deemed to be the clear fundament of commercial arbitration; as a consequence, the arbitral tribunal is deemed to have a rather restricted scope for its own initiative. This neutral role of a tribunal refraining from interfering with the autonomy of the parties, listening to the parties' arguments and deciding which of the arguments

---

[160] See van den Berg, 'Consolidated Commentary', pp. 521 2 and 523 4. Born, *International Commercial Arbitration*, p. 2770f. For ICSID arbitration, see Schreuer, Malintoppi, Reinisch and Sinlcair, *The ICSID Convention* Article 52, para. 293ff.

[161] For example, W. Wiegand, '*Iura novit curia* v. *Ne ultra petita*: Die Anfechtbarkeit von Schiedsgerichtsurteilen im Lichte der jüngsten Rechtsprechung des Bundesgerichts', in Monique Jametti Greiner, Bernhard Berger and Andreas Güngerich (eds.), *Rechtsetzung und Rechtsdurchsetzung. Festschrift für Franz Kellerhals* (Stampfli Verlag, 2005), pp.127ff.; in the context of investment arbitration, see Christoph Schreuer, 'Three Generations of ICSID Annulment Proceedings', in E. Gaillard and Y. Banifatemi (eds.), *Annulment of ICSID Awards* (IAI Series on International Arbitration, 2004), no. 1, pp. 30f, quoting a series of decisions by the ICSID ad hoc annulment Committee applying the maxim *iura novit curia*, and approving of this application.

[162] For example, C. Kessedjian, 'Principe de la contradiction et arbitrage', (1995) 3 *Revue de l'arbitrage*, 381ff.; Rubin, '"Observations" in connection with *Swembalt AB* v. *Republic of Latvia*', pp. 123ff., seems to justify an active role by the tribunal only in some contexts of public interest, such as investment arbitration; Michael Schneider, 'Combining Arbitration with Conciliation', (2003) 1(2) *Oil, Gas and Energy Law Intelligence*, 4, has serious doubts on whether an international arbitral tribunal should have the authority to identify, on its own initiative, the rules of law applicable to the claims made before it, but, in any case, deems it necessary for the tribunal to invite the parties to clarify their case.

[163] For example, Kaj Hober, 'Arbitration Involving States', in Lawrence W. Newman and Richard D. Hill (eds.), *The Leading Arbitrators' Guide to International Arbitration* (JurisNet, 2004), p. 158, affirming that in a procedure as consensual as arbitration is, it must be up to the parties to determine the scope of the dispute both as to facts and law; see also Kaufmann-Kohler, 'The Arbitrator and the Law', and Gabrielle Kaufmann-Kohler, '*Iura novit arbiter*: Est-ce bien raisonnable? Réflexions sur le statut du droit de fond devant l'arbitre international', in A. Héritier and L. Hirsch (eds.), *De lege ferenda: Eéflexions sur le droit désirable en l'honneur du professeur Alain Hirsch* (Editions Slatkine, 2004).

deserves to win, is sometimes defined as the role of an umpire.[164] The opposing role, more of a judicial and interventionist role, would consist in the tribunal taking various measures on its own initiative, rather than upon the request of one of the parties, to develop a factual and legal argumentation, as well as to identify the applicable law.

The alternative between an umpire and an inquisitor may remind one of the classical opposition between the adversarial common law systems and the inquisitorial civil law systems. The usefulness of the classical division into adversarial and inquisitorial systems, however, may be questioned: while either of these forms is rarely to be found in its pure terms in any system of civil procedure nowadays, it is dubious as to how possible it would be to apply this division to international arbitration.[165]

An adversarial approach in the strict sense is certainly not reflected in the arbitration law that mostly represents the common law systems: English law. The English Arbitration Act does not seem, in many of the respects that are relevant here, substantially different from the approach in civil law countries.[166] The Arbitration Act 1996 confers on the tribunal the power to determine a series of matters on its own initiative (provided that there is no agreement to the contrary between the parties): for example, the decision on procedural and evidential matters,[167] or the default power to determine a series of remedies, if the parties have not specified the remedies that may be awarded.[168] In addition, in drawing inferences from the evidence produced by the parties and in developing its reasoning, the tribunal is not bound by the arguments made by the parties.[169] All of these powers speak for arbitrator

---

[164] The use of this terminology may be misleading. In the strict sense, an umpire denotes under English law a system for deciding deadlocks between two party-appointed arbitrators. In case of a disagreement between the party-appointed arbitrators, the two arbitrators become advocates and the decision is taken by the umpire; prior to turning into advocates, however, the arbitrators have a duty to act impartially. This system is an alternative to the arbitration, and must be considered as being rather anomalous; see Merkin, *Arbitration Law*, pp. 449ff.

[165] The use of this classification is clearly contested by Claude Reymond, 'Civil Law and Common Law Procedures: Which is the More Inquisitorial? A Civil Lawyer's Response', (1989) 5(4) *Arbitration International*, 357ff. That international arbitration is not affected by the traditional contrast between adversarial and inquisitorial traditions is confirmed also in connection with the drafting of the ICC Rules, see Derains and Schwarz, *Guide to the New ICC Rules of Arbitration*, comment on Article 20(1), pp. 251f. See also Kaufmann-Kohler, 'The Arbitrator and the Law', pp. 632f. with further references in footnote 4.

[166] See also the ALI/UNIDROIT Principles Article 22.2.3, specifying that the court may rely upon an interpretation of the facts or of the evidence that has not been advanced by a party. This Article is actually more lenient towards party autonomy than English arbitration law, since it assumes that the court must give the parties the possibility of responding to such an independent interpretation, whereas English case law does not assume the parties' right to be heard on the tribunal's own interpretation of the facts or of the evidence: see Merkin, *Arbitration Law*, pp. 592f. Traditionally, English arbitration law has restricted party autonomy even more than other systems by allowing judicial interference on questions of law (through consultative case procedures and the judicial review of errors in law), that in the civil law systems were unknown. It follows that, in English arbitral procedures, the law is not totally subject to party autonomy, at least as long as the law in question is English law.

[167] Section 34. [168] Section 48(1).

[169] Merkin, *Arbitration Law*, pp. 592f.

autonomy, rather than for party autonomy. This, however, does not mean that the tribunal faces no limits in assuming an inquisitorial role or taking over one party's interests against the other party's: the overriding principle is that the proceeding is conducted fairly and impartially,[170] and this mandatory requirement is deemed sufficient to ensure a balance between the adversarial and the inquisitorial proceeding.[171]

A peculiar treatment is reserved, in the English system, for foreign law: foreign law is considered as a fact and has therefore to be proved by the parties. This is unknown in most civil law systems, where not only the domestic, but also the foreign law has, in principle, to be applied *ex officio* by the tribunal in accordance with the maxim *iura novit curia*.[172] However, even if foreign law is treated as a fact under English arbitration law, it does not mean that in questions of foreign law, party autonomy totally prevails over the tribunal's independent evaluation. First of all, we have seen above that the arbitral tribunal has extensive powers in procedural evidential matters and may evaluate the evidence independently. If foreign law is treated as a fact, it will be subject to the same powers as described above. Second, if the foreign law is not satisfactorily proved, the tribunal may apply the presumption that foreign law is the same as English law, and will apply (on its own initiative) English law, thus avoiding falling into the role of the umpire who would have to choose the pleadings made by the other party.[173]

Under English arbitration, therefore, the role of the tribunal in respect of the parties' pleadings does not fall into the category of the adversarial system more than

---

[170] Section 33.   [171] Merkin, *Arbitration Law*, pp. 512, 586ff.

[172] See, in respect of arbitration, Matti Kurkela, '"*Jura novit curia*" and the Burden of Education in International Arbitration: A Nordic Perspective', (2003) 21(3) *ASA Bullettin*, 485ff.; G. J. Wetter, 'The Conduct of the Arbitration', (1985) 2(2) *Journal of International Arbitration*, 24f.; and Wiegand, '*Iura novit curia v. Ne ultra petita*', pp. 130ff. On Swedish arbitration law, see Heuman, *Arbitration Law of Sweden*, pp. 323ff. See also the extensive comparative observations made by the Swiss Federal Court in its decision 4P.100/2003, ATF 130 III 35, pp. 577f. (the decision confirmed the principle of *iura novit curia* in arbitration, but set aside an award as an exception to that principle, because the award was based on elements that did not relate to the arguments presented by the parties, and the tribunal had not granted the parties the chance to comment thereon. In doing so, the Court emphasised that this exception to the *iura novit curia* principle has to be applied only in extraordinary situations). See also the Swiss Federal Court decision 4P.14/2004, referred to by G. Segesser, (2004) 3(1) *ITA Monthly Report*, confirming an award applying the maxim *iura novit curia*, even if the tribunal had not invited the parties to comment on the legal theory upon which the decision was based. The principle is also codified in a series of private international law acts; see, for example, Article 14 of the Italian, Article 16 of the Swiss and § 4 of the Austrian private international laws, as well as § 293 of the German ZPO. A notable exception until recently was represented by French law, but recent court decisions seem to have acceded to the civil law approach also in France: see E. Cashin-Ritaine, 'Editorial', in *ISDC's Letter 7* (2005) p.1. See also Maarit Jänterä-Jareborg, 'Foreign Law in National Courts: A Comparative Perspective', in Hague Academy of International Law, *Recueil des Cours* 304 (Giuffrè 2003), pp. 264ff., showing various internal inconsistencies in the various systems' approach to foreign law. That the tribunal has the duty to apply the law *ex officio* does not exclude that the law may be pleaded by the parties.

[173] Merkin, *Arbitration Law*, pp. 901f.

it would do in accordance with the international or national civilian arbitration rules that we saw in Section 3.1 above. As has been seen, tribunals have considerable powers to act on their own initiative by requesting additional information, and they are not bound to decide in favour of the participating party in the case of a default by the other party (which implies that they have the power to make their own independent evaluation of the pleadings, rather than limiting themselves to choosing between the available pleadings).

Having excluded the fact that the tribunal is expected to act as an umpire in the strict sense, it remains for us to see more specifically what kind of *ex officio* initiatives are compatible with the ultimate borders of the arbitral authority described in Section 3.2 above: the principles of excess of power, of a fair hearing and of impartiality. While it is only a breach of these principles that has consequences for the validity[174] and enforceability[175] of the award, it might be possible to identify certain guidelines for the conduct of arbitration proceedings that might be useful as an indication of a proper procedure even if violation thereof does not lead to dramatic consequences such as invalidity or unenforceability.

Below, we will go through some situations that are often encountered in practice and that might present some challenges in respect of our questions.

3.3.1 Excess of power regarding questions of law: may the tribunal disregard the choice of law contained in the contract?

The arbitral tribunal owes its very existence to the will of the parties. Consequently, it must follow the parties' instructions as to its composition, the procedure that it will follow, its jurisdiction, the scope of the dispute that it is called upon to solve and the kinds of remedies that it may grant. An award that does not follow the parties' instructions is an award that exceeds the powers that the parties have conferred on the arbitral tribunal. As the parties' instructions are the ultimate source of the tribunal's power, an award that is affected by excess of power does not have a legal basis and is ineffective.

This is the rationale of the exception of excess of power, which is listed both in the UNCITRAL Model Law, Articles 34.2(a)(iii) and 36.1(a)(iii), and in the New York Convention, Article V.I(c), as a ground to set aside the award and, respectively, refuse enforcement thereof.[176] The question is whether the exception of excess of power can be invoked to sanction the tribunal's choice of applicable of law.

---

[174] Assuming that the applicable arbitration law in this respect corresponds to the UNCITRAL Model Law, to English or Swedish law or to the ICSID regulation.

[175] In accordance with Article V of the New York Convention.

[176] The wording is, in the UNCITRAL Model Law: 'the award deals with a dispute not contemplated by or not falling within the terms of the submission to arbitration, or contains decisions on matters beyond the scope of the submission to arbitration, provided that, if the decisions on matters submitted to arbitration can be separated from those not so submitted, only that part of the award which contains decisions on matters not submitted to arbitration may be set aside'; and, in the New York Convention: 'The award deals with a

3.3.1.1 The difficult borderline between a review of the applicability of the law and a review of the merits

An excess of power is relatively easy to ascertain, as long as it is confined to the object of the dispute. What is more difficult is the question regarding the applicable law: if the award relates to an object within the borders of the tribunal's power, but the tribunal applies a law that is different from the law requested by the parties. As we have seen in Section 2 above, neither the challenge nor the enforcement of an arbitral award may be used as a basis for the courts to review the arbitral tribunal's decision, also including its application of the law. It may not always be easy to determine the borderline between the review of the tribunal's application of the law and the decision on whether the tribunal had the authority to apply that law. The former is not within the scope of the jurisdiction of the court. The latter may be evaluated by the courts when determining whether the arbitral tribunal exceeded the power that it was granted by the parties.

An analysis of the reported cases concerning the UNCITRAL Model Law and the New York Convention shows that the defence of excess of power is seldom given effect to for the purpose of sanctioning the arbitral tribunals' application of the law.[177] To the extent that the question has been given attention to, it seems that it has mainly been answered negatively, both in theory and in practice.[178] However, even if it does not happen very often, it is, in principle, possible to request the annulment of an award or to resist its enforcement on the basis of the allegation that the arbitral tribunal has gone beyond its powers in connection with the application of the law. That the governing law has an impact on the interpretation and the effects of a contract was seen in Chapter 3. The same contract may have dramatically different effects, depending on the governing law. The matters submitted to arbitration very much depend on the criteria that they have to be measured against. The dispute is to be solved on the basis of certain rules that have been agreed upon by the parties in the contract (or, failing such agreement, that are designated by the applicable private international law); if the tribunal applies a different law, and assuming that

---

difference not contemplated by or not falling within the terms of the submission to arbitration, or it contains decisions on matters beyond the scope of the submission to arbitration, provided that, if the decisions on matters submitted to arbitration can be separated from those not so submitted, that part of the award which contains decisions on matters submitted to arbitration may be recognized and enforced'.

[177] See Kronke et al., *Recognition and enforcement of foreign arbitral awards*, 'Article V(1)(c)', pp. 271f.

[178] In theory see, for example, Emmanuel Gaillard and John Savage (eds.), *Fouchard, Gaillard and Goldman on international commercial arbitration*, (Kluwer Law International, 2004), p. 1700. In practice, see the US District Court, Southern District of California, 7 December 1998 Civ. No. 98–1165-B, 29 Federal Supplement, Second Series (S.D.Cal.1998) pp. 1168–74, excluding that a decision rendered *ex bono et aequo* exceeded the arbitral tribunal's power. From the reasons of the decision, however, it appears that the court based its reasoning on the conclusion that the parties had actually empowered the tribunal to decide *ex bono et aequo* (therefore it is not surprising that the court did not see any excess of power). Additionally, a German decision decided similarly, even mentioning, in an *obiter dictum*, that the arbitral tribunal's choice of law may not be reviewed by the court. However, also in this case, the court based its conclusion on the fact that the parties had empowered the tribunal to decide *ex bono et aequo* (Landesgericht Hamburg, 18 September1997, *ICCA Yearbook Commercial Arbitration XXV* (Kluwer International, 2000), p. 512).

the two laws regulate the question in different ways, it could be considered as if the tribunal had applied a different contract. The assumptions for resolving the dispute would not be the same as those agreed upon by the parties; therefore, the decision would be on matters different from those submitted by the parties.[179]

This judicial control, however, has to be based on a careful analysis of the reasons for the award to verify that the proper criteria for the exercise of the defence are met. As we will see in the following sections, under certain circumstances, the arbitral tribunal's application of a law different from the law that was chosen in the contract cannot be seen as a disregard of the parties' choice. This may be due to the circumstance that the choice made in the contract does not cover the relevant area of law, or it may be because the law chosen by the parties gives effect to rules of other laws (for example, through the *force majeure* principle, rules on immorality or rules on illegality that extend to the violation of foreign laws). Under other circumstances, the disregard by the arbitral tribunal of the parties' choice may be qualified as a disregard of the parties' instructions. Below, we will examine various scenarios.

3.3.1.2 The tribunal disregards the contract's choice and applies national law

In the first scenario that we will examine, the tribunal disregards the choice of law made in the contract and applies rules of another law. In the second scenario, the arbitral tribunal applies sources that are not national or international in the strict sense (i.e., deriving from treaties or conventions), but that are transnational and non-authoritative, such as restatements of principles. The first scenario may be divided into two sub-scenarios according to whether the tribunal applies some rules of the law that would have been applicable to the dispute if the parties had not made a choice, or applies a law that would not have been applicable even in the absence of the parties' choice.

3.3.1.2.1 Disregard of the contract's choice in favour of the otherwise applicable law
To illustrate the matter, we can assume a contract entered into by two competing manufacturers for the licensing of certain technology; the transfer of technology is accompanied by a system for sharing the market between the two competitors, which violates European competition law. The contract contains a choice-of-law clause, according to which the governing law is Russian law, and an arbitration clause. We can assume that a dispute arises between the two parties, and that one of the two parties alleges that the contract is null and void because it violates European competition law. The other party alleges that EU competition law is not applicable to the contract, and that the choice of the Russian governing law was meant specifically to avoid the applicability of EU law. Hence, it is outside of the tribunal's power to take into consideration EU competition law.

---

[179] For a similar reasoning see Redfern, Hunter, Blackaby and Partasides, *Redfern and Hunter on International Arbitration*, para. 3.91 as well as the International Commercial Arbitration Committee, ILA Report, 2008 p. 19.

What can the arbitral tribunal do? If it follows the contract and applies the chosen Russian law, it runs the risk of rendering an award that violates the EU *ordre public* (EU competition law having been qualified by the ECJ as *ordre public* in a case similar to the one illustrated here),[180] as was seen in Section 2.6.4.4 above. As was seen above, an award that violates the *ordre public* of the court may be set aside as invalid[181] and is unenforceable.[182] If the arbitral tribunal has its seat within the EU, therefore, the award runs the risk of being annulled; and if the award has to be enforced in an EU country, it runs the risk of not being enforced.

Consequently, the tribunal might be inclined to take into consideration EU competition law, thus avoiding rendering an invalid or unenforceable award. Does the arbitral tribunal run the risk of exceeding its power or incurring a procedural irregularity if it takes into consideration EU competition law? In other words, is the arbitral tribunal forced to choose between two grounds for invalidity or unenforceability of the award; that is, excess of power or procedural irregularity on one hand, and conflict with the *ordre public* on the other hand?

In my opinion, there is room for arguing that an arbitral tribunal is, under certain circumstances, not affected by the contract's choice. The fact that the parties have chosen a certain governing law does not exclude the relevance of all rules of any other laws. As was seen in Chapter 4, Section 4, this will depend both on the substantive rules of the chosen law (such as the rules on illegality or on *force majeure*, which may make reference to the effects of foreign laws), and on the conflict rules of the private international law applicable by the tribunal (such as the scope of party autonomy, the applicability of overriding mandatory rules). A variety of approaches is possible, as we will see below.

3.3.1.2.1.1 Violation of the *ordre public* of the *lex arbitri*?

If the tribunal is located in an EU state, it cannot be expected to disregard its own *ordre public*; the award would be annulled by the courts of the state where it was rendered. Therefore, EU competition law would have to be taken into consideration, and the contract's choice of the Russian governing law would have to be restricted correspondingly. The arbitral tribunal would found the authority to do so on the applicable private international law, if this law contains a rule that renders a choice of law made in the contract invalid to the extent that the parties' choice violates the applicable *ordre public*.[183]

---

[180] Case C-126/97 (*Eco Swiss*).   [181] UNCITRAL Model Law Article 34.2(b)(ii)

[182] UNCITRAL Model Law Article 36.1(b)(ii), and New York Convention Article V.2(b)

[183] Most private international laws contain such a rule. Within European law, this is provided for in Article 21 of the Rome I Regulation on the Law Applicable to Contractual Obligations.

3.3.1.2.1.2 Application of the chosen law refers to the excluded law

Irrespective of whether the tribunal is located in a member state of the EU or not, the arbitral tribunal might apply the law chosen in the contract in full, also including any illegality rule contained therein, and allowing for the disregard of an agreement (or a choice of law) made by the parties that leads to violating the mandatory rules of foreign law, as was seen in Chapter 4, Section 4.6. In this way, the tribunal would not have exceeded its power – on the contrary: it would have given full application to the law chosen by the parties, and the instruments to restrict the effects of the choice of law would be given precisely by the chosen law.

Application in full of the law chosen by the parties may, in several situations, lead to taking into consideration the very rules of the law that the parties had intended to exclude. For example, a rule on *force majeure* of the chosen law may lead to the consideration of foreign rules restricting exports or imports,[184] and rules on immorality or illegality in the chosen law may lead to the invalidity of a contract entered into to avoid the application of a foreign law.[185]

3.3.1.2.1.3 Application of private international law

The tribunal might verify the applicable private international law to determine the borders of party autonomy. As was seen in Chapter 4, Section 2, by choosing the applicable law, the parties have exercised a choice-of-law rule (the rule of party autonomy), and the scope of such a rule is determined by the applicable private international law. In this way, the tribunal might ascertain to what extent the choice of Russian law made in the contract is valid under the applicable private international law, or to what extent it may be restricted by applying other conflict rules or by taking into consideration overriding mandatory rules of other laws. The EU competition law would be an example of these latter points: rules that the judge (or the arbitral tribunal) is entitled to apply, irrespective of the choice of law made by the parties, as was seen in Chapter 4, Section 4.3.[186]

The applicable private international law may result in further restrictions on the relevance of the chosen law, as was seen in Chapter 4, Section 4.1.

3.3.1.2.1.4 Conclusion

Based on the foregoing, it seems unlikely that, in the example made here, the award would be deemed invalid or unenforceable for excess of power, even if the tribunal has given effect to EU competition law, whereas the contract had intended to exclude

---

[184] For a more extensive discussion on the matter, as well as further references, see Fritz A. Mann, 'Sonderanknüpfung und zwingendes Recht im internationalem Privatrecht', in *Festschrift für Günther Beitzke zum 70. Geburtstag* (De Gruyter, 1979), p. 608; Lennart Pålsson, *Romkonventionen.Tillämping lag för avtalsförpliktelser* (Norstedts Juridik, 1998), p.123, and Kurt Siehr, 'Ausländische Eingriffsnormen im inländischen Wirschaftskollisionsrecht' (1988) 52 *Rabels Zeitschrift für ausländisches und internationales Privatrecht*, 41–102, 78ff., as well as Cordero-Moss, *International Commercial Arbitration: Party Autonomy*, pp.124ff.

[185] For example, Article 20 of the Swiss Obligation Code and § 138 of the German BGB.

[186] In the European private international law, the authority to apply overriding mandatory rules is regulated in Article 9 of the already mentioned Rome I Regulation.

the applicability of that law. It seems more likely that an arbitral tribunal would fear the invalidity and lack of enforceability of the award in case of a disregard of EU competition law. Taking into consideration that a tribunal should aim at rendering awards that are effective, it seems that the expectations of the parties to receive aid by arbitral tribunals in avoiding mandatory rules of closely connected laws should be disappointed more often than not, at least in those situations where the mandatory rules are of such a nature that an award disregarding them might be deemed to be against the *ordre public* in the state of origin of the award or in a state of enforcement. As seen above, the arbitral tribunal does not need to fear any excess of power, as there are many routes that are allowed under the applicable private international law to restrict the scope of the choice of law made in the contract.

3.3.1.2.2 Disregard of the contract's choice in favour of a law that is not otherwise applicable

The private international law does not always provide a means for restricting the scope of party autonomy; as a matter of fact, the restrictions that we saw above are more the exception than the rule, and in the majority of cases, the choice of law made by the parties cannot be restricted by other choice-of-law rules, by overriding mandatory rules or by principles of the *ordre public*.

We can assume that the parties, after having entered into a contract, renegotiate the price and enter into a new contract with the sole purpose of increasing the price. If the amendment agreement is governed by English law, the party that agreed to pay a higher price might claim, under certain circumstances, that the amendment contract is not binding because it did not contemplate any consideration in exchange for the promise to pay a higher price (the expectation of obtaining a performance that the other party was already obliged to carry out according to the first contract does normally not qualify as a consideration), as was seen in Chapter 3, Section 6.2. The arbitral tribunal may find this result unsatisfactory, since the expectation of the parties at the moment of entering into the second contract was clearly that the higher price should be binding. In order to avoid an unsatisfactory result, the tribunal may decide not to apply English law, but, for example, the law of the country where the contract is to be performed, because under such law, the increase in price would be deemed as binding.

In a scenario like this one, the private international law does not provide any tool with which to override the choice of law made by the parties: there is no violation of the *ordre public*, there are no overriding mandatory rules and the subject matter is clearly within the scope of party autonomy. Therefore, it is not possible to argue, as we did in the previous section, that the arbitral tribunal has not disregarded the contract's choice and has simply filled in its gaps in accordance with the applicable private international law. Moreover, in our example, the law applied by the arbitral tribunal is not the law that would be applicable if the contract had not contained a choice (this law being, at least in European private international law, not the law of the place of performance, but the law of the country where the party making the characteristic performance has its place of business).[187] The tribunal has, in other words, not used the applicable private international law to integrate or correct the contract's choice. It has simply decided that it was more appropriate to choose a different law.

3.3.1.2.2.1 Has the tribunal exceeded its power?

Once again, it is necessary to draw a line between the tribunal's application of the law and the tribunal's disregard of the parties' instructions.

If, from the award's reasons, it is possible to infer that the arbitral tribunal has applied some choice-of-law rules, and that this application has led to disregarding the law chosen in the contract, we are in the field of the application of the law; more specifically, in the field of the application of private international law. If the arbitral tribunal has applied private international law wrongly, for example, because it wrongly assumed that the English rule on consideration would be contrary to the *ordre public*, it has incurred an error in law. As already mentioned, errors in law are not subject to judicial control under the UNCITRAL Model Law or under the New York Convention. Therefore, an award that disregards the contract's choice of law on the basis of a wrong application of private international law may not be considered as invalid or unenforceable because of an excess of power.

If, however, the award does not make any considerations on private international law and there is no basis for assuming that the disregard of the contract's choice is due to an error in the application of choice-of-law rules or in the interpretation of the contract, then it is possible to argue that the arbitral tribunal has ignored the parties' instructions. This qualifies as an excess of power. There are, admittedly, only few cases where this line of thought was applied; however, this is fully compatible with the judicial control that may be exercised on arbitral awards under the UNCITRAL Model Law and under the New York Convention.[188]

---

[187] See Article 4 of the Rome I Regulation.

[188] There are at least two cases where this reasoning was applied to set aside arbitral awards rendered under the Washington Convention of 1965, establishing an arbitration mechanism for disputes between private parties and foreign states (ICSID), and providing for an independent, non-national system for reviewing the validity of awards, which includes, among others, the possibility of annulling an award if the tribunal has manifestly exceeded its powers (Article 52.1(c) of the Convention). In *Klöckner GmbH* v. *The United Republic of Cameroon and Socame* (ICSID case no. Arb/81/2), the ad hoc Committee acting as the controlling instance affirmed that the failure by the tribunal to apply the governing law is to be deemed as an excess of power, and so did the ad hoc Committee controlling the award rendered in *Amco Asia* v. *The Republic of Indonesia* (ARB/81/1). For further references, particularly on the debate that arose in connection with the *Klöckner* decision, see Cordero-Moss, *International Commercial Arbitration: Party Autonomy*, pp. 276ff.

3.3.1.2.3 Disregard of the contract's choice of law in favour of transnational sources
Application of transnational principles is not a new phenomenon in international arbitration[189] and many authors consider the *lex mercatoria* as the most appropriate source to be applied in this context.[190]

In the case presented in the previous section, for example, where the application of English law would make the amendment contract not binding, the arbitral tribunal may decide that the English doctrine of consideration is peculiar to English law, and that in an international setting, it is not appropriate to apply a rule of a municipal law, particularly when it conflicts with the expectations of parties in international trade. The tribunal may thus resolve to apply a principle that is often referred to as a generally acknowledged principle within international trade – *pacta sunt servanda* – according to which, an agreement has to be complied with irrespective of the presence of a consideration. Alternatively, the tribunal could have applied the UPICC, which in Article 2.1.1, say that an agreement is formed by an exchange of an offer and acceptance or conclusive conduct – without the requirement of consideration. The tribunal, in this case, would have disregarded the contract's choice of law by not applying the law of another country, but generally acknowledged principles or non-authoritative trans-national sources.

3.3.1.2.3.1 Would this be considered as an excess of power?
In the context of the defence of excess of power, it is not very significant to distinguish between a disregard of the choice of the law made in the contract by applying the law of another country and a disregard by applying transnational sources. This distinction becomes more relevant when the exercise of the tribunal's powers is measured not against the arbitration agreement (as is the case in the defence of excess of power), but against the applicable arbitration law (as is the case in the defence of procedural irregularity, which we will see in Section 3.5).

From the point of view of an excess of power regarding the parties' instructions, the same reasoning explained above will apply here: if the tribunal's disregard of the contract's choice is due to the wrong application of the private international law or the wrong interpretation of the contract, there are no consequences of judicial control. If, however, the application of transnational sources is due to a blunt

---

[189] Two famous and controversial cases that adopted transnational principles were the '1951 *Petroleum Dev (Trucial Coast) Ltd* v. *the Sheik of Abu Dabi*', (1952) 154 and 247 *International and Comparative Law Quarterly*, and '*Saudi Arabia* v. *Arabian American Oil Company (ARAMCO)*', (1963) 27 *International Law Report*, 117. For references and a criticism of this approach, see Gaillard and Savage (eds.), *Fouchard, Gaillard and Goldman on International Commercial Arbitration*, p. 1512. These decisions, like those mentioned in the previous footnotes, are rendered in the frame of investment arbitration and not in pure commercial disputes. Their relevance to commercial arbitration, therefore, is not direct.

[190] See Chapter 2 Section 1.

disregard of the parties' instructions, the tribunal has exceeded its powers and this can result in the invalidity or unenforceability of the award.

3.3.1.2.4 Conclusion

The above analysis shows that the arbitral tribunal enjoys considerable freedom in respect of the law that it applies to resolve the dispute, and that this freedom goes so far as to permit the tribunal to apply the chosen law wrongly or to disregard the choice of law that the parties made in the contract. However, there are certain borders to the tribunal's freedom in respect of the applicable law: the *ordre public* of the court that exercises judicial control may not be violated by the award, and the tribunal may not render a decision in equity without having been empowered to do so by the parties (as will be seen in Section 3.5). Between these two borders, there is a wide range of possibilities to integrate or correct the parties' instructions, particularly by applying various rules of private international law. The interpretation of the parties' instructions, the application of the chosen law or the choice of another law on the basis of private international law may not be reviewed by the judge, even if they are manifestly wrong. The disregard of the parties' instructions, therefore, enjoys a nearly total immunity, as long as it may be qualified as an interpretation or an error in law, because the courts have no jurisdiction thereon. If the decision to ignore the parties' instructions is not the consequence of a (perhaps erroneous) application of the law or interpretation of the contract, but is simply the result of the tribunal's overruling of the parties' will, then it is possible to exercise judicial control. The reasons for the award play a determining role in this context; unreasoned awards, to the extent that they are permitted by the parties and the applicable arbitration law, would make it impossible to evaluate what law has been applied and on what basis, thus permitting the disregard of the parties' instructions.

3.3.2 Excess of power regarding questions of law: may the applicable law be disregarded if the parties do not sufficiently prove it?

Sometimes tribunals do not consider the applicable law because it was not sufficiently proven by the parties; this approach has been subject to criticism, and with good reason.[191]

The applicable law shall be considered, even if it has not been sufficiently proven by the parties, irrespective of whether the law is deemed to be a fact (as the English system assumes, see Section 3.3 above) or not:

---

[191] For example, 'Swembalt AB v. Republic of Latvia', Stockholm Arbitration Report (SCC Arbitration Institute 2004–2), pp. 97ff., criticised in the 'Observations' by Rubins, Stockholm Arbitration Report (SCC Arbitration Institute 2004–2), p. 126, and F. Yala, Stockholm Arbitration Report (SCC Arbitration Institute 2004–2), pp. 128ff., 133ff. See also CME v. Czech Republic, criticized by Schreuer, 'Failure to Apply the Governing Law', 189 and footnote 179. For a comparative analysis of the consequences of an insufficient proof of foreign law, see Maarit Jänterä-Jareborg, 'Foreign Law in National Courts – A Comparative Perspective' Recueil des cours (The Hague Academy of International Law, 2003), vol. CCCIV, 324ff.

(i) If foreign law is treated as fact, it has to be proved by the parties. As we will see
     in Section 3.3.4 below, under English law, the pleadings made by the parties
     in respect of the facts do not bind the tribunal in its independent evaluation of
     the evidence and in the inferences that are based on those facts. It follows that
     an English tribunal is not bound by the presentation of the foreign law made by the
     parties, that it may request additional information and may build its own argu-
     mentation thereon. In the case of insufficient evidence on foreign law, therefore,
     an English tribunal will be entitled to ask for additional evidence. If the evidence
     is still not satisfactory, the tribunal will apply the presumption that foreign law is
     the same as English law; and English law is applied *ex officio* by the tribunal.

(ii) If the law is not treated as a fact, insufficient evidence does not excuse the
     tribunal from its duty to investigate it *ex officio*. This does not mean that the
     tribunal may not ask the parties to provide evidence of the law:[192] It certainly is
     in the interest of the parties to provide as exhaustive and convincing evidence
     of the law as possible, so as to substantiate their respective pleadings. This
     approach is very common in practice, and is even codified in some private
     international law acts.[193] The duty of the arbitral tribunal to investigate the law
     seems to consist in asking the parties to produce additional evidence of the
     law or appointing legal experts, rather than in directly investigating the law.[194]

This approach is consistent with the ALI/UNIDROIT Principles: According to Article
22.1, the court is responsible for determining the correct legal basis for its decision,
including matters determined on the basis of foreign law.

   To what extent the award may be set aside as invalid or deemed unenforceable
because the tribunal disregarded the applicable law on the ground that it was insufficiently proved, depends on whether the failure to apply the law falls into the category
of an error of law (in which case it will not have consequences for the effectiveness
of the award) or into one of the principles that we defined in Section 3.2 above as
the ultimate borders of the tribunal's powers. If the disregard of the applicable law
is based simply on the insufficiency of the evidence thereof, and it is not corroborated
by reasons that show that the tribunal has made some considerations on the choice,

---

[192] See, however, the comment on Article 20(4) of the 1998 ICC Rules (corresponding to Article 25(4) of the
     2012 Rules), Derains and Schwarz, *Guide to the New ICC Rules of Arbitration*, footnote 582, affirming that
     in international arbitration, the appointment of legal experts to testify on foreign law should not be
     necessary, because an international tribunal should not consider any law as foreign, and is assumed to
     know the law that it is supposed to apply. For a comparative analysis of the question of where the duty to
     prove foreign law lies, whether with the parties, the judge, or both, see Jänterä-Jareborg, 'Foreign Law in
     National Courts', 286ff.

[193] See, for example, § 293 in the German ZPO and § 6 in the Austrian Private International Law Act.
     Kaufmann-Kohler, '*Iura novit arbiter*', pp. 74f., analyses how Swiss arbitration law gives the tribunal the
     power, but not the obligation to investigate the law *ex officio*. Also, the Swedish system is based on the
     principle that the parties have to prove the law, see Heuman, *Arbitration Law of Sweden*, p. 326, even if
     the Swedish arbitrator has the authority to develop his/her own arguments of law, see p. 379.

[194] See also the ALI/UNIDROIT Principles, Article 22.4.

interpretation or application of the law, there is a basis to consider it as an excess of power (because the tribunal made its decision on the basis of legal facts that are different from those submitted by the parties) or a procedural irregularity (if the applicable law is mandatorily determined in the applicable arbitration law or investment treaty). The borderline between these remedies and a review of the merits of the award (of which the latter falls outside of the courts' jurisdiction) were examined in Section 3.3.1.1 above.

3.3.3 Excess of power regarding questions of law: may the tribunal develop its own legal arguments?

We will see in Section 3.3.4 that the tribunal is empowered to develop its own reasoning in respect of the evidence and of the facts that the parties have introduced in the proceeding. In addition, we saw in sections 3.3 and 3.3.2 that the tribunal has the ultimate responsibility to apply the law, whether the law is deemed to be a question of fact or a question of law. It follows that the tribunal is also entitled to develop its own reasoning in respect of the law, more so if the law is under the sphere of the tribunal rather than that of the parties. This is also recognised in the ALI/UNIDROIT Principles that state, in Article 22.2.3, that a court may rely upon a legal theory that has not been advanced by a party. This article requires, however, that the court must give the parties the chance to respond to such a new theory; we will come back to this requirement in Section 3.4 below.

   Under the power to develop an independent legal reasoning, it is possible to distinguish at least three categories:

(i)   *New qualifications under the same sources.* Suppose that a buyer has proved the content of the whole contract with the seller, as well as the circumstances of the non-performance of that contract by the seller. We can further assume that the buyer is claiming reimbursement of damages on the basis of Article 45 of the Vienna Convention of 1980 on the CISG. The request for damages is based on the alleged breach by the seller of the quality specifications for the goods; according to Article 45 of the CISG (combined with Article 35), breach of specifications entitles the buyer to claim damages. We assume that the evidence produced in the arbitral proceeding shows that the seller was in breach of the contractual obligation on the time of delivery; however, the buyer does not act upon this breach. The tribunal does not accept the buyer's arguments in respect of the breach of specifications. However, the tribunal deems the delay in performance as a breach of contract. The seller, therefore, is ordered to reimburse damages to the buyer on the basis of Article 45 of the CISG, as requested; however, the basis for applying Article 45 of the CISG is not Article 35 on non-compliance with specifications but Article 33 on the time for delivery. As will be seen in Section 3.3.5 below, the tribunal is not exceeding its power because the fact of the delay had been proved in the proceeding, even if it had not been invoked by the buyer. The tribunal is not exceeding its power in respect of the legal argumentation either. The tribunal is free to qualify the proven facts in accordance with the legal sources that it deems applicable, especially if these legal sources have been pleaded by the parties (we will see immediately below to what extent the tribunal may apply new sources that have not been pleaded by the parties). In our example, the tribunal is subsuming the proven facts under an article of the CISG that it deems more appropriate than the article that was invoked by the buyer. The qualification and subsumption of a fact belong to the evaluation of the legal consequences of that fact, and are part of the legal reasoning that the tribunal has the power and the duty to carry out independently.[195]

(ii) *New sources.* To take another kind of independent legal reasoning, let us assume that a buyer alleges that the contract is terminated, in accordance with Article 49 of the CISG, because of a fundamental breach by the seller. The arbitral tribunal determines that the contract may be terminated, as requested by the buyer. However, the basis for terminating is not the fundamental breach and the CISG, but the governing national law that penalises unfair contract terms with invalidity of the contract. During the proceeding, the buyer had produced evidence of the contract that contained a clause excluding the seller's liability, and the tribunal deemed this clause to be sufficient to trigger invalidity under the national governing law. Assuming that the consequences of the invalidity are the same as the consequences of the termination that had been requested by the buyer (we will see immediately below to what extent the tribunal may apply remedies that were not requested), and assuming that the tribunal is acting on the basis of facts that have been proved (even if not invoked) by the parties, it is within the scope of the tribunal's power to investigate the applicable law and apply it as it deems appropriate, even if the parties have failed to make the relevant argument.[196] A possible problem might arise in respect of the possibility for the parties to respond to the new legal sources introduced by the tribunal. We will revert, in Section 3.4 below, to the possible implications relating to the adversarial principle.

---

[195] In the same sense, see the decisions by the Swiss Federal Court referred to in footnote 698 above, and Wiegand, '*Iura novit curia v. Ne ultra petita*', p. 140; for Swedish law see Heuman, *Arbitration Law of Sweden*, p. 379 and the decision 8090–99 by the Svea Court of Appeal, published in English in *Stockholm Arbitration Report* (SCC Arbitration Institute 2003–1), pp. 251 ff., and commented upon by Wallin, in *Stockholm Arbitration Report* (SCC Arbitration Institute 2003–1), pp. 263ff.; for French law, see the judicial practice referred to by Kessedjian, 'Principe de la Contradiction et arbitrage', 404.

[196] In the same sense, see the decisions by the ICSID ad hoc Committees referred to by Schreuer, 'Three Generations of ICSID Annulment Proceedings', pp. 30f. The decision of the ICSID ad hoc Committee in *Klöckner v. Cameroon*, in *Yearbook Commercial Arbitration XI* (Kluwer International, 1986) (*Klöckner I*), pp.173f., clearly affirms the tribunal's freedom to develop its own legal theory and arguments; such freedom, however, is restricted by the 'legal framework' established by the parties. As an example of a hypothetical violation of the limits set by such a legal framework, the ad hoc Committee mentions a decision rendered on a tort ground, whereas the parties' submissions were based on the contract (*ibid.*).

(iii) *New remedies.* We can assume that the buyer is requesting reimbursement of damages for breach of contract by the seller; the tribunal, however, determines that the contract is to be declared invalid because it contained unfair terms. Whether this determination is based on the same facts invoked by the buyer, or on facts that were proved but not invoked, the evaluation does not change. There does not seem to be a unitary treatment of this situation in the various countries. In common law systems, the request of remedies made by the parties is deemed to constitute the borders for the tribunal's jurisdiction.[197] In many civil law systems, the borders of the tribunal's jurisdiction seem to be set by the parties' presentation of the facts, whereas the legal consequences of those facts are left to the tribunal to determine according to its own identification of the applicable law, subsumption and interpretation.[198] This latter approach seems to be more consistent with the powers of the tribunal, shown in the foregoing, to develop its own legal argumentation and to apply the law *ex officio*. In other words, the tribunal would not exceed its power if it grants remedies that were not requested by the parties, provided that these remedies are based on the facts proved in the proceeding and that they have not expressly been excluded from the authority of the tribunal by agreement of the parties (in the arbitration agreement, under the proceeding or in another manner expressly meant to regulate the jurisdiction of the tribunal). As we saw above, the tribunal is not expected to simply act as an umpire and choose between the parties' arguments; if it is entitled to develop its own legal argumentation, it must also be entitled to draw the legal consequences of this argumentation, and these, at times, might entail remedies that were not requested by the parties. This is, however, a dangerous area for the tribunal, since, as we just saw, the power of the tribunal to grant remedies beyond the requests of the parties is not completely uncontroversial in all legal systems. The systems that the tribunal should be concerned with are the law of the arbitral venue and the law or laws of the enforcement court or courts. While the law of the place of arbitration is known to the tribunal, the law of the place or places of enforcement is not. Since an award may be enforced in any country where the losing party has assets (assuming that enforcement is permitted by prevailing legislation or conventions, of which the New York Convention is the most significant), and this may include any country where that party has assets in transit, it is unpredictable for the tribunal as to which interpretation of the excess of power clause the enforcement

---

[197] See, for England, Merkin, *Arbitration Law*, p. 714(a).

[198] See, for Sweden, Heuman, *Arbitration Law of Sweden*, pp. 611, 736f.; for Switzerland, see the court decisions referred to in footnote 56 above, and Wiegand, 'Iura novit curia v. Ne ultra petita', pp. 135f., 140ff. extensively arguing how the legal consequences are within the sphere of the tribunal and should be determined *ex officio* (in accordance with the maxim *da mihi factum, dabo tibi ius*). That an independent subsumption by the tribunal does not lead to excess of power is indirectly confirmed by the lack of reported court decisions refusing enforcement under the New York Convention: see van den Berg, 'Consolidated Commentary', p. 512c; Born, *International Commercial Arbitration*, p. 2798f.

court will apply. Therefore, it is in the interest of the effectiveness of the award to avoid rendering a decision that, even if valid under the law of the place of arbitration, might be deemed to be in excess of power in other systems. It seems advisable that the tribunal informs the parties of its evaluation of the legal consequences of the produced evidence, and gives them the chance to comment thereon. Should the parties agree that the remedies suggested by the tribunal shall not be applied, this would clarify that the tribunal does not have the authority to grant them. Should the parties not reach an agreement thereon, they would still have the opportunity to make their cases on the points introduced by the tribunal. In this way, the adversarial principle would not be violated. We will revert, in Section 3.4 below, to the necessity or opportunity that the tribunal invites the parties to comment on new elements upon which the decision is going to be based. This should not be considered as if the tribunal was acting partially, suggesting to one party what legal arguments it should make and what legal remedies it should request. The invitation by the tribunal to comment is only a consequence of the tribunal's power to develop its own independent legal argumentation and is meant to preserve the adversarial principle.

3.3.4 Excess of power regarding questions of fact: is the tribunal bound to decide only on invoked facts?

The tribunal has to base its decision on the facts introduced and proved by the parties; otherwise, it will exceed its power. The general rule is, therefore, that an award may not be based on a fact that was not invoked by a party. This does not mean that the tribunal is bound by the argumentation made by the parties in respect of the proven facts. We have seen in Section 3.3.3 above that a tribunal is free to evaluate the evidence and to draw from it the inferences that it deems appropriate. Does this extend to facts that are proved but not invoked by a party?

Let us assume that a buyer pays only part of the agreed price to the seller on the grounds that the delivered goods did not fully comply with the specifications. The seller initiates arbitration against the buyer for breach of its payment obligations. The buyer produces evidence of the whole content of the contract, including the specifications, as well as of all the factual circumstances of the performance. From the produced evidence it appears that the seller was in breach of contract; however, the non-performance did not relate to the specifications of the goods (as invoked by the buyer), but to the delivery time. The breach of the obligations on delivery time is proved in the proceeding; however, it is not invoked as a basis for the buyer's defence. May the tribunal base its decision on a circumstance that is introduced by one party in the proceeding, but is not acted upon by that party?

In the situation described above, if we also assume that a delay in the delivery entitles the buyer to a reduction in the price, the breach of the delivery obligation is an alternative basis for the same defence presented by the buyer. The tribunal must be allowed to consider the consequences of a fact that was proved before it, even if that fact was not invoked, as long as this does not modify the scope of the dispute.[199] Would the tribunal exceed its power if the tribunal's evaluation of a proven, but not invoked fact leads it to order a remedy that was not requested? Let us assume that the arbitration is initiated by the buyer. The contract provides that, in case of non-compliance with the specifications, the price shall be reduced. The buyer had paid the whole price before it had the possibility to inspect the goods; after the inspection of the goods, it requests reimbursement of part of the price because the specifications were not complied with. The contract also contains a clause that permits termination and full restitution in case of late delivery. As in the scenario described above, the content of the whole contract as well as all the circumstances of its performance are proved in the proceeding; the buyer, however, acts only on the basis of non-conform specifications, and requests reimbursement of part of the price. If the tribunal decided that the contract had to be terminated because of late delivery, and ordered restitution of the whole price and of the goods, would it exceed its powers? The question of introducing new remedies is examined above, under Section 3.3.3(iii).

3.4 Fair hearing: inviting the parties to comment

We saw in Section 3.2.2 that one of the grounds for setting aside or refusing enforcement of an award is that the parties were not granted a fair hearing. This includes the adversarial principle, which is relevant to the questions that we are dealing with. If the arbitral tribunal renders a decision on the basis of facts or arguments that one of the parties (or both) did not have the chance to comment upon, the adversarial principle is affected. We saw in the previous sessions that the tribunal enjoys considerable room to develop its own arguments, particularly regarding questions of law (including choice of law). To avoid an unfair treatment of the parties, it may be advisable to accompany this room for development with an invitation to the parties to comment on the elements that the arbitral tribunal intends to use as a basis for the decision.

The invitation to the parties to comment on the tribunal's own legal reasoning is required in some systems,[200] recommended in others[201] and not

---

[199] Coming to the same conclusion see, under Swedish law, Heuman, *Arbitration Law of Sweden*, pp. 606f., 634 and 640, and, under English law, Merkin, *Arbitration Law*, p. 592.

[200] For example, in France, see Kessedjian, 'Principe de la contradiction et arbitrage', 399. A recent Norwegian Supreme Court decision defined the adversarial principle as a fundamental principle of due process in Norwegian law, and set aside an award that had radically reduced the amount of damages requested by the claimant without the tribunal having advised the parties that it was contemplating doing so: Rt. 2005 p. 1590. See also the Swiss decision 4P.100/2003, which, however, underlines that this requirement applies only to extraordinary cases. See also the ALI/UNIDROIT Principles, Article 22.2.3.

[201] See, for Sweden, Heuman, *Arbitration Law of Sweden*, pp. 634, 683 and 734, who considers it open as to whether this rule is mandatory. See the Svea Court of Appeal decision no. 8090–99, pp. 260ff., rejecting the existence of such a rule, commented upon by Wallin, (2003) 1 *Stockholm Arbitration Report*, pp. 266ff

considered necessary in yet others.[202] In addition, the legal literature seems to be divided between these positions.[203]

This invitation seems necessary if the tribunal's legal reasoning leads to new facts or evidence becoming relevant. If one or both of the parties may develop their cases by presenting new evidence that was not relevant in the context of the original pleadings, but becomes relevant in the context of the tribunal's reasoning, it is reasonable to expect the tribunal to give the parties the opportunity to do so, even in the systems that do not, as a general rule, require an invitation to comment.[204]

The necessity of this invitation to comment is less evident if the tribunal's reasoning remains on a purely legal level: as long as the parties' comments are limited to the legal qualification of some factual circumstances or the subsumption under a certain rule, they are a contribution to the tribunal's reasoning, but they are not binding on the tribunal and do not add anything to the sphere of authority of the tribunal, as was seen in Section 3.3.3.

If the tribunal introduces new sources of law, however, it might be advisable to request the parties to comment on the new sources, so that the parties are given the possibility of being able to evaluate the new legal dimension of the dispute. The tribunal might not be in a position to evaluate whether the parties can produce new evidence in light of the new sources, and therefore it seems advisable to leave this evaluation to the parties themselves, by advising them of the tribunal's intention to apply a certain source.

Another question is how specific the invitation to comment on the new sources should be. Should the tribunal limit itself to indicating the source in a generic way, in the example made in Section 3.3.3(ii), by making reference to the national law on unfair terms of contracts, or should it be more specific and indicate the article of the law that it deems relevant? This latter alternative seems to come close to a suggestion of the legal arguments to one party, and should, probably, be avoided.[205] What if the parties do not properly respond to the generic invitation and do not address the specific aspects of the sources that the tribunal intends to apply? In our

---

(considering it recommendable to invite the parties' comments, but deeming it not a serious procedural irregularity if it is not done, at least in respect of domestic arbitration).

[202] On Swiss law, see the judicial practice referred to in footnote 688 above and, more explicitly on this matter, the Federal Court decision no. 4P 115/1994, in *ASA Bullettin* 2 (1995), 217ff., para. 5. On English law, see Merkin, *Arbitration Law*, p. 592. In respect of German law, see Martinek, 'Die Mitwirkungsverweigerung des Schiedsbeklagten', XI. In respect of ICSID arbitration see Schreuer, Malintoppi, Reinisch and Sinlcair, *The ICSID Convention* Article 52, para. 305ff., showing that ICSID awards are consistently not deemed to be invalid even if the reasons upon which they are based come as a surprise to the parties.

[203] Considering the invitation necessary, for example, Kessedjian, 'Principe de la contradiction et arbitrage', 399ff., and Schneider, 'Combining Arbitration with Conciliation', 4. Considering it not necessary: Wiegand, 'Iura novit curia v. Ne ultra petita', pp.137ff., and Merkin, *Arbitration Law*, p. 592.

[204] In this sense, see also Wiegand, 'Iura novit curia v. Ne ultra petita', pp. 140ff.

[205] But see Heuman, *Skiljemannarätt*, p. 324, who prefers that the invitation to comment is made with reference to a specific legal rule.

scenario, this would happen if the tribunal invites the parties to comment on the applicable national law on unfair terms of contracts, and the parties comment on parts of the regulation that are not relevant to the dispute, whereas they fail to comment on the article on invalidity that the tribunal deems relevant. The adversarial principle has been taken care of in that the tribunal drew the parties' attention to the source on unfair contract terms. By so doing, the source has been introduced in the proceeding and the parties have had the possibility of being able to comment on it. Failure by the parties to recognise the relevant article may not affect the tribunal's ability to develop its own legal argumentation, as seen above. Therefore, it should not be a problem to decide on the basis of the rules the tribunal deems applicable, even if the parties have not pleaded them after they have been invited to comment on them.

3.4.1 Distinction between domestic and international arbitration?

In respect of the tribunal's ability to develop its own legal argumentation and to apply the law *ex officio*, a distinction is sometimes drawn between domestic arbitration and international arbitration, and it is suggested that the principle of *iura novit curia* should apply to a more restricted extent when the dispute is international.[206]

This suggestion is mainly based on the international character of arbitration: it is assumed that foreign parties might be used to (from their respective systems) a different procedure and might not expect that the tribunal takes an active role. The overview of the arbitration rules made in Section 3.1.2 above, however, seems to show that the tribunal's powers are not regulated in dramatically different ways in the main institutional rules as well as in the UNCITRAL Rules. It might, of course, not be excluded that other arbitration rules provide for much more passive tribunals; however, the rules analysed here are quite representative of the modern standard, at least within European arbitration rules.[207]

Furthermore, it might be difficult to assume total ignorance by the parties of the local arbitration law, let alone of the arbitration rules of the institution that the parties have chosen. That the venue for the arbitration shall be chosen out of logistical or other practical reasons and without taking into consideration the legal framework for the proceeding does not seem to comply with the important role that local arbitration law has in respect of the validity and enforceability of the award, of the tribunal's power to order interim measures or of the local court's powers to intervene in or assist the arbitral procedure, as was seen in Sections 1.4.1 and 1.4.1.1–1.4.1.3. Such an undervaluation

---

[206] See, for example, Heuman, *Skiljemannarätt*, pp. 323, 379 and 682f., Kaufmann-Kohler, '*Iura novit arbiter*', pp. 73f., Kessedjian, 'Principe de la contradiction et arbitrage', 403f., and P. Mayer, 'Le pouvoir des arbitres de régler la procédure: Une analyse comparative des systèmes de civil law et de common law' (1995) 2 *Revue de l'arbitrage*, 176ff.

[207] Kaufmann-Kohler, 'The Arbitrator and the Law', p. 632 (with further bibliographic references in footnote 4) even speaks of a transnational arbitral procedure that is developing on an international level, possibly with the exception of US arbitration.

of the local arbitration law's significance might have been encountered more often some decades ago, when arbitration was a relatively new phenomenon. Nowadays, arbitration has become a settled branch within international dispute resolution and seems to have even passed the definition as an 'alternative' method for dispute resolution over to newer forms, such as mediation and conciliation. In this context, not knowing the tribunal's powers under the chosen arbitration law seems to be rather unjustified; therefore, the suggestion that the role of the tribunal in international disputes should be restricted because of the possibility that the parties might be unprepared for an active role under the applicable arbitration rules seems to be an excessive measure that is meant to accommodate the interests of negligent parties. Should, however, the venue of the tribunal have not been chosen by or known to the parties prior to the initiation of the proceeding, this reasoning might be more flexible.

Another reason for distinguishing between domestic and international disputes in respect of the principle of *iura novit curia* is the observation that, in an international dispute, the tribunal might tend to apply to the merits transnational sources of the *lex mercatoria*, which are more difficult to determine than state law.[208] An invitation to comment on these sources, therefore, might preserve the predictability of the result. It is certainly a commendable aim to preserve predictability, and I agree that the application of transnational sources might create problems in terms of predictability. From the point of view of the validity and enforceability of the award, however, the distinction between application of transnational sources and of a state law becomes relevant only if the sources applied by the tribunal do not qualify as sources of law. As will be seen in Section 3.5, often an award that is not rendered at law is invalid if the parties have not requested the tribunal to act as an *amiable compositeur*.[209] The lack of power to render an award *ex bono et aequo* would not be remedied by an invitation to comment (unless the parties, in their comments, agree thereon). If the application of transnational sources does not prevent the award from being considered at law, invitation to comment is not required for the effectiveness of the award (although it might be highly recommendable because of the mentioned question of the predictability).

3.5 Procedural irregularity

One of the grounds for setting aside or refusing enforcement of an arbitral award is, as seen in Section 3.2.3, the violation of mandatory procedural rules of the *lex arbitri*. In respect of the disregard of the contract's choice of law, and as already mentioned

---

[208] Kessedjan, 'Principe de la contradiction et arbitrage', pp. 403f.

[209] According to a widespread opinion in the legal literature, the tribunal has the authority to apply the *lex mercatoria* on its own motion if the arbitration rules or the applicable arbitration law provide that the tribunal may apply 'rules of law', as opposed to 'law'. The SCC Rules, for example, use the formula 'rules of law', and so do the UNCITRAL Arbitration Rules as revised in 2010. The UNCITRAL Rules in the original version of 1976 use 'law'. For a more extensive analysis of this question, see below, Section 3.5.1.1.

in connection with the defence of excess of power, it is firstly necessary to remember that the tribunal's interpretation of the contract and application of law (also including the private international law) may not be reviewed by the court, irrespective of how evidently wrong they are. Therefore, disregard of the parties' instructions in respect of the governing law may not, as a rule, fall within the scope of the irregular procedure if it does not fall within the scope of the excess of power. There is, however, one context in which it is possible to differentiate: when the arbitral tribunal disregards the choice of the parties and applies transnational sources. In this case, the arbitral tribunal may, in addition to exceeding the instructions of the parties, have exercised powers that it might not have according to the applicable arbitration law.

As we will see below, the arbitral tribunal does not necessarily have the power to apply transnational sources on its own initiative; in the majority of the arbitration laws, the arbitral tribunal has to apply a national law, unless the parties have requested otherwise. Therefore, application on the tribunal's own initiative of transnational sources may result in something more than a simple wrong application of the private international law. It may result in a violation of the rules that govern the arbitration, which, in turn, is a basis for the defence of irregularity of procedure. This matter, however, requires an accurate analysis, which we will carry out below.

Moreover, mandatory procedural rules of the *lex arbitri* may regulate questions regarding allocation of the burden of proof between the parties, as was seen in Section 3.1. A too active role by the arbitral tribunal may violate these rules, as will be seen in Section 3.5.2.

3.5.1 Decision at law or in equity (*ex bono et aequo*)

Most arbitration laws, as we will see below, permit the parties to request that the arbitral tribunal renders its decision without taking into strict consideration the applicable law. This kind of decision, called a decision *ex bono et aequo*, assumes that the tribunal is not applying the provisions of a specific law, but is acting as an *amiable compositeur*; that is, taking into consideration the circumstances of the case, the interests of the parties, as well as the common sense of justice and any other sources or circumstances that it might consider appropriate. Among these sources and circumstances, it is also possible to apply the transnational sources of law described in Chapter 2. An award rendered in equity will be subject to the same regime as an award rendered at law when it comes to validity and enforceability. The same circumstances that might affect the validity of an award at law, therefore, will also affect the validity and enforceability of an award rendered *ex bono et aequo*.

3.5.1.1 Is transnational law the basis for a decision at law or *ex bono et aequo*?

We have mentioned the eventuality that the parties have directed the arbitral tribunal to act as an *amiable compositeur*, and that the tribunal, on that basis, has applied transnational sources. But what if the parties have not expressly directed the tribunal to decide *ex bono et aequo*: may the tribunal nevertheless apply transnational sources? The answer to this question assumes the answer to another question: would a decision taken on the basis of transnational law be deemed to be a decision at law or would it be deemed to be a decision taken *ex bono et aequo*? This definition is important, because, as we will see immediately below, under some arbitration laws, the arbitral tribunal may render an award in equity only if the parties have expressly instructed it to do so. If the parties have not requested a decision *ex bono et aequo*, the arbitral tribunal has no authority, under the applicable arbitration law, to render an award otherwise than at law.

Generally, both arbitration rules and arbitration laws make a clear distinction between a decision made at law and a decision made *ex bono et aequo*. A tribunal is empowered to take the latter decision (acting therefore as an *amiable compositeur*) only if the parties have expressly instructed it to do so. This is expressly stated, for example, in the English Arbitration Act (Section 46.1(b)), in the Swiss Private International Law Act (Article 187.2), in the French and the Italian Codes of Civil Procedure (respectively, Articles 1512 and 822), as well as in the Arbitration Rules of the ICC (Article 21(3)) and of the Arbitration Institute of the SCC (Article 22(3)).

The above would seem sufficient to exclude the power of an arbitral tribunal to apply transnational law on its own initiative; however, there is growing consent[210] that transnational sources may constitute a system of law, and that therefore it is not appropriate to qualify a decision taken according to transnational sources as a decision taken as an *amiable compositeur*. Therefore, a decision based on trans-national sources would be a decision taken at law, not *ex bono et aequo*, and its application by the arbitral tribunal without specific instructions by the parties would not be a procedural irregularity.

The interpretation of the transnational law as a body of 'rules of law' equivalent to a state 'law', however, is not uncontroversial.[211]

---

[210] Some court decisions seem to have followed this view: The French Supreme Court has not considered as invalid a preliminary award that decided to apply the transnational law on its own initiative (the so-called *Valenciana* case): see Clunet (1992), 177, with a note by Goldman, and *Revue de l'Arbitrage* (1992), 457, with a note by Lagarde. The Austrian Supreme Court has not considered as invalid an award (rendered in the case *Palbalk v. Norsolor*) that applied the transnational law on its own initiative: see *Yearbook Commercial Arbitration IX* (Kluwer International, 1984), pp. 159ff, with a note by Melis). A decision by the English Court of Appeal, *Deutsche Schachtbau- und Tiefbohrgesellschaft mbH v. Ras Al Khaimah National Oil Co* CA [1987] 2 Lloyds Law Rep 246, is sometimes referred to as confirming that a decision made on the basis of the transnational law cannot be considered as an equitable decision; see, for example, M. Bonell, *An International Restatement of Contract Law* (Transnational Publishers 1997), p. 201, footnote 110, and Lando, 'The *Lex Mercatoria*', pp. 576ff. In reality, this decision does not seem to qualify the transnational law, it rather seems to interpret the applicable arbitration rules (which, in the case concerned, were the ICC Arbitration Rules) in a way that does not permit one to draw conclusions on the qualification of the transnational law: see Cordero-Moss, *International Commercial Arbitration: Party Autonomy*, pp. 290f.

[211] Critical are F. Dasser, *Internationale Schiedsgerichte und Lex mercatoria. Rechtsvergleichender Beitrag zur Diskussion über ein nicht-staatliches Handelsrecht* (Sculthess Olygraphischer Verlag, 1989), p. 309; G. Gaja, 'Sulle norme applicabili al merito secondo la nuova disciplina dell'arbitrato internazionale', *Rivista dell'Arbitrato* (Giuffrè, 1994), 433ff. and 438f.; and A. Giardina, 'La legge n. 25 del 1994 e l'arbitrato internazionale', *Rivista dell'Arbitrato* (Giuffrè, 1994), 257ff., 269f.

A confirmation of this opinion is found in the terminology used by some arbitration laws and arbitration rules, as was mentioned in Chapter 2, Section 6.1 and Chapter 4, Section 2.3. Arbitration laws and arbitration rules generally permit the parties to instruct the tribunal as to what 'rules of law' shall be applied to the merits of the dispute. Failing a choice made by the parties, the laws and rules contain some indications as to the approach to be followed by the tribunal (which conflict rules shall be applied) that will result in the application of certain 'rules of law' or in the application of a 'law'. The terminology 'rules of law' would refer not only to a state law, but to any system of rules, also including transnational rules; the terminology 'law', on the contrary, would refer to state laws. If the applicable arbitration rules or arbitration law speak of the tribunal applying 'rules of law' on its own initiative, this is interpreted as if the tribunal was empowered to apply transnational law on its own initiative; if the applicable rules or law speak of 'law', this power is excluded. In addition, other languages should reflect the distinction between 'rules of law' and 'law': for example, in French, the distinction should be between, respectively, *droit* and *loi*, in German, between *Rechtsvorschriften* and *Recht*, and in Italian, between *norme* and *legge*.[212]

According to this interpretation, the tribunal would be empowered to apply transnational sources on its own initiative by the French Code of Civil Procedure (Article 1511), by the Swiss Private International Law Act (Article 187, in the French version, but not in the German or the Italian versions), as well as by the Arbitration Rules of the ICC (Article 21(1)), the LCIA (Article 22(3)), and the Arbitration Rules of the Arbitration Institute of the SCC (Article 22(1)), which all make reference to 'rules of law'. Other laws and rules, on the contrary, exclude this possibility, and assume that the tribunal applies a state law unless the parties have made reference to non-national sources: for example, the UNCITRAL Model Law (Article 28(2)) and the English Arbitration Act (Section 46(1)).

The interpretation of 'rules of law' as also comprising the transnational law has been confirmed when the UNCITRAL, in 2010, revised its Arbitration Rules, originally issued in 1976. While the parties earlier were expected to choose the 'law' to be applied to the merits of the dispute (in the original Article 33), in the revision, they are allowed to choose 'rules of law' (in the new Article 35). This was intended to extend the parties' choice, since 'law' is usually interpreted to mean a state law, whereas 'rules of law' are deemed to be any body of rules, not necessarily emanating from a state. Even under the 1976 language, the parties could instruct the arbitral tribunal to apply rules of law to the merits of the dispute. By so doing, the parties would have incorporated these rules of law into their contract, and the arbitral tribunal would have had to apply them. In the revised version, the parties' choice of rules of law is intended to have a higher rank in the hierarchy of the applicable

---

[212] See, among others, Blessing, 'Choice of Substantive Law in International Arbitration', 39ff. and 48, and 'Keynotes on Arbitral Decision-making', 39, and P.-F Weise, *Lex Mercatoria* (Peter Lang, 1990), p. 152.

sources: they should not be simply incorporated into the contract, but they should be elevated to the status of governing law. As Chapter 2 showed, however, it is unlikely that transnational law succeeds in replacing the governing law. For the sake of completeness, it should be mentioned here that the UNCITRAL Arbitration Rules permit the parties to instruct the arbitral tribunal to apply 'rules of law', but do not permit the arbitral tribunal to do so on its own initiative. In the absence of instructions by the parties, the arbitral tribunal shall apply the 'law' which it determines to be appropriate.

Following this logic, arbitration rules and legislation would provide for three kinds of decisions. Decisions in equity, which are admissible only upon the direction by the parties; decisions based on rules of law, also including transnational sources, which may, in some systems, be applied on the tribunal's own initiative; and decisions based on state laws, which in all systems may be applied on the tribunal's own initiative.

3.5.1.2 The application of transnational sources and procedural irregularity

We have seen in Section 3.3.1 that it is not possible to sanction the tribunal's disregard of the law chosen in the contract, if this was made to apply the rule of another law that the tribunal might be requested to apply by the applicable private international law, or to avoid that the award conflicts with applicable fundamental principles and falls under the *ordre public* exception. What if the tribunal's disregard of the choice of law made in the contract is not made to apply another law, but to apply transnational principles? In a case described in Section 3.3.1.2.3, the parties to a contract realise, after the contract has entered into force, that the agreed price was too low and enter into a new contract for the sole purpose of increasing the price. At the moment of paying the increased price, the payor refuses to effect the increased payment and the dispute is submitted to arbitration. If the governing law is English law, and if it is not possible to find a factual benefit that would derive out of it to the payor, the amendment contract may be deemed as not binding for lack of consideration. What if the parties have chosen English law to govern the contract: can the tribunal, on its own initiative, disregard the doctrine of consideration contained in the governing English law? The tribunal might consider it inappropriate to apply the doctrine of consideration strictly. This doctrine is peculiar to the common law legal systems and does not reflect the general expectation of the parties in the international business arena, and certainly not the specific expectations that the parties had when they entered into the amendment contract. What happens if the arbitral tribunal decides to disregard this peculiarity of one national system of law, and applies instead the generally recognised transnational principle of *pacta sunt servanda*, or the rule of Article 2.1.1 of the UPICC, which provide for the binding effect of a contract even in the absence of consideration? Is the award effective, or does it run the risk of being annulled or of not being enforced?

We have seen that the courts of law have no jurisdiction to review the application of the law made by the arbitral tribunal. Therefore, a wrong application of English law would not be subject to judicial control; neither would a wrong interpretation of the choice-of-law clause in the contract or a wrong application of private international law. However, an unsolicited application of transnational sources goes beyond the error in law, at least under the arbitration laws or arbitration rules that do not give the arbitral tribunal the power to apply 'rules of law' without having been instructed to do so by the parties. Application of transnational sources without having being empowered by the parties is forbidden by these arbitration laws, and may therefore result in a procedural irregularity.

Whether the disregard of the English doctrine of consideration is the consequence of a (perhaps wrong) application of the law (and therefore not subject to judicial control) or of the application of transnational principles (and therefore subject to judicial control if this is deemed to correspond to a decision *ex bono et aequo* or if the arbitral tribunal is empowered only to apply a 'law') has to be established on the basis of a careful analysis of the reasons of the award.

3.5.1.3 Conclusion

There is no uniform answer to the question of invalidity or unenforceability in the scenario made here. If the parties had adopted for their dispute the Rules of Arbitration of the Arbitration Institute of the SCC, the tribunal would have been indirectly empowered by the parties to apply transnational sources. Therefore, the disregard of the English doctrine of consideration and the application of the principle of *pacta sunt servanda* or of the UPICC would be treated in the same way as the disregard of the law chosen by the parties by applying another state law (as was examined in Section 3.3.1.2 above). Whether the courts would be willing to exercise their control on the tribunal's award, or whether they would consider an intervention in this context dangerously close to a review of the tribunal's accurate application of the law (which, as we know, the courts are not empowered to make), would depend on the circumstances of the case and on the reasons of the award.

If, however, the dispute was submitted to the UNCITRAL Arbitration Rules, the tribunal would have been bound to apply a state law, and an application of transnational sources would have exceeded the powers of the tribunal and could fall under the defence of irregular procedure.

3.5.2 Burden of proof: may the tribunal request additional information to undermine uncontested evidence?

As we have seen in Section 3.1.2(iii.) above, the tribunal may, under some arbitration rules, draw adverse inferences from the failure by one party to appear. We have also seen that the tribunal is not bound to accept the other party's assertions blindly. If the produced evidence is not convincing because, for example, a witness did not seem credible or a document was evidently forged, the unsatisfactory character of the evidence is apparent at a mere examination thereof. Likewise, if the produced evidence is intrinsically illogical or if it contradicts other evidence that was produced in the same dispute, it is sufficient to examine the produced evidence to determine the weight that shall be attached to it. As long as the independent evaluation of the produced evidence consists in this examination, no difficulties seem to arise in connection with the tribunal's role.

A question that might arise is to what extent the tribunal shall limit itself to an evaluation of the evidence as presented, or if it is allowed to go further and, in order to verify the soundness of the evidence, to develop arguments that should have been presented by the other party. May the tribunal avail itself of its power to request additional information in order to substantiate these arguments?

We can assume that a party wishes to prove that the value of the disputed goods has decreased during a certain lapse of time. The party produces documentation showing that equivalent goods have, during that period, been purchased at a certain price and then resold at a lower price. This is evidence of the decreased value not of the specific goods in dispute, but of equivalent goods; however, the other party does not appear and therefore the extension of this evidence to the disputed goods is not contested. If the other party had appeared, it might have produced evidence that that particular purchase/resale was not indicative of the value of that type of goods, for example, because the purchaser/reseller did not act diligently or was under a conflict of interest; or it could have produced evidence that the disputed goods were not affected by the same decrease in value because of special circumstances. Assuming that there are no *prima facie* grounds for not also applying the proven value decrease to the disputed goods, it would be the burden of the other party to prove the special circumstances that speak against such applicability. If the other party does not appear, it does not discharge its burden of proof. In such a situation, the tribunal has two alternatives:

(i) The tribunal may consider the produced evidence as satisfactory, thus giving effect to the general rule on burden of proof:

    (a) This does not create problems in the systems that permit one to draw from a party's default inferences adverse to that party;[213]

    (b) Some systems, however, expressly state that failure to appear may not be deemed as an admission.[214] To avoid violating this rule, the tribunal should verify whether the produced evidence is capable of independently proving the point made by the party: this is the case when the evidence is relevant and sufficient even without interpreting the other party's default as an indirect admission that it is not able to rebut it by producing contrary evidence. Should, however, the tribunal determine that the produced evidence does not have an independent value, because its relevance or weight depend (also) on the absence of contrary evidence, the tribunal is under a duty to raise the matter and request additional clarification.

---

[213] For example, Swedish law, see Section 3.1.2(ii) above.
[214] For example, German law and the ICSID, see above, *ibid.*

(ii) The tribunal may consider that the produced evidence is not satisfactory, and may thus request additional evidence in order to substantiate or dismiss the arguments that can be made against its soundness.

    (a) In the systems where the tribunal may draw adverse inferences from the other party's default, the tribunal remains free not to draw such inferences. Therefore, if the produced evidence does not have independent value, and the tribunal determines that it shall not be deemed as admitted by the other party, it may exercise its power to request additional information. However, if the evidence has relevance and weight, irrespective of whether it is deemed as admitted or not, a request by the tribunal for additional information may seem to violate the rule on the burden of proof;

    (b) In the systems where the tribunal has a duty not to deem as an admission the failure to appear, this alternative is not problematic; however, if the produced evidence has a clearly independent value, the request for additional information is not based on the duty to avoid drawing negative inferences from the other party's default. The tribunal remains free to evaluate the evidence and to investigate further in accordance with the powers that the applicable regulation confers on it; but it runs the risk of taking over the burden of proof of the other party.

What are the consequences for the award of a violation of the rule on the burden of proof? Of the three ultimate borders to the tribunal's power that are relevant here, it seems that the rule on procedural irregularity, or due process, might be considered. As we have seen in the explanation above, a violation of the rule on burden of proof may be assessed by reviewing the tribunal's evaluation of the pleadings and their capability of having an independent value. As is known, this kind of review is generally not allowed, neither in the phase of the validity challenge or in the phase of the enforcement of an award. It seems, therefore, that a violation of the burden of proof would have to be quite an evident violation of impartiality and cause a substantial injustice before it can be sanctioned through the invalidity or unenforceability of the award.[215] Nevertheless, a tribunal should accurately comply

---

[215] In commercial arbitration, the reported decisions establishing a violation of the impartiality standard are few and deal mainly with the possibility of both parties being heard, rather than with the rule of burden of proof; see van den Berg, 'Consolidated Commentary', pp. 521 2 and 523 4 and Born, *International Commercial Arbitration*, p. 2746ff. As an example of a lack of impartiality by a tribunal, see the Dutch decision of 28 April 1998, in *Yearbook Commercial Arbitration XXIII* (Kluwer International, 1998), pp. 731f., refusing to enforce an award based on evidence that one party had presented after the hearing, and that the other party had not had the possibility of commenting on. The ICSID ad hoc Committees have regularly rejected applications for annulment based on the allegation that the tribunal had violated the rule on burden of proof: see, for references, Schreuer, 'Three Generations of ICSID Annulment Proceedings', pp. 32f., and Schreuer, Malintoppi, Reinisch and Sinlcair, *The ICSID Convention* Article 52, paras. 323–32, referring *inter alia* to the ad hoc Committee decision in the case *Klöckner II* (unpublished), which affirmed, in theory, the possibility of being able to annul an award because of an erroneous reversal of the burden of proof, but which did not find the annulment ground applicable in the specific case.

with its duties and avoid acting in a way that might raise even the slightest suspicion of impartiality, even if the threshold for invalidity and unenforceability of the award is not reached; otherwise, the parties' faith in arbitration might be undermined.

So far, we have assumed that the evidence produced by one party was not contested, because the other party did not appear. What if the other party appears and presents its statements, but fails to contest that particular piece of evidence? It seems that, in this situation, it would be difficult to apply the rule preventing drawing adverse inferences from the failure to appear. The other party has actually presented its arguments, where it could have contested the evidence, and has decided not to contest it. This seems to be very close to an implied admission of the assertions that were meant to be proved by producing the evidence that remained uncontested. The tribunal may invite the other party to clarify whether the failure to contest the evidence is to be interpreted as an agreement on the existence of that particular circumstance or not; however, going further than that becomes dangerously close to suggesting arguments to that party.

To the extent that the parties may be deemed to agree on the existence of a certain fact, there does not seem to be any room for the tribunal to make different assumptions; however, the tribunal remains free to draw from the agreed facts the inferences that it deems appropriate, and to ask for the additional information that these inferences might render as being relevant.

3.6 Conclusion

We have seen that the tribunal enjoys[216] ample room for independently evaluating the presented evidence, legal arguments and sources, and for requesting additional information and thus introducing new elements in the proceeding. The tribunal, therefore, is not bound by the arguments made by the parties. The only border that the tribunal seems to encounter concerns the factual scope of the dispute, as well as any restrictions to the tribunal's jurisdiction that might be contained in the arbitration agreement or other appropriate instrument, such as an investment treaty in the case of investment arbitration. There are also some uncertainties in respect of introducing remedies that were not requested by the parties. It is, therefore, advisable to invite the parties to comment on the tribunal's inferences of law or new sources that the tribunal intends to apply, so as to ensure that the adversarial principle is not violated. An invitation to comment is, as seen above, requested in some systems on all the elements upon which the award is going to be based, whether they are elements of fact or of law.

---

[216] Under the Arbitration Rules of the SCC, ICC, LCIA and UNCITRAL, as well as under the ICSID Rules and the ALI/UNIDROIT Principles.

The sanctions against a misuse of such powers are few and their scope of application is rather restricted: while the rule on excess of power mainly only penalises decisions made outside the factual subject matter of the dispute, the rules on fair hearing and impartiality are not meant to permit a review of the tribunal's evaluation of the evidence or of the law. Therefore, only gross violations of the tribunal's duties may lead to the application of these penalties.

This does not mean, however, that a tribunal should feel free from any constraint in administering the proceeding: Impartiality and due process, as well as accuracy in the interpretation of the contract and the application of the law, are important principles and should always be the inspiration for any act by the tribunal, irrespective of whether a violation thereof might be considered 'only' as a wrong decision on the merits, and, as such, not leading to invalidity and unenforceability of the award.

6

Conclusion

The excursus made in this book was meant to determine the relationship between an international contract and the sources that regulate it. Even if the parties have not thought of any governing law when they drafted the contract, even if they have expressly intended to avoid a certain governing law, even if they have chosen a certain set of transnational rules to govern their transaction, even if they have made use of model contracts that are meant to be used in a variety of jurisdictions – the contract may nevertheless be subject to the mandatory rules, the overriding mandatory rules or the *ordre public* of state laws that the parties had not taken into consideration or had intended to avoid. Moreover, the contract will be interpreted on the basis of the legal tradition of the applicable law, thus attaching different legal effects to the same wording, depending on the applicable law.

What I have tried to show is that an international contract is not necessarily a phenomenon *sui generis*, responding to its own logic, and that has to be written and interpreted in a completely different way from a domestic contract. It is, admittedly, a widespread habit to adopt a different style when the contract is international and to draft in accordance with English/US contract models; but this may create more problems than it solves, particularly in connection with the interaction between a common law contract style and a civil law governing law. The practice of writing contracts so that they are supposedly self-sufficient is often the result of a cost–benefit analysis leading to the conscious assumption of the risk that the contract may not be interpreted or applied exclusively on the basis of its terms. The analysis may have shown that it would take more resources to adapt a standardised contract model to the requirements of the local law, than legal proceedings and a possible invalidity or unenforceability of the contract might cost. Sometimes, the practice of writing self-sufficient contracts may be the result of insufficient awareness of the legal framework by the drafters. In either case, there does not seem to be a basis for elevating this practice to a source of law and thus considering the contracts as actually self-sufficient. The terms of the contract are, naturally, the first and most important source of legal obligations between the parties, and shall be interpreted and applied faithfully. However, often contracts may not be interpreted or applied without also taking into consideration the principles and rules of the legal system that governs them. The ambitions relating to the self-sufficiency of contracts, motivated as they are in the assumption of calculated risk or in an unconsidered assumption of risk, do not seem to constitute a sufficient basis with which to exclude that the governing law is relevant.

Even if the ambitions of self-sufficiency constituted a basis to exclude the governing law, there would still be the need to have a legal framework within which the contract may be interpreted and applied. Transnational sources of law created by practice, legislation or the academy do not succeed in providing a uniform system of general contract law, nor may they regulate areas that are subject to mandatory rules. Many of these regulations, whether they stem from international conventions or transnational sources, are extremely useful and should definitely be taken into serious consideration. However, they should not be adopted blindly or in the belief that these sources are in any case an effective and exhaustive regulation of the transaction. The interaction with the governing law will determine to what extent this regulation is effective, and whether other principles or rules will also have to be taken into consideration. The governing law is not replaced, but is simply integrated by these transnational sources.

The relationship between the international contract and the governing law will depend on many variables. The governing law, the existence of overriding mandatory rules of other laws, the scope of party autonomy according to the applicable private international law, the forum that will have jurisdiction to decide upon disputes or, in the case of an Arbitration clause, the forum that will have jurisdiction to verify the validity of the award, as well as the forum where the award might be enforced, will all affect the validity and enforceability of a contract. The parties, when evaluating their legal position, should verify all the above-mentioned aspects of the specific transaction, which will permit the determination of to what extent the contractual terms or any chosen transnational sources might be effective in spite of a differing state law. If, due to the already mentioned assumption of risk, the parties do not proceed to this evaluation when drafting the contract, they will do so when a dispute arises.

These considerations are less stringent if the parties include an arbitration clause in their contract; however, the arbitral tribunal may be freer from state laws than a national court of law, but it is not completely detached from state law. Therefore, the parties should be aware of the relationship between an international contract and state law, even if they have included an arbitration clause. Moreover, an abuse of the freedom that the parties enjoy in arbitration would, in the long term, undermine the trust that national legal systems have shown towards arbitration. It is this trust that permits an extensive recognition and enforceability of arbitral awards in the vast majority of national systems of law, for example, by restrictively interpreting the exceptions of *ordre public* and arbitrability. An extensive use of arbitration for the purpose of avoiding mandatory rules of applicable laws would be a basis for re-evaluating the trustworthiness of arbitration as a mechanism for solving disputes, thus inducing national courts to interpret less narrowly the mentioned exceptions and, correspondingly, reducing the usefulness of arbitration.

BIBLIOGRAPHY

American Law Institute, *Restatement (Second) of Conflict of Laws* (American Law Institute, 1971).
  Restatement (Third) of Foreign Relations Law of the United States (American Law Institute, 1989).
Audit, Bernard, 'The Vienna Sales Convention and the Lex Mercatoria', in Thomas E. Carbonneau (ed.), *Lex Mercatoria and Arbitration*, (Juris Publishing, 1998), pp. 173–94.
Baratt, James and Ichilcik, Hayley, 'Bribery' (2011) *The European & Middle Eastern Arbitration Review*.
Basedow, Jürgen, 'Wirtschaftskollisionsrecht' (1988) 52 *Rabels Zeitschrift für ausländisches und internationales Privatrecht*, 8–38.
Beale, Hugh (ed.), *Chitty on Contracts*, 31st edn, 2 vols. (Sweet & Maxwell, 2012).
Beale, Hugh, 'English Law Reform and the Impact of European Contract Law' in Stefan Vogenauer and Stephen Weatherill (eds.), *Harmonization of European Contract Law* (Hart Publishing, 2006), pp. 31–8.
Beatson, Jack, Burrows, Andrew and Cartwright, John, *Anson's Law of Contract*, 29th edn (Oxford University Press, 2010).
Berg, Albert Jan van den, 'The Application of the New York Convention by the Courts', in Albert Jan van den Berg, (ed.), *Improving the Efficiency of Arbitration Agreements and Awards: 40 Years of Application of the New York Convention ICCA Congress Series No. 9* (Kluwer Law International, 1999), www.kluwerarbitration.com/document.aspx?id=ipn17561, pp. 25–34.
  'Consolidated Commentary on the New York Convention' ICCA Yearbook Commercial Arbitration XXVIII (Kluwer International, 2003)
  The New York Arbitration Convention of 1958 (Deventer, 1981).
Berger, Klaus Peter, *The Creeping Codification of the Lex Mercatoria*, 2nd edn (Kluwer Law International, 2010).
Blessing, Marc, 'Choice of Substantive Law in International Arbitration' (1997) 14(2) *Journal of International Arbitration*, 39–65.
  'Keynotes on Arbitral Decision-Making': The New 1998 ICC Rules of Arbitration (1997) 14(2) *Journal of International Arbitration*, 39–65.
Bodgan, Michael, '1980 års EC-konvention om tillämping lag på kontraksrättsliga förpliktelser – synpunkter beträffande den svenske innställningen' (1982) 95 *Tidsskrift for Rettsvitenskap*, 1–49.
  Svensk internationell privat- och prosessrätt, 7th edn (Norstedst Juridik, 2008).
Boek, Annuck de and Hoecke, Mark van, 'The Interpretation of Standard Clauses in European Contract Law' in Hugh Collins (ed.), *Standard Contract Terms in Europe: A Basis for and a Challenge to European Contract Law* (Wolters Kluwer, 2008), pp. 201–44.

Bonell, Michael, *An International Restatement of Contract Law* (Transnational Publishers, 1997).
  'Formation of Contracts and Precontractual Liability Under the Vienna Convention on International Sale of Goods', in ICC, *Formation of Contracts and Precontractual Liability* (International Chamber of Commerce, 1990), pp. 157–78.
Born, Gary, *International Commercial Arbitration*, (Kluwer Law International, 2009).
  International Commercial Arbitration: Commentary and Materials, 2nd edn (Kluwer Law International, 2001).
Bridge, Michael, 'Good Faith in Commercial Contracts' in Roger Brownsword, Norma J. Hird and Geraint Howells (eds.) *Good Faith in Contract* (Ashgate/Dartmouth, 1999), pp. 139–64.
British Institute for International and Comparative Law, 'Study on the Question of Effectiveness of an Assignments or Subrogation of a Claim Against Third Parties and the Priority of the Assigned or Subrogated Claim over a Right of Another Person' (2012), ec.europa.eu/justice/civil/files/report_assignment_en.pdf.
Brownsword, Roger, 'Positive, Negative, Neutral: the Reception of Good Faith in English Contract Law' in Roger Brownsword, Norma J. Hird and Geraint Howells (ed.) *Good Faith in Contract* (Ashgate/Dartmouth, 1999), pp. 13–40.
Bussani, Mauro and Mattei, Ugo, *The Common Core of European Private Law Project* (Kluwer Law International, 2003).
Cafaggi, Fabrizio, 'Self-Regulation in European Contract Law', in Hugh Collins (ed.), *Standard Contract Terms in Europe: A Basis for and a Challenge to European Contract Law* (Wolters Kluwer, 2008).
Canuel, Edward T., 'Comparing Exculpatory Clauses under Anglo-American Law: Testing Total Legal Convergence', in Giuditta Cordero-Moss (ed.), *Boilerplate clauses, International Commercial Contracts and the Applicable Law* (Cambridge University Press, 2011), pp. 80–103.
Carrington, Paul D. and Hagen, Paul H., 'Contract and Jurisdiction' (1997) 8 *The Supreme Court Review*, 331–402.
Carruthers, Janeen M., *The Transfer of Property in the Conflict of Laws* (Oxford University Press, 2005).
Collins, Hugh, 'The Freedom to Circulate Documents: Regulating Contracts in Europe' (2004) 10 *European Law Journal*, 787–803.
  'Social Rights, General Clauses and the Acquis Communitaire', in Stefan Grundmann and Denis Mazeaud (eds.), *General Clauses and Standards in European Contract Law* (Kluwer Law International, 2006), pp. 111–40.
Collins, Lawrence, Mase, C. G. J., McClean, David, Briggs, Adrain, Harris, Jonathan, McLachlan, Campbell, Dickenson, Andrew and McEleary, Peter, *Dicey, Morris & Collins on the Conflict of Laws*, 15th edn (Sweet & Maxwell, 2012).
Commission of the European Communities, Report from the Commission to the Council and the European Parliament (2006), ec.europa.eu/internal_market/financial-markets/docs/collateral/fcd_report_en.pdf.
Commission on European Contract Law, The Principles of European Contract Law (PECL) (European Union, 2002), www.jus.uio.no/lm/eu.contract.principles.parts.1.to.3.2002/.
Cordero-Moss, Giuditta, 'Arbitration and Private International Law' (2008) 11 *International Arbitration Law Review*, 153–64.
  Boilerplate Clauses, International Commercial Contracts and the Applicable Law (Cambridge University Press, 2011).

'Commercial Arbitration and Investment Arbitration: Fertile Soil for False Friends?', in Cristina Binder, Ursula Kriebaum, August Reinisch and Stephan Wittich (eds.), *International Investment Law for the 21st Century – Essays in Honour of Christoph Schreuer* (Oxford University Press, 2009), pp. 782–97.

'Consumer Protection Except for Good Commercial Practice: A Satisfactory Regime for Commercial Contracts?', in Reiner Schulze (ed.), *CFR and Existing EC Contract Law* (Sellier European Law Publishers, 2009), pp. 78–94.

'Direct Action Against the Insurer: A Recent Decision by the Norwegian Supreme Court Illustrates the Norwegian Approach to Private International Law', in Talia Einhorn and Kurt Siehr, (eds.), *Intercontinental Cooperation Through Private International Law – Essays in Memory of Peter E. Nygh* (Asser Press, 2002), pp. 55–67.

'Does the Use of Common Law Contract Models Give Rise to a Tacit Choice of Law or to a Harmonised, Transnational Interpretation?', in Giuditta Cordero-Moss (ed.), *Boilerplate Clauses, International Commercial Contracts and the Applicable Law* (Cambridge University Press, 2011), pp. 37–61.

'International Arbitration is not only International', in Giuditta Cordero-Moss (ed.), *International Commercial Arbitration: Different Forms and their Features* (Cambridge University Press, 2013), pp. 7–39.

International Commercial Arbitration. Different Forms and their Features (Cambridge University Press, 2013).

International Commercial Arbitration – Party Autonomy and Mandatory Rules (Tano Aschehoug, 1999).

'International Contracts Between Common Law and Civil Law: Is Non-State Law to be Preferred? The Difficulty of Interpreting Legal Standards such as Good Faith' (2007) 7(1) *Global Jurist Advances* 1–38.

Lectures on Comparative Law of Contracts (University of Oslo Institute of Private Law, 2004), folk.uio.no/giudittm/PCL_Vol15_3%5B1%5D.pdf.

'Revision of the UNCITRAL Arbitration Rules: Further Steps' (2010) 1 *International Law Review*, 96–9

'The Function of Letters of Intent and Their Recognition in Modern Legal Systems', in Reiner Schulze (ed.), *New Features in Contract Law* (Sellier European Law Publishers, 2007), pp. 139–59.

'Tvangsfullbyrdelse av utenlandske voldgiftsavgjørelser,' (2000) 1 *Nytt i Privatretten* 15–16.

Cordero-Moss, Giuditta and Echenberg, David *et al.*, *Transcript of the APA Seminar 21 Nov 2011* (2011), www.jus.uio.no/ifp/english/research/projects/choice-of-law/events/apa-transcript.pdf.

Dannemann, Gerhard, 'Common Law Based Contracts under German Law', in Giuditta Cordero-Moss (ed.), *Boilerplate Clauses, International Commercial Contracts and the Applicable Law* (Cambridge University Press, 2011), pp. 62–79.

Dasser, Felix, *Internationale Schiedsgerichte und Lex mercatoria. Rechtsvergleichender Beitrag zur Diskussion über ein nicht-staatliches Handelsrecht* (Sculthess Olygraphischer Verlag, 1989).

De Ly, Filip, *International Business Law and Lex Mercatoria* (TMC Asser Institute, 1992).

De Nova, Giorgio, 'The Romanistic Tradition: Application of Boilerplate Clauses under Italian Law' in Giuditta Cordero-Moss (ed.), *Boilerplate Clauses, International Commercial Contracts and the Applicable Law* (Cambridge University Press, 2011), pp. 227–32.

Derains, Yves and Scwhartz, Eric, *A Guide to the New ICC Rules of Arbitration*, (Kluwer Law International, 1998).
  Guide to the ICC Rules of Arbitration, 2nd edn (Kluwer Law International, 1998)
Dirk, Otto and Elwan, Omaia, 'Article V(2)', in Herbert Kronke and Patricia Nacimiento (eds.), *Recognition and Enforcement of Foreign Arbitral Awards: A Global Commentary on the New York Convention* (Kluwer Law International, 2010), pp. 345–414.
Drobnig, Ulrich, 'Das Profil des Wirtschaftskollisionrechts' (1988) 52 *Rabels Zeitschrift für ausländisches und internationales Privatrecht*, 1–7.
Echenberg, David, 'Negotiating International Contracts: Does the Process Invite a Review of Standard Contracts from the Point of View of a National Legal Requirements?' in Giuditta Cordero-Moss (ed.), *Boilerplate Clauses, International Commercial Contracts and the Applicable Law* (Cambridge University Press, 2011), pp. 11–19.
Eidemüller, Horst *et al*, 'The Common Frame of Reference for European Private Law – Policy Choices and Codification Problems' (2008) 28(4) *Oxford Journal of Legal Studies* 659–708.
Engel, Christoph, 'Die Bedeutung des Völkerrechts für die Anwendung in- und ausländischen Wirschaftsrechts' (1988) 52 *Rabels Zeitschrift für ausländisches und internationales Privatrecht*, 271–302.
Fawcett, James, Carruthers, Janeen and North, Peter, *Cheshire, North & Fawcett: Private International Law*, 14th edn (Oxford University Press, 2008).
Fern, M. D., *Warren's Forms of Agreements* (LexisNexis, 2004), vol. II.
Ferrari, F. (ed.), *The CISG and its Impact on National Legal Systems* (Sellier, 2008)
Ferreri, Silvia, 'Complexity of Transnational Sources', in Karen B. Brown and David V. Snyder (eds.), *General Reports of the XVIIIth Congress of the International Academy of Comparative Law* (Springer Law, 2012), pp. 29–56.
  The Italian National Report XVII Congress of the International Academy of Comparative Law, Section II-B1, Private International Law, Utrecht (16–16 July 2006).
Flambouras, D., 'The Doctrines of Impossibility of Performance and *Clausula Rebus Sic Stantibus* in the 1980 Vienna Convention on Contracts for the International Sale of Goods and the Principles of European Contract Law: A Comparative Analyses' (2001) 13 *Pace International Law Review*, 261–93, www.cisg.law.pace.edu/cisg/biblio/flambouras1.html.
Flessner, Alex and Verhagen, Hendrik, *Assignment in European Private International Law* (Sellier European Law Publishers, 2006).
Fontaine, Marcel and De Ly, Filip, *Drafting International Contracts: An Analysis of Contract Clauses* (Brill Academic Publishers, 2006).
Gaillard, Emmanuel and Savage, John (eds.), *Fouchard, Gaillard and Goldman on International Commercial Arbitration* (Kluwer Law International, 2004).
Gaja, Giorgio, 'Sulle norme applicabili al merito secondo la nuova disciplina dell'Arbitrato internazionale', *Rivista dell'Arbitrato* (Giuffrè, 1994).
Gambaro, Antonio and Sacco, Rodolfo, *Sistemi giuridici comparati* (Utet Giuridica, 2002).
Giardina, Andrea, 'La legge n. 25 del 1994 internazionale', *Rivista dell'Arbitrato* (Giuffrè, 1994).
Giuliano, Mario and Lagarde, Paul, Report on the Law Applicable to Contractual Obligations (1980) OJ C 282.
Goode, Roy, 'Usage and its Reception in Transnational Commercial Law' (1997) 46 *International and Comparative Law Quarterly*, 1–36.

Goode, Roy, Kronke, Herbert and McKendrick, Ewan, *Transnational Commercial Law – Texts, Cases and Materials* (Oxford University Press, 2007).

Gordley, James, *The Philosophical Origins of Moderns Contract Doctrine* (Oxford University Press, 1991).

Gorton, Lars, 'The Nordic Tradition: Application of Boilerplate Clauses under Swedish Law', in Giuditta Cordero-Moss (ed.), *Boilerplate Clauses, International Commercial Contracts and the Applicable Law* (Cambridge University Press, 2011), pp. 276–301.

Graziadei, Michele, 'Variations on the Concept of Contract in a European Perspective: Some Unresolved Issues', in Reiner Schulze (ed.), *New Features in Contract Law* (Sellier European Law Publisher, 2007), pp. 311–324.

Grosheide, W., 'The Duty to Deal Fairly in Commercial Contracts', in Stefan Grundmann and Denis Mazeaud (eds.), *General Clauses and Standards in European Contract Law* (Aspen Publishers, 2006), pp. 197–204.

Hagstrøm, Viggo, *Obligasjonsrett*, 2nd edn (Universitetsforlaget, 2011).

'The Nordic Tradition: Application of Boilerplate Clauses under Norwegian Law', in Giuditta Cordero-Moss (ed.), *Boilerplate Clauses, International Commercial Contracts and the Applicable law* (Cambridge University Press, 2011), pp. 265–75.

Hague Conference on Private International Law, 'Some Reflections on the Present State of Negotiations on the Judgments Project in the Context of the Future Work Program of the Conference', *Preliminary Document No 16 of February 2002* (2002), www.hcch.net/upload/wop/gen_pd16e.pdf.

Halpern, Joseph, 'Exorbitant Jurisdiction and the Brussels Convention: Toward a Theory of Restraint', in Michael Reisman (ed.), *Jurisdiction in International Law* (Ashgate Publishing, 1999), pp. 369–87.

Hanotiau, Bernard, 'The Law Applicable to Arbitrability', in Albert Jan van den Berg (ed.), *40 years of Application of the the New York Convention, The Hague etc.* (ICCA Congress Series No. 9, 1999) pp. 146–67.

Hartley, Trevor C., 'Mandatory Rules in International Contracts: The Common Law Approach', *Recueil des Cours* vol. 266 (The Hague Academy of International Law, 1997), vol. CCLXVI.

Hay, Peter, Borcher, Patrick and Symeonides, Symeon, *Conflict of Laws*, 5th edn (Thomson West, 2010).

Heuman, Lars, *Arbitration Law of Sweden: Practice and Procedure* (JurisNet, 2003).

Current Issues in Swedish Arbitration (Kluwer, 1990).

Skiljemannarätt (Nordstedts Juridik, 1999).

Heuman, Lars and Jarvin, S., *The Swedish Arbitration Act of 1999, Five Years on: A Critical Review of Strengths and Weaknesses* (JurisNet, 2006).

Hober, Kaj, 'Arbitration Involving States', in Lawrence W. Newman and Richard D. Hill (eds.), *The Leading Arbitrators' Guide to International Arbitration* (JurisNet, 2004), pp. 139–62.

Honsell, P., Vogt, N. P., Schnyder, A. K. and Berti, S. V. (eds.), *Basler Kommentar Internationales Privatrecht*, 2nd edn (Helbing Lichtenhahn Verlag, 2007).

House of Lords European Union Committee, Social Policy and Consumer Affairs, 12th Report of Session 2008–2009, European Contract Law: the Draft Common Frame of Refence Report with evidence (10 June 2009), www.publications.parliament.uk/pa/ld200809/ldselect/ldeucom/95/9502.htm.

Houtte, Hans van, *The Law of International Trade*, 2nd edn (Sweet & Maxwell, 2002).

Immenga, Ulrich, Mestmäcker, Ernst Joachim and Dannecker, Gerhard, *GWB Gesetz gegen Wettbewerbsbeschränkungen Kommentar* (C. H. Beck, 2001).

International Chamber of Commerce (ICC), *The International Commercial Terms (INCOTERMS)* (International Chamber of Commerce, 2010).

International Institute for the Unification of Private Law (UNIDROIT), 'ALI/UNIDROIT Principles of Transnational Civil Procedure' (2004) 9 *Uniform Law Review 4*, www.unidroit.org/english/publications/review/contents/2004–4.pdf.

    Principles of International Commercial Contracts (International Institute for the Unification of Private Law, 2010), www.unidroit.org/english/principles/contracts/main.htm.

International Law Association Committee on International Civil Litigation & the Interests of the Public, *Conference Resolution Sofia 2012* (International Law Association, 2012), www.ila-hq.org/download.cfm/docid/F784A3AA-7030-433D-96833C48F941FB28.

    Final Report International Civil Litigation for Human Rights Violations (International Law Association, 2012), www.ila-hq.org/download.cfm/docid/D7AFA4C8-E599-40FE-B6918B239B949698.

International Law Association Committee on International Commercial Arbitration, *Final Report Ascertaining the Contents of the Applicable Law in International Commercial Arbitration* (International Law Association, 2008), www.ila-hq.org/download.cfm/docid/985890F9-BF95-45C9-A47EB7B52082CDC4, pp. 4–21.

    Final Report on Public Policy as a Bar to Enforcement of International Arbitration Awards (International Law Association, 2002), www.transnational-dispute-management.com/search/get_page.asp?v2=download&v1=tv1%2D1%2Ddl%5F21%2Epdf.

    Interim Report on Public Policy as a Bar to Enforcement of International Arbitration Awards (International Law Association, 2000), www.newyorkconvention.org/userfiles/artikelen/198_ila-interim-report-public-policy-2000.pdf.

International Swaps and Derivatives Association, 'Response to Questionnaire' (2006), ec.europa.eu/internal_market/financial-markets/docs/collateral/2006-consultation/isda_en.pdf.

Jansen, Nils and Zimmermann, Reinhard, 'A European Civil Code in All But Name: Discussing the Nature and Purpose of the Draft Common Frame of Reference' (2010) 69 *Cambridge Law Journal*, 98–112.

Jesse, Katinka. and Verschuuren, Jonathan, 'Litigation Against International Business Corporations for Their Actions Abroad: Recent Environmental Cases from the Netherlands' (2011) *Tilburg Law School Legal Studies Research Paper Series No. 12*, ssrn.com/abstract=1773165, 1–7.

Jhering, Rudolf von, 'Culpa in contrahendo, oder Schadenersatz bei nichtigen oder nicht zur Perfektion galangten Verträgen' (1861) 4 *Jahrbücher für die Dogmatik de heutigen römischen und deutschen Privatrechts*.

Juenger, Friedrich K., *Choice of Law and Multistate Justice* (Martinus Nijhoff Publishers 1993).

Jung, Helena, 'SCC Practice: Challenges to Arbitrators SCC Board Decisions 2005–2007' (2008) *Stockholm International Arbitration Review* 1, www.sccinstitute.com/filearchive/2/28190/04-Art32-Jung.pdf 1–18.

Jänterä-Jareborg, Maarit, 'Foreign Law in National Courts – A Comparative Perspective', *Recueil des cours* (The Hague Academy of International Law, 2003), vol. CCCIV.

Kaufmann-Kohler, Gabrielle, '*Iura novit arbiter* – Est-ce bien raisonnable? Réflexions sur le statut du droit de fond devant l'arbitre international', in A. Héritier and L. Hirsch (ed.), *De lege ferenda – Réflexions sur le droit désirable en l'honneur du professeur Alain Hirsch* (Editions Slaktine, 2004), pp. 71–8.

'The Arbitrator and the Law: Does He/She Know it? Apply it? How? And a Few More Questions' (2005) 21(4) *Arbitration International* 631–8.

Kegel, G., 'The Crisis of Conflict of Laws', *Recueil des Cours* (The Hague Academy of International Law, 1986), vol. CII.

Kessedjian, C., 'Principe de la contradiction et arbitrage', (1995) 3 *Revue de l'arbitrage*, 382–410.

Kondring, J, 'Der Vertrag ist das Recht der Parteien – Zur Verwirklichung des Parteiwillens durch nachträgliche Teilrechtswahl' (2006) 5 *Praxis des Internationalen Privat- und Verfahrensrechts*, 425–38.

Konow, Berte-Elen Reinertsen, *Løsørepant over landegrenser* (Fagbokforlaget, 1999).

Kritzer, Albert H., *'Pre-Contract Formation'*, *CISG Database* (Pace Law School Institute of International Commercial Law, 2008), www.cisg.law.pace.edu/cisg/biblio/kritzer1.html.

Kropholler, Jan, *Internationales Privatrecht*, 6th edn (Mohr Siebeck, 2006).

Kurkela, Matti, '*"Jura Novit Curia"* and the Burden of Education in International Arbitration – A Nordic Perspective' (2003) 21(3) *ASA Bulletin*, 486–500.

Lagarde, Xavier, Méheut, David and Reversac, Jean-Michel, 'The Romanistic Tradition: Application of Boilerplate Clauses under French Law', in Giuditta Cordero-Moss (ed.), *Boilerplate Clauses, International Commercial Contracts and the Applicable Law* (Cambridge University Press, 2011), pp. 210–26.

Lalive, Pierre, 'L'ordre public transnational et l'arbitre international', in S. Bariatti and G. Venturini (eds.), *Liber Fausto Pocar* (Giuffre, 2009), pp. 599–611.

Lando, Ole, 'CISG and Its Followers: A Proposal to Adopt Some International Principles of Contract Law' (2005) 53 *American Journal of Comparative Law*, 379–402.

'The Law Applicable to the Merits of the Dispute' (1986) 2 *Arbitration International*, 104–15.

'The *Lex Mercatoria* in International Commercial Arbitration' (1985) 34 *International and Comparative Law Quarterly* 4, 747–768.

'Lex Mercatoria 1985–1996', *Festskrift til Stig Strömholm* (Iustus, 1997), pp. 567–584.

'The New Lex Mercatoria in International Commercial Arbitration' (1985) *International and Comparative Law Quarterly* pp. 747–768.

Lando, Ole and Beale, Hugh (eds.), *Principles of European Contract Law – Parts I And II* (Kluwer Law International, 2002).

Lando, Ole, Prüm, André, Clive, Eric and Zimmerman, Richard (eds.), *Principles of European Contract Law – Part III* (Kluwer Law International, 2003).

Law Society of England and Wales, The, 'Firms' Cross-Border Work' (2010), ec.europa.eu/justice/news/consulting_public/0052/contributions/224_en.pdf.

Lennep, W. Huding-van, 'Anticipatory Application of a Multilateral Treaty with Uniform Conflict Rules' (1995) 42(2) *Netherlands International Law Review*, 259–69

Lew, Julian D. M., *Applicable Law in International Commercial Arbitration* (Oceana Publications, 1978).

Liukkunen, Ulla, 'Lex Mercatoria in International Arbitration', in J. Klabbers and Touko Piiparinen (eds.), *Normative Pluralism and International Law: Exploring Global Governance* (Cambridge University Press, 2013), pp. 201–28.

Lookofsky, J., *International privatrett på formuerettens område* (Jurist- og Økonomiforbundets Forlag, 1997).

Lowenfeld, Andreas, *International Litigation and the Quest for Reasonableness: Essays in Private International Law* (Clarendon Press, 1996).

Lowe, Alan Vaughan, 'Ends and Means in the Settlement of International Disputes over Jurisdiction' (1985) 11 *Review of International Studies*, 183–98.

Lupoi, Michele A., *Conflitti transnazionali di giurisdizione*, (Giuffrè, 2002).

Mann, Fritz A., 'Lex Facit Arbitrum', in Pieter Sanders (ed.) *Liber Amicorum for Martin Domke* (Martinus Nijhoff, 1967).

'Sonderanknüpfung und zwingendes Recht im internationalem Privatrecht' in *Festschrift für Günther Beitzke zum 70. Geburtstag* (De Gruyter, 1979), pp. 607–24.

Studies in International Law (Clarendon Press, 1973).

Magnus, Ulrich, 'Comparative Editorial Remarks on the Provisions regarding Good Faith in CISQ Article 8(1) and the UNIDROIT Principles Article 1.7,' in J. Felemegas (ed.) *An International Approach to the Interpretation of the United Nations Convention on Contracts for the Internatioanl Sale of Goods (1980) as Uniform Sales Law* (Cambridge University Press, 2007), pp. 45–8.

Staudingers Kommentarzum Bürgerlichen Gesetzbuch mit Einführungsgesetz und Nebegesetzen (Sellier de Gruyter, 2002).

'The Germanic Tradition: Application of Boilerplate Clauses under German Law' in Giuditta Cordero-Moss (ed.), *Boilerplate Clauses, International Commercial Contracts and the Applicable Law* (Cambridge University Press, 2011), pp. 179–209.

Mance, Jonathan, 'Is Europe Aiming to Civilise the Common Law?' (2007) 18, *European Business Law Review*, 77–99.

Martinek, M., 'Die Mitwirkungsverweigerung des Schiedsbeklagten', in G. Lüke, T. Mikami and H. Prütting (eds.), *Festschrift für Akira Ishikawa zum 70. Geburtstag* (De Gruyter, 2001), pp. 269–92.

Mayer, Pierre, 'Le pouvoir des arbitres de régler la procédure', (1995) 2 *Revue de l'arbitrage*, 163–84.

McKendrick, Ewan., 'Harmonisation of European Contract Law: The State We Are in', in Stefan Vogenauer and Stephen Weatherill (eds.), *The Harmonisation of European Contract Law* (Hart Publishing, 2006) pp. 5–29.

Mehren, Arthur Taylor von, 'Adjudicatory Jurisdiction: General Theories Compared and Evaluated' (1983) 63 *Boston University Law Review*, 279–340.

Menyhárd, Attila, 'The East European Tradition: Application of Boilerplate Clauses under Hungarian Law', in Giuditta Cordero-Moss (ed.), *Boilerplate Clauses, International Commercial Contracts and the Applicable Law* (Cambridge University Press, 2011), pp. 302–28.

Merkin, Robert, *Arbitration Law* (Laforma Law, 2004).

Mikelsen, Anders, *Hindringsfritak* (Gyldendal, 2011)

Mustill, M. J., 'The New Lex Mercatoria: the First Twenty-Five Years' (1988) 4 *Arbitration International*, 86–119.

Møgelvang-Hansen, Peter, 'The Nordic Tradition: Application of Boilerplate Clauses under Danish Law', in Giuditta Cordero-Moss (ed.), *Boilerplate Clauses, International Commercial Contracts and the Applicable law* (Cambridge University Press, 2011), pp. 233–53.

Möller, Gustaf, 'The Nordic Tradition: Application of Boilerplate Clauses under Finnish Law', in Giuditta Cordero-Moss (ed.), *Boilerplate Clauses, International Commercial Contracts and the Applicable Law* (Cambridge University Press, 2011), pp. 254–64.

Neuhold, Hanspeter, Hummer, Waldemar and Schreuer, Christoph, *Österreichisches Handbuch des Völkerrechts*, 4th edn (Manz, 2004).

Nielsen, P. A., *International privat- og procesret*, (Jurist- og Økonomiforbundets Forlag, 1997).

Nygh, Peter and Pocar, Fausto, *Report on the Preliminary Draft Convention on Jurisdiction and Foreign Judgments in Civil and Commercial Matters, Preliminary Document No 11 of August 2000* (Hague Conference on Private International Law, 2000), www.hcch.net/index_en.php?act=publications.details&pid=3494&zoek=jurisdiction.

Paulsson, Jan, 'Arbitration Unbound: Award Detached from the Law of its Country of Origin' (1981) 30 *International and Comparative Law Quarterly*, 357–87.

    'Arbitration Without Privity' (1995) 10 *ICSID Review – Foreign Investment Law Journal*, 232–57.

    'Delocalization of International Commercial Arbitration: When and Why it Matters' (1983) 32(1) *International and Comparative Law Quarterly*, 53–61.

Peel, Edwin, 'The Common Law Tradition: Application of Boilerplate Clauses under English Law', in Giuditta Cordero-Moss (ed.), *Boilerplate Clauses, International Commercial Contracts and the Applicable Law*, (Cambridge University Press, 2011), pp. 129–78.

    Treitel on The Law of Contract 13th edn (Sweet & Maxwell, 2011).

Philip, Alan, *First Danish Decisions on the Rome Convention* (IPRax, 1994).

Port, Nicola Christine., Bowers, Scott Ethan and Noll, Bethany Davis, 'Article V(1)(c)', in Herbert Kronke and Patricia Nacimiento (eds.), *Recognition and Enforcement of Foreign Arbitral Awards: A Global Commentary on the New York Convention* (Kluwer Law International, 2010), pp. 257–80.

Pålsson, Lennart, *Romkonventionen. Tillämplig lag för avtalsförpliktelser* (Norstedts Juridik, 1998),

Queen Mary University of London School of International Arbitration, *International Arbitration Survey: Choices in International Arbitration* (2010), www.arbitrationonline.org/docs/2010_InternationalArbitrationSurveyReport.pdf.

Radicati di Brozolo, Luca 'Arbitration and Competition Law: The Position of the Courts and of Arbitrators' (2011) 27(1) *Arbitration International* 1–25.

Redfern, Alan, Hunter, Martin, Blackaby, Nigel and Partasides, Constantine, *Redfern and Hunter on International Arbitration* (Oxford University Press, 2009).

Reese, W. 'Dépecage: a Common Phenomenon in Choice of Law' (1973) 73 *Columbia Law Review* 1, 58–75.

Research Group on the Existing EC Private Law (Acquis group), *'Principles of the Existing EC Contract Law (Acquis Principles) – Contract II: General Provisions, Delivery of Goods, Package Travel and Payment Services'* (Sellier European Law Publishers, 2009).

Reymond, Claude, 'Civil Law and Common Law Procedures: Which is the More Inquisitorial? A Civil Lawyer's Response' (1989) 5(4) *Arbitration International*, 357–68.

Rogers, Catherine A., 'The International Arbitrator Information Project: An Idea Whose Time Has Come', in Roger Alford (ed.) *Kluwer Arbitration Blog* (Wolters Kluwer, 2012), kluwerarbitrationblog.com/blog/2012/08/09/the-international-arbitrator-information-project-an-idea-whose-time-has-come/.

Rubins, Noah, 'Final Arbitral Award Rendered in 2000 in UNCITRAL Ad Hoc Arbitration Swem-Balt AB v. Republic of Latvia – Observations' (2004) 2 *Stockholm Arbitration Report*, 119–27.

Rubins, Noah et al., 'Judgment by the Svea Court of Appeal, rendered in 2003 in case T8735–01, The Czech Republic v. CME Czech Republic B.V. – The CME v. Czech Republic case – Observations' (2003) 2 *Stockholm Arbitration Report*, www.sccinstitute.com/filearchive/2/21294/CME_tjeckiska_republiken.pdf.

Savigny, Friedrich Carl von, *System des heutigen römischen Rechts, 8 vols.* (Veit und Comp, 1849).

Schlechtriem, Peter, *Good Faith in German Law and in International Uniform Laws* (Rome: Pace Law School Institute of International Commercial Law, 1997).

'The Functions of General Clauses, Exemplified by Regarding Germanic Laws and Dutch Law', in Stefan Grundmann and Denis Mazeaud (eds.) *General Clauses and Standards in European Contract Law* (Aspen Publishers, 2006), pp. 41–55.

Schneider, Michael, 'Combining Arbitration with Conciliation' (2003), 1(2) *Oil, Gas & Enegy Law Intelligence*, Article 55.

School of International Arbitration, Queen Mary, University of London, *International Arbitration Survey: Choices in International Arbitration*, www.arbitrationlive.org/docs/2010_International-ArbitrationSurveyReport.pdf.

International Arbitration Survey: Current and Preferred Practices in the Arbitral Process (2012), arbitrationpractices.whitecase.com.

Schreuer, Christoph, 'Failure to Apply the Governing Law in International Investment Arbitration' (2002) 7 *Austrian Review of International and European Law* 147–96, www.univie.ac.at/intlaw/wordpress/pdf/70_cspubl_70.pdf.

'Investment Treaty Arbitration and Jurisdiction over Contract Claims – the Vivendi I Case Considered', in T. Weiler (ed.), *Leading Cases from the ICSID, NAFTA, Bilateral Treaties and Customary International Law* (Cameron May, 2005), pp. 281–323.

'Three Generations of ICSID Annulment Proceedings', in E. Gaillard and Y. Banifatemi (eds.), *Annulment of ICSID Awards* (Juris Publishing, 2004), pp. 17–42.

Schreuer, Christoph, Malintoppi, Loretta, Reinisch, August and Sinclair, Antony, *The ICSID Convention: A commentary*, 2nd edn (Cambridge University Press, 2009).

Schwenzer, I., *Schlechtriem & Schwenzer* Commentary on the UN Convention on the International Sale of Goods (CISG), 3rd edn (Oxford University Press, 2010).

Schwenzer, I., Hachem, P. and Kee, C., *Global Sales and Contract Law* (Oxford University Press, 2012).

Scoles, Eugene, Hay, Peter, Borchers, Patrick and Symeonides Simeon, *Conflict of Laws*, 4th edn (Thomson West, 2004).

Sheppard, Audly, 'Public Policy and the Enforcement of Arbitral Awards' (2004) 1(1) *Transnational Dispute Management*, www.transnational-dispute-management.com/article.asp?key=48.

Siehr, Kurt, 'Ausländische Eingriffsnormen im inländischen Wirschaftskollisionsrecht' (1988) 52 *Rabels Zeitschrift für ausländisches und internationales Privatrecht*, 41–102.

(ed.), *Intercontinental Cooperation through Private International Law – Essays in Memory of Peter Nygh* (Cambridge University Press, 2004).

(ed.), *Internationales Privatrechts* (Mueller C. F., 2001).

Sonnenberger, H. J., *'Treu und Glauben – ein supranationaler Grundsatz?'*, Festschrift für Walter Odersky (De Gruyter, 1996), pp. 703–21.

Spagnolo, Lisa, 'Green Eggs and Ham: The CISG, Path Dependence, and the Behavioural Economics of Lawyer's Choice of Law in International Sales Contracts' (2010) 6(2) *Journal of Private International Law*, 417–64, ssrn.com/abstract=1664168.

Special Commission on Choice of Law in International Contracts, 'Draft Hague Principles on the Choice of Law in International Contracts' (Hague Conference on Private International Law, 2012) www.uncitral.org/pdf/a_conf.97_5-ocred.pdf.

Staudinger, J. von, *Kommentar zum Bürgerlichen Gesetzbuch mit Einführungsgesetz und Nebengesetzen* (De Gruyter, 2009).
> Book 2: *Einleitung zum Schuldrecht, Treu und Glauben* (De Gruyter, 2005)
> Book 2: *Vertragsschluss* (De Gruyter, 2005)

Sternlight, Jean R., 'Panacea or Corporate Tool? Debunking the Supreme Court's Preference for Binding Arbitration' (1996) 74(3) *Washington University Law Quarterly*, 637–712.

Study Group on a European Civil Code and Research Group on EC Private Law (Acquis Group), *Principles, Definitions and Model Rules of European Private Law – Draft Common Frame of Reference (DCFR)* (Sellier European Law Publishers, 2009) ec.europa.eu/justice/policies/civil/docs/dcfr_outline_edition_en.pdf.

Symeonides, Simeon, 'Material Justice and Conflicts of Justice in Choice of Law', in P. Borchers and J. Zekoll (eds.), *International Conflict of Laws For the Third Millenium: Essays in Honor of Friedrich K. Juenger* (Transnational Publishers, 2001), pp.125–40.
> 'Party Autonomy and Private-Law Making: The Lex Mercatoria that Isn't' (19 November 2006), ssrn.com/abstract=946007.

Thue, Helge Johan, *Internasjonal privatrett* (Gyldendal Academic, 2002).

Twigg-Flesner, Christian, 'Standard Terms in International Commercial Law – The Example of Documentary Credits', in Reiner Schulze (ed.), *New Features in Contract Law* (Sellier European Law Publishers, 2007), pp. 325–39.

UNIDROIT Principles of International Commercial Contracts, 3rd edn (2010), www.unidroit.org/english/principles/contracts/principles2010/blackletter2010-english.pdf.

United Nations Commission on International Trade Law (UNCITRAL), 'Commentary on the Draft Convention on Contracts for the International Sales of Goods, prepared by the Secretariat A/CONF.97/5' (1979), www.uncitral.org/pdf/a_conf.97_5-ocred.pdf.
> 'UNCITRAL Model Law on International Commercial Arbitration – Explanatory Note' (2006), www.uncitral.org/pdf/english/texts/arbitration/ml-arb/07–86998_Ebook.pdf.
> 'Recommendation Regarding the Interpretation of Article II Paragraph 2, and Article VII, Paragraph 1, of the Convention on the Recognition and Enforcement of Foreign Arbitral Awards' (1956), www.uncitral.org/pdf/english/texts/arbitration/NY-conv/A2E.pdf.
> 'Report of the Working Group on Arbitration on the Work of its Thirty-second Session' (2000), A/CN.9/468, daccess-dds-ny.un.org/doc/UNDOC/GEN/V00/530/64/PDF/V0053064.pdf.
> 'Report of Working Group II (Arbitration and Conciliation) on the Work of its Forty-sixth Session' (2007), A/CN.9/619, daccess-dds-ny.un.org/doc/UNDOC/GEN/V07/818/18/PDF/V0781818.pdf.
> 'Report of Working Group II (Arbitration and Conciliation) on the Work of its Forty-ninth Session' (2008), A/CN.9/665, daccess-dds-ny.un.org/doc/UNDOC/GEN/V08/570/77/PDF/V0857077.pdf.
> 'Settlement of Commercial Disputes – Preparation of Uniform Provisions on Written Form for Arbitration Agreements – Article 2 of the Convention on the Recognition and Enforcement of Foreign Arbitral Awards' (1958), A/CN.9/WGII/WP.139, daccess-dds-ny.un.org/doc/UNDOC/LTD/V05/912/12/PDF/V0591212.pdf.

Vettese, Maria Celeste, 'Multinational Companies and National Contracts', in Giuditta Cordero-Moss (ed.), *Boilerplate Clauses, International Commercial Contracts and the Applicable Law*, (Cambridge University Press, 2011), pp. 20–31.

Vogenauer, Stefan, 'Regulatory Competition Through Choice of Contract Law and Choice of Forum in Europe: Theory and Evidence' (2013) 21(1) *European Review of Private Law* 13–78.

Wallin, Martin, 'Judgment by the Svea Court of Appeal rendered in 2000 in case 8090-99 – Observations' (2003) 1 *Stockholm Arbitration Report*, 251.

Weise, P. F., *Lex Mercatoria* (Peter Lang, 1990).

Wetter, G. J., 'The Conduct of the Arbitration' (1985) 2(2) *Journal of International Arbitration*, 7–38.

Whish, Richard, *Competition Law*, 5th edn (Lexis Nexis, 2003).

Whittaker, Simon, 'On the Development of European Standard Contract Terms' (2006) 1 *European Review of Contract Law*, 51–76.

   'Theory and Practice of the "General Clause" in English Law: General Norms and the Structuring of Judicial Discretion', in Stefan Grundmann and Denis Mazeaud (eds.), *General Clauses and Standards in European Contract Law* (Kluwer International, 2006), pp. 57–76.

Wiegand, W., '*Iura Novit Curia* v. *Ne Ultra Petita* – Die Anfechtbarkeit von Schiedsgerichtsurteilen im Lichte der Jüngsten Rechtsprechung des Bundesgerichts', in Monique Jametti Greiner, Bernhard Berger and Andreas Güngerich (eds.), *Rechtsetzung und Rechtsdurchsetzung. Festschrift für Franz Kellerhals* (Stämpfli Verlag, 2005), pp. 127–44.

Wilhelmson, T., 'International Lex Mercatoria and Local Consumer Law: An Impossible Combination?' (2004) 3 *Revue européenne de droit de la consummation*, 141–53.

Windmöller, Martin, *Die Vertragsspaltung im internationalen Privatrecht des EGBGB und des EGVVG* (Nomos, 2000).

Yala, Farouk, 'Final Arbitral Award rendered in 2000 in UNCITRAL Ad Hoc Arbitration Swem-Balt AB v. Republic of Latvia – Observations' (2004) 2 *Stockholm Arbitration Report*, 128–41.

Zimmermann, Reinhard, *The Law of Obligations: Roman Foundations of the Civilian Tradition* (Oxford University Press, 1996).

Zimmermann, Reinhard and Whittaker, Simon (eds.), *Good Faith in European Contract Law* (Cambridge University Press, 2000).

Zweigert, Konrad and Kötz, Hein, *Einführung in die Rechtsvergleichung* (Mohr Siebeck, 1996).

Zykin, Ivan S., 'The East European Tradition: Application of Boilerplate Clauses under Russian law', in Giuditta Cordero-Moss (ed.), *Boilerplate Clauses, International Commercial Contracts and the Applicable Law* (Cambridge University Press, 2011), pp. 329–43.

INDEX